Social Work in
Health Care
in the
21st Century

SAGE SOURCEBOOKS FOR THE HUMAN SERVICES SERIES

Series Editors: ARMAND LAUFFER and CHARLES GARVIN

Social Work in Health Care in the 21st Century

Surjit Singh Dhooper

Sage Sourcebooks for

the Human Services

SAGE Publications
International Educational and Professional Publisher
Thousand Oaks   London   New Delhi

For information address:

SAGE Publications, Inc.
2455 Teller Road
Thousand Oaks, California 91320
E-mail: order@sagepub.com

SAGE Publications Ltd.
6 Bonhill Street
London EC2A 4PU
United Kingdom

SAGE Publications India Pvt. Ltd.
M-32 Market
Greater Kailash I
New Delhi 110 048 India

Printed in the United States of America

Library of Congress Cataloging-in-Publication Data

Dhooper, Surjit Singh.
    Social work in health care in the 21st century/ author, Surjit
Singh Dhooper.
        p. cm. —(Sage sourcebooks for the human services; v. 33)
    Includes bibliographical references and index.
    ISBN 0-8039-5932-X (cloth: alk. paper).—ISBN 0-8039-5933-8
(pbk.: alk. paper)
    1. Medical social work. I. Title. II. Series: Sage sourcebooks
for the human services series; v. 33.
    HV687.D48 1997
    362.1'042—dc20   96-45777

97 98 99 00 01 02 03 10 9 8 7 6 5 4 3 2 1

Acquiring Editor:	Jim Nageotte
Editorial Assistant:	Nancy Hale
Production Editor:	Astrid Virding
Production Assistant:	Karen Wiley
Typesetter:	Marion Warren
Print Buyer:	Anna Chin

Dedicated to Dr. S. Zafar Hasan:
a source of sound advice and great
encouragement and an example of
fairness and objectivity

CONTENTS

PREFACE

A national effort at comprehensive reform of the U.S. health care system failed recently. That failure brought about a general recognition that the system is problematic and that the status quo is not acceptable. Despite the United States spending close to 15% of its gross domestic product (GDP) on health care, about 40 million Americans are still without health insurance, and health and health-related problems not only are persisting but are getting worse. The system is recognizing the need for change and is changing in many ways on many fronts—some changes being more obvious than others.

Advances in biomedical knowledge and health care technology are the most obvious and impressive. Americans appreciate and take pride in the medical miracles being made in the nation's hospitals. They are also spending billions on alternative methods of treatment, however, such as acupuncture, yoga, tai chi, homeopathy, massage therapy, and aromatherapy, that are not dependent on high technology.

Advances in medical science and technology have, on the one hand, the potential for turning physicians into super technicians. On the other hand, these physicians are learning to coexist with those practicing nontraditional forms of medicine. Even the pecking order within the medical profession is changing. Specialties such as family practice, geriatrics, rehabilitation medicine, psychiatry, and general medicine are becoming more prominent.

Hospitals are diversifying activities horizontally as well as vertically. They are integrating into outpatient facilities that diagnose patients prior to admission, into subacute facilities that shelter patients after discharge, and into many other forms of health care not directly linked to acute care at all. Ambulatory services are grabbing center stage. The ideas of prevention and early detection of illness, health maintenance, and wellness have started appealing to patients and physicians alike. The medical establishment is deliberating ways of encouraging medical students and residents to choose generalist careers.

Cost-containment efforts are changing the age-old concepts of "physician-patient relationship," "professional judgment," and "autonomy." Physicians are taking on the role of gatekeepers at the cost of the idea of being the agents of the patient.

Even the idea of universal health care coverage is not far-fetched anymore because a majority of the millions of uninsured Americans are no longer the voiceless poor and unemployed. They represent a broader segment of society and include the employed and those not necessarily poor. A critical mass of the population who feel personally affected by the deficiencies of the system is emerging that will create the political will to legislate universal access to health care.

Yes, change is taking place, but in an atmosphere of uncertainty. I am asked, *With the health care scene changing so fast, is it wise to forecast the future? How does one prepare for an uncertain future?*

My answer to the first question is that social workers as a profession do not have a choice. If we are ever to be proactive—and social workers are often accused of being reactive—we must not passively wait for the future to unfold. The answer to the second question is that we prepare for the future by reducing the degree of uncertainty and using the uncertainty to our advantage, by anticipating the future, preparing for it, and venturing into it with faith in ourselves, with creativity, with imagination, and with the willingness to take risks.

This book is built on a threefold belief: (a) The future is never completely divorced from the past; (b) coming events cast their shadows before them; and (c) people have power over the future—we build it both by what we do and what we do not do. The book is based on the premise that social work has much to give the health care world—and in many ways, both traditional and innovative. It looks at the four major sectors of health care—acute care, ambulatory care, illness prevention and health promotion work, and long-term care; reviews the past and present of the organizations within these sectors; projects about their future in the light of a realistic assessment of their current situation;

identifies their major needs; and discusses how social work can step in and help meet those needs.

The book is divided into eight chapters. Chapter 1 describes and discusses the already happening and likely to continue demographic and other sociological changes; advances in biomedical knowledge and health care technology; and changes in health care financing, structure, and services. It discusses health and health-related problems that are persisting, the significance of all these changes for the social work profession, and the profession's assets for taking on the relevant future roles.

Chapters 2 and 3 orient the reader about the past of the major health care organizations in the four sectors mentioned above and identify the emerging and future needs of those organizations and those of health care providers across those settings. Chapters 4 through 7 provide a brief history of social work in each of those four sectors, propose future social work roles, and discuss the required knowledge and skills for the performance of those roles. Chapter 8 presents a set of general strategies that will, over and above the role-specific skills discussed in earlier chapters, enable social workers to thrive in the health care world of tomorrow.

Throughout the book, an effort has been made to point out or suggest appropriate theoretical concepts and practice principles. Overall, an approach is recommended that incorporates (a) general systems theory, which helps in grasping the complex realities and relationships of systems at all levels, from individual clients to organizations and in-stitutions; (b) the problem-solving methodology; and (c) such powerful social work concepts as "enabling" and "empowerment." Social work perspective and methodology are being embraced by practitioners in other professions and disciplines in their efforts to enrich their theories and models for explaining health behaviors and models and strategies for intervening in the lives of people at individual and community levels.

I urge present and future social work practitioners in health care to take the initiative and expand the scope of their jobs, to take on roles not traditionally seen as social work, to help their agencies anticipate the future, to plan future relevant programs and activities, and thereby to create innovative positions for themselves and their social work colleagues. No other profession has the breadth of scope, richness of perspective, and skills appropriate for different levels of intervention. Social workers should seek positions that are not likely to be advertised as clearly social work positions, as many employers may have a restricted view of their expertise. If this book provides some direction, guidance, and a nudge to explore the unknown, it will have served its purpose.

I am thankful to many colleagues, both within the University of Kentucky College of Social Work and outside, in the field, for ideas and encouragement. Within the college, most notable are colleagues S. Zafar Hasan, Joanne Bell, and L. C. Wolfe. Outside the college, Barbara L. Worful, Coordinator of Social Work Education at the Veteran's Administration Medical Center, Lexington, Kentucky; Marylu K. Stewart, Director of Social Services, University of Kentucky Medical Center; and Peg Nethery, Director of Social Services, Saint Joseph Hospital, Lexington, Kentucky, are especially noteworthy. Discussions with them about social work in health care have always been stimulating. Equally important has been the help, support, and understanding of Jim Nageotte, my editor at Sage Publications; Charles Garvin, Sage's social work consultant; and Linda Poderski, copy editor. Finally, I am ever grateful for the understanding and support of my wife, Harpal, and our children Amrit, Devinder, Manjot, and Nimrat, who have willingly accepted the reality of my spending all my "spare" time in my office rather than at home.

Chapter 1

INTRODUCTION

Social work has been a part of the health care scene for more than 100 years. It has an impressive history of significant contributions to the field of health care in such settings as hospitals, clinics, rehabilitation centers, nursing homes, health departments, hospices, and home health agencies. Social workers have been involved in health care at all levels: preventive care, primary care, secondary care, tertiary care, restorative care, and continuing care. Depending on the major purposes and functions of each health care setting, their roles have varied, requiring differential professional skills. Their professional organization, the National Association of Social Workers (NASW), has not only promulgated standards of social work practice in health care but also has been in the forefront of the movement for reform of the health care system.

The United States recently experienced the failure of a national effort at reforming the system. Literature is abundant on why the effort failed (e.g., see Altman, 1995; Dukakis, 1995; Goldfrank, 1995; Mongan, 1995; Seward & Todd, 1995; Yankelovich, 1995) and where we go from here (e.g., see Blendon, Brodie, & Benson, 1995; Cohen, 1995; Ethnoven & Singer, 1995; Feder & Levitt, 1995; Helms & Damiano, 1995; Ignagni, 1995; Lee, 1995; Shine, 1995; Young & Sklar, 1995). In his editorial in the January 18, 1995, issue of the *Journal of American Medical Association,* Lundberg (1995) began by saying: *Everything has changed. Nothing has changed.* There is an element of truth in both of these apparently contradictory statements.

Nothing has changed in terms of the following facts about the U.S. health care scene. The number of Americans without health care coverage not only is staying high but also is growing rapidly. In 1 year

(1992-1993) alone, the number of uninsured rose by 1.1 million—to 39.7 million (U.S. Bureau of the Census, 1994). Another 50 million are underinsured and are one major illness or "pink slip" away from financial ruin (*Social Work Speaks,* 1994). Even those with adequate health insurance do not necessarily have adequate health care. This is particularly true of African Americans, Asian Americans, Native Americans, and Hispanic Americans (Randall, 1994). At the same time, health care spending continues to rise and consume a larger and larger share of the federal budget. The cost-driven system also runs the risk of compromising quality. Randall (1994) analyzed the working of managed care organizations and concluded that there is significant potential for abuse in their approaches to managing care (providing necessary care and eliminating "unnecessary" care).

Everything has changed in the sense that there is now a general recognition that the U.S. health care system is problematic and that the status quo is unacceptable. "Despite the collapse of the 1994 debate, two national election-eve surveys found that Americans still rank health system reform as the No. 1 priority for the new Congress to address" (Altman, 1995, p. 247). More and more of the uninsured are no longer the voiceless unemployed and poor. The problem affects a much broader segment of society, and the uninsured include those who are employed and not necessarily poor (Merrill, 1994). A study by Smith and associates (1992) showed that 50% of Americans with yearly incomes over $50,000 had a family member or a first-degree relative without insurance for whom they would feel some sense of financial responsibility in case of an emergency. All major actors seem to be seriously talking about doing something about the problem.

Even without a comprehensive reform of the health care system, things are changing. These changes are creating much uncertainty in the process—uncertainty about the health care system, its future shape and structure, its functions and priorities, and the roles and responsibilities of its functionaries. The trends in demography, patterns of morbidity, and advances in the technology of health care are also like straws in the wind, indicating the direction of future changes. Shapes of things to come have begun to appear, validating the truth of the adage that coming events cast their shadows before them. It is reasonable to think that the U.S. health care system in the 21st century will be significantly different from what it is today. It will be different in the philosophy, approaches, priorities, and rewards of its organizations and in the attitudes, knowledge, and skills of its care providers. Social work must prepare for those changes and turn the prevailing uncertainty into an opportunity for meaningful contributions to the health care of tomorrow. This book is a partial response to that professional need.

In this chapter, I (a) review the past and present of social work in health care; (b) forecast the future of health care by looking at the anticipated demographic and other sociological changes, advances in biomedical knowledge and health care technology, and changes in health care financing, structure, and services; (c) identify the health and health-related problems likely to persist; (d) discuss the significance of the changing health care scene for social work; and (e) talk about the assets that the social work profession can build on for its future roles.

A BRIEF LOOK AT SOCIAL
WORK AND HEALTH CARE

In all health care settings, social workers have provided a holistic perspective on problems and situations, highlighting the social antecedents and consequences of illnesses and the need to deal with the larger picture along with the immediate concern. At the level of the individual's acute or chronic illness, a social worker's focus is on the patient's physical, psychosocial, and environmental health needs. In the second half of the 19th century, social workers were in the forefront of the movement for reform in labor, housing, relief, sanitation, and health care. They were acutely aware of the interdependence of all dimensions of human life. They saw how such social factors as poor housing, neighborhoods, work conditions, family situations, and diet adversely affected health and how poor health in turn produced a host of social problems. They viewed health as more than the mere absence of illness and considered physical health as necessary for social, psychological, and economic well-being. The following quote illustrates this interrelationship:

It is bad enough that a man should be ignorant, for this cuts him off from the commerce of men's minds. It is perhaps worse that he should be poor, for this condemns him to a life of stint and scheming in which there is no time for dreams and no respite from weariness. But what is surely worst, is that he should be unwell, for then he can do little about either his poverty or his ignorance. (Kimble quoted in Haughton, 1972, p. 28)

This recognition of the importance of health care for the total well-being of the individual and the ability of social workers to make unique contributions to patient care have resulted in health social work becoming the largest field of social work practice. According to a 1987 NASW membership survey, about half of NASW members work in the health care field (*Social Work Speaks,* 1994). Of all the health care sectors, social work in hospitals has been the most remarkable in terms of number of social workers employed, variety of professional social work roles played, richness of the practice models used, strategies and approaches developed, and tasks performed—tasks aimed at enhancing the quality of patient care, as well as at contributing to the institutions' efficiency and cost containment efforts.

The emergence of social work roles and responsibilities and the development of appropriate knowledge and skills have been partly the result of an evolutionary process and partly the profession's reaction to the changing situation and needs of the health care system. Many factors have affected the development and practice of social work. The complexity of health care organizations with a number of variables such as "the organization's perception of social work practice; the resources of the organization; the organizational climate; the competencies of the social work practitioners; administrative support and interdisciplinary support" (Holosko, 1992, pp. 27-28) has resulted in the differential use of social work skills. There is also much variation in the nature and functions of various health care organizations even within each health care sector. Here, we look at hospitals as an example of this variance and how hospital-related variables affect the practice of social work.

Marked differences exist between, for example, a small community hospital and a large university-based teaching medical center or between a public general hospital and a for-profit private specialty hospital. Such differences have demanded differences in the nature and degree of involvement of social work. The standards of the Joint Commission on Accreditation of Health Care Organizations require that every hospital make social work services readily available to patients and their families; that these services be well organized, properly directed, and staffed with a sufficient number of qualified individuals; and that social work services be appropriately integrated with other units. Hospital social work departments vary considerably, however, in terms of the number of social workers employed and the extent and nature of their work. The dominance of the health care field by physicians and their perspective and approach to health care is also an important reality. Physicians and others have often tended to define social work roles and functions. Social workers have carried out the expected roles and performed the required functions, but while doing so they have also sensitized other health care professionals to the psychosocial aspects of illness and treatment and the need for dealing with the total patient rather than merely his or her illness and disease.

> In reviewing social work's goal of making the health care delivery system more sensitive to the needs of its clients, one finds that social work professionals have met with infinite success in their ability to have other professions adapt to their ways of helping, such as by considering the whole person and his or her life outside the institution. (Kerson, 1985, p. 301)

This success has had an important side effect. Part of the "what" and "how" of social work has been accepted by professionals from other disciplines and incorporated into their philosophies and practices. Meyer (1984) said that we should be glad "that some of our special values are now held in esteem by others; it means that clients will reap the gains" (p. 7). However, this loss of distinctiveness of social work perspective and methodology has weakened, to a large extent, social work's claim to a "turf" of its own within the hospital. Social work functions in hospitals have included work with patients and their families involving provision of both concrete services and intangible psychotherapy, work on behalf of patients and their families both within the hospital and outside, work regarding the hospital's mission and overall functioning, work regarding the community's health needs and resources, and education of social work students and other health care professionals. Most social work units in hospitals are responsible for at least the following functions: (a) high-risk screening, (b) psychosocial assessments and intervention, (c) interdisciplinary collaboration for coordinated patient care, (d) discharge planning, and (e) postdischarge follow-up. Despite the important relevance of these functions to the quality and effectiveness of medical care, social work has not become a core health care profession. Social workers have experienced only limited success in asserting their professional autonomy and assimilating into the medical world as occupiers of their own legitimate turf. In the words of Erickson and Erickson (1992),

Having a place to stand within the field, with a defined area of competence, a shared and recognized domain of autonomy, are all matters that are never finally settled (other than perhaps in specific sites) in the field, but rather are continuously subject to redefinition. (p. 7)

Meyer (1984) provides an explanation of this state of affairs:

Our professional problem is not that we are lacking in experience, knowledge and skills, but rather that we have for so long concentrated our efforts on the doing of our work, we have not articulated it, we have not evaluated it, and worst of all, we have not thought about it. We are still an emerging profession because we have used our feet and not our heads. In this regard, it would be well to follow the medical model; physicians write up what they do, and often because they claim expertise, they are perceived as having it. Social workers are too modest to claim the domain they have been working in for a hundred years. (p. 9)

The unpleasant reality is that, in the current turmoil of change in the health care scene, social work seems to be losing ground in the hospital sector. Hospitals are experiencing closings, downsizings, mergers, affiliations, and other forms of restructuring, and in the process of cutting costs, departments viewed as not producing enough revenue become easy prey. Ross (1993) painted the following picture of what is happening:

Social work department personnel budgets have been devastated by severe cuts, social workers are being replaced by nonprofessional staff, specialization is decreasing, and other disciplines are appropriating key social work functions. A luxury most cannot afford, clinical supervision is minimal or nonexistent; indeed, the clinical contribution of social work in hospitals seems devalued. (p. 243)

In answer to the question, Is hospital-based social work in jeopardy? Ross says that a widespread, progressive, and serious malady is threatening this professional domain and that the prognosis is uncertain. Although the status of social work in other sectors of health care is not uncertain, social workers are not making up for the losses being experienced in this sector. This is where forecasting the future and thereby hoping to influence it becomes a desirable professional activity.

FORECASTING THE
FUTURE OF HEALTH CARE

Erdmann and Stover (1993) told a story of two frogs in the meadow who fell into a pail of milk. After an hour of struggling to jump out and failing, one of the frogs gave up and drowned. The other struggled all night and churned the cream of the milk into butter and found himself sitting on a solid clump. He jumped out and went on his way. Drawing and building on the lessons from this story, the authors emphasized the importance of an optimistic outlook, hard work, perseverance, facility for assessing a situation realistically, the ability to convert facts—even inconvenient and painful facts—into a solid basis for action, and being prepared for the unexpected. We as social workers can add to this list the need to recognize our power over the future. "We ourselves build the future both through what we do and what we do not do" (Cornish, 1994, p. 60).

Forecasting can be done through four basic methods:

1. *Extrapolation* involves finding a pattern in the past that is projected onto the future. Patterns may be trends as seen in technological and economic data or cycles as those based on weather data.

2. *Leading indicators method* uses information about one time series to forecast about another time series.

3. *Causal models* incorporate information about cause and effect, rather than merely look for correlation between past and future as in the extrapolation and leading indicators approaches.

4. *Probabilistic methods* produce a probability distribution over a range of possible values (Martino, 1993).

Different types of data lend themselves to the use of different methods of forecasting. To anticipate and prepare for the future of social work in health care, I have mixed and matched these methods and used data from the past and present, as well as projections about people and the conditions of their lives in the 21st century. This mixing and matching has been done with the realization that forecasting the future is a risky affair. The risk of being wrong is high, and the rapid pace of changes in society is increasing manifold possibilities of error.

My view of the future of the health care field is based on many streams of information and conjectures. It is projected as (a) anticipated demographic and other sociological changes that will significantly affect the health care field; (b) anticipated advances in biomedical knowledge and health care technology; (c) likely changes in health care financing, structure, and services; and (d) health and health-related problems that are likely to persist. In the following section, we discuss the likely ways that the health care system will respond to these changes and social work contributions to that response.

Anticipated Demographic and Sociological Changes

The following are the major population projections until the year 2050 (in the middle series). From 80 million in 1900, the total population of the United States will have grown to 276 million by 2000. It may top 300 million by 2010 and is projected to be 392 million by the middle of the 21st century. Although the rate of population growth is projected to decrease by about 50% in the next five or six decades, the number of persons living in the United States will increase greatly (Day, 1993).

The age-group of those under 18 may increase by about 6 million by 2000 and then grow another 20 million by 2050, but this group's proportion of the total population may never again be as large as it is today. The largest growing age-group is the 45- to 54-year-olds. They will increase 44% from 1990 to 2000. During the next two decades, the rate of growth of the 65-and-over group is projected to be slower than in the past. Those 85 and older, however, will be the most rapidly growing group, their number increasing sixfold between 1990 and 2050.

In the 21st century, not only the age distribution of the U.S. population but also the race and Hispanic-origin distribution will have changed. The non-Hispanic white share of the population is projected to fall steadily from 76% in 1990 to 72% in 2000, 60% in 2030, and 53% in 2050. After 2030, the non-Hispanic white population will contribute nothing to the nation's population growth. By the middle of the century, the black population will have doubled its 1990 size to 62 million. The fastest-growing racial/ethnic group will be the Asian and Pacific Islander population, with an annual growth rate exceeding 4%. The Hispanic-origin population is projected to add the largest number of people to the population. After 1996, the Hispanic population will add more people to the country every year than any other race or origin group (Day, 1993).

By the middle of the 21st century, less than half of all births will be non-Hispanic white, 1 in 3 will be Hispanic, 1 in 5 will be black, and 1 in 10 will be Asian and Pacific Islander. It is assumed that, of the people added to the population through net immigration every year, 2 out of every 3 will be Hispanic or Asian, 1 in 5 will be non-Hispanic white, and 1 in 10 will be black (Day, 1993).

These demographic changes are likely to lead to many other changes that will significantly effect the nature, quality, and structure of health care in the 21st century. The gradual increase in life expectancy will continue. More and more people will live longer and be healthier. They will be culturally more diverse, better informed, and politically more active. Social institutions will constantly make efforts to accommodate the special needs of various groups such as the elderly, minorities, and women.

A sizeable proportion of the population will be made up of those age 65 and older. An increasingly large number of them will lead generally healthy and independent lives. More and more will respond to society's call to continue using their knowledge and skills by staying in the workforce. As a group, however, the elderly will continue being heavy users of health and medical services as they survive such illnesses as heart attacks and strokes. More than 1.5 million older adults now live in nursing homes and other long-term care facilities, and that number is expected to increase by more than 50% by the year 2020 (Osgood, Brant, & Lipman, 1991). How best to meet the needs of the elderly and where—particularly the issue of community-based versus institutional long-term care—will continue to be important societal concerns. The increased diversity *in* aging as well as *of* the aged population will be an important element adding complexity to that social reality. Even today, 40 years and three generations may separate the younger from the older "elderly" (Bass, Kutza, & Torres-Gil, 1990). These subgroups of the elderly have differing needs. The number of elderly from different racial, ethnic, and otherwise culturally diverse groups will grow, making it impossible to ignore their needs. Meeting these differential needs will be a significant challenge to policymakers and program planners. It is also possible that the attention given to the needs of the elderly and the resources devoted to meeting those needs will generate animosity toward them on the part of younger generations. Feelings of being neglected and socially starved may become part of the experience of more and more elderly. The suicide rate of the elderly is already climbing and is more than 50% higher than that of teenagers and young adults (Osgood et al., 1991). This is despite the availability of powerful antidepressant medications and various psychosocial therapies for dealing with depression, which is considered to be the major cause of suicides in the elderly. It is unlikely that the causes of depression in the elderly will be reduced in the next century.

The United States is moving rapidly from a white society of European origin to a multiracial and multicultural one. Many major cities already have nonwhite majorities, and this trend is rippling out from urban centers to suburban and rural areas (Coile, 1990). With today's minorities making up almost half of the U.S. population by 2050, not only will the country's complexion have changed but its cultural norms and power structure will have as well. Already the country contains more Muslims than Episcopalians. Spanish language will vie with English for prominence as the medium of communication. Los Angeles is now the second-largest Spanish-speaking city in the world, after Mexico City. One can prosper in southern Florida even if one speaks only Spanish. Some 1,000 publications already cater specifically to Latino audiences ("Latinos on the Rise," 1993). Similarly, Asian Americans will become much more visible and active. In the 21st century, the various minority groups—ethnically different, culturally varied, and religiously diverse—will assert their claim to their share of political and economic power more successfully than is happening now.

The same will be true of women. Their participation in the labor force will continue to increase. "Nearly three-quarters of women aged 25-34 and 35-44 are working. The shape of the curve of labor force participation is now essentially identical to the one for men. This change is most probably permanent" (Coile, 1990, p. 56). Even in the 1990s, women will have reached a critical mass in virtually all white-collar professions, especially in business, and already have established themselves in the industries of the future (Naisbitt & Aburdene, 1990). In the 21st century, women will exercise more political power and ensure the elimination of gender-based disadvantages for themselves in the educational, occupational, and political arenas. They not only will have greater employment opportunities with equal pay for equal work under conditions favorable to them but also will occupy positions of leadership at all levels of management. Traditionally "feminine" attributes, such as the willingness to share power and information, will be seen as necessary to lead in a time of rapid change (Rosener as quoted in Field, 1993). Their influence on the health care field will be manifold. Already, "women who have been the backbone of medical institutions in menial and powerless roles are now claiming more influential positions as well as seeking different attitudes and behaviors from male physicians who have dominated the health care field" (Rehr, 1991, p. 11). In the next century, they will have secured not only an easy entry into the fields of medicine and health care management but also positions of leadership. They will also be important for the application and success of many new health care technologies, such as gene therapy and chromosome manipulation, that will involve women more than men as patients.

American families will become even more diverse. The traditional family of husband, wife, and children is declining. In the 21st century, it will become impossible to determine what a "typical" family is. The current picture of the American family includes nuclear families, single-parent families, remarried and stepfamilies, nonmarital heterosexual and homosexual cohabitation families, foster and adoptive families, and multiple-adult households. Already one in four babies is born to an unmarried mother, and nearly one in three Americans is a member of a blended or stepfamily (Ahlburg & De Vita, 1992). Medical advances in the form of newer reproductive technologies are adding complexity to the familial picture. Genetic, gestational, and nurturing parents can now be separated or combined in numerous possibilities by various combinations of artificial insemination, in vitro fertilization, embryo transfer, and freezing (Chell, 1988). This picture will become much more complex in the next century. "More individuals will experience a greater variety of family situations over their lifetime. For many this will include growing up in single and multiple parent situations, living singly, cohabiting, remarrying, and widowing" (Rubin quoted in Olson & Hanson, 1990). Child custody issues and disputes will become more tangled and difficult to deal with. Already, we are seeing biological parents fighting against stepparents for custody of children, grandparents suing for visitation rights even when a child has been adopted, and an estimated 1.5 million lesbian mothers living with their children (Herman, 1990). Rates of marriage and divorce may become meaningless in the future. The marriage rate fell by almost 30% between 1970 and 1990, whereas the divorce rate increased by almost 40% (Ahlburg & De Vita, 1992). In view of the multiple forms of the family in the next century, such information will have little explanatory and predictive value in the future. If the number of single-parent households continues to increase, the associated problem of disproportionately higher rates of poverty among single mothers and their children will continue.

The average number of children per family will continue to shrink, and childless families will become more common. Even now, a majority—33.2 million of the 65.1 million U.S. families—have no children under the age of 18 living at home ("Childless Families," 1989). Overall, fewer children in the country does not mean that those children are more adequately cared for. Of all the children, 21.1% were below poverty thresholds in 1991. This problem not only persists but is getting worse. This figure has risen from 17.9% in 1980. The proportions of black and Hispanic children in poverty are much higher than the overall percentage. In 1991, 45.6% of black children and 39.8% of Hispanic children were poor (Lewit, 1993). Poverty will continue to breed numerous other problems.

The complexity of life in the 21st century will be reflected not only in the diversity of family forms but also in economic and work situations. U.S. industry will face tougher competition from abroad and will have to satisfy much more informed and sophisticated consumers while accommodating the needs and demands of its workers. Worker benefits will include insurance for or provision of health care, mental health care, child care, and elder care services. Case management and comprehensive counseling will be parts of benefits packages. AIDS in the workplace will continue to add to the complexity of the situation, with some significant results.

> One of the positive results of the AIDS crisis has been the emergence of major employers, from Akron to San Francisco, working with community groups to provide a support system that can be a model for the management of many other illnesses. The savings achieved in San Francisco, with the strong and very public participation of leaders from Bank of America, Levi Strauss, and many other recognized employers, are the result of creating an integrated employer-home-hospital-community illness-management system that is as humane as it is cost effective. (Goldbeck, 1988, p. 19)

Only large national and international corporations will be the major actors on the economic stage. Through their personnel health care policies and in other ways, these corporations will influence the structures of the health care system.

In the 21st century, the importance of groups and group work in the lives of people will grow. An estimated 14 to 16 million Americans now belong to some half-million self-help groups. That number continues to increase because people who belong to these groups are better off, emotionally and physically, than those who face their problems alone ("Self-Help Groups," 1988). That trend will persist in the next century as people continue to appreciate the benefits of acting together as groups, as well as of forming coalitions for mutual support and empowerment. Improvements in communications technology will make it easier for people to realize those benefits.

Advances in Biomedical Knowledge and Health Care Technology

Advances in social workers' understanding of human health and illness and their ability to affect those phenomena positively will continue at an astonishing pace. Already, advances in neonatal care have resulted in the survival of more than half of the live-born infants weighing less than 1,000 gm (2.2 lb), compared with less than 10% 20 years ago (President's Commission, 1983). Techniques such as cardiopulmonary resuscitation, mechanical ventilation, renal dialysis, artificial feeding, and antibiotics prolong the lives of adults (Office of Technology Assessment, 1987). Experiments being conducted in laboratories and clinics all over the world provide examples of the future advances. In his book *Rx 2000: Breakthroughs in Health, Medicine, and Longevity in the Next Five to Forty Years,* Fisher (1992), a physician, predicted not only specific improvements, inventions, and developments but also the time frames during which they were likely to take place. Some of these are happening already; others are expected to happen in the near future; and still others will involve some waiting. These anticipated changes are divided into four groups: (a) development and discovery of drugs and diets for the prevention and treatment of diseases; (b) improvements in the technology of diagnosis and treatment, both medical and surgical; (c) enhancement in the basic understanding of the human organism; and (d) changes in the approaches to health care.

New Drugs and Diets for Disease Prevention and Treatment

In the 21st century, (a) a drug for the prevention of breast cancer will be released; (b) an AIDS vaccine will be developed; (c) drugs will be able to prevent or correct osteoporosis by regulating calcium metabolism and bone formation; (d) drugs will be able to inhibit the growth of the prostate gland; (e) a vaccine against bacteria that cause cavities and periodontal disease will become available; and (f) drugs that slow cell metabolism (and thereby keep the cells alive longer) and thus slow the aging process[1] will become available (Fisher, 1992).

People will realize the relationship between improved diet and good health and will become much more diet-conscious. Recent studies have shown that 6 of the 10 leading causes of death in the United States—heart disease, stroke, cancer, adult-onset of diabetes, atherosclerosis, and cirrhosis of the liver—are linked to diet (Committee on Nutrition in Medical Education, 1985). "Nutraceuticals"—nutritional products with disease-related benefits—will come into the mainstream of medical practice and thereby become an important part of health care in the 21st century. Examples of these nutraceuticals are calcium for possible prevention of colon cancer, nicotinic acid for reduction of serum cholesterol, beta carotene for possible prevention of lung cancer, and magnesium for the treatment and prevention of certain types of hypertension ("Foods That Bring Better Health," 1991). Gottlieb (1995) recommended food therapies for all kinds of maladies as diverse as colds and prostate problems. Food and pharmaceutical companies will unite to form "pharmifood" companies. Immunologists will create foods that can treat viruses and cancer ("Forecasts for the 1990s," 1989).

Not only will newer and more effective drugs prevent and cure diseases, but they will be administered in easier ways as well. The following are some examples of future approaches to drug delivery.

A new form of oral drug delivery using hydrogels has been developed at Purdue University. Hydrogel is capable of remaining in the stomach and releasing drugs into the bloodstream for up to 60 hours, which is five times longer than current drugs ("A Spoonful of Hydrogel?" 1991).

Chemical engineers at the University of Cincinnati are working on reversible hydrogel, which could be adapted to react to blood sugar levels, releasing an appropriate amount of insulin whenever blood sugar starts to rise and shutting off the insulin when the level drops ("Hydrogel," 1989).

Manufacturers of feminine-hygiene products are considering a new vitamin-impregnated tampon to help restore iron and essential vitamins lost during menstruation ("Tampons With Vitamins," 1988).

The use of tiny pumps implanted in a patient's body that send a drug to the target site will become common. The pump can be reprogrammed by a computer and radio signals to alter the dosage of the drug released and can be refilled by hypodermic syringe when its reservoir is empty. It will help treat diabetes and heart disease, as well as Lou Gehrig's, Alzheimer's, and Parkinson's diseases ("Tiny Pumps for Drugs," 1988).

New Technologies for Diagnosis and Treatment

Technology is reshaping health care by providing more sophisticated diagnostic tools and treatment options. Already available diagnostic technologies include the following:

- *Three-dimensional and cine computed tomography (CT),* which is a vast improvement on the conventional CT. Three-dimensional CT has increased the utility of CT imaging, and cine-CT provides images at four times the speed of conventional CT.
- *Two-dimensional Doppler echocardiography,* which combines two-dimensional imaging with Doppler display of blood flow. This technique allows for a safe and definitive diagnosis of a number of cardiac problems.
- *Low-osmolality radiographic contrast agents,* which are safer than the standard media used in such procedures as angiography and myelography.
- *Magnetic resonance imaging,* which is the top-rated modality for imaging the central nervous system. Newer, low-strength magnetic resonance imaging units can even be installed in mobile labs.
- *Mammography,* which is considered a "must" technology for the diagnosis of breast cancer.
- *Single photon emission computed tomography (SPECT),* which merges nuclear medicine and CT technology and is an improvement on conventional imaging in the fields of cardiology and oncology.
- *Tumor markers,* on the basis of advances in monoclonal antibody production, are likely to improve cancer diagnosis.
- *Chorionic villus sampling (CVS),*[2] a promising replacement for amniocentesis for prenatal diagnosis.
- *Ultrasound,*[3] which is being used in combination with other diagnostic approaches such as endoscanning, which combines ultrasound and endoscopy (Coile, 1990).

Even more powerful diagnostic techniques and tests will become available in the 21st century. At Battelle's Medical Technology Assessment and Policy Research Center, researchers have developed a machine that can measure gases in parts per trillion. Even at a very early stage of many diseases, the patient's breath contains small amount of certain chemicals. If physicians can detect these chemicals, they may be able to detect a disease by analyzing the patient's breath (Olesen, 1995).

Sudden cardiac death claims more than 400,000 American lives each year. It will become possible to prevent sudden cardiac death through the use of a portable heartbeat monitor. Researchers at Northwestern University are working on such a non-invasive monitor. It will record heartrate variability 24 hours a day and enable physicians to identify and treat patients at high risk of sudden cardiac death early enough to prevent death ("Preventing Sudden Cardiac Death," 1990). While describing telemedicine already in practice, Blanton and Balch (1995) said that patients recovering at home from heart attacks can put on a headset, connect the electrocardiogram (ECG) wires to their chests, and ride their stationary bikes. The ECG information is carried to a medical technician in a hospital through telephone wires. Physicians at East Carolina University have set aside a cable channel to enable cardiac rehab patients to have visual contact with the hospital staff.

Lyme disease, which can cause neurological problems, cardiac distress, facial paralysis, and arthritis, is on the rise. Its cases have increased at an alarming rate over the past few years. It has symptoms similar to those of other diseases and is therefore often misdiagnosed. In the 21st century, a specific test for this disease will be available (Fisher, 1992).

The number of melanoma (skin cancer) cases is growing faster than that of other forms of cancer. Melanoma can be fatal within months if not detected and treated early. Newly developed ultrasonic scanners will enable physicians to examine the skin for melanomas ("Skin Scan," 1989).

Among the therapeutic technologies already being used are (a) *balloon angioplasty,* which is replacing cardiac bypass surgery for the treatment of blockages of cardiac vessels; (b) *continuous arteriovenous hemofiltration (CAVH),* which is used as an alternative to conventional hemodialysis for the treatment of acute renal failure; (c) *cochlear implants,* which are a multichannel, significant improvement over single-channel devises for those with profound hearing loss; (d) *gallstone pumps,* which are used for flushing chemically dissolved gallstones, a nonsurgical approach to that problem; (e) *lithotripsy,* which uses sound waves to shatter kidney and ureteral stones and is fast replacing conventional surgery as a treatment choice; and (f) *lasers,*[4] which are used for a number of therapeutic purposes such as closing surgical wounds and unblocking coronary arteries (Coile, 1990).

Radiation treatments will use newer devices and techniques such as the gamma knife, a non-invasive devise that delivers a single high dose of ionizing radiation from 201 cobalt-60 sources to previously inoperable brain tumors. At the point where all 201 beams intersect simultaneously, enough gamma radiation is dispensed to the tumor without affecting the surrounding tissue ("Invisible Scalpel," 1989).

Physicians at Clatterbridge Hospital, in northwest England, are testing the use of proton therapy for treating eye cancer. It is believed that beams of subatomic particles other than X rays can be used effectively against cancer. The more precise targeting of doses allows physicians to treat a tumor without affecting the surrounding tissues ("Proton Therapy," 1989).

It will become possible to cure allergies, reverse baldness, and even manipulate biological rhythms (to combat such problems as jet lag). Researchers at the University of Cincinnati have developed an implantable hearing aid no bigger than an eyeglass screw. This micromachine holds more than 10,000 transistors and requires only 20 microamps of power from its battery to operate. Replacement of the battery once in 5 years can be done through a simple surgical procedure ("Tiny Hearing Aid Developed," 1995).

Couples suffering from infertility will benefit from newer and more sophisticated noncoital reproductive technologies. Two new approaches to treating infertility—in vitro fertilization (IVF) and gamete intrafallopian transfer (GIFT)—are already being used. The Office of Technology Assessment of the U.S. Congress predicts that, in the next decade, the practice of embryo freezing as an adjunct to IVF will proliferate ("Infertility Services Boom," 1988).

New technologies will also save many more premature babies. A new ventilator developed in England monitors a baby's breathing pattern and works in harmony with it, rather than forcing air into the lungs haphazardly. By permitting these infants to breathe normally, the ventilator promotes full development of the babies' brains and bodies.

Advances in surgical approaches to treatment will be equally impressive. These will be in the areas of improved surgical techniques with fewer surgery-related risks, use of more sophisticated artificial devices, and transplantation of human organs and tissues. The following examples provide an idea of future possibilities.

A scalpel-free vasectomy technique has been pioneered in China. It allows the surgeon to reach the vasa through a small puncture in the scrotum and is an almost bloodless procedure ("No-Scalpel Vasectomy," 1988). As Ross and Williams (1991) put it, under microscopic surgery, surgeons are able to suture veins and nerves as small as the period at the end of this sentence. Also, the linking of new imaging technologies with robotic surgery will become common (Coile, 1990).

A bone-substitute material that stimulates natural bone growth has been developed. It promises to revolutionize surgery for hip and knee replacement, bone cancer, and damage caused by accidents ("Bone Substitute," 1994).

The use of artificial skin, hips, knees, finger and toe joints, Teflon ligaments, and heart valves is already taking place ("Man-Made Materials," 1988). These artificial body parts will be further improved, and others will join this list in the 21st century. An example of future improvements of artificial body parts is provided by work done at the Oxford Orthopaedic Engineering Centre in England. Researchers there have developed a new standard for artificial-hip design and manufacture that can predict how such a hip will settle in the body over the next 10 years. Artificial-hip replacement markedly improves the quality of life for patients, but in up to 30% of cases, the surgery must be redone. The design of artificial hips in the future will be based on specific factors such as body weight, inertia, forces from the muscle, and the way the patient walks so that those hips can last the lifetime of the patient ("Longer-Lived Artificial Hips," 1994).

People undergoing amputations will be able to wear more comfortable, natural-looking prostheses. For instance, the Endolite lightweight prosthesis enables its wearer to take part in strenuous activities such as squash, rock climbing, and cycling. Even those who have lost both legs can run again ("Amputees," 1990). Such prostheses may be crude examples of what will be available in the next century.

"Artificial blood" (synthetic oxygen carriers) will become the answer to the ever-present scarcity of donated human blood and the danger of contamination.

In the field of transplantations, some things that existed only in human fantasy not long ago have become a part of regular medical practice. Some 25 tissues and organs are able to be transplanted. Tissues used in transplantation include bone, bone marrow, corneas and other eye parts, ligaments, tendons and other connective tissues, blood, blood vessels, and heart valves. Organs include kidneys, livers, hearts, lungs, and pancreases, and their transplantation is already giving thousands of very sick people a new lease on life.[5] In the 21st century, researchers will have added to the types of transplants being done, including brain "implants." The ability to maximize the success of transplants will be further improved by developments such as the following:

- New approaches to keeping people alive while they wait for organs will be found. Researchers at the Massachusetts Institute of Technology are experimenting with the possibility of regenerating a diseased organ with a tiny portion of a live donor's organ, rather than the whole organ ("Organ Regeneration," 1989).
- A suitable mechanical heart will be used as a bridge between dying from heart disease and finding a transplantable heart. In most heart transplant programs, about 20% of patients die while waiting for a heart (Pizer & the Massachusetts General Hospital Organ Transplant Team, 1991).
- Transplanting organs from animals into humans will become possible. The powerful immunosuppressants being developed are likely to overcome the problem of rejection of nonhuman organs. The use of nonhuman organs as a temporary measure (until human organs become available) will become commonplace.
- The transplantation of kidneys from donors without a beating heart will become a possibility. At present, cadaveric organs come from donors who are brain dead but breathing with the help of machines.
- It will become possible to treat kidney failure by transplanting half a kidney instead of a whole organ and thereby maximizing the use of available organs. Researchers at Johns Hopkins Hospital have split pig kidneys in two and transplanted the halves with good results (United Network for Organ Sharing [UNOS], 1993).
- Maintaining the viability of recovered organs for transplantation for long periods of time will improve. At present, the preservation time is in hours—72 hours for a kidney, 8 to 24 hours for a liver, up to 12 hours for a lung, and 4 to 6 hours for a heart and heart-lungs (UNOS, n.d.).
- The discovery of more powerful immunosuppressant drugs will enable organ recipients to fight the body's tendency to reject the transplanted organ without significant side effects.
- It will become possible to induce transplantation tolerance in organ recipients. Scientists have achieved transplantation tolerance in animals across the major histocompatibility barrier and partial tolerance in cadaveric renal allograft recipients with donor-specific bone marrow transfusions (Barber, 1990).

Transplantation of organs will also be used as a preventive measure in the future. Talking about pancreas transplants, Pizer and associates (1991) said,

Now that we have established that replacing the pancreas is reasonably safe, it is time to test its long-term efficacy in people who are not yet suffering kidney failure, loss of vision, and the other terrible effects of diabetes. . . . Our hope is that by performing surgery earlier we can make pancreas transplantation a method of preventing, not just treating, the complications of this terrible disease. (p. 173)

Enhancement of the Understanding of the Human Organism

In the 21st century, medical scientists will have added to human knowledge an understanding of life at the cellular level. Physicians of the future will actually be able to look inside every one of the trillions of cells of the human body and detect abnormalities at the most basic molecular level long before symptoms of disease appear (Fisher, 1992). That ability will empower physicians to attack disease at that most basic level and thereby make the prevention of disease the most important aspect of medical practice.

Genetics will be another area in which tremendous progress will be made. It will become possible to genetically engineer and artificially construct human organs. Similarly, the genetically engineered replacement for damaged brain cells in patients such as those with Alzheimer's disease will become a viable approach to treating those patients (Fisher, 1992). All human diseases and disorders will have their linkages, if any, to the human genome identified. The intermediate biochemical processes that lead to the expression of the disease and its interaction with a person's environment and personal history will also be explicated (Coates, 1994). Scientists at Washington University in St. Louis have developed an artificial chromosome that may speed up scientists' attempts to map completely the 46 human chromosomes that carry genetic information. Genetic mapping could provide clues to such diseases as cystic fibrosis, muscular dystrophy, and Huntington's chorea ("Artificial Chromosome," 1988). In the future, such research will help in the understanding, more effective treatment, and even prevention of such complex diseases as schizophrenia, heart disease, and inherited cancers. It may also lead to programs to enhance people's overall physical and mental abilities.

Changes in Approaches to Health Care

Approaches to health care will not be restricted to the traditional medical model of treatment. Already, a third of Americans spend $14 billion per year on alternative medical methods and agencies, such as the Sharp Institute for Human Potential and Mind-Body Medicine, an offshoot of the Sharp Health Care medical conglomerate in California, that offer nontraditional health care services. The federal government has begun financing research into the effectiveness of alternative medicine. In 1992, the National Institutes of Health opened an Office of Alternative Medicine. In 1994, 30 researchers and institutions were selected from among 452 applications for grants for such projects as testing acupuncture and hypnosis to relieve pain and heal bones, massage therapy for surgical patients, dance movement for cystic fibrosis, macrobiotic treatments for cancer, biofeedback for diabetes, yoga for heroin addiction, tai chi for balance disorders, and massage therapy for AIDS babies ("Mainstream Takes New Look," 1994). Another example of newer therapies is aromatherapy. Research on the sense of smell by Shizuo Torii at Toho University in Japan has revealed that different fragrances produce different effects; some are calming and relaxing, others stimulating, and still others improve concentration ("Aromacology," 1990). "As life expectancy increases, people will not only be greatly concerned about their outer aging signs, but about learning the techniques for keeping all of their senses at peak performance" (Green, 1993, p. 17). The growing acceptance of nontraditional therapies by even the medical establishment is reflected in the appearance of the journal *Alternative Therapies in Health and Medicine.*

In the 21st century, health care personnel will not be dominated by those trained in allopathic medicine. These physicians will coexist with those practicing nontraditional forms of medicine such as acupuncture, homeopathy, and other approaches to treatment and care. Even the current health care professionals will have redefined their roles. Gender change in the health care workforce, with more women in positions of authority, will be another significant feature of the health care scene. Within the existing medical profession, pecking order will change among specialists. Specialties such as family practice, geriatrics, rehabilitation medicine, and psychiatry will become more prestigious. Newer specialties such as environmental medicine and addiction medicine will emerge. General practitioners will regain a place of honor among their colleagues. Schools of medicine and teaching hospitals are already being challenged to encourage students and residents to choose generalist careers. In 1992, the Association of American Medical Colleges created a task force to develop a policy statement for that purpose. That policy statement says:

> The Association of American Medical Colleges (AAMC) advocates as an overall national goal that a majority of graduating medical students be committed to generalist careers (family medicine, general internal medicine, or general pediatrics) and that appropriate efforts be made by all schools so that this goal can be reached within the shortest possible time. ("AAMC Policy," 1993, p. 2)

The task force also recommended several strategies for accomplishing this goal. Others (e.g., Greer, Bhak, & Zenker, 1994; Petersdorf, 1993; Schroeder, 1993) have added to these recommendations.

Within the diversity of professionals and approaches, unity will gradually grow. Considering and treating the patient as a partner will be the common theme reflected in the behaviors of all health care workers and their approaches. The informed consumers of health care of the 21st century will not tolerate another type of relationship. "Today's healthcare consumer is a sleeping giant—one who is awakening to his power. Fully awakened, he will be the master and healthcare providers will be the servants" (Leland R. Kaiser, quoted by Coile, 1990).

Ferguson (1992) presented a physician's forecast about how a health-active and health-responsible patient of the future will behave under what he called the "information age model of care." It is a 6-step model. At Step 1—using individual self-care—the person tries to deal with his or her health problem or concern on his or her own. At Step 2—tapping into one's network of family and friends—he or she asks the loved ones for help and advice if self-care does not work. At Step 3—using formal self-help networks—if advice from loved ones does not solve the problem, then he or she may seek help from community self-help programs such as a self-help hotline or self-help support group. At Step 4—using a professional as an adviser—the person seeks appropriate information, tools, skills, and support. This does not result in the health professional stepping in and taking over. At Step 5—using a professional as a partner—the health professional does the things the person cannot do for him- or herself, such as ordering tests, prescribing drugs, and performing surgery. At Step 6—using a professional as an authority—the patient is unconscious or incapacitated and would want the professional to step in and manage the situation.

This health activity and health responsibility on the part of the patient will result from an easy access to information. Self-help literature is already growing. For example, in one self-help book, Louria (1989), a physician, proposed a 17-point lifestyle regimen for what he called "taking control of your medical destiny." Included in the 17 points are specific medical tests (e.g., blood pressure, cholesterol level, mammogram) and the recommended frequency that these should be done. To these tests, he added a number of actions that people should take themselves, such as testicular or breast self-examination, daily back exercises, and seat belt use. For those over 65, his program includes yearly tests for taste, smell, hearing, and vision, as well as an evaluation of social support systems and disabilities.

Many more devices than blood pressure kits (available today) will help in such self-performed or self-directed programs. A meter that determines a person's percentage of body fat is being developed for commercial use. This handheld device uses infrared light to analyze the muscle-to-fat ratio in five places on the body. It compares the user's weight, height, age, and gender with medically established values and produces a customized health and fitness plan ("Fat Meter," 1988). Those who are ill but not in need of acute care will have personal emergency response systems based on implantable biosensors now being tested in Europe and Japan. They will also use a number of techniques and devices themselves at home as part of their treatment. This home care is already happening to an extent. "Cancers and pneumonias are now routinely treated with home chemotherapy and portable infusion therapy. Indwelling catheters allow home administration of hyperalimentation formulas and antibiotics" (Coile, 1990, p. 115).

For those needing hospital-based acute services, the *cure* will be accomplished through the use of sophisticated medical and surgical techniques and equipment, and *care* will be marked by patient-centered approaches and environment. To satisfy the patients of tomorrow, hospitals will have an atmosphere of openness and informality. Ferguson (1992) described some pilot programs[6] in patient-centered health care that may turn out to be the forerunners of the hospitals of the next century.

The provision of *patient-as-a-partner-focused* comprehensive and well-coordinated services aimed at enhancing the patient's quality of life will become the overall goal of the system at all levels of care and in all settings. Mental health and social services will have to be viewed as integral parts of this broadly conceived health care system. The futility of artificial boundaries between health and mental health and health and social welfare will become obvious. Comprehensiveness of services will be the feature distinguishing that system from what we have today. Social and psychological disorders and social diseases resulting from lifestyle, environment, substance abuse, and stress will be as much the focus of that system as the treatment of physical diseases.

Understanding of mental illness will improve, and perspectives on and approaches to dealing with mental health problems will change. The belief in the biological bases of psychiatric disorders will continue to propel the search for more effective medicines for these disorders. Already, drugs capable of targeting specific mechanisms in the brain have been developed (White, 1993). Important changes in the theoretical perspectives on mental health problems are happening already. Friesen (1993, p. 12) listed the following among the advances in child mental health:

- *From* psychological models focusing mostly on intra- and interpersonal phenomena *to* more complex biopsychosocial and ecological models
- *From* a focus on pathology and deficits *to* a focus on strengths and empowerment
- *From* a focus on "child saving" *to* a focus on preserving and supporting families
- *From* a primary view of families as objects of intervention (client, patients) *to* families as partners in the design, delivery, and evaluation of services

Similarly, the concepts of "service delivery" and "practice roles" are changing (a) from a paradigm of program-centered services to person- and family-centered services; (b) from a solely therapeutic focus on the sick person's behavior, emotional life, and family dynamics to comprehensive services that address the full range of the person's needs; (c) from an exclusive focus on formal services to a larger view inclusive of formal and informal sources of help; (d) from limited service options to a wide array of services; (e) from agency-based "expert" roles to professionals working collaboratively with families; and (f) from a specialized, fragmented set of services to the ones that are truly coordinated at the interprofessional and interagency levels with the sick and their families as full and active members of the therapeutic team (Friesen, 1993). Such approaches will be built into the system, encouraged, and rewarded.

Changes in Health Care Financing, Structure, and Services

In the last decade of the 20th century, a major effort at the national level to reform the health care system failed. That failure revealed the strength of the forces of fear, greed, and ignorance (Goldfrank, 1995). A meaningful, comprehensive reform of the system is not likely within the foreseeable future. The historical and economic factors responsible for the current system will continue to exert their influence.

Historically, how Americans financed health care was based on the goal of protecting health care providers and not on serving the consumers. Economically, the health care system is a pervasive force in society (Merrill, 1994). Health insurance in the United States is a child of the Depression and the American Hospital Association (AHA) (Law, 1976). Because of the ravages of the Depression, when people could no longer pay for their hospital care, hospitals developed what later became Blue Cross plans. As Merrill (1994) put it, "It is interesting to note that, until 1971, the logo for Blue Cross was owned by the AHA and, historically, hospital representatives tended to dominate the Boards of these plans" (p. 17). Although other motivations and concerns led to the creation of Blue Shield, the major motivation was the need of physicians for "a mechanism by which they could also get reimbursed by patients who were financially strapped as a result of the Depression" (Merrill, 1994, p. 18). The health care industry is a vital economic force. It represents close to 15% of the gross domestic product (GDP), directly employs 11 million people, and indirectly creates jobs for 17 million more—the people who manufacture products or provide services that are health related (Monheit & Harvey, 1993, as reported in Merrill, 1994). Any prospect of major changes in the financing and structure of the health care system threatens the profits and positions of powerful groups and the bread-and-butter sources of millions of people.

In the foreseeable future, the recipients of health care will continue to fall into the following four groups:

1. Insured through Medicare providing universal access to those 65 and older
2. Insured privately through employment or individual purchase
3. Insured publicly through Medicaid providing access (varying from state to state) to those eligible by category (e.g., being a child of a particular age) and by family income
4. Uninsured (Hahn & Flood, 1995)

States will continue to struggle with the needs of those in Groups 3 and 4, with varying degrees of success. However, "common sense confirms there cannot be 50 different health care delivery programs creating a nightmare of varying coverage and bureaucracy" (Seward & Todd, 1995, p. 246). And as Ignagni (1995) put it,

> If I am a Medicaid recipient, why should I be deprived of benefits in one state and entitled to them in another, or protected by quality assurance standards in one state and left unprotected in another, simply by accident of birth or residence? Similarly, should a health plan operating in fifty states be subjected to fifty different sets of regulatory requirements? And should different kinds of health care delivery systems be held to different levels of accountability? (pp. 223-224)

Gradually, the futility of leaving the burden of reforming the system to individual states will be realized. The cry for reform will continue and will become increasingly shrill. A critical mass of the population that feels personally affected by the deficiencies of the system will gradually emerge. That will create the political will to deal with the problem, and society will accept health care as a societal obligation, and not as an individual responsibility. In the meantime, changes in the system will take place albeit in a slow, incremental, and fragmented manner.

Although universal access to health care will not become a reality within the first few decades of the 21st century, access will improve. That improvement will result in (a) the demand for medical services exceeding the available resources, (b) growth in cost-containment measures, and (c) rationing of expensive medical technology (Barzansky et al., 1993). A cultural paradigm shift from "don't worry about it, the insurance will pay for it" to "we're only going to do this if you really need it and we're fairly convinced it will help" (Lundberg, 1994) will take place. Nevertheless, it will be difficult to decide what the minimal but adequate care is. Gradually, a consensus will emerge that "an adequate level of care should be thought of as a floor below which no one ought to fall, not a ceiling above which no one may rise" (Abramson, 1990, p. 10). The problem of high cost of care will continue. So far, cost-containment efforts have essentially been cost-shifting strategies, each entity trying to contain its costs by shifting them to someone else. Society has not had the political will to reduce health care costs. As Merrill (1994) put it, "It may not be in anyone's best interest to see overall costs contained and, thus, there never was the consensus needed to ensure that any of these efforts would prove successful, whether they involved regulatory approaches or more competitive strategies" (pp. 51-52).

Managed care and managed competition will continue as the major approaches to controlling costs and regulating access to health care. "Managed care is a generic term for organized system of care—usually with precertification requirements, a limited network of providers and risk-based payment—that provide health care" (Oss, 1994, p. 28). Health maintenance organizations (HMOs) and preferred provider organizations (PPOs) are popular examples of managed health care. Managed competition is a system that allows health plans to compete for the enrollment of beneficiaries, who can choose among those plans. "Thus, a sponsor—an employer, a government unit, a purchasing cooperative—acting for a large group of subscribers, structures and adjusts the market to overcome efforts of insurers to avoid competition" (Leukefeld & Welsh, 1995, p. 1210). These managed care and managed competition approaches do not seem "capable of providing universal, comprehensive, affordable, equitable coverage" (Mizrahi, 1993, p. 89). Borenstein (1990) views managed care as the rationing of care that ultimately deprives care recipients of quality care. Others see it as an effort on the part of many important entities to attain dominance of the health care world. "Providers wish to protect their sources of income; industry and government are under pressure to contain health care expenditures and the medical industry wishes to protect and increase its profitability. It is important to note that the health care consumer is conspicuously absent from this array" (Cornelius, 1994, p. 49). As a cost containment strategy, managed care will have met with limited success.

> While managed care has resulted in some savings through case management, preadmission certification, utilization review, mandatory second opinion, and other devices, these savings are primarily one-time reductions: once achieved, they cannot be replicated. These cost control measures themselves use up resources, and only a minority of companies think that they have been effective. (Aaron, 1991, p. 117)

An extensive review of the literature on the performance of managed care plans by Miller and Luft (1994) led them to conclude that no bottom-line estimates of expenditure differences per enrollee existed between managed care plans and indemnity (traditional insurance) plans. As pointed out earlier, it is definitely possible that the quality of care will suffer, the needs of patients will be neglected, and the savings realized will be negligible. In the fee-for-service world, providers make more by doing more; financial incentives encourage overtreatment. In the managed care world, providers make more by doing less; the system encourages undertreatment. The primary mechanisms used by managed care organizations are strict utilization review and financial risk shifting. "These mechanisms may operate in direct conflict with the goals of improving the health status of the underserved" (Randall, 1994, p. 225).

The health care system of the 21st century will continue to be marked by pluralism and diversity but with more logic to its organization and greater integration of its services, both within the system and in the larger human services community. In the settings for health care, on the one extreme, hospitals will provide short-term, intensive, specialized treatment, and on the other, residential facilities will provide long-term care through different service models. Between the two extremes, all kinds of ambulatory centers will provide both specialized and generic disease prevention, illness management, health maintenance, and wellness enhancement services. These centers will see more patients with more diverse problems than happens in the ambulatory care settings at present.

Hospitals of the future will be cores of high-intensity and high-technology medical care. Most diagnostic and therapeutic technology, as well as powerful computer programs, will be within the reach of most hospitals and will turn even small hospitals into medical centers. Hospitals, however, will be for only those patients who have acute problems requiring highly specialized treatment. Hence, there will be fewer hospitals with fewer beds. The volume of acute inpatient services has begun to shrink already. Inpatients' days fell from 263 million in 1982 to 206 million in 1990. In the overall scheme of things, hospitals will lose much of their preeminence in the 21st century.

> Long the central institution of the health care delivery system, the hospital is being challenged by important developments in epidemiology, technology, and economics. Individually and collectively, these changes threaten to push the hospital to the margins of the system, leaving most medical services and dollars controlled by "accountable health partnerships" that emphasize outpatient, home health, and subacute care. Alternatively, these environmental changes could provide a window of opportunity for the hospital to embark on a new mission as a health care center without walls. (Robinson, 1994, p. 259)

Although the shrinkage in inpatient services alluded to above has not yet caused an appreciable reduction in the number of hospitals, it has led to diversification of the care provided by hospitals. "Hospitals have integrated rapidly into outpatient facilities that diagnose patients prior to admission, into subacute facilities that shelter patients after discharge, and into many forms of health care that are not directly linked to acute inpatient care at all" (Robinson, 1994, p. 262). The "ambulatory hospitals" are testing the feasibility of clustering ambulatory care services away from hospital campuses. A variation on this concept of the ambulatory hospital has potential for rural hospitals. "The Montana legislature enacted in 1988 a new level of hospital licensure, the medical assistance facility. More than 30 of Montana's small and rural hospitals serving low-density populations will qualify for hospital payment but under scaled-down regulations for facilities and staffing" (Coile, 1990, p. 7).

Hospitals of the future will embark on new ventures like the ones mentioned above, as well as others such as alcohol and drug units, rehabilitation centers, occupational health centers, day hospitals for the elderly, and rape crisis centers. They will also be more effectively connected with other health and social services in the community. The connection with other health care organizations will take the form of integration, both horizontal and vertical. The idea of regionalization of medical care will also become a reality whereby, for example, a CAT scanner or a cataract surgery center is located in the institution where more patients are in need of the service and others are referred from affiliated hospitals (Rehr & Rosenberg, 1991).

Most health care will be provided through neighborhood-based outpatient programs. Ambulatory care centers, variously called emergicenters, surgicenters, and walk-in clinics, are already appearing all over the United States at the rate of a clinic a day. In 1985, there were 3,000 such centers. Their number is expected to rise to 10,000 by the year 2000 (Cetron, Rocha, & Lucken, 1988). In the future, these non-hospital health care settings will be better equipped to perform sophisticated diagnostic and treatment work and many of the functions of today's hospitals. Unlike the ambulatory centers, these settings will also be the centers of wellness-focused prevention and early detection work.

The health care system of the 21st century will also be guided and goaded by the need for efficiency. The use of computers will increase and significantly contribute to improving efficiency (by minimizing the time taken by paperwork today), cutting costs, and saving lives (because of easy access to patient data). For example, computer technology will create integrated information systems for hospitals; these systems will allow hospital personnel in any department to look at and update patient records. In emergency medicine of the 21st century, physicians will not start from the very beginning with every patient, as happens today, when emergency personnel often know nothing about the patients they treat. A typical 21st-century situation might be as follows: A patient, John, with a bleeding leg, appears in a hospital emergency room and hands his "smart card" to the nurse. By inserting that card into the computer, the emergency room staff are instantly able to see on-screen all the needed information—his medical history as well as other pertinent data—and proceed with attending to his injury. "In radiology, imaging technology allows X-rays of John's leg to be scanned and stored in digital form so that physicians in any other department can view the image. Before John is sent to surgery, physicians schedule an operating room and order the necessary materials through an on-line scheduling system" ("Hospital of the Future," 1990, p. 46).

Such use of computer technology is already taking place and proving its utility. At present, 25 telemedicine projects are in place in the United States, mostly serving rural areas. These projects make it possible for medical specialists from medical schools to provide consultation to practitioners in distant and remote areas. Blanton and Balch (1995) referred to a study showing that health care costs could be reduced by as much as $36 billion per year if technologies such as telecommunication were widely used. The computerization of Sweden's health delivery system has reduced that nation's spending on health care from 12% of its GNP to just over 7% (Diebold, 1994). The future possibilities of the use of these technologies are enormous. Discussing the future of telemedicine technology and robots, Karinch (1994) reported on the work being done by the U.S. military. In 1993, a surgeon at Fort Gordon demonstrated "telepresent surgery" by performing a procedure on a pig that was 100 ft away. High-quality video cameras, microphones, and a remote manipulator arm enabled him to perform as if he were actually in the operating room. This technology will affect all facets of health care. Osman and associates (1994) reported the use of computer-supported education for reducing the hospital admissions of asthma patients.

LIKELY-TO-PERSIST HEALTH
AND HEALTH-RELATED PROBLEMS

In the 21st century, as pointed out earlier, health care agencies will be more than the illness care places they are today. They will be responsible for the prevention, early detection, and treatment of illness, as well as for the promotion of wellness. Health care professionals will take seriously the fact that "the factors in avoiding premature death and disease are: life style, 50%; environment, 20%; human biology, 20%; inadequacies in the health care system, only 10%" (Lamm, 1989, p. 3). They will realize that social and health problems are inseparable. Our discussion of the health and health-related problems likely to persist in the next century include (a) medical problems, (b) medicalized social problems such as alcoholism, and (c) social problems such as poverty, homelessness, and violence and person abuse (child, spouse, and elder abuse). These will have tremendous impact on the scope, structure, and approaches of health care in the next century.

Although some diseases will have been eliminated, others will persist and be joined by new ones. Most of those likely to persist and continue to tax the skills of the health care community and U.S. resources are chronic diseases, such as Alzheimer's disease, arthritis, genetic defects, heart disease, stroke, and cancer.

Alzheimer's disease will not only persist in the next century but will worsen in incidence as the population of the elderly rises. It is estimated that about 1.8 million suffer from severe dementia and that another 1 to 5 million have mild to moderate dementia (Office of Technology Assessment, 1990). Alzheimer's disease is a family disease, and it is a slow killer. Most of its victims live from 9 to 15 years after the onset of the illness, and their families must live through the painful experience of watching them progressively worsen in their self-care abilities. Patients pass through the phases of forgetfulness, confusion, and dementia and put increasingly greater demands on the family's emotional, physical, financial, and social resources (Dhooper, 1991). The intensity of the stress on the family can be imagined by the appropriate description of the dementia phase of the disease as the "funeral that never ends" (Kapust, 1982). The needs of the families and caretakers of Alzheimer's patients will continue to be a challenge to the health care community.

Arthritis is a common problem and a significant cause of much suffering, a fair amount of disability, and $54 billion in cost every year. It is estimated that 38 million people had this disease in 1990. A Centers for Disease Control and Prevention (CDC) study predicted that the number of arthritis sufferers will rise to 59.4 million by the year 2020 ("Arthritis Cases to Soar," 1994). Despite the ability to apply very sophisticated technology (e.g., the use of artificial joints) to its treatment, arthritis will remain on the health care scene, claiming its share of the national resources.

The 21st century will see noticeable improvement in the heart disease and stroke picture as a result of advances in medical care and changes in lifestyle. Battelle's Medical Technology Assessment and Policy Research Center forecasts that, by 2015, these changes *could* prevent as many as 23 million cases of and 13 million deaths from these two illnesses. It is estimated that about half of this improvement would be a result of behavioral changes, 40% a result of pharmaceuticals, and 10% a result of other biomedical advances. Despite the decline in heart disease and stroke cases, these illnesses will continue to occupy important positions among major health care concerns of the 21st century because more than 600,000 U.S. children now have some form of heart disease. Lack of physical activity is an increasing problem among U.S. children. The percentage of high school students participating in vigorous physical activity at least three times a week has declined from 61.7% to 36.1% in the past decade ("Children and Heart Disease," 1994). The same will be true of a number of cancers. Some cancers will decline, but others will persist. Even with newly developed preventive vaccines and simple tests for mass screening, the United States will lag behind in its ability to bring about the drastic lifestyle changes necessary for reducing these illnesses to insignificance.

Emotional disorders and mental disease will continue to afflict Americans in the 21st century. A recent national survey involving the most comprehensive look at the mental health of U.S. citizens to date found that far more people suffer from mental disorders than previously assumed. This survey used interviews with a nationally representative sample of 8,098 people aged 15 to 54 and employed the latest official psychiatric diagnoses. Its major findings were that (a) nearly one in two adults experienced a mental disorder at some time in his or her life, (b) almost one in three suffered from a mental disorder during the previous year, and (c) roughly one sixth of the population grappled with three or more mental disorders over the course of their lives (Bower, 1994). In addition to the diseases associated with unhealthy lifestyles and the emotional problems of living is the genetic threat. Advances in medical care will result in the survival of more and more people who have congenital illnesses and disabilities. This is already happening on a smaller scale.

> Individuals who once would have died by early childhood are surviving into adolescence and even adulthood. Anticipated breakthroughs in gene therapy and genetic engineering undoubtedly will affect the course and outcome of genetic disorders and will provide affected people with longer, more active, and more fulfilling lives. (Rauch, 1988, p. 392)

As these people live longer, long enough to reproduce, they will increase the genetic burden on the society of the future. The 21st century will witness a race between genetic illnesses and genetic engineering. At the same time, the psychosocial needs of those who have such illnesses will have to be attended to. "Genetic diagnoses touch on intimate, deeply personal areas of life: sexuality, decisions to conceive, and decisions to terminate pregnancy for genetic reasons. A genetic diagnosis also may reveal family secrets, such as incest or adultery" (Rauch, 1988, p. 393).

In the 21st century, the health care scene will see the appearance of diseases different in marked ways from those known today, as well as the reappearance of some of those that had been conquered and obliterated. Ullman (1988) included among the new diseases of the future (a) diseases of the immune system, not just AIDS, resulting from the deficiency or overactivity of immune system; (b) newer viral conditions incurable with the known therapies; (c) more bacterial infections resistant to the available antibiotics; and (d) allergies to foods and common substances. Researchers at Washington University in St. Louis have discovered a new lung disease that they have labeled "reactive airway dysfunction syndrome" (RADS). RADS is brought on after an unusually short exposure to a toxic substance; its effects continue to disable the patients long after the exposure ("Suddenly Breathless," 1990). More than 90% of staphylococcus strains now resist treatment by penicillin and related antibiotics. The organisms that cause pneumonia, ear infections in children, and tuberculosis are becoming harder to kill. Researchers at the CDC estimate that infections resistant to antibiotics already add $4 billion per year to health care costs ("Report of the ASM Task Force," 1995).

Some of the old diseases may also stage a comeback. Neville, Bromberg, Ronk, Hanna, and Rom (1994) observed a striking increase in multidrug-resistant tuberculosis among patients admitted to the Chest Service of Bellevue Hospital in New York. These researchers reviewed the laboratory susceptibility test results of 4,681 tuberculosis cases over a 20-year period from 1971 to 1991 and found that combined resistance to the drugs isoniazid and rifampin increased from 2.5% in 1971 to 16% in 1991, with higher rates noted for individual drugs. George E. Schreiner, an epidemiologist, considers the hantavirus a potentially serious threat to public health that may turn out to be more devastating than AIDS. The hantavirus causes hemorrhagic fever, which carries a mortality rate of greater than 70% (Smirnow, 1994).

The 21st century will see an AIDS vaccine, as well as a cure, but that is not likely to happen soon enough. A report on the 10th International Conference on AIDS in the *Journal of the American Medical Association* begins with the statement, "Hope was hard to find" and concludes that "no conclusive clinical advances have been made." In view of the slow pace of advancement, organizers decided to postpone the 11th International Conference until 1996, skipping 1995 ("Many Clues," 1994). Even though the growth rate of the disease is declining, AIDS will continue to take its toll in terms of the suffering of its victims and their families, the helplessness of the service community, and the strain on the health and social welfare resources of the United States. For example, Getzel (1992) referred to the Teltsch (1991) estimate that as many as 20,000 New York youngsters will become orphaned because of the AIDS-related deaths of parents and will need to be placed through child welfare agencies. For the first few decades of the new century, AIDS will continue to be a major health concern and will become socially more complex. In a study by the Hudson Institute, Johnston and Hopkins (1990) explored the worst, middle, and best scenarios for the spread of AIDS in the United States. In the worst-case situation, it is projected that, by 2002, as many as 14.5 million people could be infected with the AIDS-causing human immunodeficiency virus (HIV) and there could be a million active cases. The most likely scenario would have 6 million cumulative HIV infections by 2002, with more than 400,000 active cases. Blacks and the poor will be hit particularly hard, with about 15% of all blacks aged 15 to 50 carrying the AIDS-causing virus.

Alcohol and drug abuse will continue to challenge the health care community and society at large in the 21st century despite improved knowledge about pharmacological treatment of substance abuse and development or refinement of other therapeutic approaches, such as rational recovery (Galanter, Egelko, & Edwards, 1993) and cognitive therapy (Wright, Beck, Newman, & Liese, 1993). Alcohol use alone is involved in nearly 100,000 deaths annually, including up to half of deaths from motor vehicular crashes and about a third of suicides (Institute of Medicine, 1989, 1990). The sheer number of people who drink alcohol (in light, moderate, or excessive amounts)—estimated to be 70% of the population—the heterogeneity of drinkers and drinking situations, and societal approval of moderate consumption make dealing with this problem an almost impossible task. Despite hundreds of millions of dollars spent on programs to prevent and control alcoholism, there are no fewer alcoholics today than there were 20 years ago (Cahalan, 1987). The formidability of this problem is not likely to lessen in the future.

The drug abuse scene is also not likely to change significantly in the future despite more research showing the damage done by drugs. Drubach, Kelly, Winslow, and Flynn (1993) explored the effects of substance abuse on the cause, severity, and recurrence of traumatic brain injury in 322 admissions to a large rehabilitation inpatient facility. They found that patients tended to be young and predominantly male and that although motor vehicle crashes were the most common cause of injury, those reporting drug or drug and alcohol abuse were more likely to have sustained violent injuries such as gunshot wounds. Drug abuse is also a common cause of stroke in young patients (Kokkinos & Levine, 1993). The National Transportation Safety Board, in collaboration with the National Institute on Drug Abuse, investigated fatal-to-the-driver trucking accidents in eight states over a 1-year period. That study found that one or more drugs were detected in 67% of drivers and that 33% of them had detectable blood concentrations of psychoactive drugs or alcohol (Crouch et al., 1993).

Drugs (and drinking) not only kill and maim their users but also contribute to many other problems. In the 21st century, new chemical entities will be invented to combat drug abuse and such alternatives to drug abuse as "virtual reality" will be created. Virtual reality is a computer program that takes the user to an illusional world of three-dimensional structures, an experience as powerful as any psychedelic drug but without any associated physical addictions and psychotic behavior (McNally, 1990). The drug abuse problem will persist, however.

Smoking will loosen some of its grip but will continue as a danger to the health of Americans. Researchers will learn about the many ill effects of smoking not realized before. Besides the generally known fact that smoking is the single most important cause of cancer (e.g., lung cancer, breast cancer, oral cancer), recent studies have revealed its other harmful effects as well. For example, Morgado, Chen, Patel, Herbert, and Kohner (1994) studied the effect of smoking on retinal blood flow and autoregulation in subjects with and without diabetes. They found that smoking caused significant decrease in retinal blood flow and the ability of retinal vessels to autoregulate to hyperoxia in both groups. Thus, smoking has detrimental effect on vision. A study by Howard and associates (1994) not only confirmed the strong relationship between active smoking and increased thickness of the carotid artery wall but also found that even exposure to passive smoking is related to greater carotid artery thickness. Another study (Sharara, Beatse, Leonardi, Navot, & Scott, 1994) found that women who smoke have an accelerated development of clinically detectable diminished ovarian reserve, which may be a principal mechanism reducing fertility among them. Smoking is also associated with many periodontal diseases (Mandel, 1994). Czeizel, Kodaj, and Lenz (1994) found that smoking by pregnant women raised the relative odds for congenital limb deficiency in their offspring. Other studies have also found a relationship between maternal smoking during pregnancy and intellectual impairment in children (Olds, Henderson, & Tatelbaum, 1994), maternal smoking during pregnancy and problem behaviors in children in middle childhood (Fergusson, Horwood, & Lynskey, 1993), and tobacco smoke in the home and children's cognitive development (Johnson et al., 1993). Researchers are also realizing that even secondhand smoke can adversely affect the physical health of children (Marx, 1993) and that youngsters who smoke are much more likely to use alcohol and illicit substances (Gray, 1993; Torabi, Bailey, & Majd-Jabbari, 1993). A dynamic combination of complex pharmacologic, psychological, and sociocultural factors, however, makes cigarette smoking an extremely difficult problem to deal with (Christen & Christen, 1994). The complexity of the situation will continue to challenge our ingenuity and resources.

Poverty can be considered the parent of many problems. It affects its victims in numerous ways and has a special affinity with illness. Research studies point to a causative link between poverty and ill health (McMahon, 1993). It forces the poor to live in environments that create conditions and encourage lifestyles inimical to their health. A recently published study (Durkin, Davidson, Kuhn, O'Connor, & Barlow, 1994) investigated the relationship between socioeconomic disadvantage and the incidence of severe childhood injury resulting in hospitalization or death. The study was conducted in New York and covered the 9-year period from 1983 to 1991. The average annual incidence of all causes of severe pediatric injury was 72.5 per 10,000 children, and the case-fatality rate was 2.6%. Among the socioeconomic factors considered, low income was the most important predictor of all injuries. Compared with children living in areas with few low-income households, children living in areas with predominantly low-income households were more than twice as likely to receive injuries from all causes and four and one half times as likely to receive assault injuries. The effect of neighborhood income disparities on injury risk persisted after race was controlled. A study done in France (Cloarec, Rivault, Fontaine, & Le Guyader, 1992) found cockroaches to be the carriers of 30 species of bacteria in low-income multifamily dwellings; 54% of those were pathogenic and potentially pathogenic bacteria. Contamination through external contact is sufficient to ensure bacterial diffusion. In the United States, the poor also live in dwellings that often must be shared with rats and cockroaches. One cannot assume that cockroaches in these U.S. homes are more friendly and less harmful than their French counterparts.

The poor not only live in dangerous and unhealthy environments but also have poor nutritional habits and detrimental lifestyles that leave them in poor health with multiple disease conditions. Because of the lack of resources, they cannot obtain proper health care adequate for their needs. If race (being black) is used as a proxy for poverty, its effect on health is reflected in the black infant mortality rate, which continues to be twice the white infant mortality rate (Hogue & Hargraves, 1993). A look at the quality of care for cancer patients who are poor provides another example of how poverty affects not only health but also health care. U.S. society has a special sensitivity, concern, and consideration for victims of cancer, but the poor tend to receive poor cancer care. This inadequacy is highlighted by several recent studies. Berkman and Sampson (1993) found that poor people are more likely to be diagnosed with cancer when the disease is advanced and treatment options are significantly more limited. Limited access to medical care carries the additional risk of denied access to community resources, which often require referrals from the health care system. Underwood, Hoskins, Cummins, and Williams (1994) discovered the following characteristics of cancer care for the economically disadvantaged: (a) Care was deferred because of costs; (b) care was described as "fragmented," "impersonal," and "symptomatic": (c) patients were discouraged from worrying about bodily changes; (d) patients were discouraged from seeking state-of-the-art care; (e) patients experienced difficulty communicating their needs and concerns; and (f) poverty interfered with efforts to participate in volunteer activities. A study of posthospitalization care of low-income urban-dwelling black cancer patients in the Philadelphia area (O'Hare, Malone, Lusk, & McCorkle, 1993) found that the poor had significantly greater symptom distress related to frequency of nausea, intensity of pain, and difficulty in breathing and that their personal care and home activity needs were not being met adequately. Byrd and Clayton (1993) called the state of the care of black cancer patients the "African American cancer crisis."

The problem of poverty with all its sordidness will persist in the 21st century. In 1970, 25.4 million Americans lived below the poverty level. By 1991, that number had risen to 35.7 million (*Statistical Abstract of the United States,* 1993). The overall outlook for the poor and the lower middle class is bleak (Cappo, 1990). The faces of poverty will also remain essentially the same as at present; almost one third (32.7%) of blacks and 28.7% of Hispanics lived below the poverty level in 1991. Although a rising number of blacks will attain high-status occupations and political positions, the rate of increase of the black middle class is likely to decline, and approximately one third of blacks will remain impoverished (Jaynes & Williams, 1989).

The poor include a disproportionate percentage of children. Over one fifth (22.2%) of all children below age 16 (and that includes 47% of black and 41.1% of Hispanic children) were poor in 1991 (*Statistical Abstract of the United States,* 1993). The infant mortality rate in the United States is worse than in other industrialized nations. In 1987, the infant mortality rate for blacks was over twice that for whites, and the rates for some American Indian tribes and for Puerto Ricans were also considerably higher than for whites (*Healthy Children 2000,* 1991). Psychological, emotional, and learning disorders, as well as chronic physical conditions such as hearing and speech impairments, in children are on the rise. Low-income children are at a significantly higher risk for such problems. Children in families with incomes below $5,000 per year had an average of 9.1 disability days in 1980, compared with only 4 days for children in families with incomes of $25,000 or more (*Healthy Children 2000,* 1991). The gains in children's access to health care services made during the 1960s and 1970s have eroded. Between 1977 and 1987, the percentage of children without public or private health insurance increased from 12.7 to 17.8 (Cunningham & Monheit, 1990). Stoddard, St. Peter, and Newachech (1994) studied the use of ambulatory care by children with specific common symptoms (pharyngitis, acute earache, recurrent ear infection, and asthma) who were or were not covered by health insurance. They used data on a subsample of 7,578 children and adolescents 1 through 17 years of age included in the 1987 National Medical Expenditures Survey and controlled for other variables that may affect access to care. These researchers found that children without insurance were significantly less likely than children with insurance to have seen a physician for common conditions requiring medical care.

Homelessness is another manifestation of poverty. The number of homeless has been rising constantly and significantly. On any given night, up to 600,000 people are living and sleeping on the streets, in parks, in shelters, or in darkened corners of public transportation settings (Federal Task Force on Homelessness and Severe Mental Illness, 1992). Today's homeless are younger, more ethnically diverse, and more likely to be members of families than in the past. They include higher proportions of women and minorities and a growing number of people with full-time jobs. Children under age 18, usually as part of a family headed by a mother, are among the fastest growing homeless group (Institute of Medicine, 1988b).

Factors associated with homelessness, such as exposure to adverse weather, trauma, and crime; overcrowding in shelters, often resulting in unusual sleeping accommodations; poor hygiene and nutritional status; alcoholism; drug abuse; and psychiatric illness have clear health implications. But homelessness may not be merely associated with illness. It may be the breeder of illness. Abdul Hamid, Wykes, and Stansfeld (1993) reviewed the literature on homelessness and concluded that the psychiatric needs of many of the homeless may be a direct result of poverty and homelessness. Nevertheless, health problems commonly seen in homeless adults include skin ailments; respiratory infections; chronic gastrointestinal, vascular, dental, and neurological disorders; and traumatic injuries. Homeless children may have respiratory and ear and skin diseases, as well as special problems such as failure to thrive, developmental delay, neglect, and abuse (Usatine, Gelberg, Smith, & Lesser, 1994). While discussing the health care needs of homeless adolescents, Morey and Friedman (1993) concluded that these teenagers are at risk for sexually transmitted diseases including HIV infection, hepatitis, tuberculosis, accidents, and trauma. Mental health issues of depression, low self-esteem, suicidal behavior or ideation, and hostility, often compounded by drug abuse, are also common. A study of 336 homeless people aged 18 and older found that a substantial minority claimed to have health problems and that 47% of these did not receive needed medical care (Piliavin, Westerfelt, Yin-Ling, & Afflerbach, 1994).

The United States seems to thrive on violence and has accepted it as part of its culture and—more frightening—as part of its entertainment. During his or her lifetime, a child of 12 will see more than 200,000 acts of violence on television, and many will witness well over 40,000 murders (Thomas, 1992). The reality is not less frightening. The picture of crime and violence can be imagined by the following figures: In 1992, one crime index offense occurred every 2 seconds, with one violent crime every 22 seconds and one property crime every 3 seconds. These crimes took the forms of murders, rapes, assaults, robberies, burglaries, and thefts. The United States experienced one murder every 22 minutes, one forcible rape every 5 minutes, one robbery every 47 seconds, one aggravated assault every 28 seconds, one burglary every 11 seconds, one larceny-theft every 4 seconds, and one motor vehicle theft every 20 seconds (*Uniform Crime Reports for the United States,* 1992). More and more people are at risk of personally experiencing acts of violence as U.S. crime rates remain the highest in the world overall. The crime situation is not likely to improve significantly in the next century. Certain conditions associated with rising crime such as "increasing heterogeneity of populations, greater cultural pluralism, higher immigration, realignment of national borders, democratization of governments, greater economic growth, improving communications and computerization, and the rise of anomie—lack of accepted social norms" (Stephens, 1994, p. 22) will continue to provide the stage for the enactment of crime.

People experience violence at the hands of not only strangers but also their own parents, spouses, and children. Health care professionals see, in the emergency room trauma cases, the obvious results of violence in the streets. They are also required to see and recognize often not-so-obvious cases of domestic violence. These cases of violence take the form of (a) child abuse—children may be physically abused, sexually abused and exploited, physically neglected, and emotionally abused and deprived; (b) spousal abuse—violence against women may also take the form of physical, sexual, and emotional abuse; and (c) elder abuse—which similarly encompasses physical, psychological, financial, and social abuse. The incidence and prevalence of all these types of abuse are on the rise. Four children die every day from abuse and neglect, and many of these never see their first birthday. Two million cases of child abuse were reported in 1991 (Thomas, 1992). Even this number may not reflect the reality of the child abuse situation as thousands of cases go unreported or unrecognized by police, hospitals and clinics, social service agencies, mental health facilities, and parents. According to congressional estimates, up to 2 million elderly suffer physical abuse and neglect every year (Doner, 1994). Estimates of physical abuse of women by their husbands or boyfriends range from 85 per 1,000 couples to 113 per 1,000 couples per year (Plichta, 1992). In the words of Secretary Shalala of the Department of Health and Human Services, "In this country domestic violence is just about as common as giving birth—about four million instances of each" (quoted in Doner, 1994). Victims of violence are heavy consumers of health care. It is estimated that 30% of all emergency room visits by women may be the result of battering and that 1.4 million physician visits per year are for treatment of battering-related injuries (Doner, 1994). In 1991, an estimated $1.4 billion was spent to treat the victims of firearms injuries alone (Lehrmann, 1994).

SIGNIFICANCE OF THE CHANGING
HEALTH CARE SCENE FOR SOCIAL WORK

We have discussed major changes within the health care system and in society at large that will challenge that system in the next century. These changes have the potential for creating social work opportunities of immense importance. The anticipated demographic and other sociological changes, the persistence of major social problems, and society's expectations from the health care establishment and health professionals will bring into bold relief the inadequacies of the dominant health care professions to deal with the situation.

At this point in its history, social work seems to be losing ground in U.S. hospitals, and although it has increased its presence in ambulatory care and other nonhospital health care settings, it has done an inadequate job of marketing its image and importance. Social workers must turn the challenges of the future changes into opportunities of unprecedented professional significance. From an account of the anticipated changes in society and the health care system, we identify several major themes and discuss the relevance of social work to them. The "how" of future social work contributions is woven into the material for the subsequent chapters. These themes are (a) the needs of the chronically ill, both the elderly and others with disabilities; (b) the needs of the victims of major social problems such as poverty, homelessness, violence, AIDS, and substance abuse; (c) the need of the public to change its views of health and illness and its health-related behaviors; (d) the need of health care providers to change their attitudes and behaviors for providing care that treats the patient as a partner and is family-centered; and (e) the need of the health care community—professionals and organizations—to know how to resolve ethical issues involved in the application of technology to health care and to make decisions about who should benefit from new technologies. The concept of "quality of life" will pervade all these themes.

1. *Chronic illness* in the elderly as well as in others with disabilities will be the greatest challenge for the health care system of the 21st century. Even today, roughly 35 million Americans—about one in seven—have disabling conditions that interfere with their everyday life, and disability-related expenses cost the United States more than $170 billion per year. Over an average life span of 75 years, a newborn today can expect to spend 13 years with some degree of activity limitation (Pope & Tarlov, 1991). The bulk of the current health care system is structured and rewarded for acute care. Acute illness is of short duration and generally ends in either full recovery or death. There is no full recovery in chronic illness. Physicians and nurses cannot cure the chronically ill; they feel frustrated, often secretly wish the patient away, and are then burdened with guilt (Lorber, 1975). Most of the chronically ill are cared for in their own homes, personal care homes, domiciliary homes, boarding homes, foster homes, and nursing homes with assistance from such agencies as outpatient clinics, mental health centers, adult and child day care centers, hospices, and home care agencies. Most of these are social service programs planned, directed, and staffed by social workers who have, over the years, developed some practice principles, models of service, strategies, and techniques for effective intervention with the chronically ill. Their experience can be a significant asset for the health care system of tomorrow.

2. *Social problems* such as poverty and homelessness, violence and person abuse, AIDS, and substance abuse defy easy solutions and are beyond the resources of any profession. The health care community is ill-equipped to deal adequately with even the health consequences of these problems. The need is for multipronged, multidisciplinary, comprehensive, and well-coordinated approaches. Social workers are perhaps the only professionals who have closely observed the lives of the victims of these problems. They understand the realities of these victims, know how to relate to them and intervene in their lives, and deal sometimes with the problems and at other times with the consequences of those problems. Their knowledge, sensitivity, and skills in relating to and motivating these people and in mobilizing resources on their behalf are some contributions that social workers can make to the future plans and programs for these populations.

3. *The attitudes and behaviors of the public* about illness and wellness need to change not only for people's own physical and mental health but also because the changed public attitudes and expectations will in turn force health care providers to change their attitudes and behaviors. Bringing about such change, however, is difficult because people see things from frames of reference they are familiar with, and those patterns of perception determine their behavior. Traditionally, the health care system has rewarded people for passive and unquestioning attitudes and blindly obedient behaviors. Social work macropractice involves, among other things, educating people, organizing communities, and lobbying policymakers. Public attitudes and behaviors change as a result of education, as well as in response to public laws. Social workers have more skills appropriate for these purposes than do other health care professionals.

4. *Attitudes and behaviors of health care professionals* must change to meet the challenges of the next century effectively. The needed change will involve (a) a more holistic view of people and their problems; (b) a proactive stance involving a wellness orientation and the prevention and early detection of problems; (c) willingness to treat the patient as a partner; (d) interprofessional collaboration in substance as well as in form; and (e) a commitment to the idea of quality of life, rather than mere quality of services. Despite Ferguson's (1992) claim that many of his physician colleagues will welcome the chance to climb down off their pedestals and encourage patients to get up off their knees, these changes in position will be difficult because (a) habits die hard,

(b) health care professionals in the future will function in many alternative delivery systems quite different from those of today, (c) they will be required to coexist and collaborate with many more diverse health care providers, (d) professional boundaries will be much more blurred than at present, (e) consumers of health care will themselves judge the quality of services provided to them, and (f) the continued advances in health care technology will pull the professionals in the opposite direction. A tension is bound to exist within and among the various professional groups.

The central focus of social work is on the person in his or her life-situation, which demands simultaneous attention to the individual and the environment. Social workers are trained to look at the total picture, to consider the relevant larger societal forces—malignant as well as benevolent—while dealing with the private problems of individuals, and to keep in mind the suffering of the individual while dealing with public issues. This perspective compels them to collaborate with all those who can contribute to the solutions of problems. Their unique perspective and professional expertise, particularly mediation skills, are important assets. The ethical principles that guide social work practice can help health care providers in learning how to treat patients as partners.

5. *Ethical challenges* will multiply as a result of (a) the increased cultural diversity of the U.S. population, (b) the high cost of life-expanding medical technology, (c) issues of the appropriateness of the use of that technology, (d) questions of equity in the availability of that technology, (e) divergent views about the quality of life, and (f) issues of professional authority and patient autonomy. Referring to the major ethical issues faced in the health care world of even today, Friedman (1991) said:

> It is extremely painful to seek answers to questions of care (or non-care) of the dying; prolongation of the lives of fragile, doomed newborns; euthanasia; institutional survival versus community need; confidentiality of sensitive or dangerous information; meaningful informed consent; and how patients and providers can better relate to and trust each other. (p. 44)

Situations generating such questions will increase manifold in the future. Social work experience in respecting the client's right to self-determination and the practice principles and techniques relevant to that experience can contribute to the resolution of ethical conflicts and dilemmas.

SOCIAL WORK ASSETS FOR FUTURE ROLES IN HEALTH CARE

London (1988) identified the following four conditions that can help in dealing with change and in mitigating risk: (a) respect for the past, (b) ability to adapt, (c) confidence in the future, and (d) recognition of the inevitability of change itself. Ample evidence suggests that these conditions already exist in social work and can be further strengthened easily.

Respect for the Past

Social work in health care has an impressive, proud, and rich past. In the 19th century, social workers were in the forefront of the movement for reforms in labor, housing, relief, sanitation, and health care (Wallace, Goldberg, & Slaby, 1984). They participated in the prevention, case-finding, and treatment of tuberculosis, venereal disease, and maternal and child health problems (Mantell, 1984). A social worker, Edward Devine, formed the National Tuberculosis Association and led the war against tuberculosis (*Encyclopedia of Social Work,* 1971; Lewis, 1971). Social workers opened or were instrumental in the opening of free dispensaries for the poor in many cities. The roots of social medicine are to be found in organized social work (Rosen, 1974). Their response to the epidemics of influenza, polio, tuberculosis, and venereal disease in the first quarter of the 20th century was exemplary. During and after World War I, they worked with injured soldiers, families of those gone to war, and veterans and as employees of the armed services, the Red Cross, and the Department of Veterans Affairs. Throughout the 20th century, social workers have contributed their commitment and skills to health care settings of every type: hospitals, medical clinics, nursing homes, rehabilitation centers, hospices, home health agencies, and health departments. Social workers should have no difficulty in respecting this past.

Ability to Adapt

Social workers do not lack in adaptability. An example of the ability of social workers to adapt is the way they responded to the restructure of the financing and provision of services in hospitals under the diagnosis-related group (DRG) system. That system imposed a very rigid time frame for accomplishing all medical and social objectives pertaining to a patient's admission. A psychosocial assessment had to be done, problems identified, interventions planned and carried out, and the patient's family and community readied for his or her return home within the time limit set for his or her DRG.

Within a remarkable short period, however, health care social workers rallied and prepared themselves for the delivery of needed services under vastly different circumstances. Social work departments were reorganized, priorities reordered, roles redefined and sometimes reassigned, and staffing patterns reviewed. Sometimes the results were positive and social work departments expanded; at other times the results were negative and departments contracted; and in some cases they were eliminated altogether. More significant in the long run, however, was the way health social workers reconceptualized their practice to assess client needs earlier and more rapidly to continue to provide the best social work services effectively within the new time constraints. (Carlton, 1989, pp. 228-229)

Confidence in the Future

Social workers must have confidence in the future in view of the very nature of the anticipated changes in the 21st century. Whether it is the emphasis on wellness rather than illness, the need for comprehensive approaches to problems rather than piecemeal tinkering (that is done today), or treating the patient as a partner rather than a grateful and obedient recipient of services (that he or she has been expected to be in the past), the entire health care community can benefit from social work philosophy and practice principles. Knowing *what* social workers can give to that community and *how* their values and skills can set them apart as potential leaders should enable social workers to anticipate the future with confidence.

Recognition of the Inevitability of Change

Recognition of the inevitability of change is a condition that any profession desirous of increasing its respectability and societal approval must fulfill. It has taken social work practically the whole of the 20th century to secure legal status through licensing laws in all 50 states. Much more remains to be accomplished, and social workers must accept the inevitability of change. They must become proactive enough to give change the desired direction.

In terms of the professional wherewithal necessary for effective contributions to the health care world of tomorrow, social workers' basic philosophy, knowledge, and skills provide a foundation strong enough to build newer models of practice. The remainder of this book is devoted to understanding the needs of the different health care sectors and to discussing social work knowledge and strategies appropriate for dealing with those needs.

NOTES

1. Researchers at Technion-Israel Institute of Technology in Haifa, Israel, have found that oxidation, which causes damage to body cells, is the underlying mechanism of aging. They claim to have already succeeded in retarding aging in nematodes (ringworms) with vitamin E, an antioxidant chemical. They believe that, within 10 years, intensive research on oxidation as the source of cell damage will shed light on ways to slow the human aging process ("Anti-Aging Research," 1989).

2. *Chorionic villus sampling (CVS)* is a test for early detection of birth defects; it is considered to be more powerful than the amniocentesis used today. It will increase the possibility of correcting a defect before birth or give parents more choices, such as ending the pregnancy earlier in cases of severe defects or having more time to prepare for a child with a handicap. CVS can be performed 6 weeks earlier than amniocentesis and can detect disorders in fetuses as early as the 9th week of pregnancy. According to James P. Crane of Washington University in St. Louis, "First trimester detection of abnormalities paves the way for fetal therapy, which may one day enable us to treat and correct defects before birth" ("Preventing Birth Defects," 1986, p. 47).

3. Some of the most impressive and fastest developing technology is occurring in ultrasound:

> Within the last six or seven years, technical advances in transducers and digital scan converters have made ultrasound images extremely valuable. Currently, ultrasound scanners can reproduce incredible detail, limited only by the wavelength of the sound waves that can be used. Ultrasound fluoscopy has made it possible for the heart, including valvular action, to be visualized and recorded. (Ross & Williams, 1991, p. 399)

According to Dr. David Skorton of the University of Iowa, with new computer analysis ultrasound is already providing information about the structural material that makes up the heart. In the future, ultrasound will be used to detect heart problems in a non-invasive manner. It will enable physicians to classify heart muscle in different conditions, such as healthy muscle, muscle being damaged by too little oxygen, muscle damaged in a recent heart attack, and muscle reduced to scar tissue by an old attack. ("Space Age Computing," 1988)

4. The laser modalities that will become available in the next century seem beyond imagination at this time. It will be possible to correct near- and farsightedness through cornea shaping with an ultraviolet excimer laser (Fisher, 1992). Use of other lasers will aid in the treatment of eye problems in other ways as well. For example, the Microlase, developed by Keeler Limited of Windsor, England, is fired into the eyes of a patient with glaucoma before he or she undergoes treatment. The patient experiences much less discomfort than with other methods, and the eyes stay open and still during treatment ("New Laser for Eyes," 1990).

5. More than 16,000 patients underwent successful organ transplantations in 1992 ("Spotlight," 1992). The survival rates of those transplanted with organs are consistently improving. One-year survival rates for first transplants in 1988 were 76% for liver, 83% for heart, 89% for pancreas, 92% for kidneys from cadaver donors, and 97% for kidneys from related donors (Evans, Manninen, & Dong, 1991). The survival rates beyond 1 year are impressive as well: 80% of those receiving cadaveric kidneys and 41% of those receiving heart transplants survive more than 10 years (Evans, 1990).

6. For example, at the Planetree Model Hospital Unit in San Francisco's Pacific Presbyterian Medical Center, patients wear their own robes and pajamas, sleep on flowered sheets, sleep as late as they like, and have visitors at all times; their family members cook for them in a special patients' kitchen and are trained to serve as active care partners; all things are arranged at the convenience of the patients, rather than at the convenience of the medical staff. The results of this pilot program so far show that it is working. "The Planetree unit consistently runs at 85% occupancy and has a waiting list. More than 300 Pacific Presbyterian doctors have voluntarily affiliated with the unit for patient referrals, up from an initial 75. The unit has handled every type of med-surg case, and with no more nursing staff than comparable units" (Coile, 1990, p. 270).

Chapter 2

HEALTH CARE SETTINGS
Their Past

To help the reader in adequately understanding and preparing for the anticipated changes in the health care world, I present a brief history of the main health care settings. These include acute care, ambulatory care, preventive care, and long-term care settings. The importance of some of these will wax, and that of others will wane. These changes will, in turn, create different needs for these settings. This chapter is aimed at putting the changing conditions and emerging needs of these settings into a historical perspective because organizations, like people, cannot escape their past. It affects their ability to influence the future. Social workers have played significant roles in the history of all these settings. Because of space limitations in this book, however, their place in these histories has not been pointed out. Their contributions are incorporated into discussions of the future setting-specific social work roles and responsibilities in the subsequent chapters.

ACUTE CARE SETTINGS

Hospitals are essentially the settings for acute care. The hospital, an age-old institution for the custodial care of the infirm poor, has slowly evolved as the center of the medical world. Although the history of the modern hospital can be traced back to hospital-like institutions in the ancient world, the modern hospital's recognizable predecessor is an institution of the same name found in medieval Europe. In the absence of commercial inns, lodging houses called hospitals, run by religious organizations, were set up for people going on religious pilgrimages. The travelers were expected to stay in these hospitals just for the night. In time, the local homeless were also allowed to stay and for longer periods. Because many of the homeless were physically ill, nursing care was necessary, and in time medical consultation was sought (Goldwater, 1943). During colonial days in the United States, almshouses served as hospitals. They housed the physically ill, along with the homeless, criminals, orphans, and those with mental illness. Prior to the establishment of the first almshouse in Philadelphia in 1713, "the only hospitals in America were temporary structures erected in seaport towns to contain the spread of contagious disease" (Wallace, Goldberg, & Slaby, 1984, p. 3). As the cause of infectious diseases was identified as communicable, infected patients were isolated in special wards or facilities. That was the beginning of the hospital independent of almshouses. Conditions of these hospitals were usually abominable: Persons with acute and chronic medical and psychological problems were mixed together and were cared for by those who had little training or equipment (Altman & Henderson, 1989). "The true public hospital evolved during the latter half of the 19th century, stimulated by the Civil War when huge general hospitals were constructed in the major American cities" (Blaisdell, 1994, p. 761). The image of the hospital as an asylum for the poor and the destitute, however, persisted.

The rise of modern medicine around the beginning of the 20th century changed the nature and functions of the hospital. It not only led to an improvement in the quality of *caring* through highly skilled nursing but also transformed the hospital into a place for *curing* through the use of scientific medicine. Physicians needed more precise control of patient care and treatment than was possible in the home.

> Precise and elaborate rituals of aseptic surgery could be observed more easily in a special wing of a special building than in a hurriedly rearranged bedroom or domestic kitchen. When aseptic methods made it safe for the surgeon to open the abdomen and other body cavities, there was a rapid increase in the number and complexity of operations which he dared perform. This resulted in such a great increase in the number and complexity of surgical instruments that transporting them became a problem. During the past fifty years clinical applications of research discoveries such as x-ray, the measurement of basal metabolism, the electrocardiograph, and radioactive isotopes necessitated the development of costly and bulky equipment. Laboratory examinations were becoming increasingly important in patient care and could be made available more promptly

and efficiently when the patients were gathered under one roof than when they were scattered through resident areas. (Burling, Lentz, & Wilson, 1956, p. 5)

Major changes occurred after World War II. The U.S. government actively subsidized medical education, research, and the building of new hospitals. The advent and spread of private health insurance through employment also stimulated the growth of hospitals. After 1965, when the federal and state governments greatly expanded their participation in the financing and delivery of health care services, hospitals were the major beneficiaries. They continued as centers of increasingly more specialized and technologically sophisticated medical care. During the 1970s and 1980s, hospital-based care became progressively more expensive and beyond the reach of more and more people. Now the need for accessible and affordable health care is stimulating the search for other approaches to the provision of health services. Hospitals are joining that search and exploring ways of expanding their presence beyond their boundaries.

There have been regional differences in the hospital's purpose, source of origin, and relationship with the community. Along the Atlantic seacoast, hospitals were founded by wealthy citizens as charitable institutions for the care of the poor. In the South, hospitals were founded by a local surgeon as a workshop for his use and convenience. In the far West, hospitals were often subsidized by the local community and operated on a pay-as-you-go basis (Burling et al., 1956). Hence, voluntary nonprofit hospitals have a stronger tradition in the Northeast, and for-profit hospitals have long been more strongly established in the South and West. Besides these regional differences, hospitals have also reflected the pluralism of U.S. society.

By 1900 the United States was dotted with hospitals run by hundreds of different private groups, including Roman Catholics, Lutherans, Methodists, Episcopalians, Southern Baptists, Jews, blacks, Swedes, and Germans, depending on the power structures of local populations. The patterns have also varied geographically, both within states and between regions. (Stevens, 1989, p. 8)

Although by 1900 hospitals had been transformed from asylums for the poor into modern scientific institutions, they had not completely disassociated themselves from their past in terms of the original purpose for their being, their relationship with physicians, and their place in the community. Overall, they have symbolized American ideals, "combining as they do science, philanthropy, and social obligation with technological innovation and power of the purse" (Stevens, 1989, p. 351). Governments have also had a tremendous effect on hospitals. Many private hospitals were built with governmental money acquired through the federal Hill-Burton program and local funding sources, as well as subsidies via tax-exempt bond financing. The major sources of payment for medical services are the federal Medicare and Medicaid programs and employment-based health benefits, which are subsidized by the government as these are not taxed as income to employees. Also, "health care is subject to extensive governmental regulation by way of licensure requirements, reimbursement rules, and the various conditions of participation that apply to organizations that wish to seek or maintain eligibility for government funding" (Gray, 1991, p. 2). At the same time, government's part in the actual delivery of health care services is limited. Military and Department of Veterans Affairs (VA) hospitals, state psychiatric hospitals, and county and municipal hospitals are the only major public health care systems. Most individuals and organizations providing medical services are in the private, nongovernmental sector. The nonprofit hospitals dominate the scene and provide 70% of the nonfederal short-term beds. Ownership of a hospital, however, is less important as an indicator of what the hospital does than the clients it serves and the management policies it pursues. Nonprofit hospitals are income-maximizing institutions managed as businesses, and for-profit hospitals are instruments of social policy. Hospitals use conflicting models of service that overlap both public and private domains:

> On one side is a model of hospitals as supply-driven, technological system, analogous to an electrification system or a system producing military aircraft. Hospitals produce surgery, procedures, X rays, expertise, even babies. On the other is a model of hospitals as community services, with lingering religious, humanitarian, and egalitarian goals, more analogous to a system of schools. (Stevens, 1989, p. 6)

U.S. hospitals have tried to "meet American ideals of technology, science, expertise, charity, voluntarism, equity, efficiency, community, and the privilege of class all at once, to everybody's satisfaction" (Stevens, 1989, p. 355) and understandably have not succeeded in reaching so many and such ambiguous goals.

Hospitals may be classified on several bases. They may be seen as big and small, urban and rural, rich and poor, for-profit and nonprofit, public and private, and research and nonresearch. Until the late 1960s, the typical hospital could be fairly described as an independent non-profit proprietary institution. Non-independent hospitals owned by government or by religious organizations were a few exceptions. Over the past 30 years, a new entity, resulting from mergers of hospitals into or their takeover by multi-institutional systems, has appeared on the health care scene.

> Local control declined as large numbers of independent hospitals became part of multi-institutional systems (both for-profit and nonprofit). Owner-ship of institutions by publicly traded, investor-owned companies began and grew rapidly. Various kinds of new, mostly for-profit health care organizations—ranging from ambulatory care centers to HMOs—emerged without the traditional voluntary ethos. Some of the diagnostic, treatment, and rehabilitation centers are locally owned by entrepreneurs (often physicians) or hospitals. But there is also representation by inves-tor-owned companies operating multiple facilities. (Gray, 1991, p. 4)

Therefore, current hospitals can be more realistically viewed as belonging to three major categories: (a) community hospitals, (b) hospi-tals as parts of larger multi-institutional systems, and (c) academic medical centers. Each of these has a different set of purposes, priorities, and organizational setups. Nevertheless, they all share, in varying degrees, such common characteristics as segmentation, social stratifica-tion, money standard, technological identification, division between physicians and hospitals, and an authoritative role for university medicine (Stevens, 1989).

1. *Segmentation.* We have already discussed the diversity and pluralism of U.S. hospitals. Even within the broad categories suggested above, the variety of hospitals, in terms of their affiliation, ownership, and size, is remarkable.

2. *Social Stratification.* U.S. hospitals continue to serve as vehicles for defining social class and race. Urban public hospitals such as Bellevue and Kings County in New York, Philadelphia General, Cook County in Chicago, and San Francisco General, many of these being the descendants of the late 18th-century workhouses or almshouses, remain primarily for the poor.

Even as these hospitals, like other hospitals, were "medicalized" in accordance with Progressive, scientific ideas in the late nineteenth and early twentieth centuries—and indeed, many became major teaching centers—they continued to attract a relatively large proportion of the poorest Americans and a relatively large proportion of racial and ethnic minorities. The poor, in turn, became the medical schools' "teaching material." These patterns continue today in the large proportion of Medicaid (welfare) patients treated in academic centers. (Stevens, 1989, pp. 9-10)

These hospitals, representing less than 5% of the total hospital beds, train about one fifth of all medical and dental residents and one tenth of other health professionals. Although private hospitals provide the greater proportion (70%) of Medicaid-financed care, charity care is almost entirely the responsibility of urban public hospitals, which provide 65% of all charity care in the 100 largest U.S. cities (Hadley & Feder, 1983). "In place of national health insurance, the nation has substituted a network of public hospitals as a less costly surrogate" (Altman & Henderson, 1989, pp. 1-2).

3. *Money Standard.* All aspects of hospital operations are infused by the money standard of success. Hospitals attract paying patients by presenting themselves as having something valuable to sell. Appealing to upper-class patients involves show, unnecessary extras, and even waste. The pay nexus influences decisions about services so that resources are concentrated in areas of maximum profit. People have tended to think of health care as an economic as well as a social good and have preferred the economic dimension (Eisdorfer & Maddox, 1988). Hospitals have reflected that societal preference. The language of hospital administration is filled with the jargon of economics and management, not of medicine (Alper, 1984). During the past decade and a half, the hospital's obsession with cost control has overshadowed the concern about needs for medical care. While comparing the hospital priorities of the 1960s with those of the 1980s, Kane (1988) found that they had shifted from ACCESS, QUALITY, and cost to COST, quality, and access.

4. *Technological Identification.* Hospitals have focused on acute care and technology, particularly surgery, which is the mainstay of the short-stay hospital. This focus has had diverse consequences. In the words of Stevens (1989),

The modern physician, associated with the new hospitals, was—and is—a master engineer, a hero in the American mode, fighting disease with twentieth-century tools. But the early emphasis on surgery has focused hospitals, in turn, around technical spaces such as operating rooms. Generation after generation has characterized the twentieth-century hospital in industrial terms as a factory or workshop. The success and visibility of the hospital in providing acute, specialized care has also obscured its relatively limited role in the overall picture of health and disease. (p. 12)

5. *Division Between Physicians and Hospitals.* Physicians have considered the hospital an extension of their private practice of medicine, and physicians and hospitals cooperate closely. Physicians, however, do not belong to the hospital; they are officially its guests and are given "privileges" of admitting and treating their patients. Physicians are essential for hospitals, but the goals and service agendas of the two are often different—thus, the built-in tension between hospitals and the medical profession.

6. *Authoritative Role for University Medicine.* Medical schools have a strong but informal influence on hospitals. Although only a minority of hospitals have formal affiliation with medical schools, teaching hospitals are the most powerful. They have been the centers of research, generators of new knowledge and skills, and upgraders of medical and surgical practices. The combination of medical schools and associated hospitals created academic medical centers, which are important parts of the hospital scene.

Overall, hospitals are powerful social institutions:

They are affirming and defining mirrors of the culture in which we live, beaming back to us, through the scope and style of the buildings, the organizational "personality" of the institution and the underlying meaning of the whole enterprise, the values we impute to medicine, technology, wealth, class, and social welfare. (Stevens, 1989, p. 14)

They are also sensitive to messages from their environment and have been adaptive and pragmatic organizations.

In the olden days, hospitals attempted to alleviate a broad range of human ills—poverty and hopelessness, as well as disease—but gradually narrowed their focus on bodily disease. That focus continued to narrow so that hospitals in the second half of the 20th century were treating only acute physical illness. Now that trend has been reversed.

In the 21st century, hospitals will turn around and widen their scope to cover all types of services from acute tertiary care on the one extreme to health promotion on the other. The forecast is that the demographic and other sociological changes will make new demands on the health care system, that technological advances will make it possible to treat many illnesses on an ambulatory basis that require hospitalization today, and that a more holistic approach to health and illness will emphasize wellness. These will create significant alteration in the purpose, function, and organization of hospitals in the next century. The new functions of future hospitals will justify another classification based on the type and level of health care they will provide. Some hospitals will become the nucleus of primary care activities, others will provide predominantly secondary care, and still others will become centers of tertiary care. The commitment to the concept of "comprehensiveness of care" will, however, compel most hospitals to incorporate elements of other levels of care into the level of care in which they will specialize. Even within each level of care will be variations among hospitals as their past characteristics will continue to affect their future character.

AMBULATORY CARE SETTINGS

Ambulatory care is where the patient first comes into contact with the health care system and continues in order to stay in the system. Ambulatory care has no universally accepted definition. The diversity of care providers, settings, and services makes it difficult to define. The easiest way to deal with this difficulty is to stick with the literal meaning of the word *ambulatory* and call ambulatory care the care provided to the *walking* patient irrespective of who provides that care, where it is provided, and what the level of care provided is. This care would thus encompass all services provided to non-institutionalized patients (Williams, 1991).

A physician serving the walking patient is variously called an ambulatory care physician, a primary care physician, or a general practitioner, but he or she may also be a pediatrician, an obstetrician, or a surgeon. The service provider may not even be a physician; he or she may be a nurse practitioner or a physician assistant. The setting may be the private office of a physician in solo practice, offices of physicians in group practice, a free-standing clinic, a neighborhood health center, a public health clinic, a hospital outpatient department, an ambulatory surgery center, an urgent care center, or a hospital emergency room. Roemer (1986) identified the following eight types of organized ambulatory health care on the basis of their sponsorship: (a) hospital outpatient departments, (b) public health agency clinics, (c) industrial health service units, (d) school health clinics, (e) voluntary clinics, (f) private group medical practices, (g) health centers of other public agencies, and (h) health maintenance organizations.

The services provided in ambulatory care settings may cover the whole gamut and include (a) preventive services such as screening for diseases, immunization and vaccination, and health education; (b) routine care services, including diagnostic, counseling, follow-up, and therapeutic care; and (c) more complex services involving specialized tests, procedures, and facilities (Williams, 1991). These services can also be classified as primary, secondary, and tertiary care. Although primary health services include preventive measures that may be environmental, educational, or personal - and first-encounter-with-a-provider care, in this chapter the meaning of prevention in primary care is restricted to personal prevention. "Common forms of personal preventive measures are immunization, surveillance of expectant mothers and babies, and adult examinations for detection of chronic diseases" (Roemer, 1986, p. 29).

> Primary care relates to the well, the "worried well," the presymptomatic patient, and the patient with disease in early symptomatic stages. The secondary care function relates to patients with symptomatic states of diseases . . . The tertiary care function encompasses levels of disease which are seriously threatening the health of the individual. (Reynolds, 1975, p. 893)

Primary, secondary, and tertiary care represent stages in the continuum of care from the least to the most intensified. There is room for variance, however, in the judgment about where one stage ends and the other begins. Although most of the services provided in ambulatory care settings would fall under essentially primary- and to a lesser extent secondary care categories, the services rendered in ambulatory surgery centers and emergency rooms require specialized skills and sophisticated equipment. Although such settings are increasingly vying with hospitals as sites of medical miracles, I include emergency medical services under ambulatory care because their focus is on the walking patient. The needs of patients using emergency rooms for emergency and non-emergency problems are different in their nature, intensity, and urgency from those of patients seen in other ambulatory settings. Nevertheless, the emergency room serves as the primary physician, as well as the acute and emergency care facility, for the poor and multiproblem patient (Clement & Durgin, 1987). The increasing use of the emergency room for primary care has a long-term trend (Williams, 1991). The number of visits to emergency rooms for non-emergency problems by even Medicaid recipients increased by 34% between 1985 and 1990 (Nadel, 1993).

Ambulatory care has a long history. As pointed out above, until 1900, hospitals were asylums for the poor and the destitute, and hospital-based care was dreaded and stigmatized. Ambulatory care was the preferred mode of service. In those days, the physician did not have much to give. His or her role as a healer was "predominantly one of patient supporter, occasionally providing palliative therapy and very occasionally providing effective curative therapy" (Williams, 1991, p. 4), and these services could be provided easily and equally well in the physician's office or the patient's home. Virtually no technology supplemented the art of medicine, and a physician could carry all his or her tools in a "little black bag." Moreover, "a vision of the hospital as morally stigmatizing and possibly dangerous underlined a very positive function for outpatient charity medicine" (Rosenberg, 1989, p. 2). In towns and rural areas, most municipalities and counties paid local physicians to treat the poor in their homes. Dispensaries were the places the urban poor turned to for health care. Dispensaries where private physicians treated the needy patients free of charge were originally set up in England and France in the 17th century; the Philadelphia Dispensary was the first to be established in the United States in 1786. It was followed by similar dispensaries in New York in 1791 and Boston in 1796 (Rosenfeld, 1971). Hospitals and almshouses also provided outpatient care in the form of prescriptions. The Philadelphia Hospital, founded in 1751, opened the first hospital outpatient department in 1786 (Pascarelli, 1982). Dispensaries, however, were the major source of health care for those who could not afford a physician's services privately. By the beginning of the last quarter of the 19th century, 29 dispensaries had been founded in New York and 33 in Philadelphia. These dispensaries treated increasingly larger numbers of patients. For example, whereas in 1860, 134,069 patients were treated at New York City's dispensaries, the corresponding number for the year 1900 was 876,000. These dispensaries increased not only in number but also in diversity. Ambitious would-be specialists among physicians were instrumental in opening new and reorganizing old dispensaries on specialty lines (Rosenberg, 1989).

Dispensaries reached their highest point in the decade before World War I. They were everywhere. Whereas some were devoted to providing care and curative services, others—the majority—were dedicated to the prevention of such diseases as tuberculosis and syphilis.

> Only a handful of medical graduates could find house officerships in urban hospitals; such positions were limited to a small minority of the fortunate. However, a far greater number of physicians could and did volunteer to serve in outpatient units as they accumulated clinical skills. (Rosenberg, 1989, p. 2)

In the last decade of the 19th century, clinics were established at teaching institutions such as Johns Hopkins and Massachusetts General Hospital, as well as at a few hospitals unaffiliated with medical schools. By 1900, about 150 such clinics had been founded, two thirds affiliated with medical schools (Rosenfeld, 1971).

The advent of scientific medicine brought the hospital and inpatient care into prominence. Whereas in 1873 only 178 hospitals (including mental hospitals) were available throughout the country, the number of general hospitals increased to nearly 4,400 by 1910 (Roemer, 1986). This rise in the number and prominence of hospitals eclipsed the importance of ambulatory care. Many general dispensaries were gradually subsumed into hospital emergency rooms and outpatient specialized clinics, whereas the functions of the preventive dispensaries were performed by community health centers. They also lost their importance for medical training. By the 1920s, internship and residency had become a required aspect of every physician's training, and the importance of voluntary outpatient work declined. Unlike the hospital, outpatient medicine's history of association with the poor continued to affect the status of ambulatory care. "Outpatient medicine bore the burden of its welfare origins. Never a part of normal fee-for-service medicine, and marked by an often casual and routine quality, it has always been regarded with a touch of disdain—tolerated rather than aspired to by the majority of physicians" (Rosenberg, 1989, p. 4).

Many changes, particularly since World War II, have had significant effects on ambulatory care. The federal government actively subsidized medical education, research, and the building of new hospitals and stimulated numerous medical discoveries. After 1965, the federal and state governments greatly expanded their participation in the financing and delivery of health care services. The two major approaches to governmental involvement can be characterized as an individual-based (or insurance or entitlement) approach and an institution-based (or provider or grant program/direct service) approach (Davis & Millman, 1983). The Medicare and Medicaid programs are examples of the former; VA hospitals, National Health Service Corps, and community health centers are examples of the latter. Although theoretically distinct, in reality the two approaches interact a great deal. The growth of hospitals, developments in health care technology, and insurance programs—both governmental and private—entitling more and more people to sophisticated inpatient treatment made hospital care very attractive as well as expensive. Gradually, the cost of health care, of which inpatient care accounts were a major chunk, became a major concern.

Ambulatory care is now seen as a significant part of the solution to the problem of high cost. The current picture of ambulatory care includes many entities, such as (a) physicians in solo practice; (b) health care providers in group practice—both fee-for-service and prepaid types; (c) hospital-based outpatient departments; (d) health centers and clinics—government financed and/or operated, as well as private and voluntary; and (e) emergency care centers—hospital-based and free-standing. The following are the highlights of the history of these entities.

Solo Practice

Most ambulatory care has traditionally been provided by physicians in office-based solo practice. These physicians provide what can be called routine care, follow-up or ongoing care for relatively simple primary care problems (Williams, 1991). These physicians may not all be general practitioners—family physicians, general internists, and general pediatricians—because a significant portion of women receive all of their medical care from obstetricians during their childbearing years and because many patients with single organ system diseases receive their primary care from specialists (Petersdorf, 1993). Moreover, the number of generalists has been progressively decreasing. In 1931, only 17% of physicians specialized in a single branch of medicine, but by 1970 that number had risen to 80%, correspondingly reducing the availability of primary care physicians significantly (Pascarelli, 1982). To reverse this trend, the Comprehensive Health Manpower Training Act of 1971 authorized grants to hospitals for residency training in family practice, and in 1976 Title VII of the Health Professions Education Assistance Act broadened the federal incentive to cover the development of undergraduate as well as residency training in not only family practice but also general pediatrics and general internal medicine. Despite about $50 million in Title VII grants going to medical schools annually between 1977 and 1985, the percentage of medical graduates planning certification in these generalist disciplines actually declined: in family medicine, from 17.8% to 13.3%; in general internal medicine, from 27.9% to 10.7%; and in general pediatrics, from 8.8% to 5.8% during those years (Greer et al., 1994). In 1992, the proportions of medical graduates contemplating careers in these generalist disciplines were 9% for family medicine, 3.2% for general internal medicine, and 2.4% for general pediatrics (Petersdorf, 1993).

In Chapter 1, I referred to the efforts of the Association of American Medical Colleges and others to increase the proportion of medical graduates entering generalist practice. The consensus seems to be that, to meet U.S. health care needs, the appropriate mix of specialist and generalist physicians should be 50% of each group (Schroeder, 1993). Raising the proportion of generalist physicians to 50% will involve changing the admission policies of medical schools, reorienting their preclinical and clinical curricula, reconfiguring graduate medical education, and retraining physicians originally trained as specialists. According to Schroeder's (1993) calculation, not until the year 2040 would 50% of all physicians be generalist. This picture of the current and projected availability of medical personnel for ambulatory care has relevance for the group practice as well.

Physicians in solo practice are a diminishing group. Only 31.5% of physicians under age 40 are going into solo medical practice (Jolly, 1988). In view of the evermore expensive technologically sophisticated medical equipment, the cost of establishing a practice is becoming prohibitive. In addition are the increasingly complex problems of administering a practice (Williams, 1991). In an insightful discussion of the politics of ambulatory care, Bellin (1982) listed a number of problems a solo practitioner is likely to experience in establishing and managing his or her practice, coexisting with other physicians in the area, and maintaining staff privileges at local hospitals. From a consumer satisfaction perspective, Coile said, "No doctor can take patients' loyalty for granted today. To maintain high rates of return business, physicians are turning to customer relations programs that go beyond 'charm school' for physician office staff" (Coile, 1990, p. 13). Many solo practitioners cannot afford marketing services. They opt for group practice. The following future scenario may not be far-fetched in the next century: The number of nongroup physicians has fallen to less than 10% of all physicians. The nonaligned physicians are either "superstars" whose talents are so in demand they hold privileges at several competing hospitals or "lone wolves" who subsist on the few remaining fee-for-service patients or who work for a temporary-physician personnel agency (Coile, 1990, p. 239).

Group Practice

Group medical practice is growing rapidly and more than any other type of organized ambulatory care (Roemer, 1986). This practice also represents what is called "managed care," which is seen as a solution to the problem of steeply rising health care costs. The growing popularity of group practice is in total contrast with the opposition it received from other physicians individually and their societies in the early days of its history. Pascarelli (1982) traced the history of group practice to the 1870s, when the Homestake Mining Company established a medical group for its workers in South Dakota. The Northern Pacific Railroad did likewise in 1883. The first non-industrial group practice, the famous Mayo Clinic in Rochester, Minnesota, was established in 1887, demonstrating that this type of practice was feasible in the private sector as well and "represented a reputable model for group practice in a national atmosphere of fierce independence, where group practice was viewed with skepticism and distrust" (Williams, 1991, p. 14). Skepticism had, at times, taken the form of open opposition by the American Medical Association and local medical societies. Physicians in group practice were often denied privileges in local hospitals, and patients referred by them were refused treatment by community-based specialists. Group practice also had legal constraints. In such a hostile atmosphere, group practice had difficulty growing and prospering. "The early development of group practice occurred principally in the Midwest and West and in smaller communities that lacked hospitals. The pivotal physician was often someone who had trained at the Mayo Clinic" (Pascarelli, 1982, p. 8). By the early 1930s, medical groups had grown to about 150 throughout the United States. In 1931, a national committee that was established to assess medical care needs and costs suggested that (a) group practice play a major role in the provision of medical care, (b) these groups be associated with hospitals for comprehensive care, and (c) all services be prepaid (Committee on Cost of Medical Care, 1932).

Parallel to the development of group practice was the development of medical care insurance. "Taking roots in scattered communities throughout the country in the last half of the nineteenth century, and under a wide variety of auspices, the principle of pooling risks and resources to budget and pay for the costs of medical care gradually spread" (Rosenfeld, 1971, p. I-14). Groups for mutual protection that organized primarily for providing medical care, such as La Societe de Bienfaisance Mutuelle de San Francisco (which built its own hospital in 1852), the German Benevolent Society of San Francisco, and the French Mutual Benefit Society of Los Angeles, began appearing in the 1850s. The first major prepayment programs were organized by the Southern Pacific Railroad of Sacramento, California, in 1868, the Missouri Pacific Hospital Association in 1872, and the Northern Pacific Beneficial Association in 1882. Other entities that developed group practices were unions in industries, such as the Iron Molders Union (in 1859) and the Brotherhood of Locomotive Firemen and Engineermen (in 1873). The International Ladies Garment Workers' Union organized a health center in New York in 1918. In the same year, the Endicott-Johnson Corporation developed a program that combined the organization of financing and services. A group practice plan organized and financed by the Farmers' Union Cooperative Hospital Association was established in Elk City, Oklahoma, in 1929 under the leadership of Michael A. Shadid, an immigrant physician. The members owned shares in the community hospital, and services were provided by a group of five physicians and two dentists. At about the same time, two physicians—Donald E. Ross and H. Clifford Loos of Los Angeles—organized a partnership of physicians and contracted with the city's water and power department for providing medical services to employees on a prepayment basis. One side effect of the Depression on hospitals was the birth of the Blue Cross program in 1933, which was followed by Blue Shield in 1939, sponsored by state medical societies (Rosenfeld, 1971).

The prepaid group practice, the prototype of the present-day health maintenance organization (HMO), was first organized in the late 1920s and 1930s. The Kaiser Permanente Foundation Plan, originating in California; the Group Health Cooperative of Puget Sound (Seattle),

Washington; the Group Health Plan of Minnesota; and the Group Health Association of Washington, D.C., were the earliest HMOs. The establishment in 1937 of the Group Health Association of Washington, D.C., a nonprofit membership corporation of federal employees, was a significant development. In 1938, the Group Health Association took the American Medical Association to court. It claimed that the Sherman Anti-Trust Act was being violated because the medical staff of the group were denied membership in the district medical society and appointment to a hospital staff. In 1943, the U.S. Supreme Court found the American Medical Association to be in violation of the law. This decision paved the way for the further development of prepaid groups, particularly during the years following World War II (Pascarelli, 1982).

Many labor unions and community organizations established programs of group practice prepayment after World War II. Prepaid groups were criticized as "socialized medicine practices" in which patients did not have free choice of physicians and physicians did not have any incentive to practice good medicine (Watters, 1961). HMOs did constitute a departure from free market dynamics. "The HMO is basically a strategy for complete removal from the orbit of the market of a population of patients and health care providers. Buyers and sellers make an agreement, a fixed-price contract, for future delivery (usually for one year) of needed medical care" (Roemer, 1986, p. 111). These were viewed as the first step in a broader assault on the medical market. Such opposition and restrictive state laws inhibited their growth (Bracht, 1978). The situation gradually changed. The number of group practices began to rise after World War II. These practices were found to be providing excellent care while effectively controlling the cost escalation of the free medical market. This finding led to the enactment of federal legislation in 1973 for the promotion of HMOs.

Advantages of group practice from the perspective of the provider include no heavy initial investment, shared operation of practice, centralized administrative function (performed by professional management in large groups), lesser burden of operating cost, sharing of patient care responsibilities that results in greater flexibility of working hours and more time for vacation and continuing education (Williams, 1991), and greater earnings. Physicians in group practice, on average, earn more than solo practitioners. A 1987 survey found that physicians in solo practice grossed 17% less than those in group practice and that their median income was 27% below that of group physicians (Owens, 1988).

Group practices are growing. Most groups are legal entities unto themselves; others are part of larger organizations such as hospitals. A group practice can be legally organized in a number of ways: (a) a sole proprietorship in which one individual is the owner and others are his or her employees; (b) a partnership in which all members of the group share ownership and liability; (c) a professional corporation in which stock is issued and the stockholders, usually members of the group, own the corporation; and (d) other forms, including associations and foundations. Most groups are partnerships or professional corporations (Williams, 1991). In prepaid groups such as Kaiser Foundation Health Plan, most principles of group practice are incorporated but physicians and other providers are usually salaried.

As an instrument of managed care, all models of group practice—HMO, PPO (preferred provider organization), and its variant EPA (exclusive provider arrangement)—are growing. Historically, the managed care movement has been dominated by HMOs, but starting in 1986, PPO enrollment not only achieved parity with HMOs when both reached 25 million but outstripped them (Richman, 1987). Boundaries between HMOs and PPOs are blurring. The fastest growing kind of HMO is the "open-ended HMO," which works like a PPO.

Hospital-Based Outpatient Department

In 1875, the United States had fewer than 200 hospitals. Most of the health care was provided in either physicians' offices or patients' homes. Poor people received care through dispensaries. The growing population of the country—from 9 million in 1820 to 105 million by 1920 (Pascarelli, 1982)—necessitated more health care resources. To the other settings of health care were added more hospitals and hospital outpatient departments. By 1909, the number of hospitals had grown to 4,359, with a total bed capacity of 421,000. Hospitals, particularly local government hospitals, began to establish outpatient departments that were used mostly by the poor. Teaching hospitals also provided ambulatory care to children and youth under federal grants (under 1965 Social Security Amendments and the Child Health Act of 1967).

Outpatient departments, however, have all along been of low priority for hospitals (both public and private) and their medical staff. The purpose of hospital-based ambulatory services has been to provide health care to the sick poor and to provide training for medical students and residents, often the former becoming a means for the latter. The quality of these services has been uneven. The outpatient department clinics are typically classified by medical specialties and are held at specified times each week. Most patients cannot pay high out-of-pocket fees. "The fees for hospital-based ambulatory care usually are paid from public sources and are fixed at a rate that does not cover costs. On the other hand, reimbursement often is at cost rather than at a fixed fee" (Zavodnick, Katz, Markezin, & Mitchell, 1982, p. 35). Hence, these departments have not been moneymakers and therefore hospitals or physicians have had no financial incentive to take an active interest in them.

This situation is changing rapidly. The drive to reduce health care costs, the growing proportion of elderly in the population, and the push toward preventive medicine are giving ambulatory care special significance, and hospital-based outpatient services are bound to gain unprecedented importance. The quality of outpatient services is also receiving the needed attention. In 1973, the Joint Commission on Accreditation of Hospitals adopted its first set of outpatient standards. These standards defined hospital-based ambulatory care service and dealt with its various dimensions, such as sponsorship of services and staffing, education and training of service providers, written policies and procedures, facility design and equipment, medical records, and audits and evaluation. These standards forced the hospital boards, administrators, and staff to start viewing ambulatory care favorably.

The attitudes of hospital staff toward ambulatory care are changing, and that in turn is leading to changes in their policies and functions.

A few small and well-diversified hospitals are beginning to experience 50:50 inpatient revenue to ambulatory revenue. The five-year period 1990-1995 will be a watershed time for ambulatory care. Ambulatory care has cut the umbilical cord that tied it to inpatient care. The growth of ambulatory care is no longer dependent upon shifting inpatient procedures to an ambulatory basis. Most inpatient procedures have already been shifted by changing medical practice and payer policies. (Coile, 1990, p. 7)

The above picture seems to be truer of urban hospitals than of their rural counterparts, but it may be temporarily so. Before long, rural hospitals will also begin offsetting a significant portion of inpatient hospital services by services for posthospital and chronic disease care. While discussing strategies for survival of rural hospitals and focusing on the needs of the elderly, Buada, Pomeranz, and Rosenberg (1986) said that because, historically, the hospital has been the most highly organized form of health care delivery for the elderly, it should use that strength for becoming the dominant provider of long-term care services.

Health Centers and Clinics

Health centers and clinics comprise a large group and include many ambulatory care settings, such as public health department clinics, community health care centers, ambulatory surgery centers, clinics of other public agencies (e.g., the Department of Veterans Affairs, military services, Indian Health Service), industrial health units, school health clinics, prison health centers, voluntary disease-specific clinics (e.g., cancer-screening clinics), and general health clinics established by voluntary agencies. In the sections that follow, we look at the first three of these in some detail.

Public Health Department Clinics

Public health department clinics have been around for almost 100 years. They have their origin in the health center movement of the late 19th and early 20th centuries. Public health campaigns aimed at controlling smallpox, tuberculosis, venereal disease, infant and child mortality, mental illness, and other problems were the order of the day. In 1904, the first clinic for the treatment of communicable pulmonary disease was established in New York City. This clinic pioneered the use of public health nurses for controlling tuberculosis and provided prevention, early case detection, and treatment services. A rapid growth of public health departments occurred during the years 1900 to 1920. These departments organized a variety of special clinics oriented to the prevention of disease. During the Depression, when so many people could not afford to pay for health care privately, the idea of providing comprehensive care through public health centers became attractive, and funds were made available by the Public Works Administration for building health centers. Later, in the 1940s, additional funds were provided under the Hill-Burton legislation for building health centers in rural and urban areas (Pascarelli, 1982).

Health districts were modeled after school districts, and they sought to interest local people in the health centers. "Neighborhood residents were involved in the programs of these centers in an effort to achieve a 100 percent participation in the services of the center. Household surveys were conducted by block representatives, and patients were recruited by resident 'aides' " (Rosenfeld, 1971, p. 1-10). They did not attain the prominence of school districts, however. Health centers were blamed for not providing comprehensive health services, and organized medicine opposed the public approach to medical care. For these and other reasons, these districts failed to involve their communities in the health center movement and other health care concerns. "Unlike school districts, health districts were kept firmly in the hands of municipal officials and public health officers, with little if any participation by the community. The typical board of health consisted primarily of providers" (Pascarelli, 1982, p. 6). Health districts established around health centers, however, have survived and served as an important element of ambulatory health care. Besides a state health department in each state, about 2,000 public health units are scattered throughout the United States. Their focus continues to be on prevention and early detection. "In recent years, public health agencies have broadened the scope of their clinics to include family planning service (birth control), chronic disease detection, and also the general primary care of families" (Roemer, 1986, p. 41). In fiscal year 1989, state public health agencies spent $9.5 billion for their public health programs. Of that money, 75% was devoted to personal health activities. Similarly, local health departments spent over half ($2.3 of $4 billion) of their expenditures on personal health services (Public Health Foundation, 1991).

Community Health Care Centers

Community health care centers were products of the 1960s. They appeared in the poor urban neighborhoods dominated by minority populations. Some of these were started by youth groups who were not satisfied with the services of hospital outpatient departments or public health clinics. "The young people would raise money for renting an empty store and purchasing drugs, while professional services were solicited and obtained on a voluntary basis from doctors, nurses, pharmacists, and others" (Roemer, 1986, p. 44). Others emerged out of the antipoverty programs. "The Great Society of the Lyndon Johnson era stressed the right to health care and community participation in decisions and stirred the emotions, hopes, and imagination of ambulatory care professionals" (Pascarelli, 1982, p. 9). Sponsored by the newly created Office of Economic Opportunity (OEO), these health centers set out to accomplish more than the provision of comprehensive primary care services. They operated with multiple goals, many of which were not directly related to health service delivery.

Health was defined very broadly, as including physical, mental, social, economic, environmental, and political aspects. Thus, improved housing, better sewer and water systems, employment, job training, community economic development, counseling, advocacy with other social services and, perhaps most important, personal and minority group power building were all major goals of neighborhood health programs. (Davis & Millman, 1983, pp. 25-26)

Most of these clinics did not last beyond the 1970s. Fiscal woes began to afflict them. The Johnson administration was followed by Republican presidencies, and the OEO was dismantled. Initially, these centers were prohibited from serving insured or paying patients, and later they were expected to become self-sufficient by billing and collecting for their services. For Medicaid purposes, most states refused to recognize health centers as institutional providers like hospital outpatient departments, and the centers could be encompassed under no other legal entity. Thus, most centers had to rely on billing at private physician rates, using one or more of their medical staff for billing purposes. Private physician rates were generally too low to support even solo practice physicians, much less the cost of a health center (Davis & Millman, 1983, p. 28). They also suffered from other problems, such as a lack of integration with other health care providers (their physicians finding it difficult to obtain admitting privileges at local hospitals), difficulty in recruiting and retaining professional personnel, heavy involvement of community boards in personnel issues, and poor planning and coordination. Most of these centers failed to survive. Much can be learned from their failure, however. The conditions that created these are still very much alive, and the need for comprehensive health care is as real today as it was in the 1960s.

Ambulatory Surgery Centers

Ambulatory surgery centers are another entity to join the group of ambulatory care settings. These are both hospital units and freestanding. The first freestanding ambulatory surgery center was the Dudley Street Ambulatory Surgical Center in Providence, Rhode Island, opened in 1968 by a group of five physicians. The Surgicenter established by Wallace Reed and John Fox in Phoenix, Arizona, in 1970 has become a model for other developing freestanding facilities (O'Donovan, 1976). Such centers are growing all over and are the source of a wide range of primary care as well as the answer to urgent problems. In 1987, the

Health Care Financing Administration doubled the number of surgical procedures covered by Medicare outpatient payment from 100 to 200. When an approved procedure is performed on an ambulatory basis, Medicare pays 100% of "reasonable charges," instead of the usual 80% (Coile, 1990).

Emergency Care Centers

Emergency care centers have been a part of the health care scene for quite some time. "Traditionally, most hospitals found it easy to justify the establishment of emergency services in contrast to outpatient departments. This type of treatment was not available in physicians' private offices, and for many hospitals it constituted a good source of inpatients" (Pascarelli, 1982, p. 10). About 80% of the 7,100 hospitals in the United States provide emergency services. These services have been increasing in their (a) complexity, (b) range, and (c) integration with other community resources such as alcohol and drug treatment programs, mental health centers, and social services. These changes are the result of several factors. In 1966, the National Academy of Sciences produced the document *Accidental Death and Disability: The Neglected Disease of Modern Society.* It highlighted the need for improvement in emergency medical care and provided the blueprint for subsequent work, which culminated in a federal law. The Emergency Medical Services Systems Act of 1973 and its amendments in 1976 and 1979 provided mechanisms and funds for communities to establish emergency medical services systems aimed at reducing death and disability rates from all types of emergency illnesses (Boyd, 1982). The law mandated that emergency medical care programs must address, plan, and implement a "systems approach" to the provision of services and specified a number of requirements to assist planners, coordinators, and operators in establishing comprehensive programs (U.S. Department of Health, Education and Welfare [DHEW], 1975). That led to the development of a new specialty—emergency medicine—with more than 100 residency training programs and nearly 100 million patient visits per year (Young & Sklar, 1995).

The number of patients using hospital emergency room services has been steadily rising although most patients use these services for nonurgent reasons (Roemer, 1986; Williams, 1991). According to Boyd's (1982) calculations, of the millions who enter the emergency medical service system each year, at least 80% cannot be considered "true" emergencies, "another 15 percent constitutes real emergencies who require urgent care (minor trauma or infectious diseases, for example); the remaining 5 percent includes the critically ill and injured (trauma, burns, cardiac, poisonings, etc.)" (p. 114). The diversity of patients seen in emergency rooms may include "patients with severe trauma or a sore throat, patients who are intoxicated or psychotic, transients looking for a warm place to stay, and elderly people who are merely confused" (Clement & Durgin, 1987, p. 500). Many of these patients have legitimate health needs for which they have nowhere else to go. Many of them have no private physician, and appropriate outpatient clinics have no concurrent hours. Even those who have a private physician come to the emergency room when either the physician is not available or the physician suggests that they go there for evaluation of their condition. A study of the access of Medicaid recipients to outpatient care (Medicaid Access Study Group, 1994) found that these patients have limited access to ambulatory care outside hospital emergency departments. Moreover, the law (COBRA, 1986) requires that all emergency department patients be treated regardless of their ability to pay. The importance of the emergency room as a site for ambulatory care is likely to continue.

ILLNESS PREVENTION AND HEALTH PROMOTION AGENCIES

To understand the past of the major organizations involved in illness prevention and health promotion, we look at the history of (a) the significant worldwide events to which these organizations can trace their origins, (b) the significant ideas that have guided their philosophy, and (c) public health in the United States.

Significant Events

According to Taylor, Denham, and Ureda (1982), the history of health care can be divided into three eras: era of disease treatment, era of preventive medicine, and era of health promotion. The *era of disease treatment* goes back to 35 centuries B.C., when evil spirits were exorcised, war-wounded limbs were cauterized or amputated, and various minerals, plants, and animal parts were used to treat the ill. Later centuries added to these therapies of disease treatment. The 18th and 19th centuries saw a shift of thinking from treatment to prevention.

Widespread implementation of smallpox vaccination was followed by Pasteur's discovery that attenuated chicken cholera organisms could bring protection against virulent bacteria, setting the stage for the many vaccines later developed. In 1901, Walter Reed in Havana confirmed that the *Aedes aegypti* mosquito was the vector of yellow fever; subsequent public health measures confirmed that malaria could be prevented by mosquito control. In 1914 Dr. Joseph Goldberger discovered that pellagra was caused by a dietary deficiency and that it could be prevented by consuming foods containing a "pellagra-preventive" factor, which we now know as niacin. Public health efforts to ensure safe water and milk supplies reduced morbidity and mortality due to typhoid fever. Diphtheria, pertussis, and tetanus vaccines were developed during the 1930s and 1940s. Then came the Salk polio vaccine in 1952 and the Sabin oral polio vaccine in 1960. Measles, mumps, and rubella vaccines were introduced in 1958, 1967, and 1969, respectively. Efforts to develop safe, effective vaccines for a broad variety of diseases continue in laboratories across the country. (Taylor et al., 1982, p. 4)

The past two or three decades have witnessed, on the one hand, changes in the patterns of morbidity and mortality, with infectious diseases no longer topping the list of major disablers and killers and, on the other hand, a concern with the quality of life. More and more people are now willing to take responsibility for their health. Factors that have contributed to the emergence of this era include the following.

1. *Worldwide inflation was reflected, in the United States most vividly, in the ever-rising costs of medical treatment and rehabilitation without corresponding gains in health and mental health.* This reality was highlighted by uninspiring outcome studies of health and mental health treatments. These, in turn, generated cost-containment concerns and efforts in the 1970s and 1980s.

2. *The returns on investments in medical care and communicable disease control were diminishing.* This plus the rapid diffusion of scientific evidence linking lifestyle and chronic disease, and the development of skills and techniques for behavioral and lifestyle changes led to selected efforts of health, hospital, and industrial groups to redirect medical care funds toward prevention-oriented programs.

3. *The community development and mass communications movements and technologies of the 1950s and 1960s were beginning to affect large segments of the population.* Recognition was growing that prevention was easier and less costly than treatment and that many people were suffering from preventable illnesses and problems. This was happening

in the midst of a growing disillusionment with conventional medical approaches and the appearance of imaginative concepts encompassing social, mental, and spiritual qualities of life. A shift to an emphasis on holistic health resulted in changes in cultural norms about health and fitness among large groups of the population.

4. *The inequality in the availability and quality of treatment for people of different social classes, cultures, and races was documented.* This came at the time of the civil rights and women's movements. On the one hand, these movements demanded transfer of authority and resources to people previously deprived of these; on the other hand, they emphasized self-help and taking charge of one's life (Bloom, 1987; Bracht, 1987; Green & Raeburn, 1990).

In short, the country seemed to be ready for the challenge of what Terris (1983) called the "second epidemiological revolution"—the fight against chronic diseases. Alternative health interventions that were appearing also fit in with the consumer movement and were empowering. "Self-help is empowering, anti-expert, anti-authority, choice-oriented, and it increasingly questions the external world-view" (Riessman, 1994, p. 54). A new era had begun, the era of health promotion. "More than the other two eras, the era of health promotion has been ushered in as a social movement, and much of its impetus has arisen from persons and institutions outside the medical mainstream: joggers, weight control groups, Alcoholics Anonymous, tobacco opponents, and others" (Taylor et al., 1982, p. 5).

Significant Ideas

Although the importance of *health promotion* was recognized as early as the first quarter of the 20th century, the concept was narrowly defined and operationalized as primary prevention activities. Even the scope of primary prevention activities remained narrow. It covered only the prevention and early detection of specific diseases. That scope gradually widened. The term *health promotion* was used almost 50 years ago by a medical historian, Sigerist (1946), when he defined the four major tasks of medicine as the (a) promotion of health, (b) prevention of illness, (c) restoration of the sick, and (d) rehabilitation. He spelled out the conditions for health promotion—a decent standard of living, good labor conditions, education, physical culture, means of rest and recreation—and called for the coordinated efforts of politicians, labor, industry, educators, and physicians for ensuring these. Kelly, Charlton, and Hanlon (1993) identified four levels of health promotion—environ-mental, social, organizational, and individual—and urged that all four be understood and integrated for successful health promotion. It has taken several decades for health professionals to appreciate the richness of the concept of "health promotion."

Back in 1920, C. E. A. Winslow's definition of *public health* not only captured the changing scope of public health but also reflected the direction of that change:

> Public health is the science and art of (1) preventing disease, (2) prolong-ing life, and (3) organizing community efforts for (a) the sanitation of the environment, (b) the control of community infections, (c) the education of the individual in personal hygiene, (d) the organization of medical and nursing services for the early diagnosis and preventive treatment of diseases, and (e) the development of social machinery to insure to every-one a standard of living adequate for the maintenance of health, so organizing these benefits as to enable every citizen to realize his birthright of health and longevity. (Winslow, quoted in Hanlon & Pickett, 1984)

The terms *public* and *health* provide the themes for what public health is all about. *Public* does not refer to the auspices under which a health program is carried out, but rather to the public it serves (Rice, 1957). The agency providing services may be governmental (federal, state, and local) or voluntary and private. *Public* also involves organized community effort. Individual effort is important but must be augmented by communitywide work because "neither treatment of lung disease nor exhorting individuals to avoid smoking could have achieved the reduc-tion of smoking in public places made possible by organized community effort to adopt laws and regulations restricting smoking" (Institute of Medicine, 1988a, p. 39). Public health is also public in terms of its long-range goal of optimal health for the whole community. Beauchamp (1976) saw the mission of public health as social justice and the protec-tion of all human life. Similar to the concept of "public," "health" has been variously defined. The World Health Organization (WHO) defini-tion of *health* as "physical, mental, and social well-being, not merely the absence of disease or infirmity" widens the scope of public health work.[1]

Until 1960, the *infectious disease model* guided the public health approach and activities. This model views the disease process as the interaction between host, agent, and environment and focuses on one agent, a microbe or traumatic event that precipitates the disease process.

By the 1960s, it was realized that infectious diseases were no longer a threat to the public's health. Chronic diseases had become the major culprits. Attention shifted to dealing with chronic diseases in whose etiologies a single cause or agent could not be identified. Hence the *chronic disease model* was created, emphasizing processes that would identify factors associated with a specific health problem. By the 1970s, questions about the appropriateness of these models were raised (e.g., see Terris, 1975). It was suggested that the disease orientation of public health efforts should be replaced by a wellness orientation and that public health approaches should be strength oriented. By the 1980s, a broadened view of primary prevention appeared that not only included *health promotion* but also gave it a place of prominence.

A related concept is "wellness," which is defined as "the process and state of a quest for maximum human functioning that involves the body, mind, and spirit" (Archer, Probert, & Gage, 1987, p. 311). Several models of wellness have been proposed. For example, Ardell (1988) described eight dimensions of wellness: psychological, spiritual, physical fitness, job satisfaction, relationships, family life, leisure time, and stress management. Earlier, Hettler (1984) had proposed a six-dimensional model; its dimensions were intellectual, emotional, physical, social, occupational, and spiritual wellness. All these models of wellness seek to describe the "whole" or "total" person. Witmer and Sweeney (1992) tried to trace the origin of the idea of this wholeness to the writings of Adler, Jung, and Maslow and proposed a holistic model for wellness and prevention over the life span: "The characteristics of wellness are expressed through the five life tasks of spirituality, self-regulation, work, love, and friendship. These life tasks dynamically interact with the life forces of family, community, religion, education, government, media, and business/industry" (p. 140). The concept of "wellness" is akin to the WHO definition of health as a state of complete physical, mental, and social well-being, and not merely the absence of disease or infirmity. "The definition viewed health as a multidimensional (holistic) phenomenon, with multiple determinants, one that can be defined by its positive (well-being) rather than negative aspects" (Green & Raeburn, 1990, p. 33). The concepts that have guided the wellness movement in the United States include "self-responsibility for personal health," "physical fitness," "nutritional awareness," and "stress management." The future will find health workers building on these ideas as the field of health promotion and wellness grows.

History of Public Health

Organizationally, public health is a system of programs, policies, and personnel whose goal is to prevent disease, prolong life, and promote better health (*Social Work Dictionary,* 1991). It has been a part of the impressive disease prevention work, and "were it not for the organized public health efforts, our nation would not be as stable, as successful, or as livable as it is" (Raffel & Raffel, 1989, p. 273).

If public health is broadly defined as conscious efforts by an authority to protect the health of the community, the history of public health can be traced back to ancient times:

> Crete, Egypt, Greece, and Rome, all, at some time, built model towns and had finely developed sanitary systems. In Rome public baths were available to everyone; here the workers went in the evening "to wash and to undo the fatigues of the day." Inoculation against smallpox was practiced in India and China before the Christian era. Rome built leprosaria and, like Greece, sought to regulate prostitution. The latrine and the flush closet were invented not as some have said during the European Renaissance, but in Crete 3,000 years before, or earlier. The Arabic civilization carried on where Rome and Greece left off; Cordoba and other Arabian cities had health departments with sanitary inspectors. (Brockington, 1975, p. 1)

If defined as efforts to apply social, scientific, and medical knowledge to the protection of the community's health, however, public health is a modern phenomenon. Before the 18th century, although there were sporadic public efforts to protect people from epidemics such as plague, cholera, and smallpox through isolation of the ill and quarantine of travelers, these diseases were often considered a sign of poor moral and spiritual condition, to be corrected by prayer and piety (Goudsblom, 1986). By the 18th century, isolation of the ill and quarantine of the exposed became an accepted method of containing contagious diseases. In 1701, Massachusetts passed laws for that purpose. Prior to the 19th century, however, diseases were largely undifferentiated and unclassified, and no records of births and deaths were kept. Environmental hygiene as conducted from the ancient days had little scientific basis except in the practice of inoculation against smallpox. The 19th century witnessed the identification of filth as being responsible for the cause and spread of diseases, and cleanliness as the answer:

Illness came to be seen as an indicator of poor social and environmental conditions, as well as poor moral and spiritual conditions. Cleanliness was embraced as a path both to physical and moral health. Cleanliness, piety, and isolation were seen to be compatible and mutually reinforcing measures to help the public resist disease. (Institute of Medicine, 1988a, p. 58)

The efforts of Edwin Chadwick, secretary of the Poor Law Commission in Britain in 1838, greatly influenced the sanitary reform movement. The commission conducted studies of the life and health of the working class of the entire country. The findings of those studies led to the passage of the Public Health Act of 1848, which "must forever be a landmark in the history of world public health" (Brockington, 1975, p. 4). Chadwick's ideas emphasizing environmental aspects of hygiene also influenced developments in North America. Local sanitation surveys were conducted in several American cities. A report of the Massachusetts Sanitary Commission based on a survey done by Lemual Shattuck led to the creation of the state board of health in 1869. Many of the principles and activities, including the maintenance of records and vital statistics, proposed by Shattuck later came to be considered fundamental to public health (Rosenkrantz, 1972). By the end of the 19th century, scientific knowledge about causes and prevention of many diseases had significantly advanced. As pointed out earlier, bacteriologic agents of such diseases as tuberculosis, diphtheria, typhoid, and yellow fever were discovered, and it was learned that both people and the environment could be agents of disease (Institute of Medicine, 1988a).

Thus, public health began in the United States in the 19th century with the need to control such communicable diseases as smallpox, typhoid, and diphtheria. The first public health activities were in large cities, and their focus was on improving sanitation. Local boards of health were formed for the purpose.

They developed ordinances regarding waste disposal, street drainage, removal of filth, drainage of swamps, and other measures that would improve the sanitary environment. Quarantine of homes and ships, and much later immunizations, were also important functions of local boards of health aimed at preventing the spread of infectious diseases. (Raffel & Raffel, 1989, p. 263)

The first state board of health was formed in Massachusetts in 1869, and by 1900 all states had boards of health. These boards were concerned with the statewide control of communicable diseases. Departments of public health with full-time staffs evolved to carry out the functions of boards of health. These functions gradually expanded to include (a) environmental sanitation surveillance, (b) school health and immunization, (c) maternal and child health care, (d) limited care for indigent patients, and (e) screening for and control of such diseases as tuberculosis and venereal diseases (Bracht, 1978). Their thrust was illness prevention.

Each state is sovereign in its authority and responsibility for protecting the health of its citizens. Not only are the power and authority of local governments regarding health derived from the state, but the powers of the federal government in the field of health are also delegated by the states (Grant, 1987). In reality, all levels of government—state, local, and federal—as well as many nongovernmental agencies are involved in public health work.

State Public Health Departments

State health departments vary significantly in their organization. Raffel and Raffel (1989) found three basic models of organization operating. In the first, a board of health (typically appointed by the governor and approved by the state senate, a majority of whose members tend to be physicians) has policy or administrative functions. These boards either appoint or strongly influence the appointment of key personnel of the department. They have the authority for not only the overall direction of the department but also the enforcement of public health laws "by holding hearings on violations, hearing appeals on health officer actions, and by issuance of board orders for compliance with the laws. Board orders must be enforced by law enforcement agencies, although the recipient of a board health order can, of course, appeal it in the state courts" (Raffel & Raffel, 1989, p. 266). These boards function well when the professionalism of their members prevails over their political agendas. In the second model, the department is headed by a secretary or commissioner of health appointed by the governor. The success of this model also depends on the quality of both the appointed official and the governor who appoints him or her. "If a governor avoids tough issues, if a governor tends to appoint incompetents or political hacks, then the board system might be preferred. If, on the other hand, there is an unprogressive board, then a strong governor with a competent secretary of health would be preferred" (Raffel & Raffel, 1989, p. 267). In the third model, an umbrella organization such as a department of human resources is created that includes health along with other agencies such as mental health, education, and welfare. This department is headed by a secretary. The state health officer reports to that person. Improved coordination of services provided by related agencies is the rationale for this model, but the organization of the department alone does not necessarily result in improved coordination. Many other variables come into play.

Miller and associates (1977) analyzed state public health laws and identified 44 areas as the responsibility of state health departments. These included communicable disease, venereal disease, chronic disease, alcohol and drug addiction, rabies, and air and water pollution control; food, housing, and health facilities inspection; health personnel registration and facilities licensure; dental, home, maternal/child, mental, occupational, and school health; compulsory hospitalization and quarantines; care of the indigent, ambulance, and emergency medical service; and vital statistics. Some of the health programs (particularly state tuberculosis, mental health, and mental retardation hospitals, and licensure of health personnel, hospitals, nursing homes, and other health care facilities) are operated directly by the state health department; the operation of others is shared with the local health agencies, with the state health department setting the standards of performance for the local agencies and providing state funds to supplement the local resources. The Committee for the Study of the Future of Public Health found that whereas some state health departments are active and well equipped, others perform fewer functions and have meager resources (Institute of Medicine, 1988a).

Local Public Health Departments

The degree of autonomy enjoyed by local agencies varies greatly among states. Physicians dominate local health agencies. Almost two thirds of the heads of these are physicians although only one third of them have had training in public health (Raffel & Raffel, 1989). The organizational pattern of these departments varies greatly.

In New England, local departments tend to be on a city or town basis, county government being weak or nonexistent. In the South, local departments tend to be organized on a county basis. And there are in-between arrangements, as in Pennsylvania, in which there is a provision for county health departments (but very few in existence), local government (sub-county, town, borough, etc.) units with largely environmental respon-sibilities, as well as regional state health department offices. In some parts of the country, we find metropolitan and other kinds of multijurisdictional departments, that is, multicounty or combined city-county departments. (Raffel & Raffel, 1989, p. 273)

This variance goes beyond the organization. Some local health departments are technically very sophisticated and provide impressive services. "But in too many localities, there is no health department. Perhaps the area is visited occasionally by a 'circuit-riding' public health nurse—and perhaps not" (Institute of Medicine, 1988a, p. 3). A local health department profile prepared by the National Association of County Health Officials showed that, in 1985, there were 2,932 or-ganized local health units in the United States, most of them too small to have adequate funds from limited local tax bases. Only 11% of them can rely on the professional assistance of an epidemiologist (Koplin, 1993). These departments also vary in their relationships with other local health care agencies and private care providers.

Federal Public Health Service

Over the years, the federal government has acquired tremendous power in the field of health. Although the federal government has no constitutional authority to provide direct health services, it does provide some health services but mostly buys the action it wants by providing money to state and local governments and nongovernmental agencies. The "Powers of Congress" part of the U.S. Constitution gives the federal government authority to (a) raise and support armies, provide and maintain a navy, and make all laws "necessary and proper" to carry out those powers; and (b) regulate foreign and interstate commerce. These powers have been used to establish and operate military, naval, air force, and veterans hospitals and services, as well as to regulate foods, drugs, product and occupational safety, and some environmental health ac-tivities. "The power to control federal lands, along with the presidential power to make treaties (with the advice and consent of the Senate) are the sources of federal activity in providing health services for Native Americans and Eskimos. Other direct service activities also rely on these clauses for legitimization" (Raffel & Raffel, 1989, p. 285). The federal government was also helped by the Supreme Court decision in *McCulloch v. Maryland* (1819), which set out the doctrine of implied powers, powers beyond those specifically delegated in the Constitution but reasonably implied by the delegated powers (Institute of Medicine, 1988a).

The mission of the federal government's Public Health Service is to protect and advance the health of Americans by (a) preventing and controlling disease, identifying health hazards, and promoting a healthy lifestyle for the nation's citizens; (b) assisting in the delivery of health care services to medically underserved populations and other groups with special health needs; (c) administering block grants to the states for preventive and health services; alcohol, drug abuse, and mental health services; maternal and child health services; and primary health care; (d) ensuring that drugs and medical devices are safe and effective and protecting the public from unsafe foods and unnecessary exposure to humanmade radiation; (e) conducting and supporting biomedical and behavioral research and communicating results to health professionals and the public; (f) monitoring the adequacy of health workers and facilities available to serve the nation's needs; and (g) working with other nations on global health problems (Public Health Service, 1980).

The Public Health Service began in 1798 when a law was passed to provide for the relief of sick and disabled seamen. This law led to the establishment of what later came to be known as Public Health Service hospitals. The establishment of a one-room laboratory at the Marine Hospital in Staten Island, New York, in 1887 was the beginning of the current National Institutes of Health. The functions of the Public Health Service broadened after the passage of the Social Security Act, which authorized annual grants to the states for the investigation of disease and problems of sanitation (Raffel & Raffel, 1989). A significant milestone in the history of the federal government's involvement in health is the Public Health Service Act of 1944, which broadened the scope of previously established Public Health Service functions and reshaped it to meet the requirements not only of the day but also of the future. It authorized the Public Health Service to make grants and contracts (leading to the growth of extramural programs) and authorized it to work with and support the efforts of state health departments; strengthened and expanded its Commissioned Corps (to include nurses, sanitarians, and other specialists); and expanded the office of its surgeon general, "which has proved to be such a bully pulpit for educating our people in good health habits" (Lee, 1994, p. 466). The Public Health Service is now a part of the U.S. Department of Health and Human Services and operates the following six agencies:

Alcohol, Drug Abuse, and Mental Health Administration
Centers for Disease Control and Prevention
Agency for Toxic Substances and Disease Registry
Food and Drug Administration
Health Resources and Services Administration
National Institutes of Health

The federal Public Health Service has been active in the following components of national leadership in public health: (a) identifying and speaking out on specific health problems, (b) allocating funds for national public health objectives, (c) building constituencies to support action on those objectives, and (d) supporting the development of knowledge and databases. The federal government has sometimes bypassed the state and local agencies in carrying out federal health priorities, however, and at other times has reduced federal funds earmarked for public health activities by turning over more public health decision making to states (Institute of Medicine, 1988a).

Nongovernmental Organizations in Public Health

The other element of the illness prevention and health promotion picture is made up of numerous private, nongovernmental entities. These include health-related agencies and private physicians and their organizations. The line between public and private responsibilities for public health has never been hard and clear. It has shifted and blurred over the years. When public health activities were essentially matters of sanitary engineering and environmental hygiene, private physicians were active participants in the joint public and private efforts.

> With the discovery of bacteria and the development of immunization techniques, however, disease prevention could no longer be so easily defined solely as a communitywide affair. The line between prevention and treatment began to fade, and the domains of public health and private medicine could no longer be easily separated. This development created a certain amount of tension between the two that has never fully been resolved. (Institute of Medicine, 1988a, p. 51)

Of the other agencies involved in public health work, some are quite old, whereas others are comparatively new; and some are generic in their activities and scope, whereas others are concerned with the prevention and treatment of specific diseases. The following is a partial list of prominent agencies.

American Cancer Society
American Diabetes Association
American Heart Association
Epilepsy Foundation of America
March of Dimes
National Association for Mental Health
National Council on Alcoholism
National Easter Seal Society for Crippled Children and Adults
National Kidney Foundation
National Society for the Prevention of Blindness
National Tuberculosis and Respiratory Disease Association
Planned Parenthood
United Cerebral Palsy Association

The United States is in the era of health promotion, and the factors that gave birth to this era still prevail. They will continue as forces encouraging the health promotion and wellness movement in the next century. There is a long way to go. Many people in communities all over the country do not have access to the benefits of illness prevention and health promotion activities and programs. Threats to public health not only persist but are increasing. "These threats include immediate crises, such as the AIDS epidemic; enduring problems, such as injuries and chronic illness; and impending crises foreshadowed by such developments as the toxic by-products of a modern economy" (Institute of Medicine, 1988a, p. 1). Recently, the Institute of Medicine of the National Academy of Sciences released study findings that address the concern that the country "has lost sight of its public health goals and has allowed the system of public health activities to fall into disarray" (Institute of Medicine, 1988a, p. 1). These findings highlight the need for improvement in all aspects of public health in the United States. A significant reason for the sorry state of the country's public health system is misplaced priorities and resources. More than 75% of federal health care dollars are spent on the care of people with chronic illnesses such as cancer, heart disease, and stroke, whereas less than 0.5% is spent on preventing those same diseases.

LONG-TERM CARE SETTINGS

Long-term care (LTC) seems to have no boundaries in terms of settings of care, types of services, diversity of service recipients, and variety of service providers. Below, we discuss the three major groups of LTC facilities: (a) nursing homes as representatives of institution-based long-term care, (b) community residential care settings as representatives of "quasi-institution"-based care, and (c) home-based/near home-based care provided in recipients' homes or within their easy reach.

Nursing Homes

Although the name and existence of nursing homes is a recent phenomenon, county homes and almshouses can be viewed as their predecessors. Those institutions were society's response to the needs of people who could not care for themselves and had no family to care for them. These people included "the disabled, handicapped, aged, widows with children, orphans, the feebleminded, the deranged, the chronically ill and the unemployed" (Brody, 1977, p. 31). With the exception of a few of these categories, such as widows with children and the unemployed, today's nursing homes care for persons who would have had to live in almshouses and county homes in the 19th and early 20th centuries. By the 1920s, nonprofit homes for the aged, caring for the indigent "well aged," appeared under sectarian auspices. Almshouses, county homes, and mental hospitals were the homes for those with physical and mental impairments. Social Security legislation in the 1930s led to the creation of the nursing home as the successor of the almshouse. The law prohibited those living in government-supported institutions from receiving Social Security. Nursing homes appeared as the answer. These were private businesses that provided custodial care for the elderly who did not have their own homes and families (Clark, 1971) and were too frail to be cared for in the community. The federal government's main concern at the time was with the poor old (and the need to remove them from almshouses), and not the frail old.

As it turned out many of these poor elders were also frail and required supportive care. The combination of cash income and need for care led not to home care, but to the birth of modern proprietary nursing homes. . . . Then as now, some form of home care would have been the preferred alternative of many frail old. But the manifest concern was poverty, not frailty, so the issue and alternative solutions were never joined. Thus, nursing homes grew up over the ensuing 20-year period addressed to the frail old. (Hudson, 1990, p. 273)

Other factors also contributed to this growth. Interest in old people was growing, as exemplified by the first National Conference on Aging in 1950. The Hill-Burton Act (1946) gave financial aid, the Small Business Act and Small Business Investment Act (1958) provided loans, and the 1959 amendment to the National Housing Act provided mortgage insurance to facilitate the construction and equipment of nursing homes. The passage of Medicare and Medicaid in 1965 made federal funds available for purchasing long-term care (Clark, 1971). In the 1960s, states had started discharging the elderly from mental hospitals to the community. Community services were not adequate for the increased demand, and many of the discharged patients needed round-the-clock care. Many of these patients went to nursing homes. The power of the nursing home lobby also helped the expansion of the nursing home industry (Vladeck, 1980). A contrast between the number of nursing home beds in 1939 and 1970 illustrates the dramatic growth of nursing homes. It is estimated that 25,000 nursing home beds were available in 1939. In three decades, that number jumped to almost 1 million in 1970 (Brody, 1977). Now, 19,700 nursing homes with 1,624,000 beds (Mezey & Knapp, 1993) are occupied by persons requiring differing levels of care—very intense to moderate to minimal.

All nursing homes provide four basic types of services: (a) nursing care, (b) personal care, (c) residential services, and (d) medical care. *Nursing care* includes giving medicines orally and by injections, tube feeding, catheterization, and wound care and may also involve physical, occupational, and speech therapy services. *Personal care* includes help in walking, bathing, dressing, and eating. *Residential services* encompass protective environment, supervision, and appropriate social services. *Medical care* includes visits by a physician who orders and monitors medications, special diets, and restorative and rehabilitative procedures.

The quality of care provided by nursing homes varies greatly. Although along with government financing nursing home care has come regulation of the nursing home industry by both federal and state governments, it has not ensured a high level of quality of care throughout the industry. Both lay and professional literature is full of material pointing to abuses of basic human rights of nursing home residents. Former Senator Claude Pepper, who devoted most of his political career to championing the cause of the elderly, included the following among these rights: (a) the right to complain and seek redress of grievances; (b) the right to make basic personal choices; (c) the right to privacy: (d) the right to maintain personal possessions; (e) the right to freedom from verbal abuse; (f) the right to adequate and appropriate medical and nursing care; (g) the right to freedom of movement; (h) the right to a clean and safe living environment; (i) the right to freedom of speech, assembly, and religion; and (j) the right to freedom from physical and sexual abuse. It is alleged that nursing homes are more concerned about profits than the quality of services. The bulk of care is provided by personnel who are ill-trained, grossly overworked, and poorly paid (Pepper, 1986).

Many research studies have investigated differences between for-profit and not-for-profit nursing homes in terms of such dimensions as access, cost, efficiency, and quality. O'Brien, Saxberg, and Smith (1983) reviewed several of these studies and found that not-for-profit nursing homes had higher quality but lower efficiency (higher costs). On the other hand, Davis (1991) analyzed the findings of several other studies and concluded that "in light of the data, it would be premature to conclude that nonprofit nursing homes provide higher quality care, *ceteris paribus*" (p. 147). A more recent study of for-profit and not-for-profit nursing homes in Pennsylvania by Aaronson, Zinn, and Rosko (1994) found that not-for-profit nursing homes provide significantly higher quality of care to both Medicaid beneficiaries and self-pay residents than do for-profit nursing homes. An Institute of Medicine (1986) study looked for other causes of poor quality of care in nursing homes and identified inadequate supervision of care by physicians and professional nurses as a primary reason for poor quality. Sheridan, White, and Fairchild (1992) explored human resource management factors for an understanding of why some nursing homes, both for-profit and not-for-profit, fail to provide adequate care. They found that staff members' job attitudes, opinions about elderly residents, and perceptions of the organizational climate varied between the successful for-profit and not-for-profit homes. Among other things, the organizational commitment was much higher in successful not-for-profit than in successful for-profit nursing homes.

Nursing homes perform a social function, and they receive public money through several channels. Medicaid and Medicare programs are the major source of payment for their services. Not-for-profit nursing homes are also publicly subsidized through tax exemptions and tax-exempt capital financing. Therefore, they are subject to governmental regulation and scrutiny. The reason why regulation of nursing homes and inadequate quality of care can coexist lies partly in the lack of commitment to collecting accurate information on the well-being of nursing home residents:

- The regulations do not require assessment of the quality of care, only assessment of the facility's structural capacity to provide care.
- The survey process used for assessment emphasizes paper compliance, rather than observation and interviews with nursing home residents.
- Many of the standards are vague and depend too much on unguided judgments by surveyors. Many of the surveyors are untrained, and their judgments are frequently inconsistent: What is deemed acceptable by one surveyor may be unacceptable to another (Katz & Committee on Nursing Home Regulation, 1986, p. 70)

Nursing homes will continue as an important element of long-term care in the next century, but they have a long way to go to improve both their services and their public image.

Community Residential Care Settings

Long-term care in non-institutional settings takes many forms. Although the advent of Social Security led to the creation of nursing homes, it also encouraged several other more informal arrangements for the nonsick homeless elderly. The origin of a residential arrangement within a private home—a sort of adult foster care—has been traced back to A.D. 600, and such foster homes have been used in the United States for almost 100 years for the care of those with mental illness (McCoin, 1983). Application of the "foster care" concept to the elderly and persons with mental retardation is a recent phenomenon. The formal beginning of the use of foster homes for the care of the elderly can be traced to 1967, when a demonstration program was authorized by the Department of Health, Education and Welfare in the state of Washington to provide foster home care for the elderly (Fenske & Roecker, 1971). This type of care for the elderly still has room for further growth. Foster family care is now recognized as a viable and cost-efficient approach to the residential care of people with mental retardation (Best-Sigford, Bruininks, Lakin, Hill, & Heal, 1982). This type of care, nevertheless, still lacks a precise definition.

> Adult foster care is a community-based living arrangement in which an individual who is not fully capable of self-care is taken into the home of a nonrelative, often referred to as a provider, operator, a caretaker. In this setting, the client receives room, board, daily care, and supervision as needed. The provider, in turn, is compensated for his or her duties. (Brockett, 1981, pp. 4-5)

The familylike environment is the major characteristic of this type of care. Originally, the arrangement between the resident and the care provider was private and informal even though the resident's method of payment was usually government financed. This arrangement gradually changed. Several factors influenced the development of the concept of "foster care" and its many operationalizations.

The legislative response to the deinstitutionalization movement provided for community mental health centers for outpatient supervision and follow-up of patients discharged from mental hospitals. Communities were not ready for the housing and other needs of these patients. Many hospitals, state mental health departments, and cities began establishing foster care programs for the deinstitutionalized population (Fenske & Roecker, 1971). Creation of the Supplemental Security Income (SSI) program theoretically made possible the national-level oversight of the quality of life of SSI recipients. Later, the concern with the quality of these and other living arrangements led to the enactment of the Keyes legislation, which mandated states to set standards for SSI recipients living in foster homes (Sutherland & Oktay, 1987). No federal role was established, however, to review standards or to enforce the legislation (Oktay & Palley, 1988).

Currently, these non-institutional living arrangements include small homes caring for one to six residents, board and care homes, domiciliary care homes, sheltered residential facilities, and group homes. There is no consensus about how each type of care is different from others. The number of persons cared for seems to set one type of home apart from others. McCoin (1995) viewed many of these as representing a continuum of community-based (non-institutional) care for adults and covered them under the umbrella term *adult residential care.* Notwithstanding the importance of the *care* component of foster care homes, I label all of these as quasi-institutional because they must maintain a minimum standard of care and are subject to the monitoring and accountability mechanisms of some governmental agency. The degree of regulation of and support provided to these sources of long-term care varies greatly despite the fact that most recipients of this type of care are vulnerable. They have mental impairment, developmental disability, and/or are frail elders. Most studies of this type of care fall into two groups—one concentrating on the homes caring for veterans, and the other investigating homes caring for residents from the general population.

The VA has the most experience in establishing, fostering, regulating, and supervising foster care homes. Haber (1983) described the VA Community Residential Care program. These VA homes are carefully evaluated and inspected, their care providers (called sponsors) are trained and given ongoing advice and assistance, and the veterans placed there are regularly visited by social workers. Linn, Caffey, Klett, and Hogarty (1977) conducted an extensive study of five VA residential care programs and found these homes a viable family substitute and a stepping stone to other community life. Sickman and Dhooper (1991) studied 46 sponsors providing residential care to veterans in Kentucky and found a vast majority of them doing an admirable job of caring for veterans living under their roofs. Studies of nonveterans in foster home care have investigated the socioeconomic characteristics of home operators, their reasons for taking on this responsibility, the degree of integration of residents in the family life of the operators, and the extent of their acceptance in the community (e.g., see Blaustein & Veik, 1987; Bradshaw, Vonderharr, Keeney, Tyler, & Harris, 1976; Thompson et al., 1989). Oktay and Volland (1987) described the startup of a hospital-based community care program for frail elderly and evaluated it as a viable alternative to nursing home care. These homes are largely free from the abuses of patients' rights and other negatives generally associated with nursing homes. They do provide a more familylike environment and add to the choices of those who cannot live independently and want to avoid nursing home placement.

The degree of "familylike" atmosphere in these homes varies, however. Dhooper, Royse, and Rihm (1989) studied 50 adults with mild and moderate mental retardation living in four types of community residential settings and found that type of setting is associated with the subjects' perception of the extent to which their needs are being met and the degree of choice they exercise in everyday activities. Setting also has an influence on the other objectives of placement. Willer and Intagliata (1982) compared deinstitutionalized adults with mental retardation in two residential alternatives—family care and group homes—in terms of the improvement in their self-care, social, and community living skills. Those in the family care home were significantly more likely to improve their maladaptive behavior, whereas those in the group home were more likely to improve community living skills. Residents in both settings displayed essentially no improvement in self-care skills. All these homes need to do a better job of working toward a greater integration in the community of those in their care. Their importance is likely to increase in the future.

Home-Based/Near Home-Based Care

The category home-based/near home-based care is used broadly to include care provided in the home of the person, as well as care within his or her easy reach. *In-home* care includes "a very complex and varying series of services, responsibilities, costs, and relationships" (Williams, 1990, p. ix). The services may be aimed at improving, restoring, or maintaining the person's functioning and independence. These may be directed toward the person and/or his or her family caregiver and may be provided by formal caregivers from health and human services professions and organizations and/or informal caregivers from the person's own social network. *Near-home* services may be provided through health clinics, mental health centers, and social service agencies. The degree of comprehensiveness and coordination of the services provided varies greatly. The history of these services can be traced to different laws providing for the needs of different population groups. The Federal Vocational Rehabilitation Act of 1920 focused on the vocational retraining and job placement of disabled service personnel; its amendment (the Barden-Follette Amendment), in the early days of World War II, extended the provisions to civilians. The Vocational Rehabilitation Act of 1954 provided for additional services. The Rehabilitation Act of 1973 represents the most significant societal mandate for the civil rights of individuals with disabilities (Hirschwald, 1984), and the 1978 amendments to that act expanded the meaning and scope of services. The Older Americans Act of 1965 has been the cornerstone of federal involvement in a number of community services for older persons. The Older Americans Act, Title III, provides for funding for congregate meal sites, senior citizens' centers, home care, home-delivered meals, transportation, chore services, telephone reassurance, home visits, and the Nursing Home Ombudsman Advocacy Program (U.S. Senate Special Committee on Aging, 1991). Medicare and Medicaid (Titles XVIII and XIX of the Social Security Act) have also been the source of funds for many long-term care services for the aged and those with disabilities, both old and young. Title XX of the Social Security Act funds a variety of social services, including adult day care, adult foster care, protective services, homemaker services, transportation, and home-delivered meals.

In the case of infants, toddlers, and children with disabilities, the need for home-based services gradually decreases as the venue of care shifts to schools and other outside-the-home settings such as sheltered workshops. In the case of older persons with disabilities, failing health, and increasing self-care limitations, the need gradually increases. The need for home-based care occurs more commonly among older adults. The services they need may range from assistance with activities of daily living to high-tech medical care to maintaining their homes as viable settings for care. An ample description of home care services would include medical diagnosis and treatment; nursing care; medication; physical, occupational, and speech therapy; mental health care; provision of medical supplies and equipment; personal care; health aide and homemaker assistance; home repair and maintenance service; adult day care; respite care; and even social companionship (Kane & Kane, 1987).

Formal care is provided by professionals and paraprofessionals who are either from different service organizations working together, or representing a single service agency, or are self-employed. Informal care providers are unpaid relatives, friends, or neighbors. "Home care varies in scope, intensity, and duration. Sometimes it consists of no more than a single service, delivered intermittently, for a short period of time. Alternately, home care can include many different forms of service provided around the clock for months and even years" (Caro, 1990, p. 26).

Types of home care services can be classified in several ways. Yessne (1994) suggested four major segments: (a) home health services as diverse as nursing and homemaking; (b) hospice care; (c) home medical equipment, including respiratory therapy; and (d) home infusion therapy. Hughes (1992) similarly described four models: (a) high-tech home care, (b) hospice, (c) skilled home health care, and (d) low-tech custodial care. In terms of specific services, "home care encompasses a potential list of 101 services" (Handy, 1995, p. 49). Focusing on the nature of care provided yields two major models of care: one emphasizing *home health* services and the other *personal assistance* services. In the home health model, the treatment of health conditions is the primary concern and self-care limitations are of secondary importance.

Besides the type, nature, frequency, and intensity of home care services and the service providers being diverse, arrangements for payment (to formal service providers) are numerous as well. With his focus on the degree of consumer control, Kapp (1990) identified the following home care delivery models:

- *Home care provision by a governmental agency.* Care providers are governmental employees, the funding for whose services comes from state appropriations for home care services or a combination of federal and state Medicaid dollars. The consumer (care recipient) has no choice about who provides the services.

- *Purchase of service from an agency.* The governmental unit responsible for the home care program contracts with a private for-profit or nonprofit agency to provide the needed services on a case-by-case basis. The consumer has more control because his or her satisfaction is likely to be important for the home care agency.

- *Direct consumer contract with a home care or other agency.* In this model, the consumer selects the service agency that is certified for Medicare and/or Medicaid participation. The third party (Medicare, Medicaid, or an insurance company) pays for the service. The consumer's choice is often constrained by the limited availability of qualified agencies.

- *Independent provider model, with government as fiscal agent.* The consumer recruits independent service providers who are not employees of a home care agency. The governmental agency responsible for the home care program pays for the services. This model gives the consumer much greater autonomy than those listed above.

- *Independent provider is hired, supervised, and paid by the consumer with money given by a governmental agency.* This model is the same as the independent provider model except that the consumer pays the independent provider directly with money given by the governmental agency responsible for the home care program.

Eligibility for home-based services varies by program, age, geography, income level, physical condition, and previous experience

(Brody, 1977). The care provided is defined by the payor. Home health care provided by certified home health agencies is covered by Medicare. More socially oriented home care may be covered by Medicaid waivers, state programs, and programs under the Older Americans Act or may have to be paid for by the client him- or herself.

Kane and Kane (1987) used the following set of criteria in looking at long-term care and discovered significant variations.

Goal of functioning, with services being directed at preventing, correcting, or compensating for functional impairment

Focus of service being either the person with the impairment, his or her family, the environment, or some combination of all three

Locus of service, which may be the person's home or apartment, some congregate living arrangement, a senior center, a clinic, or a nursing home

Mix of services and service providers, which may involve a few or many personnel from one or many agencies

Duration and intensity of services, which may vary from life-long minimal monitoring to short-term intensive work

Nature of public sector involvement, which may be viewed as governed by the belief that long-term care is a private matter and that governments are involved only when problems are beyond the private resources

In terms of the organization and overall quality of services of home care agencies, again the variation is significant. Handy (1995) described several organizational models. That variation is understandable in view of the fact that 15,027 home care agencies operate in the United States (National Association for Home Care, 1994). Delivery of services is complex and often fragmented. Grant and Harrington (1989) listed six types of providers of home care in California: (a) licensed only (not certified) agencies, (b) licensed and certified home health agencies, (c) nurses' registries, (d) employment agencies, (e) unlicensed and temporary personnel agencies, and (f) public contract providers. These differ in how they are regulated. Even state licensing standards, if they exist (many states do not require any licensure), do not go beyond the federal Medicare standards for home health care (U.S. House, 1986). Those standards have given the lion's share of attention to nursing procedures (Eustis, Kane, & Fischer, 1993), whereas 70% to 80% of long-term home care is provided by paraprofessionals such as personal care aides, home health aides, homemakers, and personal care attendants (Applebaum & Phillips, 1990). Home care agencies may voluntarily seek accreditation from the Joint Commission of Accreditation of Health Care Organizations, the National League for Nursing, and the National Home Caring Council (Spiegal, 1987), but until recently few sought accreditation mainly because of the cost and the lack of incentives (Balinsky, 1994).

Recent studies have found that home care workers have minimal contact with their supervisors, have inadequate knowledge about client status and care plan, and lack the authority to take the initiative (Cantor & Chichin, 1990; MacAdam & Yee, 1990). The result is not only inadequate care but also the possibility of unprofessional conduct on the part of these workers. A study by Grant and Harrington (1989) identified shortcomings in the quality of in-home care in California. These included

> problems with the delivery and supervision of patient care; poor coordination of patient services; inadequate staff screening, supervision, and training; theft and fraud; drug or alcohol abuse; tardiness or absenteeism; high rates of personnel turnover; unprofessional and criminal conduct; the dispensing of medications and treatment by inappropriate personnel; inadequate clinical records; and failure to meet minimum training or education requirements. (p. 135)

It is not likely that things are any better in other states. Nevertheless, despite deficiencies, in-home care is a major piece of community long-term care. This type of care allows for the preference of most elderly and others with disabilities to stay out of nursing homes. It recognizes the contributions of informal caregivers and enhances their resources. The need for home-based/near home-based services is bound to grow in the future.

NOTE

1. The constitution of WHO begins with a set of principles, the first of which is, "Health is a state of complete physical, mental and social well-being and not merely the absence of disease or infirmity" (World Health Organization, 1958, p. 459).

Chapter 3

FUTURE NEEDS OF HEALTH CARE

This chapter brings into bold relief the important emerging needs of health care. As did the previous chapter, it focuses on settings in the four main health care sectors: acute care, ambulatory care, preventive care, and long-term care. It discusses major needs of these settings and identifies major common needs of health care providers across settings. Finally, it points out potential social work contributions to the meeting of those needs—both the care settings and care providers.

FUTURE NEEDS OF ACUTE
CARE SETTINGS (HOSPITALS)

Although acute care hospitals will change in significant ways in the 21st century, some of their characteristics as discussed in Chapter 2 will persist. Those characteristics are diversity and segmentation, social stratification, the money standard, technological identification, division between physicians and hospitals, and the authoritative role of university medicine (Stevens, 1989). The diversity of hospitals will continue. Many hospitals will expand their role to become more comprehensive in their services and to improve their responsiveness to societal needs. In the short run, while shying away from universal access to health care, the United States will allow for more expanded access than is currently the case. With that will come greater regulation and standardization of the health care industry. That, coupled with the expanded role of hospitals, will reduce the degree of *segmentation and social stratification*. At least during the first few decades of the new century, however, demand for medical services will exceed available resources, cost containment measures will increase, and expensive medical technology will be rationed (Barzansky et al., 1993). Patients with money will continue to have special appeal for hospitals that will, thus, continue to be *income-maximizing* institutions. *Technological identification* will persist but will be tempered by a shift toward a holistic approach emphasizing the concepts of "wellness" and "quality of life." The *tension between physicians and hospitals* over issues of finances and quality of care will persist (Barzansky et al., 1993). This tension will extend beyond the current concerns. Hospitals will venture into ambulatory care, and physicians will perceive anything outside the hospital as their market. Hospitals and physicians will compete to provide services (American Hospital Association [AHA], 1990). Although computer technology will make it possible for many more physicians and other health care professionals to participate in clinical research and although many more hospitals will provide health care to the poor, the *authoritative role of the academic medical center* will continue. On the basis of these observations, the following are the anticipated needs of hospitals in the future:

1. *Venturing into new areas and activities* will be the most important need of hospitals in the first few decades of the new century. As the limelight shifts from inpatient acute care to different types of outpatient services, hospitals will diversify their missions and activities. They will try to control as many pieces of the continuum of care as possible by developing a comprehensive array of health programs and related services. Many hospitals will expand into multifaceted health care complexes. Speaking about community hospitals, Eisdorfer and Maddox (1988) said that "many hospitals are exploring new ways of organizing care vertically and horizontally in order to supply a wide range of services to the community and to reach people not typically associated with the community hospital" (p. 6). The focus of health care in the future will be on nonacute ambulatory services emphasizing wellness, prevention of illness, and early detection and treatment. Even secondary and tertiary care hospitals will incorporate these elements into their activities for meeting the health care needs of their communities and for improving their image. The need for such change has been felt for some time. As a hospital director put it,

Hospitals are badly in need of image boosting. A broader look at hospitals' role in communities can do much for changing their image. One way is to consider medically underserved areas or target communities for satellite primary care facilities, as the hospitals have done in Syracuse. With appropriate community involvement and restrained public relations, the hospital may find itself in an enviable position of doing good and looking good at the same time. Primary care and decentralized hospital nonacute care services are some of the most pressing needs in high growth areas, such as many of the suburbs or small rural communities. (Yanni, 1979, p. 103)

In the opinion of a hospital president, "Perhaps more of our future than most of us ever imagined lies in this particular area" (Klima, 1992, p. 51). Examples of such efforts include hospital-sponsored primary care (Drew, 1979; Yanni, 1979), home care (Bayles, 1979), health promotion, and wellness (Lazes, 1977; Strait, 1979). The danger, however, is that while diversifying and expanding their activities, hospitals will neglect populations with special needs, such as the poor, the elderly, women, and minorities (Coile, 1990). Understanding their community and its problems, accommodating its needs, and seeking its acceptance and recognition will be the important foci of hospitals' future planning.

2. Serving diverse patient populations satisfactorily will be another vital need of hospitals in the future. Most—particularly secondary and tertiary care hospitals—will continue to provide short-term intensive high-tech care, but that care will be more comprehensive, reflecting changes in the philosophy and nature of the hospital involvement. Note 6 in Chapter 1 gives examples of the Planetree Model Hospital Unit of the Pacific Presbyterian Medical Center as a precursor of things to come. While concerned with the alleviation of the immediate medical problem, hospital care will be expected to enhance the quality of a patient's life. That will involve shifting the focus from the problem to the *person-with-the-problem in his or her life situation.* That shift will lead to the conversion of today's patient—a compliant but passive recipient of treatment—into an active partner in the therapeutic endeavor.

The patient's life situation will be minimally operationalized as the presence and active participation of the family in his or her care and treatment. Hence, the hospital-based medical care of tomorrow will be family centered. "Family-centered care means that all patients are important and have a right to be in control of all aspects of their lives; that they also have a right to have those they love with them wherever and however they wish" (Harden, 1979, p. 94). That will make the patient care situation much more complex, however. Involving the family means understanding the antecedents and consequences of the patient's illness and assessing and mobilizing the family's internal and external resources. As patients become increasingly culturally diverse, their care will also have to be culturally sensitive. Thus, a constant need of the hospitals of tomorrow will be the successful provision of acute care services that (a) combine high-tech with high-touch, (b) treat patients as partners, and (c) are comprehensive.

3. *Meeting the special needs of the elderly* will be another important need of hospitals. Older patients have had a special significance for hospitals. Although those aged 65 and above comprised only 13% of the U.S. population in 1988, they accounted for 34% of the average hospital's admissions, 45% of inpatient days, and 48% of revenues. In terms of actual numbers, these percentages translate as 11 million hospital admissions, 98 million patient days, 8.8 days per average hospital stay, $8,000 per average admission, $53 billion in Medicare payments to hospitals, and $35 billion in Medicare payments to physicians (American Hospital Association, 1989). Hence, hospitals can be viewed as de facto geriatric institutions and will become more so in the future (Vladeck, 1988). It is forecast that a sizeable proportion of the U.S. population in the next century will be made up of people aged 65 and older. The majority of them will live in the community and depend on its network of health and social work agencies. The same will be true of other non-elderly chronically ill members of the community. The number of older adults and others suffering from chronic illnesses will represent a substantial proportion of the population. They will require a system of comprehensive, integrated, and continuing care that recognizes the chronicity of their illness and their desire for functional independence. Hospitals will have to be an important part of the community's service network. For their efficiency, cost effectiveness, and image, most secondary and tertiary care hospitals will find it necessary to (a) provide inpatient services that are medically sophisticated, organizationally well coordinated, psychosocially comprehensive, and philosophically person-centered and (b) be involved in activities outside their four walls either as sole providers of outpatient services or as collaborators with other agencies in joint service projects. How to accomplish these goals successfully will be another need of hospitals in the 21st century.

4. *Taming the computer* will be another challenge for hospitals in the future. An increased role of computer technology is forecast in the health care of tomorrow. Computerization of hospital operations and records will lead to greater efficiency. Also, patients' access to their records will increase their involvement in their diagnosis and treatment and help in the operationalization of the concept of "patient-as-a-partner." The ease of transmitting information electronically, however, will intensify ethical concerns about the maintenance and sharing of patient data (Barzansky et al., 1993). Computer technology will aid in the standardization of patient care, which in turn may involve the risk of increased impersonalization of that care. Dealing with such concerns and guarding against the undesirable side effects of computer technology will be another major need of future hospitals.

5. *Ensuring quality of care* will continue as another important need of hospitals in the 21st century. The concept of "quality" will have a much broader meaning. *Quality of care* will be defined as more than the quality of service in terms of the correctness of the service procedure and appropriateness of the expertise of the service provider or even the quality of the outcome of service. It will include the quality of service and its outcome as it affects the quality of the patient's life. The push for demonstrating the quality of care thus defined will be constant. It will be necessary to quantify quality and to resolve such issues as perceived versus real quality and provider-defined versus consumer-defined quality (Friedman, 1991). Expanded access to health care will bring the issue of rationing of expensive medical technology into bold relief. Resolving ethical conflicts and dilemmas pertaining to the quality of life and rationing of care issues will be a constant challenge for future hospitals.

6. *Involving minorities* will become an important political necessity for hospitals in the future. In the 21st century, today's minorities will have grown stronger in their numbers, political activities, and claims on the sources of power and authority. Even 18 years ago, a hospital trustee expressed his caution, concern, and advice thus:

> Various community activist groups are developing nationwide, and their requests must be taken seriously and at least evaluated. A private, not-for-profit hospital in North Carolina is undergoing some very severe challenges by a group that maintains that there are not enough poor people on the

hospital governing board. This same phenomenon is developing in other areas. In New Jersey, for example, a health systems agency declined to review a hospital's application because the HSA did not like the makeup of the hospital's board. These signs must be taken seriously. Hospital boards should be reviewed to ensure that they properly represent their particular communities. (Ewing, 1979, p. 12)

Hospitals of the future will have difficulty remaining noncontroversial, quiet industries as in the past. How to operate effectively in an increasingly more political environment and satisfy their constituents will be among their important needs. That need will have to be met at two levels: (a) adequate representation of the various sections of the community on the hospital's policy-making bodies and (b) satisfaction of the hospital's consumers with its practices, procedures, and services.

7. *Contributing to the solutions of social problems* will become the community responsibility of future hospitals. The health consequences of such social problems as poverty, homelessness, violence, substance abuse, and AIDS will continue to be the concerns of hospitals, but the intensity of that concern will deepen. The paradox of medical success intertwined with social failure will persist.

> Hospitals signify achievements in American science and technology, but they also represent a breakdown in the public's health. In their beds lie, inter alia, victims of accidents, violence, poor nutrition, lack of knowledge, carelessness, overindulgence, poverty, and addiction, translated into damaged hearts, babies, lungs, and livers. (Stevens, 1989, p. 356)

Hospitals will be forced to examine this paradox. Hospitals have been conceived of as a high-technology system—an extended emergency service—(providing short, intensive, and acutely needed medical care) and, alternately, as a community resource for caring. Hospitals have been strictly neither a technological system nor a community-service system. Ramifications of being neither will continue to challenge the creativity and resources of hospitals. Improving the technological sophistication of hospital-based medical care will be easier in the future, but responding to the community's social health needs will be much more difficult. The idea of medicine as a "science," with hospitals as its major instrument, represented in standard definitions for prospective payment (diagnosis-related groups [DRGs]) and standard expectations about hospital use (Stevens, 1989, p. 357) has very little relevance for complex social health problems, which defy such standardization. Even within the problems of health, although medical technology may have an enormous effect on the health of the individual, it has very little effect on the health of the population. How to be the instruments of medical science (a system of standardized problems and reproducible results) and also combatants of social problems or exploring what their appropriate role in combating social problems is will be another major need of future hospitals.

8. *Retaining a position of leadership* will be an abiding need of hospitals in the future. Hospitals have been leaders of health care organizations. Jones (1979) listed roles played by hospitals to justify their claim to leadership. Changing societal conditions, however, are likely to challenge that claim in the next century. Most hospitals will try to retain their leadership by becoming the hub of the community care system. While discussing the roles of hospitals in the community care of the aged, Eisdorfer and Maddox (1988) said, "Hospitals are already the principal gathering place for professionals, technicians, equipment, and support services that can be focused on packaging an individual's care in an infinite variety of ways" (p. 8). Hospitals are the predominant entry points for nursing home and formal home care (Vladeck, 1988). Some marketing experts recommend that hospitals sponsor *senior membership plans* offering senior discounts, free health screenings, Medicare copayment write-offs, and the use of a senior activity center (Coile, 1990). Taking on new roles will become a necessity for the continued existence and prominence of hospitals. Deciding on the "what" and "how" of the new roles will be an important need of future hospitals.

Social workers can make significant contributions to the efforts of future hospitals in meeting each of these needs. Their professional knowledge, sensitivity, and skills give them an edge over many other health care professionals in understanding and dealing with social problems, working with diverse populations, involving minority groups, and improving the patient-centeredness of hospital care. Their values and ethical principles have relevance for dealing with quality-of-life issues and moral dimensions of health care technology. Their experience as the bridge between the hospital and the community is an added asset for hospitals' efforts to venture into community-based activities and seek positions of leadership.

FUTURE NEEDS OF
AMBULATORY CARE SETTINGS

The various entities providing ambulatory care differ in their auspices, organization, scope of service, clients they serve, and sources of their funds. Some are governmental, others are voluntary, and still others are proprietary. In the scope and organization of their services, some provide general (all essential basic) services, whereas others deliver only special services (of a single medical specialty or for a particular medical condition). General services may be comprehensive or piecemeal. In terms of the clients they serve, they again vary greatly. Some serve all members of the community, whereas others cater to special populations, with their eligibility dependent on such factors as income, age, membership of various groups—prepayment, geographic, categorical, and others. Similarly, the sources of financing are many—both public and private and combinations thereof (Rosenfeld, 1971). Roemer (1986) attributed this complexity to three major features:

> First, since the United States is an affluent industrialized country, its health care system has abundant resources, and it spends a great deal of money. Second, since this is a federated nation, the governance of the system is highly decentralized to numerous states, counties, and communities. Third, since this nation has a free market economy, very permissive laissez-faire concepts are incorporated throughout its health care system. (p. 2)

Despite its affluence, the United States is increasingly realizing that the money spent on health care is not producing the desired results. There is much unnecessary suffering, illness, and disability. Despite the health care system being a trillion-dollar industry, 15% of the gross national product being expended on medical and health care, and "an angle of that spending slope becoming nearly asymptotic to the vertical" (Lundberg, 1994, p. 1533), nearly 40 million Americans are without insurance coverage for health services. This number is unacceptable. Change is in the air. Noting that "not since the debates over Medicare 25 years ago has medicine been in such ferment," Coile (1990, p. xiii) listed the following signals of change: (a) The Harvard Relative Value Scale study may establish national physician prices; (b) national health insurance is back on the policy agenda; (c) rationing of medical care is state law in Oregon; (d) national expenditures for physician services are rising at a 10% rate; (e) Medicare spending on physician services is rising at an 18% rate; (f) a federal "cap" on physician payments is likely; and (g) outcomes of medical care are published in newspapers. The system is responding to the need for reform.

Nevertheless, proceeding on the assumption that the future is never completely divorced from the past, it is safe to say that, in the 21st century, "the heterogeneity and pluralism of the U.S. health culture will certainly not vanish" (Roemer, 1986, p. 36) but that major changes will occur in the organization and patterns of health care. Already, a structural change is taking place in the health care industry, a change that will continue whether or not health care is legislated. The following have been forecast for the next century:

Changes will occur in the organization of medical and health care practice so that (a) ambulatory services will become more popular with providers of care and hospitals will compete with other organizations for a share of the ambulatory care market; and (b) group practice will become more prominent and generalist medical practitioners will be in great demand. This prediction has started to happen already. Earlier, we talked about more and more hospitals venturing into ambulatory care and about hospital outpatient departments starting new or expanding into special programs for such patient groups as alcoholics and drug abusers, abused spouses, the elderly, and rape victims. We also discussed more and more physicians going into group practice, both fee-for-service and prepaid types. Even in dealing with hospitals, an increasing number of physicians are realizing that, as groups, they can negotiate with hospitals more advantageously. In the future, we will see hospital-based group practices or even physician groups contracting to run hospital services—inpatient and outpatient. "In tomorrow's dynamic health care enterprise, hospitals and physicians will create new ventures and develop new clinical and business relationships" (Coile, 1990, p. 248).

Changes will occur in the nature and pattern of health care services so that (a) comprehensiveness of services will be a necessity rather than an ideal; (b) coordination of health services within each setting, as well as between the setting and community health and social services, will become a must; (c) illness prevention and promotion of healthful lifestyles will become important parts of the primary care services; and (d) it will become necessary to accommodate the special needs of major health care consumers, programmatically as well as by changing the attitudes and skills of care providers.

The United States will move toward universal access to health care leading to those, hitherto outside or on the periphery of the system, demanding high-quality health care services. That will result in

(a) a strain on the system's resources, (b) questions of equity, and (c) issues of quality of service.

Because the focus of health care will have shifted onto ambulatory care, the anticipated changes will make special demands on ambulatory care settings. Meeting those demands will be the greatest overall need of these settings. That need may be divided into the following three: (a) the need to expand their services so that some basic primary care is provided to everyone; (b) the need to provide patient-centered services that are marked by comprehensiveness, coordination, and continuity; and (c) the need to accommodate the special needs of hitherto neglected groups.

1. *Expanding services:* Hospital outpatient departments, private group practice offices, health maintenance organizations (HMOs), and other community-based clinics and health centers are some of the settings for ambulatory care. This diversity will persist in the next century, and diversity will also increase in the scope of services provided that may include primary care, ancillary care, and preventive care services. Minimally, however, all these settings will be responsible for providing primary care. Some settings may have to focus on primary care and add wellness and prevention activities to their services yet retain their secondary care functions. Others, such as maternal and child health programs and public health centers, which have been essentially prevention oriented, will have to expand the scope of their services. Recent amendments to Titles V and XIX of the Social Security Act (Omnibus Reconciliation Budget Act of 1989) mandate that the scope of maternal and child health services be expanded from pure prevention to include primary care. Such changes are like straws in the wind, indicating the direction of change and adding weight to this prediction about the future.

Because the provision of primary care will be the most common feature of most ambulatory care settings, it is appropriate here to elaborate on the definition of primary care. *Primary care* has been defined as the care of the well, the worried well, the presymptomatic patient, and the patient with disease in early symptomatic stages. This definition tells something about the patient in relation to illness but nothing about the elements or attributes of the care. The *Journal of Public Health Policy* listed the essential elements of primary care as (a) correct diagnosis as the precondition of treatment; (b) appropriate treatment for maximum possible restoration of function: (c) relief of pain and suffering and alleviation of illness-related anxiety; (d) appropriate referral for specialized diagnostic, treatment, and rehabilitation services; (e) management responsibility for overall health of the patient; (f) preventive services, including immunization, multiphasic screening for early detection, and preventive supervision; and (g) health education and advice for health promotion, disease prevention, treatment, and rehabilitation (Milton, 1983). The Institute of Medicine (1978) defined *primary care* as accessible, comprehensive, coordinated, and continual care provided by accountable providers of health services. It thus identified accessibility, comprehensiveness, coordination, continuity, and accountability as the attributes of good primary care. Such care will be expected to result in the care of the "whole person," and not merely the treatment of an illness.

2. *Providing patient-centered comprehensive services:* All types of ambulatory settings will be expected to provide comprehensive and well-coordinated patient-centered, high-quality services. In terms of their past experience, health care organizations and providers will not have much to go on. The record of the U.S. health care system on the provision of comprehensive coordinated services at the community level or even at the individual patient level has been far from satisfactory despite the importance of such services. More than 60 years ago, one major recommendation of the Committee on Cost of Medical Care (1932) was that,

> the study, evaluation, and coordination of medical service be considered important functions for every state and local community, that agencies be formed to exercise these functions, and that the coordination of rural with urban services receive special attention.

From time to time, coordinating councils formed at the community and state levels have focused on special problems or needs of special groups. These have had minimal impact. The Comprehensive Health Planning Act of 1966 and its follow-up law, the National Health Planning and Resource Development Act of 1974, established a nationwide network of health system agencies for assessment of community health needs, coordination of programs, and stimulation of actions to respond to unmet needs. These laws failed to achieve their objectives. Under the Reagan administration, planning efforts at the local level were "greatly eroded, leaving mainly skeleton agencies at the state level" (Roemer, 1986, p. 137). The integration of health care with other human services has remained a noble ideal.

The answer of the medical establishment to the need for "total patient-oriented" basic health care has been the creation of the family practice specialty. As pointed out earlier, however, an unimpressive proportion of medical graduates are going into family practice despite incentives and encouragement. This trend is likely to change in the next century, and ambulatory care will gradually become more attractive. It will be many decades, however, before the supply of adequately trained family practitioners and other generalist physicians is adequate. "Having too few generalists means that Americans have less access to primary care, miss opportunities for prevention, and receive inappropriate, uncoordinated care when they have complex or chronic conditions" (Schroeder, 1993, p. 120). While discussing ways of correcting the imbalance in the medical workforce—the United States being flooded with specialists at the expense of generalists—Schroeder (1993) presented several possibilities, such as (a) making energetic efforts to achieve an appropriate generalist-specialist balance (50% of each), (b) increasing the generalist capability of specialists, and (c) replacing the missing generalist capability with such nonphysician substitutes as nurse practitioners and physician assistants. The goal of 50% of all physicians being generalists is not attainable in the foreseeable future, and the option of specialists filling in the gap will not ensure comprehensive and coordinated health care. "Many specialists who are forced to practice outside their special areas of competence will not take pleasure at straying from their fields" (Schroeder, 1993, p. 120). At the same time, physicians and the medical establishment will resist the idea of nurse practitioners and physician assistants replacing physicians even as primary care providers.

Even when (possibly by the middle of the next century) the number of primary care ambulatory physicians is adequate, their training, orientation, and resources may not suffice to provide comprehensive services. It is forecast that families in the future will be much more varied and complex in their form and weaker in their resources, and the medical problems of major groups of patients will be intertwined with powerful social needs. According to Cassata and Kirkman-Liff (1981), 30% to 36% of all patients treated by family physicians have psychosocial problems that tend to be ignored. Even for providing minimally acceptable services effectvely to their clients, the professional resources of primary care medical personnel will have to be supplemented by the resources of others.

3. *Accommodating the special needs of different groups of patients:* The elderly, non-elderly with disabilities, AIDS patients, and victims of social problems such as homelessness, substance abuse, and violence will be the groups with special needs requiring special consideration. These groups will be heavy users of ambulatory as well as acute care services. For identifying the needs of these major groups of consumers of ambulatory services, we look at the most often encountered situations in ambulatory care settings. I have divided all ambulatory care settings into two categories: (a) settings providing acute care and (b) settings providing nonacute care. The former include hospital emergency departments and trauma centers and freestanding emergicenters, urgent care centers, and ambulatory surgery centers. The latter include hospital outpatient departments, private group practice offices, HMOs, and public health centers and clinics. In acute care, particularly emergency care settings, the following three kinds of situations are generally encountered: (a) true medical emergencies with powerful social consequences, (b) social emergencies with vital medical dimensions, and (c) non-emergency health or social needs. Persons in each of these situations make different demands on the care setting and care providers. In nonacute care settings, chronic problems dominate, interspersed by crises that are often more social than medical. As emphasis shifts from illness management to wellness maintenance, many patients will need to be encouraged, goaded, and motivated to prevent illness and crises.

Social workers are superbly qualified to help ambulatory care settings meet their needs as discussed above. Their assets include (a) the know-how of the comprehensiveness, coordination, and integration of services; (b) a health orientation that is much broader than the illness focus of many other health care providers; (c) the ability to treat the total patient rather than merely as a carrier of a disease; (d) the understanding of the characteristics and problems of major patient groups; (e) a refined tendency to look for strengths, rather than dwell on deficiencies; and (f) the skills to intervene appropriately in the lives of patients beyond the immediate medical concern.

FUTURE NEEDS OF ILLNESS PREVENTION
AND HEALTH PROMOTION AGENCIES

As the wellness movement grows stronger and health care priorities shift more strongly to illness prevention and health promotion in the next century, more and more agencies will appear on the scene. More than 325 national membership organizations, besides state public health departments, are listed as part of a consortium for achieving the *Healthy People 2000* goals (Public Health Service, 1992). For conceptual clarity, all agencies involved in illness prevention and health promotion work are divided into the following three groups: (a) public health departments, which will make renewed and concerted efforts to regain prominence; (b) hospitals, which will continue to diversify their functions to include health maintenance and health promotion as important complements to their illness care activities; and (c) other organizations that will either be expanding their programs to include illness prevention and health promotion or specializing in these activities. All of these will work toward and contribute to the attainment of the broad goals of *Healthy People 2000* much beyond the year 2000. These goals are (a) to increase the span of a healthy life for Americans, (b) to reduce health disparities among Americans, and (c) to achieve access to preventive services for all Americans. These goals have been divided into 300 specific objectives in 22 priority areas addressing a broad range of issues, including the following:

- Health promotion through the reduction of high-risk behaviors and improvement of health behaviors related to physical activity, nutrition, smoking, alcohol and other drugs, family planning, mental health, and violence
- Health protection through prevention of injuries and environmental risks and improvement of food and drug safety
- Preventive services focused on diverse areas, including maternal and infant health, heart disease and stroke, cancer, diabetes, HIV infection, sexually transmitted diseases, infectious diseases, and immunization
- Surveillance and data systems for improving data collection efforts at the national, state, and local levels (Public Health Service, 1993)

We draw on the material in *Healthy People 2000* that has relevance for our discussion of illness prevention and health promotion. As is evident from the above list of objectives, *Healthy People 2000* uses health promotion, health protection, and preventive services as organizing categories. For our purposes, all the items included in the three categories can be subsumed under the rubric "illness prevention and health promotion."

The three groups of agencies identified above will provide different combinations of services in the above categories. These groups will have some common and some unique needs. Their common needs in varying degrees will be (a) having access to adequate financial resources for their services, particularly in the first few decades of the new century and (b) knowing how best to implement the known illness prevention and health promotion approaches and to develop new approaches that provide the best match between an agency's resources and the needs of the individuals and groups it serves.

Their unique needs will be determined by the particular constellation of such factors as purpose of the agency's activity, its client group, and its resources, both material and professional. We discuss separately the major needs of each group.

Public Health Departments

Unlike other health care organizations that are either already in or likely to enter the field of illness prevention and health promotion, public health establishments are the only entities whose very reason for existence has been the prevention of disease and the promotion of health. The core missions of public health are monitoring the occurrence and spread of disease, promoting infant health, immunizing children, controlling infectious diseases, and conducting health education and promotion activities (Lee, 1994). Although large sections of the population are becoming a part of the wellness movement, as a nation the United States has had no commitment to the concepts of "prevention" and "health promotion." As pointed out earlier, less than 1% of federal dollars spent on health care is allocated to public health. The financial allocation for public health activities at the state and local levels is not very generous either. Although the federal government can set the tone and provide the resources for health promotion efforts, action will be at the state and local levels, much more at the local than at the state level. Our focus in this discussion, therefore, is on local health departments.

That there is a lack of resources affecting the ability of local health departments to address even their core functions is supported by the findings of a recent study. Using a stratified random national sample of local health departments, Turnock and his associates (1994) surveyed those departments' compliance and roles with respect to 10 public health practice performance measures. These measures pertained to the three major health department practices—assessment, policy development, and assurance. They analyzed their data by focusing on (a) individual performance measures, (b) groups of measures reflecting performance in the three practice areas, and (c) the department's role as the lead agency, collaborator, or minimal. They found that very few (3%) local health departments reported compliance with all 10 of the performance measures. Overall, 31% reported compliance with seven or more performance measures, and only 19% reported compliance with the majority of performance measures for each core practice. For only one practice did more than half the departments characterize their role as the lead agency. The researchers viewed their findings in relation to the *Healthy People 2000* objective (8.14) that calls for 90% of the population to be served effectively by a local health department and concluded that extensive capacity-building efforts are necessary for that to happen by the year 2000.

In the meantime, the persistence or reappearance of communicable diseases such as AIDS and tuberculosis; the growth of noncommunicable conditions such as cancer, heart disease, and stroke; and ever-present environmental hazards are making added demands on these departments. Greenberg, Schneider, and Martell (1995) surveyed the local health officers (LHOs) of 436 Northeastern and Midwestern cities with populations between 25,000 and 500,000 about their priorities for promoting health through prevention. They also looked for differences between LHOs of the most economically stressed cities and those of the least economically stressed cities. The priority lists of the two groups were remarkably similar. The five most important public health prevention goals were (a) reducing the incidence of HIV infection and AIDS, (b) improving maternal and infant health, (c) controlling sexually transmitted diseases, (d) reducing violent and abusive behavior, and (e) immunizing against infectious diseases. LHOs of the most stressed cities, however, were more pessimistic about achieving these goals. "Parenthetically, the lack of expert personnel has made it difficult for local health departments to collect and analyze the information required to accurately measure health status and program needs" (Koplin, 1993, p. 394).

Public health practitioners have not succeeded in selling and marketing the simple truths of illness prevention and health promotion. Unlike other health care issues, public health programs have lacked an effective and supportive constituency. As Gordon (1993) so aptly put it,

Public health has always been a rocky road, as it provides no immediate gratification or feedback. It requires the ability to look to the future, which is not a commonplace trait of our political leaders who are looking to the next election rather than the status of their constituents' health in coming decades. Public health, thus far, lacks the glamour associated with hospitals, organ transplants, emergency medicine, diagnosis, treatment and rehabilitation and does not compete well with crisis health care. (p. 263)

In the next century, the logic of prevention will make more sense to the public and politicians alike, and health promotion and illness prevention will permeate and be integrated into every component of the health care system. This will happen slowly and gradually over several decades, however, and not without concerted effort on the part of public health professionals. On the one hand, overall public and professional attitudes, acute care-oriented training of most health care professionals, organization of health care systems, and the system of rewards for health professionals and organizations will be slow in changing. On the other hand, the self-interest of powerful economic forces will not allow them to give up their modes of making profit even when these involve risk to people's health and lives. Roberts (1994) discussed at length how, in the matters of tobacco and smoking, car passenger safety, and guns and violence, the United States has "allowed a variety of forces to contaminate any meaningful effort to prevent the major killers of children and adults" (p. 269). Curbing the power of these forces to contaminate illness prevention and health promotion efforts will be an ongoing challenge. Public health professionals will need to keep reminding themselves that they must constantly "explain, promote, market, sell, interpret, propose, advocate, and communicate the need for improved public health and environmental health and protection services" (Gordon, 1993, p. 264).

In Chapter 2, it was mentioned that nearly 3,000 local public health units existed in the United States in 1985, of which 42% served populations of fewer than 25,000 and 65% served populations of up to 50,000 (National Association of County Health Officials, 1990). Most of these units do not have the financial and organizational resources to do an adequate job. Koplin (1993) agreed with Emerson (1945), who had proposed that a population of about 50,000 would be optimal for one efficiently run public health unit. Hence, public health organizations at the local level can benefit from restructuring. The Institute of Medicine report *The Future of Public Health* (1988a) also found that the infrastructure of state and local health units is limited and restricts their capacity to ensure protection of the public's health. These units lack the trained people to coordinate the collection and analysis of data for identifying problems and setting priorities (Lee & Toomey, 1994).

The major needs of public health departments can be summarized as

- Generating more funds for personnel and programs
- Reorganizing for greater efficiency and effectiveness
- Intensifying their health promotion and wellness activities

Hospitals

In the next century, as the limelight shifts from inpatient acute care to other forms of health care, hospitals will diversify their activities to include illness prevention and health promotion. Their mission will become the provision of comprehensive health care services. This has begun already. The American Hospital Association (AHA) has established the Center for Health Promotion with the purpose of encouraging and assisting hospitals to create and implement effective health promotion programs. In 1979, it published the association's policy statement on the hospital's responsibility for health promotion. Many hospitals are rewriting their missions to strengthen their roles in maintaining and improving the health of their communities. In the words of Behrens and Longe (1987),

> Some are redefining the business that they are in, recognizing that in the past they had engaged in the "illness business" rather than the "health business." Today, these hospitals state confidently that they are in the health business—helping people in their communities regain health when they are sick or injured, helping them maintain good health when they are well, and helping them improve their health at every stage in their lives. (p. 3)

Longe and Wolf (1983) listed the following reasons for hospitals to engage in health promotion efforts: (a) improve the health of the community, (b) improve the image of the hospital, (c) change the hospital's service mix, (d) reduce health care costs, and (e) achieve specific financial goals for the hospital. Behrens and Longe (1987) discussed how health promotion programs for children bring new patients to the hospital and its physicians and give it a competitive edge. Earlier, I gave some examples of how hospitals are reorganizing themselves and expanding their activities horizontally as well as vertically. Coile (1990) mentioned hospitals that are able to generate 50% of their revenues from activities other than inpatient acute care services. Many hospitals—community hospitals more than the others—are venturing into outpatient services. This trend is likely to continue. These hospitals are providing outpatient services through hospital-based as well as community-based satellite clinics. To the extent that these clinics offer primary care, they are participating in illness prevention work. There is also some room for health promotion during a health care provider's encounter with the patient in these clinics. However, "patient's medical needs, physician's work loads, reimbursement constraints, and ambulatory practice norms all conspire to make health promotion a low priority in the medical encounter" (Currie & Beasley, 1982, p. 143).

To be effective, health promotion programs must be independent entities. At present, only some hospitals are entering health promotion programs in the community. Some of these expect their health promotion programs to generate profit, others expect them to break even, and still others offer these programs as a community service. Although the financial goal of a hospital regarding its health promotion program determines its program-related planning and operation, every hospital that ventures into this area can expect to make some gains. Even the hospital that provides health promotion as a community service stands to improve (a) its image as an agency concerned about the health of the community, (b) the goodwill between itself and the community, (c) the community's familiarity with its services, (d) the cooperation between itself and other health and human service agencies, and (e) its base for referrals for its other services. Perhaps the most important benefit for such a hospital is its enhanced ability to "prepare for future trends in health care that rely on having a solid foundation in areas of ambulatory and health promotion services" (Longe & Wolf, 1983, p. 18).

In the 21st century, more and more hospitals will enter the health promotion business. Their major need in this regard will be twofold: (a) deciding the "what," "where," and "how" of the health promotion services and (b) designing and implementing the decided-upon programs.

Other Organizations

Other organizations engaged in illness prevention and health promotion work are the various voluntary and professional associations, some of which were listed in Chapter 2. Some of these, such as the American

Cancer Society, American Heart Association, and American Lung Association, have been among the most ardent health promotion advocates that have contributed significantly to the current levels of awareness about different diseases and measures for their control. These organizations and others that will join this category in the future do not suffer from the constraints and faults of public health departments or hospitals. Public health departments must satisfy the bureaucratic requirements and whims of politicians, and for hospitals, illness prevention and health promotion represent one of several, and often low-priority, missions. Moreover, voluntary organizations can be closer to the people and are generally simpler in their organization, clearer in their mission, and more single-minded in their pursuit of that mission. All these attributes enable them to make their services accessible to people more easily and less expensively.

> The low cost and wide availability of the services offered by these organizations, coupled with their institutional experience and commitment to disease prevention and health promotion, makes them a natural ally of other groups initiating such efforts, and should ensure the growth of their involvement in future health promotion activities. (McGinnis, 1982, p. 413)

The more established of these organizations are quite good at both raising money and providing services. The new ones generally struggle in both of these areas. Their major needs are (a) creating adequate fiscal resources and (b) overcoming deficiency in the best available knowledge and skills for their job.

Social workers have much to offer to illness-prevention and health-promotion organizations in dealing with their major needs. The concept of "resource" is basic to social work thinking (Siporin, 1975), and social workers understand its various meanings and how to operationalize it. The ability to create, mobilize, and maximize resources is their greatest asset. Similarly, for designing and implementing illness prevention and wellness promotion programs, their *person-in-environment* perspective, grasp of the *systems theory* and the concepts of "enabling" and "empowerment," and "community organization" skills will give them an edge over many others.

FUTURE NEEDS OF
LONG-TERM CARE FACILITIES

Although community-based long-term care is viewed as a viable alternative to costly institutional care, both its financing and delivery systems are in need of reform. The cost of nursing home and home-based care is essentially not covered by Medicare or private insurance. Those who need this care must use their own resources, and when those resources are used up, they are forced to turn to Medicaid, a welfare program.

Weissert and Hedrick (1994) reviewed 32 well-designed studies of community-based long-term care programs and concluded that this type of care does not increase survival and does not affect the rate of deterioration in functional status of care recipients. It does reduce unmet needs and increase the life satisfaction of patients and their familial caregivers, but the higher life satisfaction levels diminish with time. Even if the use of institutions (hospitals and nursing homes) is decreased, the decrease is too small to outweigh the costs of additional community-based care. Weiner and Illson (1994) asserted that the long-term care system is broken and needs to be fixed: "Indeed, no other part of the health care system generates as much passionate dissatisfaction as does long-term care" (p. 403). The challenge for long-term care is to become so "good"—appropriate, effective, efficient, and normal—that institution-based care starts being viewed as the alternative care. We look separately at the major needs of the three groups of long-term care settings: nursing homes, community residential care homes, and facilities providing home-based and near home-based care.

Nursing Homes

The essential elements of the nursing home picture and the important needs of nursing homes can be summarized as the following.

The quality of care provided by nursing homes varies greatly—excellent in some and far from acceptable in others. Almost any intervention in nursing homes seems to yield measurable benefits for their residents, which possibly reflects the general deprivation of the environment (Kane & Kane, 1987). The public image of a nursing home as a place farthest from "home," dirty, cold, impersonal, and a place where people go to die persists. The greatest need of nursing homes is to change that image.

Nursing homes have not yet realized the importance of linking with other community services to provide a continuum of care that benefits patients, payors, and providers (Clapp, 1993). We have discussed the health care system of the future being marked by an integrated continuum of comprehensive services. This will be at two levels: one emphasizing continuum, and the other integration. Depending on a patient's condition and needs, the principle of continuum of care would ensure his or her smooth movement among hospitals, nursing homes, retirement communities, foster homes, or own residence fortified by appropriate home health and social services. The principle of integration would guide the provision of services by community-based health and human services. This change will particularly affect the care of the elderly. Nursing homes, being an important subacute care setting, will be a significant part of the continuum of care. Nursing homes will need to prepare for this change toward an integrated continuum of comprehensive services.

Nursing homes will also need to extend themselves into the community by making use of their facilities and equipment and the services of their personnel available to home-based needy—young and old with disabilities and frail elderly—and other community groups. This can be done directly or through other agencies and programs, some of which may even be willing to pay for those services. Some agencies and programs find purchasing some services less expensive than establishing their own. For improving the quality of life of their residents, nursing homes will have to foster the involvement of the community in the lives of those residents.

Thus, the major needs of nursing homes are (a) improving their public image, (b) becoming a part of an integrated continuum of services, and (c) extending themselves into the community.

Community Residential Care Homes

Community residential care homes are viable residential alternatives to institutional care. For several reasons, however, they have not received the recognition and support they deserve. While discussing adult foster care, McCoin (1995) said that this type of care suffers from "the unsocial Darwinistic ethos of being (a) small, (b) qualitatively oriented, and (c) cost effective. These qualities are antithetical to the 'bigness' which seems so necessary to feed that survival of the greediest forces tantamount in today's quantitative/computer/information/politically correct age" (p. 3). It is estimated that over 90% of public expenditures for long-term care go to institutions (Callahan & Wallack, 1981) and that the nursing home industry "sucks up" half of the Medicaid budget (Johnson, 1991). Whereas nursing homes are paid directly from Medicaid, much of the funding for community residential care comes from the residents' Supplemental Security Income (SSI), a much smaller source. These residential care homes lack the organization and voice of the powerful nursing home industry. The advent of the National Association of Residential Care Facilities is an attempt to organize these, but this organization is still in its infancy. The major need of these facilities is to organize themselves, improve their visibility, and increase their resources.

Although community residential care homes do provide a familylike atmosphere for their residents, no clear evidence suggests that those residents are integrated into the family of the operator. These settings vary considerably even in the degree of warmth and familistic atmosphere. Some are like boarding homes, and others are like homes. Ample evidence does suggest, however, that the integration into the community of adults with mental illness and mental retardation residing in the various non-institutional community living settings has not happened. These settings will need to work for this integration.

Nevertheless, community residential care is proving to be an appropriate and least restrictive option for most children and youth who cannot live with their natural families. Foster care homes serve as the hub of a network of developmental and therapeutic connections for these children (Hess, 1994). This success can be attributed to the training, supervision, and support for the care providers. Similarly, the success of community residential care homes for the elderly sponsored by the Department of Veterans Affairs results from the careful recruitment, training, and ongoing support of "sponsors." Sickman and Dhooper (1991) also found that a significantly higher percentage of sponsors who had undergone formal health care training were more competent than those without such training. These settings must improve their performance through systematic training and support. They must ensure that the nurturing environments they provide for those in their care is age-appropriate and not infantalizing.

The major future needs of community residential care homes are (a) improving their visibility, (b) increasing their resources, and (c) improving their performance.

Facilities Providing Home-Based
and Near Home-Based Care

As is evident from our earlier discussion, there are many variations in the arrangement and provision of home-based services. On the one hand, services provided by hospices are marked by appropriateness, comprehensiveness, coordination, and sensitivity. On the other hand, service goals of many other home care agencies are more often related to the priorities of payors than to the needs of those being served. Even the services approved for payment often lack coordination.

Several models of home-based care have been proposed, with different rationales, philosophies, and approaches (Malone-Rising, 1994). These models are a definite improvement over the simplistic approach reflected, for example, in Brody's (1977) statement about the aged that "the 'well aged' went to homes for the aged, the physically ill to nursing homes, and the mentally impaired to state and private psychiatric hospitals" (p. 262). The narrow perspective of the dominant service model, however, results in the neglect of needs not emphasized by that model. The long-term care needs are often seen as either health or social as if the two dimensions of life are independent and separate and must compete with each other.

Neither the health nor the social service model adequately addresses the functional needs of service recipients. Chapter 2 mentioned studies that found home-based care marked by not only inefficiencies but also shortcomings of a more serious nature, such as unprofessional and criminal behavior on the part of care providers. Although incidents of physical injury, inappropriate care, financial exploitation, intimidation, and disrespect by the care provider may not be frequent, this type of care tends to result in the loss of the autonomy and independence of service recipients. Home care agencies must address these quality-of-care issues in view of the following factors.

Home care will continue to be viewed as cost-effective and financially more desirable than institutional care. Almost 6,500 Medicare-certified home health agencies existed in 1993; this number represents a more than 600% increase over the number of such agencies on record at the end of 1966, Medicare's first year (Balinsky, 1994). As in the past, proposals for health care reform will continue to advocate for the expansion of home care. The demand for this type of care will rise, too, because the advances in health care technology will make it increasingly possible to care for more and more sick persons at home who currently must be treated in hospitals and nursing homes. Already those on dialysis, IV chemotherapy, total parenteral nutrition, and ventilators are being cared for at home.

At the individual client level, this care will continue to appeal to people's desire to remain in familiar surroundings, to carry on with many activities of daily living, and to retain the ability to make small decisions about daily life, such as when to get up, what to wear, what and when to eat, what and when to watch on television, and if and when to turn off the light (Balinsky, 1994; Brickner, 1978). My forecast about the leaner structure and weaker natural resources of the family also suggests that the basic care provided by family members in the past will not be available in the future. Agencies providing home-based care will be needed for providing more and more of the basic care. They will be seen as helping families stay together.

The need for improvement in the quality of services by in-home and near-home care agencies can be viewed from two angles: one broad, the other narrow. The broad view is represented by the movement away from *quality assurance (QA)* and toward *continuous quality improvement (CQI)* or *total quality management (TQM)*. The Joint Commission on Accreditation of Healthcare Organizations is creating new sets of conditions for accreditation that reflect the philosophy of care that CQI represents. It is based on the premise that "If it ain't broke, it can still be improved" (O'Leary, 1991a, p. 74). CQI demands that customers must come first, which means that the organization must have a formal process that enables it to meet all customer needs and expectations. No longer is the order of priorities structure, process, and outcome; instead, outcome comes first, process second, and structure last (Kirsch & Donovan, 1992). This requirement involves fundamental changes, and all health care organizations will need to prepare for and implement those changes. The narrower view brings to light the major shortcomings of most in-home and many near-home long-term care agencies. Their major needs are (a) improving their assessment of client needs/problems; (b) increasing their ability to provide comprehensive and well-coordinated services; and (c) sharpening their sensitivity to issues of clients' autonomy, independence, and options.

Social workers have much to give to the long-term care sector. Because the major recipients of long-term care services are the elderly and persons with disabilities, social workers can contribute their (a) understanding of the needs of these populations, (b) grasp of the major philosophical shifts in the field of disabilities, (c) comprehensive perspective on clients' reality (encompassing both the person and the environment as well as a life span view), and (d) skills in working with these groups effectively. The social work client-worker relationship can become the model for equal partnership between clients and helpers. Social workers can also help long-term care agencies in improving their visibility and community image.

FUTURE NEEDS OF HEALTH CARE
PROVIDERS ACROSS SETTINGS

To meet their needs, health care organizations of the future will require the services of personnel who have the necessary knowledge, skills, and commitment. These assets, generally specialized and profession-specific, often have to be tailored to the needs of specific client groups for optimal effectiveness. Here, we discuss the major future needs of health care providers on the basis of projections about (a) major consumers of health care services, (b) the state of the art and science of medical and health care, and (c) quality-of-life issues.

Major Consumers of Health Care Services

The major consumers of health care services that most care providers, to varying degrees, will have to know and understand fall broadly into the following groups: (a) the elderly; (b) non-elderly with disabilities; (c) victims of social problems such as homelessness, violence, alcohol, and drug abuse; (d) victims of AIDS and similar new diseases; and (e) children. These groups are likely to be heavy users of all types and levels of health care.

The Elderly

A substantial proportion of the U.S. population in the future will be made up of the elderly. Those 85 and older are already the most rapidly growing group of the elderly. Although the majority of the elderly will be women, they will not be a homogeneous group. They will reflect the cultural, ethnic, and religious diversity that will characterize the United States in the 21st century. Some facts about the elderly relevant for health care providers, particularly hospital-based, are as follows:

- Each year, 25% of people admitted to a hospital are over 65. Of these, 50% are readmitted within the next 12 months.

- Older adults are highly susceptible to iatrogenic illness.
- Older adults take an average of 3.2 prescribed medications and an uncounted number of nonprescribed drugs; 20% to 25% of hospital admissions of older adults are a result of adverse drug reactions.
- The primary health problems of older adults are chronic—for example, heart conditions, high blood pressure, hearing loss, glaucoma or cataracts, arthritis, and diabetes; 80% have at least one chronic condition. The average older adult has four or five such conditions,
- The acuity of all five senses declines with age, independent of disease.
- Any acute episode of illness experienced by older adults or their spouses may trigger stress-related deterioration and loss of functional ability.
- The health problems of older adults are compounded by financial, legal, emotional, familial, or ethical issues.
- Maintaining good health is consistently ranked by older adults among their top three priorities, and independent functioning is extremely important to most of them.
- Elder abuse is being recognized as a serious social problem. (AHA, 1989)

Hospital-based service providers must know that despite the centrality of older patients for the economic health of hospitals (these accounting for nearly 50% of hospital revenues), most hospitals have not been very good at serving geriatric clients.

Perhaps most importantly, the increasing body of experience with home- and community-based long-term care services continually reminds us of the capacity of hospitals to mess up even the best-managed long-term care cases. Sooner or later, frail elderly long-term care clients are going to end up in the hospital for treatment of acute problems, and in such instances even care that is minimally adequate by prevailing professional standards may undo months of successful service in terms of functional dependency, self-esteem and self-image, management of depression, or even cognitive orientation and functioning. (Vladeck, 1988, p. 42)

Non-Elderly With Disabilities

Persons with disabilities are a large, noncohesive group whose members may have only one thing in common: Each has a disability. Because of their disability, however, they all are vulnerable and share the chronicity of their problems. It is estimated that 36 to 40 million Americans are physically, mentally, or emotionally disabled. It is difficult to classify disabilities into clear-cut, neat groups. For example, although most physical disabilities fall into three anatomical categories—involving the skeletal system, the muscular system, and the neuromuscular system—some involve more than one anatomical category, and others are independent of these systems.

The classification of the developmentally disabled includes those with mental retardation, autism, cerebral palsy, epilepsy, and neurological impairment (Velleman, 1990). Public Law 95-502 (Rehabilitation, Comprehensive Services, and Developmental Disabilities Amendments of 1978) defines a developmental disability in terms of functional limitations:

> A severe, chronic disability of a person which (a) is attributable to a mental or physical impairment or combination of mental and physical impairments; (b) is manifested before the person attains age twenty-two, (c) is likely to continue indefinitely; (d) results in substantial functional limitations in three or more of the following areas of major life activity:
>
> 1. self-care, 2. receptive and expressive language, 3. learning, 4. mobility, 5. self-direction, 6. capacity for independent living, and 7. economic self-sufficiency; and reflects the person's need for combination and sequence of special, interdisciplinary or generic care, treatment, or other services which are of lifelong or extended duration and are individually planned and coordinated.

In the future, advances in medical and health care will save many more from death but not from disabilities. Therefore, the number of people with disabilities will grow. They will need services from all types of health care settings for their share of health problems. Care providers must know that people with disabilities may be alike in the social consequences of their disability but that each is different in the nature of his or her problem and the range of the functional abilities.

Victims of Social Problems

Poverty in all its manifestations, violence in all its forms, and abuse of all kinds of harmful substances will continue to plague the United States in the next century. All these problems are interrelated, with each feeding the others. In a recent study of 443 impoverished medical patients, Gelberg and Leake (1993) found that 24% were frequent alcohol users and that 18% had recently used illegal drugs. Other associated variables included a previous felony conviction and psychiatric hospitalization. I earlier alluded to the health consequences of poverty and homelessness and to the role of alcohol and drug abuse in the incidence of injury, death, and disease. The National Committee for Prevention of Child Abuse (NCPCA) estimated that 675,000 children are maltreated by an alcoholic or drug-addicted caretaker every year (NCPCA, 1989). Among the confirmed cases of child maltreatment, the estimated proportion involving substance abuse averages 40% nationwide (Daro & McCurdy, 1991). Health care providers, and hospital-based providers more than others, will continue to deal with victims of these problems. They will need to know who these patients are.

Poverty has many faces. As Harrington (1987) put it, "Poverty is an 'integrated' problem: over two-thirds of the poor are white and just under one-third are black, Hispanic, Asian, and American Indian. But minority people are significantly over-represented among people in poverty" (p. 14). The problem of poverty will persist in the 21st century and will continue among people of color at higher rates than among whites. Many of them will continue to "live in a world of self-contained, self-reinforced misery, victims of the hopelessness and the violence which accompanies extreme deprivation" (Harrington, 1987, p. 15). To appreciate the reality of poverty, one can look at homelessness—its most blatant manifestation.

It is estimated that 250,000 to 300,000 people in the United States are homeless. The homeless are not the skid row alcoholics and happy wanderers as they used to be thought of. Families comprise approximately one third of the homeless population (Mihaly, 1991; National Coalition for the Homeless, 1989), and even this may be a conservative estimate. Many homeless families live in cars, campgrounds, or motels. They avoid contact with social service agencies for fear of losing their children and so are not counted among the homeless (Edelman & Mihaly, 1989). Of the 919 rural homeless adults studied by First, Rife, and Toomey (1994), 247 headed family units. More than two thirds of those families were headed by single parents (mostly women). In a study based on in-depth interviews with 26 street mothers, Ray (1993) concluded that they were proud and devoted mothers but under economic, social, health, relationship, and emotional stresses. An increasing number of the homeless are even employed but are not able to escape life on the streets. A statewide study of the homeless at 25 shelter facilities in Maryland by DiBlasio, Belcher, and Connors (1993) found that 35% of the sample were employed—24% full-time and 11% part-time. In a study of the homeless in rural areas as well, First et al. (1994) found that 90% of adults had worked for pay previously in their lives and that nearly one third had worked for pay (two thirds in permanent full-time or part-time positions) in the month preceding the study.

Health and mental health problems abound in the homeless poor. Harris, Mowbray, and Solarz (1994) studied the users of four of Detroit's largest homeless shelters and found that these homeless are a multiproblem group with many physical health problems, drug and alcohol abuse, and psychological distress. Dental and vision problems were the most prevalent, followed by neurological, gastrointestinal, and female reproductive problems. Alcohol abusers were significantly more likely to have low blood pressure, symptoms of liver disease, and a history of tuberculosis treatment. No differences were found in the health problems of those with and those without a history of psychiatric hospitalization. These researchers used only a nonintrusive health screening examination to determine the health status of the homeless; this tactic might have resulted in underrepresentation of less-visible or hard-to-detect disorders. The health status of the poor who are not even sheltered—street people—must be even worse. "Those who are too dysfunctional to seek or recognize their need for shelter may have much more serious problems" (Harris et al., 1994, p. 43). Health care providers in many settings and programs will continue to see the victims of social problems and must learn to relate to them with sensitivity and understanding.

Victims of AIDS and Similar New Diseases

At least for the first two or three decades of the 21st century, AIDS will continue as a compelling reality. The health and human services professionals will continue to be challenged by the suffering and tragedy at the individual patient/client level and by the social, economic, and political ramification of this disease for their agencies and programs. AIDS is no longer the disease of homosexual males concentrated in a few large cities. Its victims include heterosexuals, both male and female, young and old, white and nonwhite, drug users and drug-free, living in urban as well as rural areas. Demographic shifts have occurred in the prevalence of infection with the human immunodeficiency virus (HIV) from homosexual males to injection drug users, males and females, non-drug using women, and children. Larger proportions of minorities (black and Hispanic), both male and female, are represented among the HIV-positive and AIDS patients. Minorities will continue to be among the major groups of sufferers.

Even after a vaccine and a cure for AIDS have been found, the health care system will continue to be challenged by other diseases of the immune system. Service providers in hospitals, outpatient programs, and long-term care facilities will continue as a part of the treatment and care of the victims of AIDS and similar other diseases. They will need to look for more effective ways of serving these victims and their families, as well as themselves surviving the emotional stress of that work. They must address such complex, persistent, and at times over-whelming themes/concerns as (a) their attitude toward homosexual lifestyles, as well as the fear of being stigmatized because of their work with homosexual patients, (b) their feelings about drug users, (c) their attitude toward women with AIDS, (d) sexuality and intimacy, (e) death and dying, and (f) existential issues such as quality of life, meaning of life, loneliness, isolation, and abandonment (Dworkin & Pincu, 1993).

Children

In the 21st century, the proportion of children (those younger than age 18) in the total population will decline from almost 26% in 1990 to 23% in 2050 (Day, 1993), and as a nation, the United States will value children more than it does now. In view of the complexity and general lack of stability of the family, however, ensuring the health and well-being of children will continue to be a societal challenge. Despite the impressive progress made during the 20th century, the United States lags behind many other industrialized countries on major indicators of child health. In 1988, 17.1% of U.S. children lived below the poverty line, which was the highest percentage among such countries as Australia, Canada, Norway, Sweden, Switzerland, the United Kingdom, and Germany (Children's Defense Fund, 1991). Edelman (1991) high-lighted several painful facts about U.S. children, such as the following:

Every 35 seconds, an infant is born into poverty.
Every 2 minutes, an infant is born to a mother who received late or no prenatal care.
Every 2 minutes, an infant is born at low birthweight (less than 5 lb, 8 oz).
Every 11 minutes, an infant is born at very low birthweight (less than 3 lb, 8 oz).
Every 14 minutes, an infant dies in the 1st year of life.
Every 14 hours, a child younger than age 5 is murdered.
Every 5 hours, a 15- to 19-year-old is murdered.

Earlier, we discussed the extent of poverty among children and its adverse physical, psychological, and emotional effects on them. Similarly, we have discussed the magnitude of the problem of child abuse (physical, sexual, and emotional) and neglect. These problems are likely to persist in the next century. Health care providers will share the responsibility of ensuring the well-being of children.

In general, at all levels and in all health care settings, service providers will need to understand the complexity of the problems of these groups of patients. They will need to change their orientation and responsibilities to serve these groups effectively. That orientation will have to be guided by a new vision of patient care, a vision in which they not only provide their piece but also ensure that the piece fits well in the total picture of patient needs and resources. They will need to recognize, understand, and accommodate patients' situations and problems that impinge on their medical and health needs and to coordinate their services with other community sources of care. Recognizing the need for better integration of the different types of health care and the better use of health and social interventions will involve a conceptual change. It will involve unlearning some ways of thinking about people, their problems, and solutions to those problems. For example, to serve the elderly effectively, hospital-based service providers will need to (a) improve their knowledge about the elderly and their sociomedical needs because "ageism, therapeutic nihilism, and lack of adequate preparation and knowledge in geriatric care" (Hirschfeld, 1988, p. 113) pervade the hospitals; (b) realize that their "traditional motivation to cure must be complemented by the idea that caring rather than curing is the reality of later life, and that maximization of function is the most appropriate goal to achieve" (Eisdorfer & Maddox, 1988, p. 9); (c) appreciate that a comprehensive assessment of the elderly cannot be based on a traditional pathological diagnosis—rather, it has to result from the use of skills of many professionals working as a team; (d) recognize the importance of better integration of hospital-based and community-based care; and (e) accommodate elderly patients' expectation for sympathy and understanding, clarity and completeness of communication, sensitivity about their functional difficulties, comprehensive assessment and intervention, support and guidance in decision making, and ability to balance the use of high-tech measures with quality-of-life considerations (AHA, 1989). As Eisdorfer and Maddox (1988) put it,

> The practice of adequate medical care for older persons must involve the recognition that a different style of practice is needed. This style of practice would appreciate the range of variables that affect functional capacity and incorporate into patient management a similar range of nonmedical adaptive approaches—from prostheses to socialization, day care, homemaker services, and "friendly visitors." (p. 17)

Similarly, service providers will need to change their attitudes toward other patient populations, such as the poor, the homeless, the abused, and substance abusers. These patients are often viewed as responsible for their problems. For example, it is not uncommon for health care providers to hold on to such myths about the poor as (a) only welfare mothers and their children are poor, (b) most welfare recipients are too lazy to work, and (c) families on welfare spend their money on luxuries. Nor is it uncommon for health care professionals to believe that victims of abuse, rape, and other forms of violence had somehow brought their painful experience on themselves. Health care professionals will need to (a) learn not to be blinded to the plight of the victim of these problems by their beliefs in the myths, simplistic explanations, and half-truths about these problems; (b) realize that blaming the victim does not help in generating patient trust for the professional and the patient's faith in him- or herself necessary for the success of the intervention; (c) understand that, given the deficits of their internal and external resources, these patients require the use of more intensive, coordinated, and multidisciplinary skills for even minimal impact of the intervention; and (d) consider the coming of these patients for medical assistance as an opportunity to help them go beyond the immediate problem.

State of the Art and Science of Medical and Health Care

In the next century, advances in biomedical knowledge and health care technology will make the medical miracles of today commonplace occurrences. The ability of physicians to diagnose and treat most diseases will have improved manifold. They will be able to detect diseases long before symptoms of those diseases appear and, thereby, prevent the degree of damage caused. They will also be able to monitor the functioning of organs of patients at high risk for failure of those organs. The therapeutic tools at their disposal will be many and more sophisticated.

They will treat illnesses with more powerful drugs administered in newer, more reliable, and better controlled ways. They will use more sophisticated surgical instruments and techniques, as well as human and artificial organs and tissues for repair, correction, and replacement of damaged and diseased body parts. If the required replacement part is not available, physicians will have found newer approaches to keeping a patient alive while he or she waits for the needed part. For illnesses that do not respond to chemotherapy and do not lend themselves to be treated surgically, physicians will use more powerful radiation and laser treatments with more effective devices and techniques. What is high-tech now will be considered old-fashioned in the next century.

To deliver the much more sophisticated high-tech medicine, physicians of the future will be the masters of these life-saving machines and techniques, each specializing in the use of a particular set of machines and methodology for correcting a particular part of the body. The science of medicine will have reached its pinnacle and, in the process, reduced its practitioners to super technicians. The tendency to treat the damaged and diseased body parts rather than the whole person will continue to pull physicians away from a holistic view of people and their problems. This pull will persist as a threat to the art of medicine. Physicians will need to discover and rediscover the importance of caring as a vital part of the curing business. High-powered physicians will also experience ambivalence about treating the patient-as-a-partner. This ambivalence and the struggle in the task of combining the caring and the curing—the art and the science of medicine—will be reflected in the behaviors of many other health care providers as well. Studies of hospital-based professionals have found that all professionals are strongly influenced by the attitudes, stances, and behaviors of physicians.

Looked at from another perspective, the practice of high-tech medicine may also be a source of frustration for the practitioner. Mishel and Murdaugh (1987) called modern medicine a halfway technology because, no matter how wonderful, it does not completely cure illness. Patients do live longer, but medical illness is often replaced by psychosocial problems.

In the 21st century, the institution of the family will have undergone so much change that it will be hard to agree on what a "normal" family is. The image of the family as a symbol of cohesion, stability, and everything positive in life will be a thing of the past. People will search for warmth of concern and understanding from all kinds of formal and informal groups and health and human service organizations. Health care organizations, dictated to by the needs of the consumers of their services, will demand that service providers shift their focus from problem to person-with-the-problem. Service providers will need to make that shift and to deal with whatever such a shift will entail. A more holistic view of the patient and the patient's problems will force physicians and other health care providers to realize that the expertise of any one professional is inadequate for the job of treating the whole patient and that meaningful sharing and collaboration among many professionals are necessary for effective service. Similarly, determining how medical care will enhance a patient's quality of life will require the input of many disciplines. Hospital-based service providers will need to change many of their attitudes and behaviors accordingly.

Quality-of-Life Issues

Quality of life will become a touchstone for quality of medical and health care services in the next century. Health care organizations and professionals will be judged, not by the adequacy, correctness, and efficiency of their equipment and procedures, but by the outcome of their service as it affects the quality of the patient's life. What is quality of life? There is no consensus about what it is and what it entails. Andrews and Withey (1976) identified more than 800 overlapping dimensions of quality of life. Today, transplantation of vital organs such as hearts, kidneys, livers, and lungs is considered the miracle of medical care that saves and prolongs life, but does it improve the quality of life of the organ recipient? Divergent views abound. For example, on the one hand, Simmons and Abress (1990) compared 766 patients on one of the three treatment modalities—center dialysis, continuous peritoneal dialysis, and kidney transplantation—and found that transplant patients scored significantly higher on almost all measures of quality of life than both dialysis groups. On the other hand, Baumann, Young, and Egan (1992) studied the recipients of heart transplants and concluded that the experience of living with a heart transplant should be understood as a chronic condition. They found that although life improved for the majority of their sample, transplant recipients continued to experience work problems, financial burdens, family role changes, lifestyle changes, and side effects of the long-term drug treatment. According to Johnson (1990), transplantation does not cure disease: "It extends life by trading one chronic disease (of the organ) for another (a chronically compromised immune system). Under these circumstances, the quality of life for those who survive surgery and their families will vary dramatically" (p. 177). The necessity for operationalizing the concept of "quality of life" will continue to provide a challenge and an opportunity to health care providers.

> For other caring health professions, such as nursing, social work, and occupational and physical therapy, it [quality of life] provided a firm set of criteria to demonstrate more convincingly their contribution to patient health and well-being. And for medicine it represents a reaffirmation of one its most important missions. (Levine, 1987, p. 5)

The objective and the subjective are the two dimensions of quality of life that everyone agrees on. Objective indicators of quality of life include a return to work, functional ability, and health status, whereas subjective indicators of quality of life include well-being, life satisfaction, psychological affect, and happiness (Evans, 1991). Both dimensions, the subjective more than the objective, are influenced by a person's culture—values, worldview, and meaning of life. In the 21st century, the challenge for determining the quality of life of recipients of health care will be monumental. The populations to be served will be much more culturally diverse, and many more people will have chronic problems. The situations demanding the (a) incorporation of the individual's subjective dimension of the quality of life into the decisions for medical care when it is at variance with ideas and values of the professionals, (b) appropriate use of high-cost health care technology, and (c) equitable distribution of technological and other resources will create a host of ethical conflicts and dilemmas for health care providers. The providers will need to seek solutions to such problems from joint deliberations. That will involve sharing with, depending on, and benefiting from everyone's knowledge and skills.

In all the problem areas discussed above, social workers can help other health care providers improve their understanding, skills, and performance. A deeper knowledge of the lives and needs of victims of social problems and unique perspective on ethically challenging situations and quality-of-life issues, as well as a willingness to cooperate, skills for collaboration, and strategies for conflict management qualify social workers for that helping role. Also, "their grounding in systems theory, expertise in working with diverse systems, knowledge of small group theory, and skills in communication and tension reduction are significant assets" (Dhooper, 1994b, p. 106).

Chapter 4

SOCIAL WORK IN ACUTE CARE

Chapter 3 identified the future needs of health care settings and health care providers. The major needs of acute care hospitals include (a) reorganizing to gain or retain a position of leadership in the community, (b) delivering ambulatory care to the sufferers of chronic medical ailments and the victims of social health problems, (c) providing effective and comprehensive patient-as-a-partner as well as family-centered inpatient care, and (d) maintaining a quality of both inpatient and outpatient services that meet the highest professional standards and that are technologically sophisticated, ethically correct, and financially cost-effective. The future needs of hospital-based service providers include (a) understanding their patients, patients' problems, and situations and relating to their patients as partners; (b) coexisting and teaming up with other professionals for providing comprehensive patient care; (c) knowing how best to deal with ethically problematic patient care situations; and (d) contributing to the hospital's community-oriented activities.

HISTORY OF SOCIAL WORK
IN ACUTE CARE SETTINGS

Acute care is generally provided through emergency rooms, trauma centers, intensive care units, newborn nurseries, general medical and surgical departments, and other specialty care units of hospitals. Emergency rooms, urgent care centers, and outpatient surgery clinics are included among ambulatory care settings. (The past and future of social work roles in those settings are discussed in Chapter 5.) In this chapter, our focus is on hospitals which are the centers of most of the acute care activity. The presence of social workers in hospitals can be traced to 1905 when the first social worker was hired by Dr. Richard Cabot for his clinic at Massachusetts General Hospital in Boston. Dr. Cabot, the chief of medicine at the hospital, believed that the effectiveness of medical treatment depended on a complete diagnosis, for which it was necessary to have information on the patient's home, family, work, and problems. He had been associated with the Boston Children's Aid Society and observed social workers in action. He had listened to their case discussions and studied their case records. "Later, when he saw some of the same children in his clinic, he realized how much better he was able to understand them and their home backgrounds and other environmental factors" (*Encyclopedia of Social Work,* 1971, p. 90). His venture was considered an experiment. The social work program was referred to as an "unofficial department" in the hospital's 1896 annual report, and funds for it came from Dr. Cabot, his personal friends, and other contributors (Cannon, 1952). The experiment was highly success-ful, and the social work unit at his hospital became a model for the establishment of similar units in other hospitals across the United States. Within a decade, more than 100 hospitals employed social workers (*Social Work Dictionary,* 1991). Initially, social workers were not allowed on the hospital wards and were not involved with inpatients. The realization that they could make positive contributions to the care of inpatients came slowly. Massachusetts General Hospital officially recognized social work activities on the wards in 1914.

World War I also created a need for social workers. They were needed in army hospitals overseas to work with injured soldiers and in U.S. Public Health Service hospitals at home to work with returning veterans and their families (Kerson, 1979). In 1920, the American Hospital Association (AHA) sponsored a formal survey of hospital social ser-vices that led to the formation of a committee on training for hospital social workers. The American Association of Hospital Social Workers, formed in 1918, set standards for the curriculum components designed to prepare medical social workers at the schools of social work, several of which had been established by then. The Association also pioneered the working relationship between schools and hospital social service departments regarding the field work of students (Bernard, 1977; Shev-lin, 1983). In 1928, minimum standards for social service departments were included in the hospital standards published by the American College of Surgeons (Nacman, 1977). The standards of social work practice in hospitals have changed over the years to reflect the evolution of that practice in response to the changing needs of patient populations and of hospitals.

From the 1930s on, medicine became increasingly more specialized and resulted in the fragmentation of health care. No one was responsible for coordinating the care a patient could be receiving from many different specialists and facilities simultaneously. "Patients may as a result receive incompatible medications and conflicting instructions: families may be treated in an atomized fashion, as though the baby's illness or the father's unemployment had nothing to do with the mother's ulcer, headaches, or mental illness" (Furstenberg, 1984, pp. 28-29). Although their activities were a part of the solution to the problems of specializations in medicine, social workers were not unaffected by the idea of specialization. Social workers also became more specialized, and "serious fractures between medical and psychiatric social work were well established by the 1940s" (Bracht, 1978, p. 13). During the 1940s and 1950s, social workers became involved in health care teams and comprehensive health care projects to address the lack of coordination of care (Bracht, 1978). By the 1950s, newer illnesses such as heart disease, stroke, and cancers had replaced tuberculosis, polio, and other infectious diseases, and medical care of acute and chronic problems was becoming infused with the concept of "rehabilitation" (Nacman, 1977). In the 1960s, the civil rights and welfare movements led to changes, including the passage of Medicare and Medicaid, which in turn created more demand for social workers in hospitals. In the 1970s, the establishment of a patient's bill of rights sanctioned the advocacy role of social workers (Nacman, 1977). In the 1980s, societal concern about rising health care costs led to the institution of prospective payment systems (using diagnosis-related groups [DRGs]), social workers became involved in hospitals' utilization review work, and their discharge planning function acquired an unprecedented importance. The problem of providing increasingly technologically sophisticated care and of cutting costs for that care is persisting in the 1990s.

Throughout its history, while responding to the demands of its environment, hospital social work has created a professional repertoire consisting of theoretical explanations (and a conceptual grasp of the various realities—of patients, health care providers, and their institutions), practice principles, models of intervention, strategies, and techniques. The needs of patients and of organizations have guided the development of the various models of practice. "Some of these provide general approaches and tools for psychosocial assessment and interventions. Others are site, problem, and population specific. Still others focus on the major social work functions such as case management, interdisciplinary collaboration, discharge planning, documentation, and community liaison" (Dhooper, 1994a, p. 50). Still others are aimed at improving social workers' effectiveness and efficiency, professional accountability, and autonomy.

> The early "friendly visitors" have been succeeded by well-trained, qualified social work practitioners who provide services to patients and their families through a multiplicity of professional techniques. The role of social worker as assistant to the physician has evolved into the social worker as a dynamic contributing member of the interdisciplinary team. (Shevlin, 1983, p. 13)

Despite this impressive history of growth and development, social work has not become a core profession in hospitals and other health care institutions. In view of projections about the demands of the 21st century on hospitals and hospital-based health care providers, where should social work fit into the world of the hospital of tomorrow, what roles should social workers take, and what functions should they perform?

While discussing the domain of social work in the health care field, Meyer (1984) said that the social worker's unit of attention (the individual, family, group, population-at-risk), social work method (casework, group work, community organization), and social work processes (direct practice, policy analysis, program planning, administration) are not sufficient as explanations of domain because "other disciplines share our interests in all of them, often even in the arena of values . . . that which we have held so dearly and have thought to be uniquely held by social workers" (Meyer, 1984, p. 7). The blurring of professional boundaries, mentioned earlier, will continue in the next century. Hence, the search for a social work domain in health care must continue. We as social workers must constantly remind ourselves that we do have a perspective on the reality of individuals, families, organizations, and communities that is peculiarly social work.

> The bio-psycho-social framework that characterizes our work governs the way we perceive the phenomena, the goals we construct, and the interventions we employ. That is how we recognize the social work domain in whatever field of practice we work in. But domain is not the only territory

to be staked out . . . it is not social work because we have planted a flag on it. It is only social work if social workers apply themselves to defining it, to understanding it, to working with it effectively, and to assuming responsibility for it. (Meyer, 1984, p. 11)

Changes in society and health care institutions in the next century will offer new opportunities for social workers to define their domain and take responsibility for it. Social workers are qualified to make significant contributions to the efforts of hospitals and hospital-based health care providers to serve their constituents and clients effectively. As Huntington (1986) put it,

Well-trained social workers can work with intra-personal issues raised by a particular illness or condition, those of body image, stigma, and self-esteem; the interpersonal issues involved in the patient's relationships with his most significant others; the person-institution issues of his relationship to work, education, recreation and other social institutions; and the person-environment issues of relationship to neighborhood, community and society. Social work's focus and targets of intervention include institutions and environments outside the patient which can facilitate or inhibit his well-being. (p. 1155)

FUTURE SOCIAL WORK ROLES
IN ACUTE CARE SETTINGS

Social workers will play several roles regarding the needs of acute care settings. The scope of those roles will depend on such factors as the intensity of specific needs; size, purpose, and location of the hospital; and the resources of its social work component. Whether a hospital is a part of a large multihealth corporation or an independent entity will also determine the role of a social work administrator, the scope of social work activities, and the resources for the social work unit.

Multihealth corporations are characterized by horizontal and vertical integration made possible by mergers or takeovers of several health care organizations:

An example of a health care system that is integrated horizontally and vertically would be a corporation that includes a number of acute care hospitals of varying sizes and with various specialties (horizontal), as well as urgent care centers, a home health care agency, a hospice, a nursing home, and a rehabilitation facility (vertical). (Kenny, 1990, p. 23)

The job of social work administrators in hospitals that are parts of multihealth corporations is likely to be more difficult because of the complexity of the organizational structure and a different set of demands made by the nature, goals, and priorities of the corporation. Kenny (1990) included in those demands the need to balance three often conflicting identities: corporate, institutional, and professional. Social work administrators will have to sharpen their skills appropriate for operating within a political arena of multihealth systems. (In Chapter 8, we discuss approaches to gaining and retaining power that social workers, in both administrative and nonadministrative positions, will find helpful.) Social work administrators in all hospitals should function as patient advocates at the corporate level and seek to influence the direction of the organization by their expertise and information on psychosocial aspects of patient care, gaps in service, unmet needs, and issues of access (Rosenberg & Clarke, 1987). By doing so, they will be advocating for social work and social workers. They should also diversify their departmental activities and services.

> Strategically, diversification balances the vulnerabilities of our departments. Providing only one product or service is a risk few can afford. The specialties of today may become extinct tomorrow. Departments that demonstrate sensitivity in meeting the needs of their institution as well as the needs of their clients are most likely to endure. (Butcher, 1995, p. 5)

Although for different reasons, both independent community hospitals and those owned and operated by multihealth corporations will go beyond the traditional boundaries and extend themselves into the community. This expansion will provide social workers excellent opportunities for improving their value for those institutions. Thus, they will widen the definition and scope of their work and take on newer roles while retaining the traditional ones.

Cost consciousness will continue to pervade all hospital operations, and efforts to find ways of maximizing efficiency will be ongoing. Already, many hospitals are experimenting with unit-based management, and physician assistants and nurse practitioners are performing more and more of the functions traditionally seen as a physician's responsibility. Besides being a part of the hospital's newer cost-effective ventures, social workers will critically examine social work functions to determine which of those can be delegated to others who do not have formal social work training. These others may be volunteers and/or less highly paid personnel with or without people-oriented skills. Training and supervision of these assistants or extenders of the social worker will become a part of social work responsibilities.

Social workers will continue their involvement with individual patients and their families (in both inpatient and outpatient programs), and through this case activity they will act as nonthreatening role models for other service providers regarding family-centered comprehensive patient-as-a-partner care. Besides the role of case worker, they will play many other professional roles, including that of coordinator of services, discharge planner, coordinator of multi- and interdisciplinary teams, advocate, community organizer, consultant, and researcher. These roles will involve the performance of several functions.

We discuss social work roles in relation to the future needs of hospitals and hospital-based health care providers. The hospitals will need to (a) venture into the community, (b) provide patient-centered, high-quality care, and (c) meet the special needs of major patient groups. The major need of care providers will be understanding and relating to patients as partners, coexisting with other professionals, and dealing effectively with ethically challenging situations.

Social Work Role in the Hospital's Expansion Into the Community

The role of social work in hospital expansion into the community will involve such functions as assessment of the community's social health needs, participation in community coalitions for change, participation in planning for community activities, and involvement in joint programs with other agencies demonstrating the hospital's commitment to an integrated network of care, and/or laying the groundwork for its solo efforts. Examples of such ventures include an early intervention program for infants with chronic health impairments and developmental disabilities, a pain management clinic, a rehabilitation program for substance abusers, a rape crisis center, a program for abused women, a day hospital for the elderly, and a home health program for the elderly and chronically ill. It is unlikely that all hospitals will offer hospital-based ambulatory programs or venture into joint projects with other community agencies. A hospital's commitment to the provision of comprehensive health care services, however, will give social workers many opportunities to play many more roles than is possible today. Social workers will be not only the bridge between the hospital and the community but also the vehicle to take the hospital into the community. Their major roles will be as the hospital's *community liaison* and *community organizer.*

Social Work Role in the Hospital's Patient-Centered High-Quality Care

The social work role in the hospital's patient-centered high-quality care will require the social worker to act as a collaborator and a consultant. The collaboration will be aimed at bringing about a unity in the diversity of health care professionals and approaches through teamwork. The relevant functions will include (a) coordinating teamwork, (b) exploring the patient-as-a-partner practice, (c) demonstrating family-centered care, (d) planning and monitoring comprehensive services, and (e) dealing with quality-of-life questions and resolving ethical conflicts and dilemmas. Besides the work with the patient care team, there will be room for the social worker's contribution to the hospital at the organizational level as well. He or she will function as a member of its continuous quality maintenance and ethics committees.

The consultation will also be a case-level as well as an issue-related organizational-level activity. It may be related to the hospital's (a) ambulatory care work—both the ongoing programs (e.g., emergency medical services) and new programs of non-emergency health services, illness prevention, and primary care; (b) quality assurance and cost-effectiveness activities that would require participation in the utilization and review work and involvement in the work of the ethics committee; and (c) research (disciplinary and interdisciplinary) on patients, their care, and its outcomes. The social worker's major roles will be as a *collaborator* and *consultant.*

Social Work Role in the Hospital's Response to the Needs of Special Patient Groups

The special patient groups that will tax the creativity and resources of hospitals in the future are the elderly, patients with disabilities, those with AIDS, and victims of violence and abuse.

The Elderly

The elderly will continue to be major consumers of hospital services and will demand comprehensive services in terms of both inpatient treatment and after-discharge care. The elderly in the future will be healthier, better informed, more diverse, more politically active, and generally more assertive than they are today. At the same time, their kinship support networks will be much thinner and weaker because there will be fewer younger people and more of the traditional care-givers will become a part of the workforce.

Social work is the only profession whose primary responsibility is to attend to the psychosocial needs of patients and their families. Every other profession has as its central task the delivery of physical interventions (Brown & Furstenberg, 1992), and "practitioners of psychiatry and geriatric psychotherapy have not yet fully overcome Freud's skepticism about the treatability of those who are aging, despite the vigorous and at times overoptimistic reactions against this skepticism" (Monk, 1981, p. 62). Hence, minimally, hospital-based social workers will (a) enrich the understanding of other professionals about the patient and his or her total situation encompassing medical and psychosocial needs, (b) attend to the psychosocial aspects of the patient's medical condition and hospitalization, and (c) plan for the patient's postdischarge care.

Patients With Disabilities

Like the elderly, the medical problem necessitating hospitalization for patients with disabilities is superimposed on the existing disability. Its etiology, nature, and consequence must be understood in the context of that disability, and treatment must accommodate the limitations caused by the disability. Social work in these cases would involve (a) a thorough psychosocial assessment, (b) assistance to other professionals in understanding and dealing with the patient, (c) liaison between the hospital and the community service system active with the patient on an ongoing basis, and (d) discharge planning.

Patients With AIDS

Social workers have been pioneers not only in establishing HIV/AIDS services but also "in creating the very definition of AIDS as a biopsychosocial phenomenon that goes beyond an entrenched, narrow bio-medical perspective" (Getzel, 1992, p. 2). Much has been done in understanding and meeting those needs, and much more remains to be done. The major areas of hospital-based social work involvement in AIDS cases will continue to be (a) the patient's need to accept and adapt to the reality of his or her illness, (b) the needs of his or her family, (c) assistance in applying for Medicaid, Social Security Disability, and other benefits, and (d) discharge planning and case management.

Victims of Violence and Abuse

Admittance of victims of violence and abuse to the hospital depends on the medical seriousness of their injuries. Abused children may be admitted to the hospital until protective services can ensure the safety of their homes or find alternative arrangements for their discharge; most adult victims of violence—abused spouses, abused elderly, and casualties of street violence—are treated in emergency departments and discharged or transferred to intensive care units for necessary medical and surgical intervention. Hospitals have clear protocols for dealing with cases of child abuse, and the social work role and functions are specified. The next century will see a similar uniform approach to cases of elder abuse and spousal abuse. The Joint Commission for the Accreditation of Health Care Organizations already requires that, to qualify for accreditation, hospitals have a program in place for identifying and treating patients who are victims of domestic violence. This requirement has not yet created universal compliance (Doner, 1994). Some hospitals may even have hospital-based special units for serving adult victims of abuse. Minimally, the social work functions will be (a) attending to the psychosocial needs of the victims, (b) mobilizing their social support system, and (c) hooking them up with the appropriate community resources. Social workers can also help in the formulation of institutional protocols for dealing with such cases and for creating special units to serve these patients. The major social work roles regarding these special patient groups will be *clinician, discharge planner,* and *resource mobilizer.*

Social Work Role in Demonstrating Viable Approaches to Patient-as-a-Partner and Family-Centered Care

Social workers will be involved in case activity in both inpatient and outpatient care. Their major case-related functions in inpatient care will include (a) preadmission screening/planning, (b) psychosocial assessment, (c) short-term social work treatment, (d) advocacy for patient and family, (e) discharge planning, and (f) postdischarge follow-up. The case-level activity in outpatient care will minimally include (a) psychosocial assessment, (b) crisis intervention, (c) ongoing counseling, and (d) coordination and monitoring of social, psychological, and medical services. The counseling of patients and families (in both inpatient and outpatient care) will include helping them (a) adjust to ever-changing health care technology and advances in the science of genetics, (b) make difficult personal decisions, and (c) act as partners of service providers and organizations. The difficulty of decision making can be imagined by the choices a young woman at genetic risk for conceiving an unhealthy child has: She may choose not to have children, to adopt, or to have children anyway. "Other options include artificial insemination by donor, egg donation, in vitro fertilization and implantation, surrogate motherhood, and selection and/or freezing of only healthy embryos" (Weiss, 1995, p. 16). The social work activities will demonstrate how to treat clients (patients and their families) as equals and how to encourage them to participate in their treatment and care as active partners. The major social work roles will be as *case worker* and *counselor.*

SOCIAL WORK KNOWLEDGE AND SKILLS

In this section, we discuss the knowledge and skills needed for hospital-based social work in relation to the major roles identified in previous sections.

Social Worker as a Community Liaison and a Community Organizer

In the 21st century, most hospitals, particularly primary and secondary care hospitals, will be actively involved in the community. This involvement may take several forms, such as (a) the creation and implementation of new hospital-based, as well as community-based, services that are needed in the community; (b) the coordination of community health and human services; and (c) collaboration with other health and human services agencies. Several examples of such activities are already available.[1] Some of these examples of hospitals' successful community-oriented programs are the result of the creativity of social workers. In the next century, the hospital's community service orientation and social work's increased emphasis on the integration of micro and macro modes of practice will converge. No specific delineation exists between micro and macro social work. Macro issues are just micro issues that have been repeated many times (Butcher, 1995). The potential for social work contributions is endless.

Given the hospital's resources and commitment to community service, a critical look at the community's social health needs will reveal many avenues to explore. Spitzer and Neely (1992) described the role of hospital-based social work in developing a statewide intervention system for first responders delivering emergency services. The realization that fire, rescue, medical, and law enforcement personnel serving as first responders to often dangerous situations are highly vulnerable to acute and cumulative stress led to the creation of a statewide program. "The social work contribution, which received state and national recognition, united local fire, ambulance, clergy, mental health and medical professionals into one of the largest critical stress debriefing teams in the United States" (Spitzer & Neely, 1992, p. 56). Most social workers will not be expected to be this ambitious. They should realize, however, the importance of a thorough community needs assessment because each community is different. The uniqueness of the community must guide the development of the hospital's community programs.

An extensive literature describes approaches to community needs assessment. These approaches have been variously classified. For example, Rubin and Babbie (1993) categorized these as (a) the key informant approach, (b) the community forum approach, (c) the rates under treatment approach, (d) the social indicator approach, and (e) the community survey approach. Siegel, Attkisson, and Carlson (1995) divided these into (a) indicator approaches, involving analyses of social and health indicators as revealed in the available secondary data; (b) social survey approaches, involving analyses of service providers and resources and citizen surveys; and (c) community group approaches, using community forums, nominal groups techniques, delphi technique, and community impressions. Social workers should keep abreast of the know-how of these approaches and other community needs assessment methodologies. It will be helpful to remember that the existing data in the form of demographic and other vital statistics are generally in the public domain and easily available. The approaches involving contact with key informants and the general public in community forums and focus groups require the use of social casework and group work skills. For using the community survey approach, they will have to use their knowledge of the research methodology.

Once the needs have been determined and the hospital's new role agreed on, the organizational response to those needs may take several forms. Jones (1979) suggested a number of new hospital roles classified by different levels, such as local system, organization, medical model, programs, capacity management, and resource management. For example, programmatically, hospitals can start a hospice, a rehabilitation center, an innovative emergency medical service, a day care, and a home care program. From a capacity management perspective, they can create swing beds, convert to ambulatory care, and change into a long-term care facility. The role options from the medical model of care perspective can include preacute/acute/postacute, wellness, and holistic care. From an organizational perspective, multi-institutional systems, merger, innovative medical staff alternatives, and corporate reorganization are some possible options.

Social workers serve every health and human service agency, and hospital-based social workers, in their role as case workers, deal with social workers and other professionals in other agencies. These client- and program-related dealings, as well as other formal and informal contacts within the local professional community, create a network of relationships. Most social workers are also members of various coalitions and special interest groups. Hospital-based social workers should build on these existing contacts and relationships to perform functions pertaining to their community liaison and community organizational roles.

They should also recognize and address the barriers to interagency collaboration. The first step in addressing the problem is to initiate or renew communication. "Once two or more agencies agree to talk, the next step is to assess the problem, and to identify both obstacles to coordination as well as favorable factors" (Bond & Duffle, 1995, p. 48). Various tools aid in accomplishing this. The tool of focus groups is quite common. Another tool is the "organizational mirror." Agencies prepare lists for each other covering strengths and weaknesses as well as an empathy list that states the perceived difficulties of the role of the other (Iles & Auluck, 1990). The next steps are to formulate mutual goals and to plan strategies for working toward those goals.

For progress to occur, a "level playing field" is necessary. This may not happen easily; it may be necessary to address negative attitudes towards each other. Conflict may occur. Working through the conflict is necessary to developing trust. The change agents need patience and the ability to focus on the goal despite frustration. Frustration with the process may cause people to drift away. The change agents need to keep bringing people to back the effort if this occurs. (Bond & Duffle, 1995, p. 49)

Social workers should realize that their group work skills and their basic problem-solving expertise not only are good for micro situations but also are invaluable for their community liaison and community organizational work. Social work differs from other health professions primarily in its acceptance of responsibility to vulnerable people (Caroff, 1988). That responsibility has meant sensitivity and empathy for and an ability to relate to and work with vulnerable populations. These assets of social workers plus their networking and community organizational skills will enable them to identify leaders of the poor and minorities who can enrich the public representation on the hospital's policy-making bodies.

Social Worker as a Collaborator and a Consultant

In the 21st century, teamwork will be the hallmark of health care. A more holistic view of the patient and patient problems, the need to relate health care to the patient's quality of life, ethical issues raised by complex medical technology, and the necessity for coexistence among many diverse professionals will highlight the importance of collaboration. Despite its need and importance, however, collaboration will not happen easily. Everything encourages competition that "in Western society has become so ingrained in the fabric of our culture that it has become a primary value" (Kraus, 1980, p. 25). Collaboration—a cooperative venture based on shared power and authority—is the opposite of competition.

In the 1990s, the term *teamwork* is commonplace in health care organizations. Teams are viewed as important functioning units, and the current and potential benefits of teamwork are recognized and applauded. At the same time, the nature and quality of teamwork varies tremendously, and there is much truth in the conclusions that "interprofessional health care teams may never have been fully and consciously planned, tried or studied" (Brown, 1982, p. 17) and, at times, "the team is only an illusion held by more powerless providers who are dependent upon an integrated practice" (Nason, 1983, p. 26). The need for collaboration expressed as teamwork will continue to create opportunities for social workers in the role of collaborator. No other professionals have the assets for this role that social workers possess. Social work values mediation, cooperation, mutual respect, participation, and coordination (Abramson 1984). Social workers are grounded in systems theory, understand small-group theory, have experience working with many different systems, and have skills in communication. They are superbly qualified to be the coordinators of and consultants on various efforts and activities. We discuss the social worker's collaborator role at two levels: with other professionals around case activity, and in organizational committees on policy and procedural issues.

Collaboration is the best type of teamwork—working together in a joint venture. Collaborative teamwork requires communication, cooperation, and coordination. Collaboration can also be conceptualized as one end of a continuum; at the other end is competition, with communication, cooperation, and coordination falling between the two extremes and each representing an increasingly higher level of working together (Dhooper, 1994b). Thus, there are degrees of teamwork. Collaboration has a level of integration of the knowledge and skills of the various team members that results in a synergy—the total being more than the sum of the separate knowledge and skills of the individuals involved. Depending on the level of integration, teamwork is distinguished by such terms as *multidisciplinary, interdisciplinary,* and *transdisciplinary.* In *multidisciplinary teamwork,* individuals from different disciplines are involved but each is responsible for his or her disciplinary activities alone, relationships between disciplines are not explicated, and each member is affected very little by the efforts of others (Clark & Connelly, 1979; Halper, 1993). *Interdisciplinary teamwork* presupposes interaction among various disciplines. The members perform their disciplinary activity but also are responsible for the group effort and common group goals. It has a fluidity of disciplinary boundaries and flexibility of roles. *Transdisciplinary teamwork* has these characteristics to a greater extent. "Representatives of various disciplines work together in the initial evaluation and care plan, but only one or two team members actually provide the services" (Halper, 1993, p. 34).

Social workers as team builders must determine whether interdisciplinary or transdisciplinary teamwork is the desired goal for the collaborative effort. Teams go through a sort of "evolutionary" process in their development, major elements of which are leadership, communication pattern, approach to conflict resolution, and decision-making strategy. They should also monitor that process. Two sets of variables—people-related and place-related—influence teamwork and determine the unique characteristics of particular teams. People-related variables include the individual characteristics of team members such as personality, attitude, knowledge, and skills. Place-related variables include the setting, resources, stability, goals, organizational culture, and reward system. Both sets of variables can be manipulated. Similarly, communication, cooperation, and coordination, the major components of teamwork, can be improved and enhanced. These are facilitated by (a) clear common purpose, goals, and approach; (b) an understanding of the roles, functions, and responsibilities of all members; and (c) continuous team-building efforts directed both at monitoring team development and seeking organizational support.

Social workers as coordinators of patient care teams can benefit from the following suggestions:

1. *Apply the problem-solving approach, which social workers are so well versed in, to teamwork.* The generic components of the collaborative problem-solving approach are (a) problem specification—specifying the patient's condition or problem that requires interdisciplinary cooperation; (b) statement of the collaborative purpose—identifying the interdisciplinary services and the form of collaboration needed; (c) goal specification—specifying the objectives necessary for realizing the collaborative purpose; (d) task identification—identifying the specific activities essential for providing and/or coordinating services; (e) role designation and intervention—designating specific roles and responsibilities for each member; and (f) evaluation and revision—continuously assessing each component of the process and revising if required (Carlton, 1984).

2. *Be aware of the barriers to teamwork and consciously work on removing or reducing them.* These barriers can be organizational and structural, philosophical and professional, or what Stewart (1990) called "bureaucracy of the mind" and practical. Many hospitals are experimenting with unit-based management, and it is likely that, in the future, decentralized organizational structures will become more popular. Despite other faults, such structures can create an environment in which teamwork as a concept is understood, studied, and practiced (Lowe & Herranen, 1981) and interprofessional collaboration becomes possible in substance and not merely in form.

The influence of organizational and structural factors can be minimized by twofold efforts directed *within* at the team members and *outside* at the organizational bosses. Given our definition of collaboration as a cooperative venture based on shared power and authority, within-the-team efforts should be directed at encouraging participative decision making. This can be done by (a) de-emphasizing roles and focusing on the functions of the various members in relation to the problem in hand; (b) recognizing the importance of the process as well as the product—both the teamwork and the taskwork (teamwork emphasizes the interactions among team members essential for coordinated action; taskwork focuses on behaviors related to the tasks to be performed by the individual members); (c) fostering mechanisms for building, recognizing, and supporting interdependence; (d) operating as an open system with many channels of formal and informal communication; and (e) continual ongoing feedback, evaluation, and modification of both the group and the individual. Outside-directed efforts should be aimed at securing recognition, autonomy, resources, support for teamwork from the top officials, and a shift in the reward system from "hierarchical components to explicit positive recognition of the team delivery model" (Lowe & Herranen, 1981, p. 6). This can be done by (a) keeping top officials informed of the accomplishments and successes of the team; (b) highlighting the tangible and intangible benefits of the team approach; (c) negotiating for resources, change in the institutional award system, greater consonance between institutional and team goals; and (d) using appropriate institutional change strategies.

3. *Work on changing the "bureaucracy of the mind" by becoming nonthreatening teachers of other professionals.* This task can be facilitated by (a) reminding them of the purpose, the common goal of the team; (b) focusing on the needs of the patient/client and the problem in hand; (c) highlighting the different dimensions of the problem and how they are beyond the expertise of any one professional; (d) emphasizing the appropriateness of different skills for effective problem solving; (e) respecting the knowledge and skills of other team members; (f) providing much-needed emotional support and understanding; and (g) demonstrating how decisions are better implemented when implementers are decision makers as well.

4. *Attend to the practical barriers that may be the cause or the effect of a lack of congenial environment for team meetings and deliberations.* Finding a comfortable place at a time convenient for team members is an example of overcoming a practical barrier. The social work skills of resource creation and mobilization and of manipulating the environment can easily deal with these barriers.

5. *Remember that team building is a continuous process and that the relationships among team members must be constantly nurtured.* The most important skills are "communication skills (listening, reflective questioning, restatement), conflict resolution skills, information gathering skills (brainstorming, networking), and decision-shaping skills (negotiating, consensus-building)" (Carlett, 1993, p. 30). Teams progress through identifiable stages variously labeled as orientation, accommodation, negotiation, operation, and dissolution (Brill, 1976); and forming, storming, norming, and performing. The social worker should monitor these stages and ensure that the movement is from "I" to "WE" to "IT" (the task). Conflict in the team should not be denied or ignored. It should not be defined as any one member's problem. It should be viewed as belonging to the whole group and dealt with in a way that avoids win-or-lose solutions. Chapter 8 provides more strategies for thriving in interprofessional settings.

This section ends with a list of major attributes of teamwork that the STEAMWORK model proposed by Maple (1992) is built on: *Sensitivity*—being sensitive to the problem-solving process and to each other; *Tolerance*—listening for similarities among differences; *Empathy*—putting oneself in the place of the other; *Acceptance*—making efforts to accept others; *Maturity*—sitting back and observing one's own behavior and having a willingness to change; *Wisdom*—recognizing that one does not have all the answers, having the willingness to learn, and knowing when to speak and when to be quiet; *Ownership*—owning a piece of the picture to complete the process; *Responsibility*—accepting that where we are is not always someone else's fault; and *Kindness*—being kind even when familiarity tends to breed contempt (Maple, 1992, p. 146). Social workers should realize that they already possess in abundance many of these attributes.

Social workers can also assist the team in dealing with ethical issues at the case level. Exploring the psychosocial dimensions of the illness experience of patients and their families gives social workers a special understanding of those patients and their situations. The value system of social workers has generated such moral imperatives as the client's right to self-determination, respect and acceptance, caring, confidentiality, and regard for individual differences (Goldstein, 1987), and throughout their history social workers have had to struggle with and resolve value conflicts (Reamer, 1991). Their understanding of patient situations, their sensitivity to human problems, and their value system can enrich the deliberations and decision making of the team in ethically challenging cases. Social workers can draw upon the increasing social work literature on approaches to resolving ethical conflicts and dilemmas. For example, Bennett (1988) listed the following guidelines from which all helping professionals can benefit:

- Accept the idea of the adequate—not perfect—condition.
- Choose the least restrictive intervention when the need for protective measure is obvious.
- Accept the idea of limited or partial decision-making capacity in clients.
- Provide desirable decision-making environments.
- Search out what the individual's "best interests" are when he or she is unable to participate in planning.

At the organizational level, as members of hospital committees, social workers can use some of the same skills of collaboration that are valid for creating and functioning in patient care teams. The purpose of each committee, however, will determine the type of knowledge appropriate for meaningful contribution to the process and product of committee work. We discuss the potential social work role on the hospital ethics committee as an example. Following the recommendation of the President's Commission for the Study of Ethical Problems in Medicine (1983) that hospitals try committees to improve decision making regarding clinical care, many hospitals have established these committees, often called ethics committees. In a few states (e.g., Maryland), social work representation on these committees is mandated by law. In others states, social workers are sometimes included among the committee members. In the 21st century, the need for such committees will grow, and the social work perspective will have significant relevance for their work. To be effective as members of ethics committees, social workers should do the following:

1. *Improve their understanding of the "what" and "why" of these committees.* Whereas Furlong (1986) identified education, policy development, and case consultation and review as the major functions of these committees, Levine (1984) listed many more functions that these committees can perform. He divided these into prospective consultation on individual cases and retrospective review of decision-making functions. The *prospective consultation* functions include determining that all relevant information has been obtained and communicated to decision makers; suggesting additional sources of infor-

mation where appropriate; identifying ethical issues, as opposed to emotional, legal, religious, or professional; spelling out conflicting values, interests, and duties at stake; facilitating communication and helping resolve disagreements resulting from lack of information or misunderstanding of facts or principles; providing support to staff and families; and recommending, wherever appropriate, that the hospital seek recourse to courts. In *retrospective review,* these committees may determine that appropriate decisions were made; identify cases involving inappropriate decisions; formulate guidelines for difficult types of cases or procedures; and educate hospital professionals about the moral issues in clinical care. Some committees are also concerned with issues of social justice—questions of equitable allocation of expensive medical technology.

2. *Use their knowledge and understanding of the realities of patients and their situations, including quality of life concerns based on comprehensive psychosocial assessments.* Social workers should always remember that they represent the only profession with a history, mission, and qualification for advocating and intervening on behalf of vulnerable populations.

3. *Familiarize themselves with the major approaches to ethical reasoning and resolving ethical issues to better appreciate the perspectives of others.* At the same time, they should develop personal ethical guidelines based on social work values and standards.

4. *Deepen their understanding of group dynamics and sharpen their group work skills.* As Baker put it,

> Here [in the Institutional Ethics Committee], the social worker uses knowledge of group dynamics and functioning and the skills of purposeful exploration and non-judgmental listening to help balance the group and to enable each member to express his/her opinion despite possible intimidation from stronger, more powerful group or staff members. (quoted by Furlong, 1986, p. 98)

5. *Develop or refine the skills for building value consensus.* Helpful techniques include reviewing the codes of ethics of other professions and having informal discussions with other committee members; encouraging fellow members to learn a common moral language (shared meanings of such concepts as "autonomy," "confidentiality," and "quality of life"); encouraging them to spend time clarifying and

prioritizing their own and the group's values and ethical principles; helping the group develop a procedure for analyzing complex ethical dilemmas; and creating an atmosphere that allows for the expression of thoughts and feelings, reduces ambiguity, and tolerates disagreement (Abramson, 1984).

In many situations, both at the case and the organizational level, social work collaboration will take the form of consultation. *Consultation* is the activity in which expert knowledge, experience, skills, and professional attitude and values are transmitted in a relationship between consultant and consultee (National Association of Social Workers [NASW], 1981). Its purpose is to enhance the skill of the consultee to do his or her job that requires the consultant to be a *content expert,* as well as a *process helper.* Each—content and process—mode of consultation involves a different set of activities. A distinction is made between internal and external consultants, and there are differences in working as an internal or an external consultant. Most principles and processes used, however, are the same. Consultation is work related, issue focused, voluntary, and nonjudgmental. Most of the literature, theory, and models relating to consultation focus on the relationship of the consultant to the consultee (Kurpius & Fuqua, 1993). Kurpius (1978) identified the following four generic modes of consultation: (a) *provision*—the consultant provides direct service or product; (b) *prescription*—the consultant diagnoses the problem and gives direction for its treatment; (c) *collaboration*—the consultant works with the consultee in defining, designing, and implementing a planned change process; and (d) *mediation*—the consultant identifies a need, gathers data, and shares relevant data and observations as a means of focusing the consulting effort. The mediation mode is more applicable to internal consultants. Social workers should learn about the various models and theories of consultation (e.g., Brack, Jones, Smith, White, & Brack, 1993; Caplan & Caplan, 1993; Fuqua & Kurpius, 1993; Kurpius, Fuqua, & Rozecki, 1993; Lippitt & Lippitt, 1978; Rockwood, 1993).

The following practice principles can be suggested for effectiveness of consultation:

- The consultant should discuss with the consultee each other's expectation of the process, objectives, and respective roles so that there is clarity about these.
- The consultant should be sure that he or she has the needed competence to provide the requested consultation.

- "Occasionally it becomes clear that the consultee is really seeking supervision, therapy, or even a substitute to take over a troubling situation; it is important that the consultant not assume these roles" (Germain, 1984, p. 206). Instead, he or she should convey the willingness to help through a mutual process of problem solving.
- The consultant should ask the consultee for specific data about the problem, what has previously been done about it, and how it is like or different from his or her usual array of problem situations (Germain, 1984).
- The consultant should avoid rushing in with a solution of the problem, as the questions asked may alone help the consultee understand the situation better, think about it differently, and come up with his or her own solution (Collins, Pancoast, & Dunn, 1977).
- The consultant should present his or her ideas as possibilities, rather than as the right solution to the problem. "Presenting the consultee with several ideas increases his own cognitive and decision-making powers and hence his competence in his own profession" (Germain, 1984, p. 207).

Social workers' familiarity with and skills in problem solving can be used in consultation. Problem-solving approaches to consultation have been of great value to people in organizations (Kurpius & Fuqua, 1993). Similarly, their understanding of systems theory can be a definite plus as "whether implicitly or explicitly, current models of organizational consultation are based upon systems theory" (Brown, Pryzwansky, & Scultz, 1987, p. 99).

Social Worker as a Discharge Planner and Resource Mobilizer

Weak social support systems, as well as the large numbers of elderly and chronically ill people living in the community, will force hospitals to expand the definition of discharge planning in the future. Discharge planning will begin even before a patient comes into the hospital and will continue after he or she has gone back into the community. It will include preadmission planning, discharge planning, and postdischarge follow-up, and that expanded definition will also fit into the hospital's efforts to go beyond the provision of illness care and provide wellness and health maintenance services as well. Social workers' current discharge planner role will grow into the role of social health care manager, the provider of psychosocial services aimed at helping patients and families with the transition to and from the hospital.

The expanded discharge planning role of social work is conceived as having three major parts. The first provides social health care services to complement medical treatment beginning prior to admission where possible and in at least the emergency room. The second encompasses the social health care services normally provided during hospitalization. In the third part, post-hospital social health care and treatment services are included for those chronically ill patients and their families who are connected to hospital physicians or to hospital services. (Blumenfield & Rosenberg, 1988, pp. 38-39)

Our discussion of the knowledge and skills needed for the expanded discharge planner role is woven into an account of the social work efforts to conceptualize and operationalize discharge planning in the past. Social workers have a rich past on which to build the future. The "what" and "how" of preadmission planning and discharge planning are addressed in this chapter; postdischarge follow-up is discussed in the next chapter as part of case management.

Preadmission planning is a method of increasing the efficiency and effectiveness of social work with hospitalized patients. Theoretically, this is possible in all non-emergency admissions. A social work contact with a patient prior to his or her admission can result in an initial psychosocial assessment of the patient, the beginning of the patient-worker relationship, the determination of the type and extent of social work involvement needed, and the setting of the stage for social work activity, including discharge planning. It would allow social workers to alert physicians and others to psychosocial problems that may be important to consider before performing medical procedures. It can accomplish the psychosocial preparation of the patient for (a) upcoming hospital experience (by providing the planned procedure-related education, reducing preoperative anxiety, and increasing pain tolerance) and (b) posthospital experience (Berkman, Bedell, Parker, McCarthy, & Rosenbaum, 1988). For the hospital, social work preadmission screening can shorten the length of hospital stays and reduce unnecessary readmissions and/or emergency department visits.

Despite its importance, preadmission screening has not been a part of regular social work activity in hospitals. A national study of hospital discharge planning found that very few hospitals (17%) screen patients prior to admission (Feather, 1993). Not much has been written about preadmission screening and planning in the social work literature. Studies by Reardon and his colleagues (Reardon, Blumenfield, Weissman, & Rosenberg, 1988) and Berkman and her associates (1988), and the ideas of Blumenfield and Rosenberg (1988) are indicative of future possibilities but are not reflective of the current reality. Reardon et al. (1988) found that patients viewed preadmission screening as an indication of genuine concern for them and as a commitment to help ease the transition in admission to and discharge from the hospital. In the next century, preadmission screening and planning should become an important element of hospital-based social work. It will give patients a greater sense of control, and making them a part of the planning, even before admission, will be part of the process of treating the patient-as-a-partner.

Combining the tools used for postadmission high-risk screening done by hospital social workers today with appropriate psychosocial assessment tools can accomplish the purpose of preadmission screening and planning. In view of the advanced telecommunication technology in the next century, it can be done by social workers themselves or by social worker extenders. This service can be marketed to prospective patients via the media, by word of mouth, and by referral from outpatient clinics and physicians' offices. As Blumenfield and Rosenberg (1988) suggested, hospital support can be sought because "it fits well with strategies to (1) attract patients, (2) prepare them for the hospitalization experience and (3) begin planning for post-hospital care prior to admission" (p. 41).

The institution of preadmission screening and planning will make a significant difference to the process of *discharge planning* but is not likely to change its nature. Discharge planning is part of the history of the hospital. Even in the middle ages, the person leaving the "hospital" was given "bread for the road" (Mullaney & Andrews, 1983). Discharge planning has all along been one basic function of hospital-based social work although its importance has waxed and waned among social workers. Back in 1913, Ida Cannon recognized that a patient who left the hospital too early or without convalescent plans risked "grievous results of an incomplete recovery" (Cannon, 1913). In the 1920s, social workers embraced Freud's theoretical framework that directed attention to intrapsychic causes of suffering, and to establish themselves as experts on psychosocial aspects of health care, they began regarding discharge planning as an unprofessional chore (Blumenfield, 1986). Nevertheless, they retained the discharge function because of its relevance for patient care but accorded it a low professional status (Davidson, 1978). Until the introduction of the prospective payment system (using DRGs), the discharge planning activity also did not receive organizational appreciation and encouragement. In those days, the integration of acute services and long-term care did not benefit hospitals directly. On the contrary, hospitals had a financial incentive in keeping patients hospitalized longer (Hall, 1985). In the 1970s, social workers rediscovered the importance of discharge planning as reflected in the following words of Fields (1978):

> Discharge planning is where medical care interfaces with quality-of-life concerns. It is where human care needs clash or mesh with our technical cure capability. It is where institutions must validate their mission and raison d'etre. It is where the action is, and we belong there. Let us hold that territory with courage, compassion, resourcefulness, and pride. (p. 5)

Now, discharge planning is required by both the Joint Commission on Accreditation of Health Care Organizations and the Professional Standards Review Organizations, and the institution of DRGs has made it a key element of hospital survival. The Omnibus Budget Reconciliation Act (OBRA) of 1986 made discharge planning a separate condition of hospital participation in Medicare programs rather than a part of quality assurance. In the future, the law will provide for uniform needs assessment aimed at evaluating (a) the functional capacity of each individual, (b) his or her nursing and other care needs, and (c) his or her social and familial resources to meet those needs (Feather, 1993). The importance of discharge planning will increase in the next century because people will live longer and medical technologies will enhance the ability of hospitals to ameliorate and cure diseases.

> Indeed, stays in hospitals will become part of the expected life experience rather than an exception. Institutional care for some part of life may become the norm rather than a failure of the medical system to cure, and discharge planning will become an increasingly significant role for social workers in health care settings. (Ciotti & Watt, 1992, p. 502)

Discharge planning helps ensure not only the optimum use of hospital beds but also the continuity of care by providing for the posthospital needs of patients. Research studies have demonstrated its importance for reducing the hospital length of stay, as well as readmission rates (Andrews, 1986; Cable & Mayers, 1983; Morrow-Howell, Proctor, & Mui, 1991; Proctor & Morrow-Howell, 1990).

What does discharge planning involve as a social work activity? The position statement of the Society for Hospital Directors, issued in 1985, includes the following components:

- Development of systems that ensure timely and efficient identification of patients who require discharge planning
- Assessment of the psychological, social, environmental, and financial impact of illness on patients and families
- Provision of psychosocial services to patients and families
- Coordination of the contributions of the health care team
- Development and maintenance of liaison with local, state, and federal resources
- Establishment of systems to monitor and evaluate the effectiveness of the discharge planning process
- Identification of services that are not available to meet the posthospital needs of patients and families with a view to effecting the development of needed resources. ("Role of the Social Worker," 1986)

The specific case situations determine the degree of emphasis on any of the above components, and the complexity of discharge plans varies from case to case. The above-named document describes four levels of outcome of discharge planning: (a) patient and family understanding of the diagnosis, anticipated level of functioning, prescribed treatment, and plan for follow-up; (b) specialized instruction so that the patient and the family can provide posthospital care; (c) coordination of the essential community support system; and (d) relocation of the patient and coordination of support systems or transfer to another health care facility.

The above lists highlight only some things that social workers do. Social work activity with the patient and the family is based on a grasp of the psychosocial context within which illness or injury, hospitalization, and discharge occur. Viewing this phenomenon from the role theory perspective, Blazyk and Canavan (1985) said,

Hospitalization validates the definition of the patient as "ill." The need for discharge, therefore, is often seen as incongruent with this identity. Discharge planning demands a sudden reversal of the patient role, in that the individual, family, or society must quickly resume responsibility for activities and burdens suspended during hospitalization. (p. 491)

Discharge often involves substantial life reorganization and is not simply a return to the life before hospitalization. It may represent a crisis, and the worker must treat it as such.

Discharge planning may also involve ethical conflicts and dilemmas for the worker. The very idea of DRG raises the issue of "averageness versus individualization" (Blumenfield, 1986)—all patients having the same diagnosis are assumed to have similar needs, strengths, and resources, and patients are not given the right to refuse a discharge. In some situations, the obligation to the institution and the needs of the patient conflict. Blumenfield and Lowe (1987) listed several ethical conflicts involved in discharge planning. Similarly, the social worker may have to deal with legal issues (e.g., see Mullaney & Andrews, 1983). In working with patients and their families, social workers should use all the necessary therapeutic skills. Discharge in the case of victims of catastrophic illnesses "where recovery is minimal or moderate and significant deficits remain, is often viewed by the patient and/or family as symbolizing failure, loss of hope, and abandonment on the part of the medical staff" (Blazyk & Canavan, 1986, p. 23). The social worker should help them reframe the meaning of discharge and shift from a loss orientation to one of problem solving and planning for the future.

Resource mobilization for effective discharge planning can be conceived of as a two-pronged activity directed at human and material resources within the hospital and at the sources of support in the patient's social world and the larger community outside. Work on behalf of the patient takes special significance in discharge planning. It calls for collaboration with other professionals within the hospital and health and human services outside. In his study of hospital discharge planning effectiveness, Feather (1993) tested the importance of four sets of variables: role and procedural clarity, power, discharge planning model, and hospital characteristics. He found that the power and role clarity variables were the most important. These explained almost 50% of the variance in effectiveness. The power variables included discharge planner influence, physician support, and hospital administration support. Of these, support and cooperation from physicians was the most important factor. Feather recommended:

> Instead of concentrating solely on improving the process within the discharge planning program, they [discharge planners] must devote substantial effort to enhancing their visibility in the hospital at large. . . . In the long run, effectiveness will be enhanced through activities that in-

crease power and clarity, such as participation in hospital-wide committees, providing seminars on discharge planning for physicians and other
hospital personnel, or developing a brochure that clearly explains the
function of discharge planning. (p. 12)

Chapter 8 reviews strategies for attaining and retaining power that
social workers in all health care settings can practice. Here, it will
suffice to point out that the sensitivity and skills that social workers
bring to bear on their work with clients are equally effective in educating and influencing other professionals.

> To the extent that we help patients leave the hospital because "the doctor
> wants the bed" or "UR is pushing us," we act as demeaned instruments of
> a system we neither understand nor can hope to impact. To the extent we
> look behind those presenting requests and identify the sources of pres-
> sures, assessing their nature, strength, and legitimacy, we will be able and
> trustworthy helpers to patients and families, and responsible colleagues
> to physicians and administrators. (Fields, 1978, p. 5)

In teaching physicians and others, social workers may emphasize the
patients' rights related to discharge planning:

> A right to receive certain basic services that will facilitate and optimize
> transfer from the hospital, a right to receive information about his or her
> illness and what he or she needs to do about it, a right to understand the
> support he or she needs and the resources available to provide that support,
> and a right to secure those resources. (Rehr, 1986, p. 47)

Social workers should sensitize physicians and others to the complexity of discharge planning by helping them realize that (a) all patients
who are bright and alert may not be financially and/or mentally competent; (b) all family members who profess to want their relative home
with them may not be guided by the best interests of the patient and may
have other motives, such as guilt or greed; (c) families that do not want
the responsibility of care for their relative do not say so clearly—their
indirect signals often fail to change the conviction of discharge planners
that home is the best place for the patient to go; (d) patients who are
dependent on frail elderly spouses for care are putting themselves and
their spouses at risk; (e) the information given by patients or families
with memory impairments cannot be taken at face value; and (f) the
weak and the infirm may be abused, neglected, or taken advantage of at

home, and if this possibility is unheeded, the patient is being returned to a dangerous environment (Ciotti & Watt, 1992).

Discharge planning work on behalf of the patient and family outside the hospital requires knowledge of community resources and the skills of identifying or creating and mobilizing resources, advocacy, linking and matching patients and resources, and monitoring. Formal and informal contacts with community agencies, updated resource manuals and continuously refined information systems, and streamlined procedural matters will help improve these skills. Quality discharge planning will be a mark of the quality of hospital-based care in the future, and social work has much to contribute to that.

Social Worker as a Case Worker and Counselor

In the *case worker and counselor role,* the social worker not only serves the patient and the family but also demonstrates a service that is patient- and family-centered, comprehensive, and well coordinated. Differences will exist in the intensity of social work involvement, depending on the level of care provided by the hospital. In general, however, (a) advances in medical technology, (b) the use of diverse health care approaches and personnel within, and (c) the need to be more closely bound with the health, mental health, and social service systems outside will make hospitals more complex. The following observations and suggestions will be helpful for this role:

1. In the future, patients, the consumers of health care, will be better informed, more active, and demand to be treated as partners in their treatment and care, and health care organizations will accommodate those demands. Patients, thus, will have more choices and consequently greater difficulty in making decisions. The counseling aspect of social work activity will involve not only helping patients understand and cope with their illness and its treatment—the hospitalization, medical procedures, and their consequences—but also teaching them and their families how to make decisions. Ways of helping them gain greater control and decision-making power can include (a) consulting and involving the patient and the family in the establishment and implementation of the daily care routines; (b) providing accurate and clear information about the illness, the "what," "why," and "how" of the treatment plan, and alternatives, if any; (c) manipulating the environmental arrangements so that the patient has both greater privacy and less isolation; (d) pointing out the validity of their decisions and highlight-

ing their efforts and progress; and (e) encouraging their meaningful participation in discharge planning.

2. Advanced technology will add to the importance of the within-the-institution advocacy part of social casework. Social workers should use their knowledge, values, and skills to demystify sophisticated medical technology. While noting that the principle of respect of human dignity is particularly vulnerable to the press of technology, Abramson (1990) said,

> By nature of the fact that social workers are not responsible for applying the technology as are doctors, nurses, physical and occupational therapists and other health care personnel, social workers can hold onto the thread of autonomy and dignity by questioning the purpose of the technology, and encouraging dialogue and negotiation amongst all the participants, and by advocating for the patient when s/he is not able to do so for him/herself. (pp. 12-13)

3. The personal social support systems of patients will be much thinner and weaker in the future. Social work practice has always recognized the role of the family in the illness, coping, recovery and wellness of the individual, and the reciprocal impact of illness on the family. The changed family forms and weaker social supports, however, will make it necessary to put extra efforts into identifying, involving, and mobilizing patients' families and making the care family-centered. The family will have to be defined more broadly, such as "a social system comprised of individuals related to each other by virtue of strong reciprocal affect who share a permanent household or group of households that endure over time" (Caroff & Mailick, 1985, p. 20). Such a definition covers all kinds of familial structures and membership that may emerge in the next century.

4. The social work literature is rich with ideas for effective assessment of and intervention with families of hospitalized patients (e.g., Caroff & Mailick, 1985; Dillon, 1985; Germain, 1984; Kemler, 1985). On the basis of an extensive review of the relevant literature, Bergman and her associates (1993) identified four key family characteristics that may have significant impact on the course of recovery and ongoing functioning of patients: family cohesion, adaptability, social integration, and degree of family stress. *Family cohesion* is the degree of emotional bonding between family members and of individual autonomy experienced by each member. Cohesive families are marked

by mutual appreciation, commitment and support, open communication, individual differentiation, and group consolidation. They avoid the extremes of enmeshment and unconcern. Family *adaptability* is the degree of flexibility in terms of the family's structure, roles, and relationship rules that allows it to respond to situational and developmental stress. A family's *social integration* is its degree of involvement with its social network, which is a significant source of support. The *degree of family stress* existing at any given time affects the family's response to stressful events. Exploring these characteristics can easily be made a part of the psychosocial assessment, and a variety of assessment tools are available (e.g., see McCubbin & Patterson, 1981; Olson et al., 1982). Such an assessment will help the worker target the particular dimensions of the patient's social reality for intervention.

5. Advances in medical technology will continue to result in more patients surviving serious injuries and diseases, substituting chronic illnesses for life-threatening conditions, introducing a strong element of uncertainty and unpredictability in the situation, and adding another layer of stress for the patient and the family. The social worker should use a systems perspective for a comprehensive view of the total impact of illness on the patient and his or her family and for planning to intervene at different points and levels of the familial system. "Working within a family systems perspective can be especially useful in terms of opening lines of communication, helping family members support each other in the tension of the uncertainty, and dealing with disynchrony when it occurs" (Kemler, 1985, p. 49). In the desire to protect their members from anxiety, many families do not allow open talk and discussion of a member's illness, its prognosis, and consequences. This reluctance often results in the family's failure to deal with its situation realistically, to use its internal and external resources optimally, and to protect its members from avoidable anxiety, suffering, and disease.

6. For helping the hospital and fellow professionals from other disciplines provide family-centered care, social workers should build into their casework, teamwork, advocacy work, and other activities the following principles. These have been adapted from the critical components of family-centered care defined by the Association for the Care of Children's Health (Shelton, Jeppson, & Johnson, 1987):

- Recognize that the family is the constant in a patient's life, whereas service systems and their personnel fluctuate.

- Facilitate family/professional collaboration at all levels of hospital, home, and community care: (a) care of the individual; (b) program development, implementation, and evaluation; and (c) policy information.
- Provide families complete and unbiased information in a supportive manner at all times.
- Incorporate into policy and practice the recognition and honoring of cultural diversity, strengths, and individuality within and across all families, including ethnic, racial, spiritual, social, economic, educational, and geographic diversity.
- Recognize and respect different methods of coping and implementing comprehensive policies and programs for meeting the diverse needs of families.
- Encourage and facilitate family-to-family support and networking.
- Ensure that hospital, home, and community service and support systems are flexible, accessible, and comprehensive in responding to diverse family-identified needs.
- Appreciate families as families and patients as patients, recognizing that they possess a wide range of strengths, concerns, emotions, and aspirations beyond their need for health services and support.

Below, we discuss the knowledge and skills required for the social worker's caseworker and counselor role in relation to the special needs of major patient groups. These groups include the elderly, patients with disabilities, patients with AIDS, and victims of violence and abuse.

The Elderly

To serve elderly clients more effectively, social workers will find the following suggestions helpful:

1. Social workers should know that the general principles of aging are that (a) functions decline and (b) variability increases. Although decline in the body's functioning is inevitable in old age, the degree and form of decline varies immensely among the aged. A person's chronological age does not tell much about him or her.

2. Social workers should know that most elderly, when hospitalized, tend to experience confusion and a sense of loss of control. The unfamiliarity of the hospital may precipitate mental confusion, and hospital routines may enforce dependency and disrupt self-care patterns. Patients may feel overwhelmed emotionally by their situation, and surgical anaesthesia may exacerbate confusion (Furstenberg &

Mezey, 1987). A study of adverse events in the hospitalized elderly by Foreman, Theis, and Anderson (1993) found that 54% of their sample had experienced some degree of acute confusion during hospitalization.

3. Social workers should know that physical illness necessitating hospitalization may come on the heels of losses of family, friends, and valued roles that the elderly patient was struggling to cope with.

4. Social workers should realize that depression is very common among the elderly and that the prevalence rates of major depression and depressive symptoms in hospitalized medically ill elderly are high. Depressive symptoms, when combined with medical illness, have additive effects on the patient's function and well-being (Kurlowicz, 1994).

5. Social workers should sharpen their assessment skills and use them so that a comprehensive picture of the patient's life situation emerges. With a view to ensuring effective discharge planning, social workers should enrich their assessment skills with elements of functional assessment. The gerontological literature contains several models of and tools for functional assessment. Functional assessment is evaluative in its thrust. "There is an implied asset-versus-liability, positive-versus-negative judgment made about every attribute being assessed" (Lawton, 1986, p. 39). Lawton proposed a framework for functional assessment that he called "the good life." The good life is indicated by positively assessed qualities in four sectors: (a) behavioral competence, (b) psychological well-being, (c) perceived quality of life, and (d) objective environment. Weissensee, Kjervik, and Anderson (1995) devised a tool to assess the cognitively impaired elderly whose legal competency is in question.

6. In their dealings with elderly patients, social workers should guard against ageism creeping into their approach to working with them. Behaviors that indicate ageism include pigeonholing the elderly and not allowing them to be individuals, avoiding them, and discriminating against them in terms of access to services. Social workers should always remember that the rationale for a distinctive social work purpose with regard to the aged is the premise that "the individual has the right to complete his or her natural life cycle, with its expectable flow and sense of continuity, without culturally imposed inhibiting restraints" (Monk, 1981, p. 11).

7. Social workers should be conscious of the possibility of countertransference and other attitudes affecting their professional behavior. The following reasons for negative staff attitudes toward treat-

ing older persons that the Committee on Aging of the Group for the Advancement of Psychiatry (1971) report listed are still valid: (a) The aged stimulate the therapist's fear about his or her own old age; (b) they arouse the therapist's conflicts about his or her relationship with parental figures; (c) the therapist believes he or she has nothing useful to offer older people because he or she believes they cannot change their behavior or that their problems are a result of untreatable organic brain disease; (d) the therapist believes that his or her skills will be wasted because the aged are near death and not really deserving of attention; (e) the patient may die while in treatment, which could challenge the therapist's sense of importance; and (f) the therapist's colleagues may be contemptuous of his or her efforts on behalf of aged patients. In the next century, geriatric medicine and geriatric psychiatry will have gained unprecedented respectability, and no one will consider the work of these disciplines to be a morbid preoccupation with death. Some of the above attitudes will persist, however, and the scope of geriatric medicine and psychiatry's activities will continue to be narrower than social work's.

8. In view of the sensory losses and other physical impairments of elderly patients, social workers should learn to use nonverbal communication along with various "leads" that encourage the elaboration of feelings, thoughts, and concerns. These leads include restatement, clarification, interpretation, general leads, and summary leads (Kermis, 1986). The use of computers and other communication devices in the future will make communication with such elderly easier. Social workers will have to acquire the skills to use those devices.

9. Social workers should make their intervention with the elderly empowerment-oriented, one that enhances the patient's sense of control and capability to exert influence over the hospital and its service providers. Empowerment can be understood both in terms of the content—the specific activities—and the process of empowerment. We discuss both of these aspects of empowerment at length in the next chapter. Tactics of empowerment suggested by Brown and Furstenberg (1992) include contracting, setting small goals, encouraging client self-monitoring, creating room for decision making, reinforcing the perception of control, and organizing for self-advocacy.

10. Social workers will continue to be responsible for discharge planning (we earlier discussed the knowledge and skills appropriate for discharge planning). In planning the discharge of elderly patients, social workers should take into consideration the unique needs of the in-

dividual patient and try to find the best possible match between those needs and the available resources. They should also familiarize themselves with the various approaches to resolving ethical conflicts and dilemmas, because several ethical issues can be involved in discharge planning. Blumenfield and Lowe (1987) and others (e.g., Abramson, 1983; Reamer, 1985) have discussed these and suggested ways of resolving them.

11. Social workers should constantly enrich their professional repertoire with ideas for therapeutic interventions from the gerontological literature.

Patients With Disabilities

Work with patients with disabilities demands extra sensitivity and commitment to the principles of individualization and to comprehensive assessment. While discussing persons with mental retardation who are also old, Howell (1987) wrote,

> Some health problems in clients with mental retardation arise as a consequence of institutional care. Obesity, for instance, may be in part the result of a diet scant in fresh fruits and vegetables and whole grain foods, and overburdened with simple carbohydrates; sugary foods may have been given as rewards. Similarly, addiction to tobacco or to caffeine may reflect the use of these substances as positive reinforcers. Dental problems may be a consequence of the unavailability of dental care. Cardiovascular and musculoskeletal fitness may be less than optimal if the client has had little access to exercise facilities, and little encouragement. A history of use of psychotropic medications may result in impaired function of liver, kidneys, or thyroid, cataracts, or tardive dyskinesia. Other health problems related to institutionalization include exposure to hepatitis B and the possibility of a residual carrier state; a history of sexual and/or physical abuse; and habits of public masturbation or self-inflicted injury, sometimes (but not always) associated with boredom and lack of opportunities for social, physical, sexual, and mental engagement. (p. 101)

In assessing and working with inpatients with disabilities, social workers should seek and build on the information, assistance, and involvement of community-based service providers active with the patient. Social workers should be aware of their attitudes toward those with disabilities and consciously guard against their negative attitudes influencing their professional behaviors.

Social workers should ensure that people with disabilities are treated with respect and dignity like everyone else. Disability does not make these patients less human. Levitas and Gilson (1987) said people with mental retardation are often treated as if cognitive development were the only dimension of their lives.

Social workers should (and urge others to) practice the principles of individualization and avoidance of overprotection in treating patients with disabilities because "normalization" and "mainstreaming" are the goals as well as the major principles of work with them in the community. They should realize that allowing the hospitalized person with a disability to do as much as he or she can with respect to personal hygiene, individual activities, planning for treatment, and care may require much patience and time.

The need for comprehensive services in response to the unique problem and situation of each patient highlights the importance of (a) the principle of individualization, (b) the necessity of a comprehensive assessment, and (c) concerted efforts to coordinate services. In the future, hospitals will be committed to providing comprehensive patient- and family-centered care, and patients will insist on being treated as partners. With client autonomy and self-determination as the essential philosophical bases of their practice, social workers will also have opportunities for helping the organization and other professionals in the creation of an atmosphere appropriate for that type of care.

Patients With AIDS

The need for self-awareness on the part of the social worker is perhaps nowhere as real as in working with patients with AIDS. Social workers should, therefore, practice the principle of self-awareness, which involves bringing into their consciousness and examining their own attitudes, beliefs, and feelings and the ways these affect their actions and responses (Furstenberg & Olson, 1984).

The principle of individualization is of immense significance in working with AIDS patients. Social workers should know that patients' adaptive tasks include maintaining a meaningful quality of life, retaining intimacy, coping with the loss of function, confronting existential and spiritual issues, and planning for the survival of family and friends (Moynihan, Christ, & Gallo-Silver, 1988; Siegel & Krauss, 1991). Patients who are gay men, injection drug users (IDUs), women, and children, as well as the families of these patients, have differing needs and adaptive tasks. For example, individuals with transfusion-related HIV infection have the additional adaptive tasks of "coping with feelings of victimization, sadness, anger and isolation; decision-making concerning their medical treatment in the context of pre-existing medical condition; and rebuilding trust in relationships with health care professionals" (Gallo-Silver, Raveis, & Moynihan, 1993, p. 66). Most women with AIDS are IDUs or the sexual partners of IDUs. Their needs are different from those of other groups. In many cases, children and adolescents with AIDS feel guilty about having the disease, about their past behavior and lifestyle, and about the possibility of having infected others. They experience sadness, hopelessness, helplessness, isolation, and depression (Lockhart & Wodarski, 1989). Haney (1988), an AIDS patient himself, said, "AIDS has become closely associated with horrifying negative pictures of incapacitation, abandonment, rejection, hatred, physical and mental deterioration, and deformity. When one is faced with these bleak and barren prospects associated with AIDS, suicide becomes a viable alternative" (p. 251).

While working with AIDS cases, social workers must define families as more than families of origin and families of procreation and include what Bonuck (1993) called a "functional family," a group marked by committed relationships among individuals that fulfill the functions of family (Anderson, 1988). The emotional and tangible effect of AIDS on the family varies by the type of family and such factors as social stigma and isolation, fear of contagion on the part of family members, fear of infecting one's loved ones, fear of abandonment, guilt, and psychological and physical fatigue (Bonuck, 1993). Social workers should know that the family's ability to be involved in the care of the patient also depends on such factors as coping characteristics and resources, perceptions of self-efficacy, perceived adequacy of social support, familial obligation and affection, fears of being infected, the degree to which the patient is held responsible for the illness, and acceptance of homosexuality (McDonnell, Abell, & Miller, 1991).

Social workers should use their casework and counseling skills in meeting the differential needs of patients and patients' families. To counteract the pervasive helplessness, hopelessness, and isolation, the techniques of empowerment should be built into the work done with these clients. Some of these techniques can focus on the positive and less fatalistic aspects of AIDS, connect patients with sources of support, and help them regain and retain power and control over their lives and illness. Others include

massage therapy, acupuncture, holistic medicine, meditation, creative visualization, affirmation, nutrition, emotional support, coping skills training, anxiety and stress reduction, relaxation exercises, individual counseling, group therapy and group support, and experimental drug treatments. (Haney, 1988, p. 252)

Borden (1989) recommended life review and reminiscence as a helpful technique for working with young adults with AIDS because reminiscence processes work to preserve a sense of ego integrity, order, coherence, and cohesiveness.

Discharge planning for AIDS patients requires extra work and care. Social workers should supplement their skills with measures to deal with the following obstacles to effective case management that Roberts, Severinsen, Kuehn, Straker, and Fritz (1992) identified: (a) stigma of AIDS and homosexuality; (b) lack of family support; (c) impact of AIDS dementia, which has been observed in 60% to 80% of AIDS patients; (d) ethical dilemmas in discharge planning, such as the patient's wish for confidentiality about his or her disease and the need to involve his or her family; (e) conflicts in advocacy process within the hospital (if the patient insists that his or her familial visitors not know of his or her AIDS and if dementia makes his or her behavior unpredictable); (f) lack of adequate resources; and (g) issues of countertransference, which may include fear of the unknown, fear of contagion, fear of death, denial of helplessness, homophobia, overidentification, anger, and the need for professional omnipotence (Dunkel & Hatfield, 1986). Many gay patients who have not fully accepted a personal identity as gay may put geographic distance between themselves and their kinship networks and thereby deprive themselves of their natural supports, as well as local gay support. That deprivation makes discharge planning more difficult. Social work advocacy skills become much more important in such cases.

Victims of Violence and Abuse

I suggest a twofold social work contribution to the hospital's service to victims of violence and abuse: direct work with the victims and creating a special program or unit to address their needs. We discuss the social work crisis intervention skills appropriate for dealing with victims of violence and their families in Chapter 5. For creating a center or program for the service of the abused, social workers can benefit from a few impressive examples. Edlis (1993) described a hospital-based rape crisis center in Haifa, Israel. That center has been in existence since 1980, and its success has encouraged the development of similar centers in other hospitals in that country. Such a center has several advantages: (a) It is open and accessible to rape victims 24 hours a day, 7 days a week; (b) skilled professionals are on duty at all times; (c) it provides access to a full range of needed medical examinations and tests; and (d) it has the ability to centralize services and liaison with agencies outside the hospital. The hospital's social work department developed procedures, guidelines, and protocols for the center, conducted training seminars for the staff of the hospital and community organizations, and created a plan for crisis intervention (Edlis, 1993). To establish and run such programs, social workers should increase their understanding of the different approaches to battered women and models of women's shelters (e.g., N. J. Davis, 1988).

Wolf and Pillemaer (1994) presented four "best practice models" in elder abuse programming: (a) a multidisciplinary team approach of the San Francisco Consortium for the Prevention of Elder Abuse; (b) the Senior Advocacy Volunteer program in Madison, Wisconsin; (c) the Victim Support Group of the Elder Abuse Project of the Mount Sinai Medical Center, New York; and (d) a Social Work Master's Level Training Unit within Adult Protective Services in Hawaii. Two of these [(a) and (c)] can easily be hospital-based.

I have chosen to postpone the discussion of social work with culturally diverse patients. Cultural diversity will pervade all dimensions of life and will need to be accommodated at the case as well as organizational levels in all sectors of health care. Ideas about effective social work approaches to working with culturally diverse populations are presented Chapter 8.

NOTE

1. Some hospitals have established hospital-based hospice programs; others have gone into the nursing home business by creating both swing beds within the hospital and separate entities in the community. Some hospitals provide home care services; others are trying ambulatory care options such as hospital-based primary care centers; HMOs; specialized clinics for chronic pain, sleep disturbance, and so forth; as well as community-based satellite clinics and health promotion programs (Bayles, 1979; DeSpiegler, 1979; Drew, 1979; Justins, 1994; McInerney, 1979; Smith, 1979; Wilson, 1979; Yanni, 1979). Rock, Haymes, Auerbach, and Beckerman (1992) described a hospital-sponsored community residence program for the chronically mentally ill.

The possibilities for a hospital becoming the coordinator of community health and human services or for collaborating with other agencies and programs are immense. Long and her colleagues (1993) described a hospital-based program for family-centered early intervention in infants with chronic health impairments and developmental disabilities.

Patterson (1995) described the University of Maryland Hospital's comprehensive family-centered pediatric AIDS program.

Rubin and Black (1992) described a joint program of two hospitals in Pittsburgh designed to provide community-based health education to seniors. Those hospitals conduct a semiannual town meeting, one or the other taking the lead in its organization, and costs are divided equally and topics and format are developed jointly. This program has benefited both hospitals by enabling them to improve their services for the elderly. All such ventures have a social work component and call for either initiative or input from social workers. The Pittsburgh Town Meeting program had used the skills of a social worker as its part-time executive director.

Chapter 5

SOCIAL WORK IN AMBULATORY CARE

Ambulatory care is perhaps the most important element of the health care system. This is where the patient first comes in contact with the system and continues to stay in it. Ambulatory care services are also a major source of intake of patients for other health care sectors. Chapter 2 described the various definitions of and the different services encompassed by ambulatory care, the long history of this type of care, and the numerous settings through which it is provided. In the future, the demand for ambulatory care will increase, leading to growth not only in the number and popularity of services but also in the variety of care providers and organizations. Even though the provision of primary care will be the minimal expectation from ambulatory care settings, the increased demand for services will put greater strain on the system's resources, accompanied by questions of equity and quality of services. Provision of patient-centered, comprehensive, and coordinated services and attention to the special health care concerns of major population groups will be the main needs of all ambulatory care settings in the future (see Chapter 3).

HISTORY OF SOCIAL WORK
IN AMBULATORY CARE SETTINGS

Social work has been a part of many ambulatory care settings for a long time. In 1893, Jane Addams established a free medical dispensary at Chicago's Hull House. Other social workers were involved in the opening of similar dispensaries in many other cities (Bracht, 1978). From the late 1800s onward, social work, "medicine's first professional ally from the social field" (Simmons & Wolff, 1954, p. 12), contributed impressively to the development of social medicine and public health. Physicians and medical establishments began seeing the utility of social work methodology and social workers for improving their understanding and treatment of poor patients. Since the middle of the 19th century, physicians such as Dr. Elizabeth Blackwell of the New York Infirmary, Dr. Dwight Chapin of the New York Postgraduate Hospital, and Dr. William Osler of the Johns Hopkins Hospital and University in Baltimore have used hired help, volunteers, or medical students as "friendly visitors" for reporting home conditions of patients to the physician and for interpreting the physician's instructions to patients and their families (Cannon, 1952). In 1903, Dr. Richard Cabot, chief of medicine at Massachusetts General Hospital in Boston, introduced a social worker into his medical clinic. He was convinced that a person's personal difficulties may be the cause and not the result of his or her illness (Nacman, 1977). He considered medical and social work to be "branches split off a common trunk: the care of people in trouble" (Cabot, 1915, p. 91). Serving the poor—essentially, the entire clientele of health centers and clinics—was a frustrating experience for both service providers and recipients because of the social and cultural gap between the two. The giver was frustrated because of the lack of appreciation and the absence of expected results. The recipient was frustrated because of the lack of opportunity for self-expression and the unwillingness to accept the stipulations required for receiving service (Ginker et al. as in Nacman, 1977).

The social work role in outpatient clinics involved four major functions: (a) educating the physician about the patient's domestic and social conditions, (b) helping the patient comply with the physician's orders, (c) alleviating the patient's social problems that interfered with medical care, and (d) providing a link between the health care setting and community agencies. Although the earliest health social workers, mostly nurses, had little or no formal training in social work, they were expected to be "all-around human beings who can supplement the necessary and valuable narrowness of the physician" (Cabot, 1915, p. 176). Ever since, social workers have been adding a unique dimension to health care. "The contribution that social work makes to health care is in its holistic approach to problems of both body and mind. . . . Social work's uniqueness comes from its persistent focus on the physical, sociopsychological, and environmental health needs of clients" (Bracht, 1978, p. 13).

That was the beginning of social work's involvement with ambulatory care settings. With the growth of these settings in their numbers, auspices, foci, and purposes came increased presence of social workers. The creation in 1912 of the U.S. Children's Bureau (the first five chiefs of which were social workers) led to the discovery that infant and maternal mortality rates were significantly related to social and economic factors. That finding resulted in the birth of the first grant-in-aid programs in the health field under the Maternal and Infancy Act of 1921 (Kerson, DuChainey, & Schmid, 1989). Social workers were employed in public health clinics as part of the maternal and child health programs. Similarly, after World War I, the National Venereal Disease Control Act provided financial assistance to state and local health departments for clinics for surveillance, early diagnosis, and treatment of venereal disease. Social workers were a part of those clinics as well. Their interventions were focused on educating victims and families about the causes and dissemination of syphilis, tracing the syphilitic's sexual contacts, and encouraging the patient to comply with the treatment (Kerson, 1979). Earlier, social workers had been heavily involved in tuberculosis control programs, working with both patients and their families. In 1935, the Social Security Act created the maternal and child health program and the crippled children's program. In the 1950s, programs to coordinate medical and social services for unwed mothers were developed. Now, such comprehensive programs are mandated by Title V of the Social Security Act (Kerson et al., 1989). In the 1960s, new health care organizations and programs appeared. These included Office of Economic Opportunity (OEO) neighborhood health centers, expanded programs for the prevention of maternal and infant problems, special outreach programs for the rural poor, and community mental health centers. Social workers made substantial contributions to all of these (Bracht, 1978).

Thus, social workers have been important elements of many ambulatory care programs. They have worked not only in generic settings such as public health departments, health centers, and health maintenance organizations (HMOs), but also in specialized settings such as clinics for genetic counseling, family planning, prenatal and postnatal care, care of the newborn, diagnosis and treatment/management of persons with disabilities, service to those with AIDS, and work with victims of child abuse, rape, and spousal abuse. They have also been involved in acute care ambulatory settings such as emergency rooms and ambulatory surgery centers.

Both nonacute care and acute care settings are likely to continue as the sites for ambulatory care in the future, providing varied opportunities for social workers to make significant contributions to those settings. Social workers will be able to take on important roles in helping these settings meet their needs. Their knowledge and skills will be appropriate for (a) comprehensiveness of care—they will assess the total situation of the patients and attend to the psychosocial dimensions of patients' health needs; (b) coordination of care—they will be responsible for ensuring that all the pieces of care for and on behalf of the patient are coordinated; (c) integration of care—they will be the major link between the ambulatory care setting and other health and social service resources; and (d) patient-centered patient-as-a-partner care—through their involvement with patients, they will demonstrate how to relate to patients as partners in their care. They will also help in meeting the special needs of major patient groups. Social work contributions will be equally valuable for acute and nonacute ambulatory settings.

The needs of patients using acute care settings such as emergency rooms for emergency as well as non-emergency problems are different in their nature, intensity, and urgency from those of patients seen in other ambulatory settings. Social work's contribution to the care of the two groups would be different in the degree of involvement, as well as in the use of knowledge and skills. Ambulatory care, therefore can be divided into (a) acute ambulatory and (b) nonacute ambulatory care. We discuss social work roles and functions in each of these separately.

FUTURE SOCIAL WORK ROLES IN
ACUTE AMBULATORY CARE SETTINGS

In the next century, with expanded access to health care, all kinds of nonacute ambulatory care settings will try to attract and retain patients. Also, coordination of services between those settings and other community health and human services will be better. Those changes will reduce somewhat the inappropriate use of acute care settings. Acute care ambulatory settings, like emergency rooms, however, will continue as a part of the infrastructure of primary care in the United States. Their greatest attraction will be convenience of access to care. "No physician will be available 24 hours a day, 7 days a week for his/her patients" (Young & Sklar, 1995, p. 669). Moreover, advances in information technology will ensure continuity of information for patients with chronic problems coming to acute care settings. Thus, these settings will add *continuity of care* to the *convenience of access to care* as their attributes. Then there will always be patients whose problems do not fit into a neat service category, who misjudge the nature of their need or exaggerate the seriousness of their problem, and who end up in acute care facilities. They will need someone to listen to their story, help them put the situation in the correct perspective, and steer them in the right direction. In all the situations described above, the social worker will continue to play professional roles distinct from those of others, roles for which other professionals do not have the appropriate and necessary attitudes, knowledge, and skills. In dealing with people with non-emergent health and nonhealth needs, the social worker's attitude is often a complete contrast to that of others. These patients are generally viewed as abusing the facility, inappropriately taxing its resources, and threatening its routine order. This attitude tends to get translated into impatience, intolerance, and callousness on the part of the staff. Sometimes even the legitimate health-related complaints of these patients would be ignored if the social worker did not intervene.

In acute ambulatory care settings, three distinct situations are encountered: (a) true medical emergencies, (b) social emergencies, and (c) non-emergency health and social needs. Social work intervention will be different in each of these.

Social Work Role in True Medical Emergencies

Burns, cardiac problems, poisonings, and traumas are among the true medical emergencies. All of these have some common characteristics: They are generally unexpected, happen suddenly, endanger the patient's life, and the patient and/or the family were not prepared for their occurrence. Discussing trauma patients, Moonilal (1982) said that these patients may experience shock, excessive blood loss, severe respiratory distress, or cardiac arrest.

> Victims of multiple trauma are usually products of motor vehicle accidents, shootings, stabbings, or suicide attempts and are generally in shock, unconscious, or near death. Most arrive at the hospital with paramedics—a few are brought in by family or friends. (p. 16)

Immediately on their arrival, these patients become the object of intense life-saving medical activities on the part of physicians, nurses, and paramedical staff. The situation, at the same time, also generates important nonmedical needs. These include notifying the family if they are not aware of the sudden illness or injury of the patient and dealing with their reaction to what generally is experienced as an acute emotional crisis. In all emergency care settings, although physicians and nurses are specially trained and skilled for the medical treatment and care of severely ill and injured patients, a person is seldom clearly designated and trained for contacting the family of the critically ill, dying, or dead patients. That job is performed by different persons in an ad hoc, generally inconsistent, and sometimes haphazard manner. Part of the reason for inconsistency is the differing access to information and different perspectives on the situation:

> For example, the physician focuses on diagnoses and prognoses; the nurse is familiar with the patients's vital signs and observable behavior; and the registration staff members are most informed about the location of the incident and have firsthand reports relayed by ambulance personnel. (Robinson, 1982, p. 616)

Clark and LaBeff (1982) studied how different professionals—physicians, nurses, law enforcement personnel, and members of the clergy—delivered news of death and discovered five strategies of delivery. The strategy chosen seemed to depend on such factors as the personality of the person and the circumstances of the situation. The inconsistency in the manner of notification of families of acutely ill and dying or dead patients, whether because of different information, perspective, or personality of the notifier, can have adverse effects on the family. In the next century, with computers taking over many functions performed by people today, the likelihood of this need of such families being handled impersonally and insensitively will be ever greater.

Depending on the nature of the emergency, the family's immediate reaction may be disbelief, confusion, anxiety, fear, anger, guilt, or grief. "Unanticipated medical emergencies can overwhelm the unsuspecting family, making coping impossible" (Silverman, 1986, p. 312). Thus, the need for intervention is urgent. A family faced with the possible loss of a loved one needs help.

The emergency may end in the patient (a) dying; (b) being transferred to a hospital's intensive care unit with an uncertainty about survival, the prospect for survival with long-term disability, or the hope for complete recovery; (c) being transferred to a medical facility for less intensive further treatment; (d) being sent to a penal institution in the case of crime-related injuries; or (e) being discharged home. All these possibilities involve uncertainty, numerous questions, a flood of emotions, and the need for the family to plan a response to the situation. Families need help in reducing the degree of uncertainty, in understanding and gaining control over the situation, in expressing and getting validation of their emotions, in obtaining honest answers and consistent information, and in preparing for whatever may be happening and being planned for the patient. They must be prepared for even looking at the loved one, who may have been badly disfigured by the trauma and is sure to be hooked up to several machines. Acute care units "generate fear, provoke anxiety, and heighten the family's awareness that the patient is seriously ill and may not live" (Dhooper, 1994b, p. 42). Discussing the powerful impact of these units, Hay and Oken (1972) said,

> Initially, the greatest impact comes from the intricate machinery, with its flashing lights, buzzing and beeping monitor, gurgling suction pumps, and wheezing respirators. . . . Desperately ill, sick and injured human beings are hooked up to that machinery. And, in addition to mechanical stimuli, one can discern moaning, crying, screaming and the last gasps of life. Sights of blood, vomitus and excreta, exposed genitalia, mutilated wasted bodies, and unconscious and helpless people assault the sensibilities. (p. 110)

A social worker's services should be made available to the families of seriously ill patients.

> If a social worker is not available, the family will find another, perhaps less professionally trained, supportive liaison. At some point, the barrage of outside stimuli will begin to overwhelm the system. Once saturated, the family system will close, making intervention difficult. (Silverman, 1986, p. 311)

Social workers in all acute care settings, including acute ambulatory care centers/units, should consider attending to the needs of families as their major function and take on this responsibility. Their understanding of the crisis theory, sensitivity for individuals in crisis, and skills in crisis intervention would make them the best qualified for the job. Moreover, their contacting the family can set the stage for their subsequent activity with the family. Their focus should be on alleviating the impact of the crisis-created stress and helping the family grasp the situation and mobilize its internal and external resources to deal with it. This function would involve activity with the family and on behalf of the family both within the center and outside. Social work activity with the family would include assessment, consultation, crisis management, grief counseling, and termination (Moonilal, 1982). Although the focus of social work intervention is on the family, depending on the nature and severity of the patient's medical condition there may at times be room for some social work activity with the patient him- or herself. That would usually involve a psychosocial assessment (to enrich the medical personnel's understanding of the patient) and discharge planning. The activities in cases of acutely ill, dying, or dead patients (for which the anxiety level of the patient's family, friends, and relatives is high), as suggested above, would represent the social work role of a *family crisis counselor, provider of concrete services,* and *liaison* between the family and others inside and outside the health care setting.

Social Work Role in
Social Emergencies

Ours is a culture of violence that is "reflected in the history, attitude, belief systems, and coping styles of the population in dealing with conflicts, frustration, and the quest for wealth and power" (Shachter & Seinfeld, 1994, p. 347). Our society is not likely to disown or reform this culture in the next century. Violence will continue to be legitimated and rationalized. When violence is directed toward those who are weak and defenseless, however, it results in social emergencies that, of course, have significant medical dimensions.

I include in social emergencies cases of child abuse, spousal abuse, elder abuse, and rape. These are invariably encountered in ambulatory acute care settings, particularly emergency departments and centers. Sometimes the reality of these emergencies is obvious, but many times it has to be looked for. Physicians and nurses are generally quite good at looking for the signs of physical abuse in children, easily detecting the incidence of physical neglect in children and often suspecting child sexual abuse. The same may not be true of their ability to look for or their sensitivity to the possibility of spousal and elder abuse in the cases they treat.

Similarly, every state has legal requirements with clear institutional protocols for reporting cases of child abuse. Several states have parallel reporting requirements regarding elder abuse, but hardly any have the same regarding spouse abuse. Most acute care settings lack clear procedures and protocols for intervention in cases of these types of abuse despite the Joint Commission for the Accreditation of Health Care Organizations requirement regarding the treatment of victims of domestic violence. This situation will improve in the 21st century. However, social workers will continue to add to the health care setting's ability to identify cases of abuse, manage the emergency situation, improve the quality of its responsiveness to the victim's need, and set in motion the process of correction.

Child Abuse

Child abuse in all its forms—physical abuse, physical neglect, sexual abuse, and emotional abuse—is a problem that continues to defy efforts to prevent and correct it, and it is likely to persist in the next century. Children are seen in acute care settings for all types of urgent and nonurgent health problems, including abuse. Sometimes a child is brought in for the confirmation and validation of abuse because it has been suspected and child protection officials are already involved. The social workers's role in ambulatory acute care settings in such cases is to (a) attend to the emotional (and informational) needs of the child and his or her parent if accompanying the child; (b) interview the child and/or others and supplement the findings of the medical examination and tests with a psychosocial assessment; and (c) coordinate the setting's case activity with that of the child protection agency. Very often, a child is brought in for a health complaint that may or may not be the result of abuse. The discovery of abuse may depend on the suspicion of the health personnel. The suspicion may be substantiated by medical examination and tests or may remain a suspicion. The major social work functions in these cases are as follows:

- Raising the index of suspicion of the medical personnel
- Reducing the likelihood of an abuse situation going undetected and unconfirmed by a thorough psychosocial assessment that adds to the diagnostic work of the physician
- Attending to the emotional needs of the child and the parent
- Preparing them for the sequence of events that follow the suspicion of abuse
- Informing and cooperating with child protective agency personnel

Spouse Abuse

As pointed out above, cases of spouse abuse, which are mostly battered women, are not looked for and treated with the same degree of concern as shown to victims of child abuse. Battering accounts for more than 25% of emergency room visits by women, yet even in hospitals with protocols for dealing with such cases, fewer than 1 in 25 are accurately diagnosed (Stark et al., 1981). An extensive review of the literature on women battering by Pagelow (1992) included several studies that found nonidentification of victims of spousal abuse by medical personnel. Randall (1990) quoted one physician as saying, "The only physicians who ask about violence are psychiatrists, and they're only interested if it occurs in a dream. They rarely ask about the violent events that occur in real life" (p. 939). Pagelow (1981) found a pattern of disdain for battered women and considerable victim blaming on the part of physicians and nurses, who often attributed victims' returning home with abusing men to psychological defects in them. Pagelow (1992) concluded, however, that the situation is slowly changing, with nurses in emergency settings voluntarily reporting cases of wife abuse to police departments. This situation is likely to continue to change in the next century, with more women in positions of authority—as physicians and managers—in health care settings. The perspective of medical personnel, however, is not expected to equal that of a social worker in its comprehensiveness. Social workers will also continue to be the best liaison between the health care setting and mental health and social services in the community. The social work functions in cases of spousal abuse will include the following:

- Sensitizing other staff about the plight of abused women
- Doing psychosocial assessment in cases of abuse
- Attending to the emotional needs of victims
- Enlarging the scope of intervention beyond the treatment of the medical problem
- Empowering victims with encouragement, information, and options
- Connecting victims with the appropriate abuse-related sources of support in the community, including spouse abuse shelters
- Linking victims with regular health care resources

Violence against women has both short-term and long-term effects on their physical and psychological well-being. Victims of abuse are much more likely than nonvictims to have poor health, chronic pain problems, addictions, problem pregnancies, depression, and suicide attempts (Plichta, 1992).

Elder Abuse

Elder abuse encompasses physical abuse and neglect, psychological and social abuse, and financial exploitation. Except in cases where the signs of physical abuse are obvious, the detection of even physical abuse in the elderly is difficult. Cognitively impaired and often confused elderly cannot tell about the abuse, and even those not so impaired often do not share their unpleasant secret because of denial, shame, or fear of a consequence worse than abuse. It is not uncommon that the abuser is the elderly person's caregiver. Other forms of abuse generally go unrecognized. The denial and improper assessment by health care professionals also is a factor in the nonidentification of elder abuse (Benton & Marshall, 1991). All 50 states have legislation to protect elderly victims of domestic abuse and neglect, and 42 states have mandatory reporting laws, but there is significant inactivity in response to the legal mandate. Ehrlich and Anetzberger (1991) surveyed state public health departments on procedures for reporting elder abuse. All 50 states responded. Although 94% of respondents were aware of the state law, only 20% to 28% reported the use of written procedures or training materials specifically designed for health care personnel.

It is forecast that, in the 21st century, the social scene will be dominated by more and more longer-living elderly who will assert their claim to societal resources, younger generations will become resentful of the elderly, the traditional caregivers will become increasingly less available, and care giving will become more impersonal. This forecast gives little hope of the elder abuse situation improving in the future. However, there will be a comprehensive approach to the detection of elder abuse through the use of standard assessment instruments such as the one proposed by Fulmer (1984). This instrument has eight sections that together cover assessment of all dimensions of an elderly person's life, such as mental status; hygiene and nutrition; usual lifestyle; interactions of significant others; the presence of bruises, contractures, pressure sores, and lacerations; and other medical signs and symptoms of possible abuse or neglect. Despite the use of such instruments, the difficulty in determining the reality of abuse will persist. When an alert and oriented elder chooses to deny or deliberately hide the existence of abuse, its detection requires extra sensitivity for, strong ability to relate to, and sharp skill in assessing the situation of that patient. Social workers in acute care ambulatory settings can make a significant difference to the need for early detection of and appropriate intervention in cases of elder abuse. Because of their training and the major purpose of their activity, social workers possess these professional attributes more than other health care providers. Their functions in these cases would be similar to the one in the case of spouse abuse and will involve the following:

- Supplementing the medical diagnosis with psychosocial assessment
- Attending to the immediate nonmedical needs of the patient
- Reporting abuse to the appropriate authorities
- Coordinating the acute care setting's case activity with the work of the adult protective agency
- Planning for discharge of the patient

Rape

Rape as a traumatic experience is, in some ways, unique because it is the quintessential violation of a person that leaves the victim feeling used, damaged, and defiled (Soskis, 1985). Norris (1992) examined the frequency and impact of 10 potentially traumatic events among 1,000 adults and found that whereas tragic death occurred most often and the motor vehicle crash presented the most adverse combination of frequency and impact, sexual assault yielded the highest rate of post-traumatic stress disorder. Although men are raped with equally devastating effects, the majority of victims seen in health care settings are women. Frazier and Cohen (1992) reviewed research on prevalence and effects of three types of sexual victimization of women—child sexual abuse, sexual assault, and sexual harassment—and concluded that these experiences are quite common among women and have serious detrimental effect on their mental health.

The societal picture of rape as a major problem is not likely to change substantially in the 21st century. Two parallel but opposing forces will continue to operate. On the one hand, historically, the trend has been toward a gradual decrease in the prosecution and penalty for rape. During the 17th, 18th, and 19th centuries, rape was not as prevalent as it became in 20th-century America, but it was viewed with horror and was severely punished (Crossman, 1992). *Rape myths,* defined as prejudicial, stereotypical, and false beliefs about rape, rape victims, and rapists, continue to be accepted by people from varied walks of life, including women (Tabone et al., 1992). The convicted sexual offenders are extremely heterogeneous, which makes focused preventive work impossible. On the other hand, social workers will continue to improve their understanding of the phenomenon of rape (Ellis, 1991; Haggard, 1991; Lakey, 1992; Malamuth, 1991; Prentky & Knight, 1991), leading to better preventive and therapeutic programs. Steinberg (1991) suggested that Title IX be amended to define rape as sex discrimination. Such efforts will be made to increase rape prosecution rates.

Rape victims being seen in the ambulatory acute care settings often have no physical injury and are there for a physical examination and specimen collection necessary for evidentiary reasons. They invariably are in a state of acute emotional crisis, which must be handled with utmost care and understanding. Responding to such crises is in the appropriate domain of social work expertise. Social work functions in these cases are as follows:

- Ensuring that the rape patient is not kept sitting in the waiting room like most patients with nonurgent medical problems
- Listening to the patient with empathy and acceptance of her emotions
- Helping her deal constructively with feelings of guilt and shame
- Restoring her sense of control in whatever ways the situation will permit
- Contacting the local rape crisis center and putting the resources of that agency at her disposal
- Helping her identify and mobilize her own social supports
- Being available for follow-up and linking her with the appropriate mental health, legal, and social services

The social work functions in social emergencies discussed above will require the social worker to assume the role of a *helper with the crisis* that the patient is in, an *advocate,* and a *coordinator of services* of the health care setting and other appropriate agencies.

Social Work Role in Non-Emergency Health and Social Needs

Earlier, we talked about a large proportion of the patient population of acute care settings being made up of those who do not have an emergency situation. Most of these people come to the acute care settings because they have nowhere else to go. They all have a need that they believe deserves immediate attention and assistance. Some have medical problems that could be treated at a nonacute ambulatory setting if one were accessible to them financially and logistically. Others have nonmedical problems that they are able to couch in medical terms. Still others have problems that are simply nonmedical that cannot be taken to social service agencies because these agencies are not open in the evenings, at night, and on the weekends. The greatest attraction that acute care ambulatory settings, particularly emergency rooms, have is that they are open 24 hours a day, 7 days a week. As Soskis (1985) put it,

> A sizable proportion of people visiting emergency rooms have no major medical complaint or sometimes no medical complaint at all, and often few or no resources—social, economic, or otherwise—to help them cope with the problems that brought them in. This group comes to the emergency room because the emergency room is always open, because they can usually get there (by police, fire rescue, or similar transport), and because they know that they will be seen. (p. 3)

In the group of people who come to these settings without legitimate health problems, Soskis (1985) included alcoholics, the homeless, runaways, persons with psychiatric conditions, and "space cases." The space cases are the chronic former mental patients living on the streets but shunned by other homeless. All these are unwelcome because they are seen as inappropriately using and abusing the resources of an acute care setting. Some are more unwelcome than others, however. They include (a) those who have chronic and complex problems and who come frequently and are demanding and hostile, (b) those who are emotionally disturbed or have drug and alcohol problems who come in after fights or accidents and who have attempted suicides and homicides and are disruptive, and (c) the elderly whose presenting problems are related to aging, such as sleeplessness, loss of mobility and memory, aches and pains, malnutrition, and feelings of being unable to cope (Soskis, 1980). Social work activity in regard to these patients is fourfold: (a) assessing their needs; (b) ensuring that they are medically screened and treated, if need be; (c) providing the necessary concrete social services; and (d) referring them to an appropriate community social service, mental health service, or other health care resource (discharge planning). As we will see later in the chapter, advocacy skills of the social worker become the most important in dealing with patients who come to acute care settings for nonacute and nonmedical needs. The social worker has to advocate for these patients while contacting resources outside as well as within the unit because these patients do overtax the emotional resources of the staff. Therefore, in cases of these "abusers" of the facility, the social work role is that of an *advocate* within and outside the setting, a *broker,* and a *provider of concrete services.*

Other Social Work Roles in Acute Ambulatory Care

Besides the patient-oriented roles, the social worker will continue to play two other roles: one focused on other professionals/service providers and the other related to the environment of the setting. The social worker plays the role of an *educator* when he or she (a) provides information on the patient's social, emotional, and demographic situation; (b) interprets the patient's needs and/or helps the patient articulate those needs beyond vague complaints; (c) enables medical professionals to discover the not-so-obvious cases of physical, sexual, and other forms of abuse; and (d) helps those professionals not be blinded to the real health problems by stereotypical views of the homeless, substance abusers, those with chronic mental illness, and difficult patients. By managing the social dimension of the ever-occurring crises, the social worker also helps fellow care providers keep their morale high and stress low. By attending to the patients and/or their families who must wait, at times, for hours, the social worker contributes to making the setting's atmosphere less aversive and more supportive (Soskis, 1985). The social worker thus also plays the role of a *stabilizer* of the health care setting.

FUTURE SOCIAL WORK ROLES IN NONACUTE AMBULATORY CARE SETTINGS

In the 21st century, health care will have changed so that most care will be (a) provided by groups or teams of professionals, (b) geared to accommodate the peculiar needs of special groups, and (c) marked by such attributes as accessibility, comprehensiveness, coordination, and accountability. The limelight will be on ambulatory care settings, and they will be expected to demonstrate and reflect these changes and attributes. Social workers will significantly contribute to that reality.

This chapter elaborates on the above attributes of care to highlight social work roles and functions.

"Accessibility refers to the responsibility of the health provider team to assist the patient or the potential patient to overcome temporal, spatial, economic, and psychologic barriers to health care" (Wallace et al., 1984, p. 29). With some type of national health insurance in place in the next century, financial barriers to care will have been removed, but other barriers will persist. Social work skills will be valued in helping patients overcome those barriers.

An Institute of Medicine report (1978) defined comprehensiveness as the ability and willingness of the primary care team to handle most of the health problems in the population it serves. It is estimated that between 20% and 70% of all visits to general medical clinics involve such problems as substance abuse, domestic violence, sexual dysfunction, stress reactions, grief, anxiety, and depression (Rosen, Locke, Goldberg, & Babigian, 1972), which are more psychosocial than medical. Comprehensiveness demands that these problems be handled and monitored at the health care setting itself.

> Since such patients appear with problems at medical settings, and since such problems are intertwined in a complex fashion with bodily symptoms and feelings, the responsible course is to develop a strategy for patient management at the point at which help is sought. (Mechanic, 1980, p. 18)

Moreover, many patients do not want to go to mental health or social service agencies because of the stigma attached to seeking help there. Social workers are skilled at handling these problems. They can enhance the setting's ability to provide comprehensive services.

Coordination of services is the next attribute of primary care that involves the responsibility for ensuring that all the pieces of care provided to the patient (within the setting and outside by medical specialists and others) fit together and yield the maximum benefit. Even if the care coordinator is a medical person,

> the role of patient care coordinator at times calls for the contribution of the team social worker, particularly when environmental/network/systems issues both within and without the health care establishment appear to threaten, disrupt, or preclude the process of diagnosis and treatment. (Wallace et al., 1984, p. 31)

Continuity of services is dependent on their accessibility, comprehensiveness, and coordination, as well as the setting's ability to accommodate other subjective and objective patient-related variables affecting the patient's willingness to continue. It may require individualizing, reaching out to, and understanding the unique reality of patients and their families. Social workers have an edge over other professionals in accomplishing these tasks. Again in the words of Wallace et al. (1984):

> The contribution of social work to primary care is essential when it comes to ensuring continuity of care with poor, uneducated, perpetually crisis-prone, or barely functioning patients. Intervention with these cases often requires experience with a particular set of values and with a lifestyle which is distant from middle class proprieties and preoccupations. (p. 32)

Accountability is an attribute not unique to primary care. An Institute of Medicine report (1978) recommended that, to ensure accountability, the primary care practice should regularly review the process and outcomes of its care; establish a policy of providing information to the patient about the risks, undesirable effects, and unexpected outcomes of treatment; and follow sound fiscal management policies and procedures. Social workers will have as much to offer to the realization of accountability as other members of the group.

Ambulatory care settings will make concerted efforts to acquire, incorporate, and practice these attributes and, in the process, experience a shift in the perspective on care from biomedical to biopsychosocial. As it is acknowledged that the social element can be as life threatening as the physical and psychological illness, the "social" dimension of care will become as important as the "biological" and the "psychological," and with that will come a deeper appreciation of the contributions of nonmedical health care providers such as social workers.

> The true foundation of primary care lies in the realization that operationalizing comprehensive models of health care requires collaborative effort beyond the expertise of medicine no matter how less specialized it becomes. The foremost responsibility of medicine and its unique area of expertise will be the biological dimension of health care. In essence, the primary care physician is the biomedical specialist as part of the primary care team, appreciative of the psychosocial and social dimensions but not inexpertly attempting to provide them. (Wallace et al., 1984, p. 65)

Social workers will have made tremendous contribution to that bio-psychosocial model. The major social work roles in nonacute ambulatory settings will include both patient-focused and other roles.

Patient-Focused Social Work Roles

Patient-focused social work roles will be the following:

1. *Clinical work with patients and their families:* This work may be necessitated by (a) concerns of the well and the worried well, (b) difficulties in coping with the stresses of life that find expression as somatic and psychosomatic complaints in some patients, (c) primary psychosocial problems of others threatening to jeopardize their physical health, and (d) psychosocial problems accompanying disease—problems in understanding and accepting diagnosis, coping and following through with treatment, living with its physical and emotional effects, and dealing with the social consequences of illness. Work with families has been a neglected area of primary care. Even physicians trained as family practitioners have, in actual practice, focused on the individual rather than on the family. Social workers will be able to fill that gap. Their clinical work may involve diverse modalities, such as providing information, crisis intervention, short-term therapy, and long-term casework. The strength orientation of social work will pervade these interventions and will be viewed as a distinguishing and valued mark of the contribution of social workers.

2. *Coordination of services for patients and families provided by several agencies and programs:* Other agencies may be hospitals and medical centers providing more intensive secondary and tertiary health care or mental health centers and social work programs providing nonmedical services. There will always be patients whose problems are so complex as to make the resources of an ambulatory health care setting inadequate.

3. *Education as part of disease prevention and health promotion activities:* Most nonacute ambulatory care facilities will have disease prevention and health promotion programs as part of their comprehensive services. These programs will offer health education and social support groups for those struggling with different types of problems. "Health related problems, such as obesity, substance abuse (including smoking), prolonged stress, child abuse, child sexual abuse, terminal illness and behaviors leading to high risk pregnancy, could be the focus

of such group activities" (Greene, Kruse, & Arthurs, 1985, p. 63). Social workers will be involved as organizers, facilitators, and educators of these groups.

Other Social Work Roles

The most prominent other social work role will be that of a consultant, performing *consultation work with fellow professionals* from other disciplines. Consultation may be about psychosocial problems or psychosocial dimensions of health problems in response to the need for a comprehensive diagnosis, or about exploring and involving community resources in comprehensive treatment plans. Greene et al. (1985) included the following areas where social work consultation can enrich a physician's diagnostic and treatment skills: (a) psychosocial aspects of the patient's functioning; (b) individual and family dynamics affecting the etiology and treatment of health problems; (c) transitions of life stages of a family that tend to create stress and generate problems; (d) the physician's interviewing skills with a view to recognizing psychosocial problems masked by physical complaints, dynamics of the interactions between him- or herself and the patient, and body language signals of emotional stress focusing on the whole person; and (e) community resources and approaches to accessing them.

SOCIAL WORK KNOWLEDGE AND SKILLS

In discussing the knowledge and skills appropriate for the various professional functions that social workers in ambulatory care settings are likely to perform, we discuss the major social work roles identified above.

Social Worker as a Crisis Counselor/Manager

As pointed out earlier, two kinds of major emergencies are encountered in acute care ambulatory settings: one created by a sudden serious physical illness or injury, the other resulting from various types of person abuse that may or may not be accompanied by physical trauma. Both types of emergencies thrust the patient and his or her loved ones into a state of crisis. Even in the nonacute health care settings, patients and their families seek help when they cannot handle life's crises with their own resources.

Poorer, less educated, more disorganized and chaotic individuals and social networks are increasingly resorting to health care providers . . . to obtain problem-solving help, often for complaints which are only tangentially medical. Even when presenting complaints are emphatically medical, the psychosocial component is commonly so integral that medical attention cannot be provided without immediately addressing the nonmedical issue as well. (Wallace et al., 1984, p. 71)

In acute care settings, management of the medical aspect of the crisis is the focus and responsibility of the medical professionals, whereas its nonmedical dimensions, including emotional, social, economic, and legal, are often not given adequate attention. This unevenness in the treatment of emergencies is likely to disappear in the 21st century. Commitment to the concepts of "comprehensiveness of care" and "treating the total patient" will result in the filling of the gaps in the current system of care. Social workers will be instrumental in correcting the situation. In nonacute settings, wherever they are part of the establishment, social workers already provide a significant part of crisis intervention services. In the future, their presence on ambulatory care teams will increase, and being responsible for the psychosocial aspects of health care, they will play the role of *crisis counselors and managers.*

Knowledge of crisis theory and principles of crisis intervention is necessary for effective help in the management of crises. Because all social workers have acquired that knowledge as part of their training, it will suffice to list here the basic pieces of that knowledge and to reiterate some "shoulds" of crisis intervention. This material is drawn from several sources (Dhooper, 1990; Golan, 1969; Morrice, 1976; Rapaport, 1967; Smith, 1977; Soskis, 1985; Wallace et al., 1984).

- There are stages in the development of crisis and an identifiable event precipitates the crisis.
- The normal coping abilities of the individual have either broken down or are inadequate to deal with the situation.
- The person in crisis is more susceptible, vulnerable, and dependent than usual, and this makes him or her more accessible to intervention.
- The crisis period is time-limited, and the availability of help in time is crucial. Without help, the crisis may result in a poorer level of the individual's functioning.
- Even a little help has a lot of positive effect. Intervention is more likely to be successful if made during the acute crisis.

- The major tasks necessary for crisis resolution are (a) cognitive—viewing the situation accurately and realistically; (b) emotional—acknowledging, accepting, and discharging one's feelings; and (c) problem solving—considering and weighing the available options, developing adaptive behaviors, and seeking and using formal help and informal support.

The following are some of the important "do's" and "should's" for social work crisis intervention. The social worker should

- Believe that something positive must come out of the person's crisis experience. Hence, he or she should intervene with the purpose of enabling the patient to turn the painful life event into an opportunity for survival, growth, and improvement.
- Try to stay with the crisis (provide the maximum help as close to the precipitating event as possible).
- Recognize and meet the patient's need for emotional support, use empathic listening, encourage expression of feelings, validate those feelings, and provide hope.
- Convince and remind the patient that seeking and using help is a sign of strength, not a mark of weakness.
- Be active and direct, rather than passive or neutral and indirect, without the fear of fostering dependence.
- Focus on the current situation and encourage planning and action, rather than dwelling on past actions and memories.
- Mobilize for the patient the patient's own informal social supports, as well as formal sources of help inside and outside the health care setting.

Although the above suggestions are worded as if the focus of social work activity were on the patient, the focus may be on the patient's family, in which case the family's understanding, needs, resources, and strengths will have to be assessed and worked with. In situations of a patient's impending death from unexpected injury or illness, it is difficult to think of the family crisis as yielding something positive. Social workers based in acute care settings, however, know of the ever-present need for human organs and tissues for transplantation and that families who donate the organs and tissues of their deceased loved one find solace in that donation and view it as something positive coming out of their tragedy. Therefore, the social worker in ambulatory acute care settings who deals with such families should mention organ donation as an opportunity for them to have some choices and regain some control over their situation. These families have the choice of donating or not donating, and if they choose to donate, they have the option of donating all or some of the organs and tissues and deciding how the donated body parts will be used—for transplantation, medical therapy, or research.

Earlier, it was proposed that notifying the family of a seriously ill or injured, dying, or dead patient should be one of the functions of the social worker. Bearer of bad news is not a pleasant role, but the social worker is the best qualified to play that role. He or she should remember that the news may trigger a crisis for the family. Here are a few helpful suggestions based on my experience and the work of Soskis (1985). The social worker should

- See the patient before calling the family so that he or she can give a firsthand visual report to the family, if needed.
- Identify him- or herself and the place he or she is calling from.
- Explain the reason for calling briefly, clearly, and specifically leaving no gaps for the listener to fill with own imaginings.
- Ask only those questions that need to be answered immediately, such as the patient's past illnesses or present medications.
- Tell the family that the patient is critically ill (even if the patient has died) and that they should come in immediately. This information will give them time to prepare for the worst news.
- Assume that the shock and fear may cause many listeners to miss or distort much of what is told them and to ask the person to repeat what has been said.
- Find out whether the family can actually get to the emergency care center and whether they need assistance with transportation, directions to the center, information about parking, and so on.
- Assess the listener's ability to drive safely, and accordingly advise that the person either wait until emotions have settled or get someone else to drive and come along.
- Make the call the beginning of his or her activity with the family. Offer assistance with concrete needs; if they are from out of town, they may need help with lodging and long-distance communication.

Social Worker as a Clinician and Caseworker

Even in busy and, at times, chaotic acute care ambulatory settings, there is room for meaningful brief, even one-shot, clinical casework. Discussing the importance of how a patient is treated in an emergency room, Soskis (1985) said,

> It is here that he or she receives his or her first and probably lasting impression of how the system works: helping, supporting, confusing, blaming, punishing, humiliating. . . . The social worker's attitudes and activity here may make a tremendous difference in how the patient views and copes with what is happening to him or her. (p. 53)

The social worker should remember that an acute medical condition often sets the stage for vital changes in people's lives. The old saying "Strike while the iron is hot" represents a profound truth about human behavior. The social worker's basic assessment and intervention skills must be tailored to the realities of the acute setting. He or she should be able to do a quick psychosocial assessment and undertake an appropriate clinical activity that may involve (a) giving the patient an insight into the psychosocial antecedents or consequences of the patient's medical problem, (b) intensifying the patient's awakened motivation to deal with the problem beyond the medical treatment, (c) sharing with the patient ideas and suggestions for help, and (d) referring the patient to an outside professional resource.

In nonacute care ambulatory settings, it is forecast that a biopsychosocial model of care will gradually replace the current biomedical model. That shift, plus the fact that a large proportion of patients seen in these settings present problems that are more psychosocial than medical, will create new opportunities for significant contributions by social workers. Their professional philosophy and skills are in tune with the biopsychosocial model, their expertise lies in dealing with psychosocial problems, and their interventions may be more appropriate for nonmedical problems. For effective clinical work, however, they will need to supplement their basic knowledge with greater understanding of biomedical and psychiatric issues—for example,

> The social worker must appreciate that sexual dysfunction can be secondary to (that is, caused by) diabetes mellitus and does not always represent a "psychological" problem. Working with patients who have substance abuse problems requires a knowledge of the appropriate use of toxicology screens, symptoms indicative of withdrawal states, behavioral manifestations of different toxi-cotives, and so on. (Wallace et al., 1984, p. 37)

While understanding the psychodynamics of patients' problems, the social worker should also know when to seek consultation from a psychiatrist or to refer a patient to a mental health facility for specialized services. The worker should strengthen his or her assessment skills with the use of appropriate instruments for identifying patients at high risk for social, psychological, and physical problems.

The medical needs of most nonacute patients will pertain to chronic problems. "Understanding the difference between illness and disease is a prerequisite to the care of patients affected by incurable disorders. Even though many chronic conditions are incurable, the discomfort or disability they produce may be substantially modified" (Conger & Moore, 1988, p. 108). The social worker should understand and develop sensitivity for the characteristics of chronic conditions that cannot be cured but must be managed. Buada et al. (1986) listed the following as the mandates of chronic conditions:

- Chronic conditions are long-term, and the affected patient has an ongoing need for service.
- Chronic conditions often fluctuate and thereby create the need for differing levels of services simultaneously.
- Chronic conditions involve subjectively experienced discomfort, pain, and disability, and therefore the measures of relief must address those subjective elements.
- Chronic conditions also significantly affect the patient's family and significant others, and the focus of service must also be on the needs of those informal caregivers.
- Chronic conditions require a service package that includes a large variety of support services, along with medical services.

Patients who are disabled because of chronic illness react to their condition in a number of ways, depending on the severity and type of disability. The pattern of reaction has such elements as (a) uncertainty, (b) anxiety, (c) depression, (d) anger expressed directly, (e) anger expressed indirectly, (f) desire for the feeling of competence, (g) helplessness and hopelessness, (h) threatened sociability, and (i) variance in good feelings (Viney & Westbrook, 1981). The social worker should be sensitive to the presence of these elements. He or she should explore and deal with these as a part of the assessment and treatment of chronically ill patients. Although it is difficult to predict a patient's reaction to disability, the more global the disabling condition, the more psychologically devastating it is likely to be (Conger & Moore, 1988).

Social workers well recognize the importance of resources for coping with stress. Those who work with the chronically ill should also remember that self-controlled resources are more effective than other-controlled resources for such patients. "Whatever the demands, ultimately it is the individual who is constantly confronted by them, interprets them, assigns them a subjective meaning, and constantly has to respond to them. The greater an individual's control of resources, the greater will be his or her capacity to cope successfully" (Conger & Moore, 1988, p. 105). Therefore, social work intervention should include the creation and strengthening of resources within the patient's control.

In view of the broader service missions of ambulatory care settings in the future and for dealing with the varied problems of patients and families, the social worker will have to master many skills. These should include skills in using short-term problem- or task-focused therapies, in manipulating the patient's environment, and in helping in the maintenance of those with chronic problems.

Among the "difficult" patients or families that all human services professionals must deal with are those who are crisis-prone. Their lives seem to be a series of crises. The practice principles derived from crisis theory and other therapeutic approaches are often not very effective in working with these people. Even systems theory, which guides the overall social work perspective, sometimes fails to explain their behaviors and situations. Social workers should familiarize themselves with and learn to use other potentially more useful approaches. Chaos theory promises to provide important clues to understanding and working with "chaotic" systems (e.g., see Gleick, 1987; Goldberger, Rigney, & West, 1990; Hoffman, 1988; Kagan & Schlossberg, 1989; Olson, 1989; Pietgen & Richter, 1986; Wood & Geismar, 1989).

Social Worker as an Advocate and a Broker

The need for comprehensiveness of services will, on the one hand, propel the shift of health care toward a biopsychosocial model of diagnosis and treatment, and on the other hand, emphasize the importance of mobilizing the patient's illness- or wellness-related resources inside and outside the health care setting. The mobilization of resources calls for professional roles of advocate and broker. By their history and training, social workers are the best equipped to play these roles. They have practiced advocacy at two levels: at the individual case level and on behalf of a whole class of people. *Class advocacy* is used to secure and protect entitlements for a group of people who share a common status and problems (Connaway & Gentry, 1988). It is a form of social action. Within *case advocacy,* Wallace et al. (1984) made a distinction between social advocacy and clinical advocacy on the basis of the breadth and depth of the assessment and intervention.[1] In a health care setting, it is assumed that the need for advocacy is in response to patient deficits that have clear clinical relevance to the patient's health problem. Hence, it is *clinical advocacy.* I agree with J. Cohen (1980) that the purpose of clinical social work is to maintain and enhance psychosocial functioning by "maximizing the availability of needed intrapersonal, inter-personal and societal resources" (p. 30).

Although there is a lack of consensus about the "what," "why," and "how" of advocacy within the social work profession, social workers will be able to draw helpful ideas from the currently available literature to enrich their advocacy skills. The easiest thing is to apply to the task of advocacy the problem-solving approach that social workers are good at. McGowan (1987) suggested a number of variables[2] that should be assessed for decision making in case advocacy. Connaway and Gentry (1988) included educating, persuading, negotiating, and bargaining among the strategies for case-level advocacy. Sosin and Caulum (1983) proposed a typology of strategies based on the context which may be one of alliance, neutral, or adversarial. The social worker should use the various strategies and techniques of advocacy purposefully and selectively. As Hepworth and Larsen (1986) put it, "In a given situation, a practitioner may employ several interventions but a rule of thumb is to employ no more than are necessary and to cause no more disruption than is required to achieve a given objective" (p. 571). The worker should communicate his or her concerns in a factual and nonabrasive manner, try to understand the feelings and position of the other party, and consider realistic options and alternatives proposed by that party (Sheafor, Horejsi, & Horejsi, 1988).

Because advocacy is an activity on behalf of the patient, the most important "should" is to ensure that it does not undermine the patient's autonomy and sense of mastery. Such sabotage would be contrary to social work's basic belief system, as well as to the need of the health care system to treat the patient as a partner.

The social worker's broker role involves activities designed to link clients to needed resources. To perform this role effectively, the social worker should know the various resources relevant to the patient's need and how to link the patient to those resources. The resources can be classified into three categories: (a) formal health and human services in the area, (b) various self-help groups, and (c) the patient's own natural support systems.

Hepworth and Larsen (1986) grouped the formal health and human services by the following needs:

Income maintenance
Housing
Health care
Child services
Vocational guidance and rehabilitation
Mental health care
Legal services
Marital and family therapy
Youth services
Recreation
Transportation

Some self-help groups found in most communities include the following:

Al-Anon/Alateen (for families and friends of alcoholics)
Alcoholics Anonymous (for alcohol abusers)
Compassionate Friends (for bereaved parents)
Fresh Start (for smokers quitting their habit)
Gamblers Anonymous (for those with gambling problem)
Lost Chord Club (for laryngectomees)
Mended Hearts (for heart disease patients)
Overeaters Anonymous (for compulsive overeaters and those with other eating disorders)
Parents Anonymous (for abusive parents)
Parents Without Partners (for single parents)
Parkinson's Disease Support Group
Reach to Recovery (for breast cancer patients)
Recovery, Inc. (for former mental patients)
Synanon (for substance abusers)
United Ostomy Association Group (for patients with ostomies)

Many other disease-specific self-help groups are available for patients and/or their families. Natural support systems include the patient's family, relatives, friends, neighbors, fellow workers, and associates from school, church, and other social groups.

Most social work departments and units maintain a list of all the health and human service resources in the area, with brief descriptions of the "where," "when," and "how" of their services and eligibility requirements. The social worker should create and/or update such a resource list and add the names of specific persons to be contacted at the most often used agencies and programs. It is wise to know as many of them personally as possible. That would result in a smooth linking process and reduce the ill effects of the darker side of many human service organizations reflected in "complex application procedures, needless delays in providing resources and services, discriminatory policies, inaccessible sites of agencies, inconvenient hours of service delivery, dehumanizing procedures or behaviors by staff" (Hepworth & Larsen, 1986, p. 16).

Besides knowing community resources and the people who represent those resources, the social worker should practice the principle of appropriate use of those resources.

> Many community resources are not useful with difficult to manage patients because the resources cannot handle them, are not equipped to make clinical interventions, and the patient has usually worn out his or her welcome there already. Inappropriate referrals often make the situation worse and, moreover, ruin the reputation of the clinician in the community where credibility in urgent situations and emergencies is crucial. (Wallace et al., 1984, p. 199)

Linking the patient with the needed resource requires selecting the appropriate resource that will match the patient's needs and referring him or her to the selected resource agency. The preconditions of a successful referral include (a) the patient's readiness for referral, (b) his or her agreement with the appropriateness of the selected resource, and (c) his or her ability to follow through with the referral. The social worker can benefit from the following suggestions for meeting these conditions. The social worker should

- Reiterate his or her assessment about the patient's need for referral.
- Give information about the resource agency, its policies, procedures, and services without any false promises or unrealistic reassurances.
- Share his or her reasons why that agency would be an appropriate match for the patient's needs.

- Encourage the patient to express his or her feelings about the need to seek help elsewhere and about the resource agency itself.
- Deal with any misconception about the agency and its services and other doubts, ambivalence, and apprehension that the patient may have.
- Arrange for transportation, if lack of that is likely to be problematic.
- Suggest and arrange for someone—family member, neighbor, friend—to accompany the patient if that would make a difference.
- Use cementing techniques (Weissman, 1976) selectively for increasing the chances of the patient continuing with the resource agency beyond the first contact. These techniques include (a) checking back—contacting the patient after the initial contact about what has been accomplished, (b) haunting—calling the patient at the resource agency after his or her initial and subsequent contact with that agency, (c) sandwiching—planning an interview with the patient before he or she goes for the initial contact with the resource agency and immediately after that contact, and (d) alternating—planning a series of interviews with the patient intermittently during his or her involvement with the resource agency.

Mobilizing the patient's own natural support system is often more difficult than approaching a formal source of help. The following suggestions are likely to be helpful in this task:

1. *Realize the complexity of people's natural social support systems.* People are the active shapers of their social networks. Those who do not reciprocate the support they receive are less likely to ask for help, and they feel guilty if they do. Those who place high value on self-reliance have difficulty asking for help. Those who have difficulty discussing their problems with others are reluctant to seek support. Those who have sought help from some of their social network members and have not received it are discouraged from asking for help even from others. The effects of expecting the needed support that is not forthcoming is more upsetting than the perception that the support is not available. Potential support givers (a) may not know how the patient feels about his or her situation and need for help, (b) may feel uneasy and unsure about their helpfulness, (c) may not know how to provide appropriate help and support, and (d) may feel resentful for having to provide support (Antonucci & Israel, 1986; Brown, 1978; Dhooper, 1983, 1984; Lehman, Ellard, & Wortman, 1986; Wortman & Lehman, 1985).

2. *Identify the patient's natural supports and analyze their potential for helpfulness.* While exploring the patient's social network, the social worker should individualize the patient's situation and give attention to

the structural features of the network, the dynamic features of relationships, the patient's subjective view of the network, and significant life events that might have affected the network (Snow & Gordon, 1980). Different network structures are more or less important, depending on the nature of the need. The dynamic features of relationships indicate the positive and negative nature of interactions within the network. Significant events such as death, retirement, and change in physical or mental health, or even change in residence of important network members can seriously disrupt a patient's social network. Several approaches to network analysis (e.g., Dhooper, 1990; Gottlieb, 1985; Maguire, 1983) can be used. This exploring and analyzing would result in a list of potential helpers who, the patient believes, can provide the needed support.

3. *Help the patient in deciding how to approach and request the identified network members for help and how to overcome any obstacles.* Those in greatest need are often the least able to structure their interactions to facilitate support from others (Lehman et al., 1986). This may require giving the patient suggestions or even role playing effective ways of communication, helping him or her deal with guilt, rehearsing a backup plan, and encouraging the expression of appreciation for the help received (Dhooper, 1990).

4. *Enable the patient's helpers to be supportive.* Mobilizing the patient's social supports, at times, also involves work with the members of the social network. The distress of those in difficult situations tends to create or increase the anxiety of potential helpers. The social worker can, with the consent of the patient, give the helpers information about the patient's problem and needs, encourage them to discuss those needs, prepare them for the patient's behavior, teach them how to manage their anxiety, facilitate communication among the helpers, and support their helping efforts. Impressive work on social network interventions has been done in mental health practice (e.g., see Biegel, Tracy, & Corvo, 1994; Tracy & Biegel, 1994), which can be a source for supplementing the worker's professional repertoire.

Closely related to advocacy and brokering is the concept of "case management," which has become prominent over the past few decades. In the field of aging, case management was identified as a basic service under the Older Americans Act of 1965 (P.L. 95-478), and the case management approach has also been practiced in several other fields, such as health care, mental health, and rehabilitation (Loomis, 1988; Roessler & Rubin, 1982; Sanborn, 1983; Steinberg & Carter, 1983).

Many evaluation studies of case management programs and services have shown the effectiveness of the case management approach to service delivery (e.g., see Berkowitz, Halfon, & Klee, 1992; Bond, Miller, Krumwied, & Ward, 1988; Goering, Wasylenki, Farkas, & Ballantyne, 1988; Macias, Kinney, Farley, Jackson, & Vos, 1994; Marcenko & Smith, 1992; Quinn, Segal, Raisz, & Johnson, 1982). With the general trend toward maximizing the quantity, quality, and types of community-based care, newer technologies increasingly making it possible to provide more and more services on an ambulatory basis, and the increasing number of the elderly in the population, it is very likely that the importance of case management will grow in the future. In view of that importance, we discuss the social worker's role as a case manager separately.

Social Worker as a Case Manager/Service Coordinator

The commitment of ambulatory care settings to the concept of "comprehensiveness of services" and their responsiveness to the needs of vulnerable populations, such as the elderly and those with disabilities, will bring case management services into bold relief in the future. Social workers are superbly qualified to serve as case managers because of their knowledge of community resources; their skills in communication, advocacy, and brokering; and their professional commitment to helping people obtain resources, facilitating interactions between individuals and others in their environments, and making organizations responsive to people (Hepworth & Larsen, 1986). This role will be played at two levels, depending on the needs of the individual patient. At one level, the social worker will refer the patient for case management services in the community and will use the knowledge and skills we discussed above under the advocate and broker role. At the other level, the social worker will serve as case manager and will use many other skills, along with the advocacy and brokering skills. New models of case management mix and match the skills appropriate for both these levels. White, Gundrum, Shearer, and Simmons (1994) described a project in which a social worker in the role of a case manager functioned as a liaison between primary care physician offices and community services. The case manager provided in-person, on-the-spot assistance and consultation to physicians and their office staff. Kramer, Fox, and Morgenstern (1992) reported on two HMOs that use social work expertise to provide access to resources, home visits, and monitoring for high-risk patients.

The concept of "case management" is still evolving as it is being operationalized in serving different groups of clients with different needs in varied situations. Some basic common functions, however, are involved in all types of case management. These include assessing need, identifying and planning for services, linking clients with services, advocating for the client's best interest, coordinating services, and monitoring and evaluating the process and result of case management. On the basis of an assessment of the individual case situation, case management may also involve significant therapeutic activities such as emotional support and counseling. For example, case managers for families of children with both a developmental disability and a chronic health condition (Marcenko & Smith, 1992) acknowledged the chronic sorrow, social isolation, and emotional, physical, and financial stress experienced by such families and included in case management the organization of parents' support groups and informational and skill-building activities. Similarly, the case management model for serving drug-exposed infants and their chemically dependent mothers described by Berkowitz et al. (1992) included many more than the usual brokering, referring, and follow-up functions to ensure comprehensiveness, continuity, and coordination of services.

A critical look at the basic functions of case management listed above reveals the relevance of problem-solving skills that all social workers have acquired and practiced as a part of their training. A comprehensive psychosocial assessment of the patient will uncover all of his or her needs and the extent to which they are being met. Planning will involve discussing and exploring with the patient the available resources—formal as well as informal, the patient's own as well as the community's—relevant to the unmet needs. Implementation of the plan may involve the use of advocacy and linking skills described earlier. Wherever there is a dearth of essential resources in the community or the community lacks interagency linkages and coordination, the social worker as a case manager should also become involved in community-level groups.

Participation in community-based advocacy groups and advisory boards supports system-level case management by broadening the potential scope of resources for the population. Participation on these boards is helpful for establishing interagency linkages and networks necessary for effective coordination and collaboration; facilitating referrals among community agencies, and enhancing community standards of practice. But ultimately, participation on community boards is a way to shape policies that are advantageous to the meeting the needs of the client population. (Berkowitz et al., 1992, pp. 113, 115)

The coordination and monitoring of services are the other important functions of case management. Coordination involves collaboration and teamwork, and the suggestions for sharpening social work skills for collaborative work made in Chapter 4 are relevant for coordination as well. Johnson (1989) listed the following as blocks to effective coordination:

> lack of respect for or confidence in other helpers involved; lack of adequate sharing of information among the helpers; differing perspectives or values about what is to be done regarding clients; lack of capacity to share and work together; lack of time to develop cooperative relationships; and lack of agency sanctions and support for coordination. (p. 357)

In view of the need for comprehensive and coordinated services in the next century, the lack of agency sanctions and support is not likely to be a problem. Social workers as case managers will be able to negotiate the time and other resources required for effective coordination of services. For overcoming the other blocks to coordination, they will find the following suggestions helpful:

- Learn as much as possible about the perspectives, services, and skills of all the help/service providers involved in the case. This would help in knowing, accepting, appreciating, and respecting their contributions.
- While appreciating the differences among the various help providers, look for commonalities and highlight those. Concern for the patient's well-being is the central theme in everyone's activity. From time to time, highlighting that common purpose would help communication.
- Express appreciation for the commitment and efforts of all service providers, both formally and informally, and encourage the patient and/or his or her family to do likewise.
- Remember that communication is the soul of coordinated effort and open many channels of communication with and among the various services providers. These channels can be both formal and informal, as well as direct and indirect. Encourage and facilitate communication among all involved.
- Understand the differences in the functioning of informal helpers from the patient's natural support system and service providers from formal agencies and programs. In terms of the communication between the informal and formal systems, the balance theory of coordination (Litwak & Meyer,

1966, 1974) suggests that a midpoint be sought in the social distance between the two. If they are too far apart, they do not communicate; if they are too close, they hinder each other's functioning.

- Be conscious of the differences in the ways men and women communicate.

The natural helping system seems to be more often a female system. The formal system, while staffed with both men and women, seems to function in a formalized manner that is more akin to traditional male communication. Male social workers should be particularly aware of their difference in communication styles when working with the informal helping system. (Johnson, 1989, pp. 356-357)

- Appreciate the unique contributions to the patient's care of the informal helpers. Do not expect them to function as formal service providers.
- Use innovation and creativity in opening new channels of communication and finding new ways of strengthening coordination among service providers.

Monitoring is the ongoing evaluation of the process and product of intervention. It is an ethical as well as a technical responsibility of the social worker and refers to the periodic observations and feedback in checking and reviewing how things are going and what progress is being made (Siporin, 1975). Unlike the evaluation at the end of an activity, monitoring is a self-regulatory activity. As Egan (1990) put it, "Appraisal that comes at the end of the process is often quite judgmental: 'It didn't work.' Ongoing evaluation is much more positive. It helps both client and helper[s] learn from what they have been doing, celebrate what has been going well, and correct what has been going poorly" (p. 181). Monitoring also depends on effective communication and honest relationships among the people involved in the helping situation. The suggestions for improving communication given above are equally effective for monitoring purposes. The social worker, as a case manager, can do the following to perform the monitoring function:

- Remember that the purpose of monitoring is improvement in the service delivery, its quality, and efficiency.
- Ensure that the process and short-term goals of all service providers are clear and empirically measurable to the extent possible.
- Build into the monitoring plan as many relevant variables as possible— patient-related, problem-related, and situation-related.

- Concentrate on two major tasks: determining whether the service plan is being completed and whether the original goals are being met (Kirst-Ashman & Hull, 1993).
- Gather information from all available sources by using many methods of communication—formal and informal meetings, telephone calls, case records, reports, and formal evaluation devices and tools.

As in hospital-based social work, there is also room for innovation for maximizing the resources and skills of the social work staff in ambulatory care settings. Some case management functions can be performed by paraprofessionals with appropriate training and supervision. In the interest of efficiency and cost-effectiveness, social workers will delegate some of their functions to others.

We discussed the necessary knowledge and skills for effective performance of the social work role of consultant in Chapter 4. Earlier in this chapter (p. 185), we briefly discussed the social worker as an educator of medical colleagues. The worker's patient-related educator role is discussed at length in Chapter 6. As in other settings, social workers will be able to make significant contributions to the efforts of ambulatory care settings to maintain quality. The "what" and "how" of continuous quality improvement approaches are discussed in Chapter 7.

NOTES

1. As an example of clinical advocacy, Wallace et al. talk about a 27-year-old married Jewish orthodox woman who presented in the emergency room with sleep and appetite disturbance, depressed mood, and intrusive suicidal thoughts. The social work assessment revealed a conflict between the patient's religious obligations on the one hand and her family and personal obligations on the other as the primary issue. She had been trying for 5 years to get pregnant, with no success because her religious sect restricted sexual contact to a limited number of calendar days. The worker called her rabbi, who granted the patient a dispensation from her religious obligations. Her symptoms disappeared.

2. The variables are (a) problem definition, (b) objective, (c) target system, (d) sanction, (e) resources, (f) potential receptivity of target system, (g) level of intervention, (h) objective of intervention, (i) strategy and mode of intervention, and (j) outcome of prior advocacy efforts.

Chapter 6

SOCIAL WORK IN
ILLNESS PREVENTION
AND HEALTH PROMOTION

In the next century, the health care system's current treatment orientation, which determines the point of intervention too late in the course
of many diseases, will be replaced by an orientation toward disease
prevention and health promotion. It will move toward the realization of
health as "physical, mental, and social well-being," an idea proposed
by the World Health Organization (WHO) almost 50 years ago. That
movement will involve not only a vital shift in the philosophy and
priorities of the health care system but also a significant change in the
nature of the roles and relationships of health care providers and
recipients. The system has been philosophically treatment- and
procedure-centered and driven by incentives for costly and often excessive treatment of mostly preventable morbidity (Gellert, 1993). As the
system's focus gradually shifts from illness to wellness, the patient will
become a true partner of health care providers in the joint effort to stay
healthy. In the past, the patient put all the faith and confidence in health
care providers to keep him or her healthy. This dependence resulted in
the failure to take responsibility for healthy living. As Taylor et al.
(1982) put it,

> The past generation of men and women have consumed nutritionally
> deficient foods, accepted increasing weight as a natural consequence of
> aging, used tobacco despite well-documented hazards, ingested unneces-
> sary and sometimes dangerous drugs, failed to get necessary rest and
> sleep, exercised infrequently, and accepted prolonged stress as though
> immune to its damaging sequelae. (p. 1)

On the other hand, health care providers, particularly physicians, have restricted their role to only diagnosis and treatment of disease. Illness prevention and health promotion have not been parts of their role as healers. For most of them, advising the patient in proper nutrition and exercise has lacked the professional self-fulfillment of managing a serious illness episode such as an asthmatic attack or excising an inflamed appendix (Taylor et al., 1982). All this has been a part of the larger cultural context.

> Industrial societies have placed their management of health and human welfare issues into the hands of "experts," who in turn are typically associated with large, centralized bureaucracies. Thus a relatively impersonal service takes over some of the most intimate and important human concerns—birth, death, sickness, health, education, care of the elderly and disabled, to mention just a few. (Green & Raeburn, 1990, p. 37)

This will gradually change. Besides the illogic of the way things are, the cost (in every sense of the term) to the individual and to society of waiting until problems become full blown will increasingly become unbearable.

Conceptually, illness prevention and health promotion are distinct. Health promotion is a much wider concept than illness prevention. In *health promotion,* intervention is directed at improving the general well-being of people, and no specific disease agent or process is targeted. "Health promotion transcends narrow medical concerns and embraces less well defined concepts of wellness, self-growth, and social betterment. Concepts related to illness prevention are more specific" (Bracht, 1987, p. 318). Health promotion is a prepathogenic level of intervention, whereas in *disease prevention,* the known agents or environmental factors are the focus of intervention with the aim of reducing the occurrence of a specific disease (Leavell & Clark, 1965). *Illness prevention* involves actions to eliminate or minimize conditions known to cause or contribute to different diseases.

In the public health literature, all health-related activities are conceptualized as preventive and categorized as primary prevention, secondary prevention, and tertiary prevention. *Primary prevention* involves actions to keep conditions known to result in disease from occurring, thus preventing the disease process from starting; *secondary prevention* involves actions to limit the extent and severity of an illness, after it has begun, by early detection and treatment; and *tertiary prevention* involves efforts, during and after the full impact of illness, that would minimize its effects and preclude its recurrence (*Social Work Dictionary*, 1991; Watkins, 1985). In this scheme, health promotion and illness prevention are two phases of primary prevention. Together, they refer to actions and practices aimed at *preventing* physical, psychological, and sociocultural problems; *protecting* current strengths, competencies, or levels of health; and *promoting* desired goals and the fulfillment or enhancement of human potentials (Public Health Service, 1979). These actions and practices are concerned with the total population generally and the groups at high risk particularly. For their effectiveness, they must be comprehensive and multi-focused—aimed at changing individual health behaviors, creating a positive climate for health in the community, and bringing about policy change in favor of a social and physical environment free of health hazards.

HISTORY OF SOCIAL WORK IN ILLNESS PREVENTION AND HEALTH PROMOTION

As we have seen in Chapter 2, public health has been the main actor on the illness prevention and health promotion stage. Because of the congruence between the broad goals of social work and public health, social work has been a part of public health activities and programs for more than 100 years. As Bracht (1987) put it,

> Interest in health promotion and illness prevention is certainly not new, especially to social workers whose professional role has historically been targeted on the broader aspects of health and social betterment. Jane Addams engaged the first woman physician graduate of Johns Hopkins Medical School to come to Chicago in 1893 to open the country's initial well-baby and pediatric clinic. In Ohio, the Cincinnati Social Experiment, a neighborhood health center, was established by a group of social workers stressing neighborhood and environmental health. (p. 316)

In the second half of the 19th century, social workers collaborated with others in organized efforts to control communicable diseases. Their help was considered essential for the success of public health programs that required the cooperation of citizen groups. They not only collaborated with health professionals but also demonstrated the utility of social work approaches and methods for health-related work. The major social work approaches of those days were illustrated by the work of charity organizations and settlement houses. The Children's Bureau, created in 1912, had its origins in the settlement house movement. Four of the first five chiefs of the bureau were social workers. The fourth, Martha May Eliot, a physician, had worked as a social worker in the Social Service Department at Massachusetts General Hospital before entering medical school (Hutchins, 1985). During the influenza epidemic of 1918-1919, social workers tracked and reached out to children in the community who were at high risk because their parents had died of the flu (Harris, 1919). After World War I, the passage of the National Venereal Disease Control Act led to the development of clinics for surveillance, early diagnosis, and treatment of venereal disease. As part of those clinics, social workers educated the victims of venereal disease and their families about the cause and dissemination of syphilis (Kerson, 1979).

Social workers also participated in political advocacy, at times at great cost. They had to work against societal biases and prejudices. In the early 20th century, for their efforts to increase government's role in maternal and child health, social workers of the day were maligned by their opposition as communists, subversives, endocrine perverts, and derailed menopausics (Siefert, 1983). Nevertheless, they led a campaign culminating in the passage of the Sheppard-Towner Act of 1921. The work made possible by this law contributed substantially to the reduction of infant mortality, demonstrated the effectiveness of preventive health services, and established the principle of shared federal-state responsibility in health and social welfare (Doss-Martin & Stokes, 1989). Passage of the Social Security Act of 1935, which created the Maternal and Child Health and Crippled Children's Services, brought social workers into public health programs much more prominently. They have worked in public health and other health care organizations not only as case workers with the ill and the disabled but also as case finders, planners of outreach services, prevention workers (in maternal and child health, family planning, alcohol and drug abuse, and mental health programs), health educators, advocates for and planners of comprehensive health projects, consultants, researchers, and trainers of paraprofessional personnel (Bracht, 1978).

Social workers have believed in the widest definition of *public health*. In 1981, the National Association of Social Workers (NASW) adopted, with minor modifications, Winslow's definition of public health (given in Chapter 2) as part of its official policy statement on social work in health settings and laid down the standards for social work practice in public health. In general, objectives of public health social work include the following:

- Ensuring the provision of psychosocial services for individuals and families
- Providing information and knowledge about community service networks to consumers and health care providers
- Collaborating with professionals from other disciplines in delivering comprehensive care
- Promoting social work values, such as self-determination, within the health care system
- Encouraging consumer participation in the planning and evaluation of services
- Discovering systemic factors that prevent access or discourage use of services
- Documenting social conditions that interfere with the attainment of health and working for program/policy changes to address those conditions (Morton, 1985)

These objectives have demanded that social workers assume different and varied roles, such as provider of direct services, case manager, administrator of a program, coordinator of services, program planner, consultant, and program evaluator. Social workers work in all kinds of illness prevention settings/programs, such as prenatal and postnatal clinics, health centers, HMOs, clinics for children with developmental or physical disabilities, and special programs for genetic counseling, bereavement work, prevention of child abuse, teenage pregnancy, teenage suicide, AIDS, and substance abuse.

Social work has also contributed to the theory and technology of illness prevention and health promotion. While incorporating the principles of epidemiology into social work practice, social workers have applied the philosophy, principles, and methods of their profession to public health work. The work of social work theoreticians such as Bloom (1981), Bracht (1990), Germain (1984), and Germain and Gitterman (1980) is noteworthy. Basic social work philosophy, theory, and techniques have significant relevance for the illness prevention and health promotion field, and social workers can enter this field with a high degree of confidence in their abilities. The major elements of their professional repertoire are highlighted below.

The philosophy of social work is based on democratic values, as well as the values of science. In the words of Weick (1986), "The profession has developed an intellectual heritage based on two separate but related intellectual approaches: a commitment to scientific inquiry spawned by the rise of an empirical, technical world view and a commitment to philosophical principles motivated by humanistic, democratic beliefs" (p. 551). This philosophy, on the one hand, generates the belief that people can change if given the reason and the wherewithal and creates such practice principles as self-determination, individualization, and participation of people (as individuals, groups, and communities) in the change efforts. On the other hand, it emphasizes the need for rationality, objectivity, and nonjudgmental attitude and the study and assessment of people and their situations for professional intervention. This philosophy is essentially optimistic and strength-oriented, as is reflected in the social work axioms "Let people determine the course of their own lives," "Work with people's strengths," and "Consider people within their social environment." In illness prevention and health promotion work, whether the emphasis is on increasing personal strengths, decreasing personal weaknesses, increasing social environmental resources, or decreasing social environmental stresses, the overall social work philosophy would keep the worker on the right professional path. Moreover, this theme blends well into the philosophical basis of health education practice, which is founded on democracy as a political philosophy and citizen participation as a professional principle (Steckler, Dawson, Goodman, & Epstein, 1987).

Because the focus of social work is on person-in-environment, systems theory provides a useful model for conceptualizing social work practice. This theory offers a holistic view of people and their problems and situations; it (a) helps social workers in perceiving and better understanding the social environment, (b) helps in identifying practice principles that apply across different contexts, and (c) can help in integrating social work theories and in unifying the profession (Martin & O'Connor, 1988). Therefore, social workers engaged in illness prevention and health promotion work can apply the systems perspective to their assessment, planning, and intervention, yielding significant results at all levels of their activity. This perspective fits into the ideal health promotion approach, the ecological perspective that seeks to influence intrapersonal, interpersonal, institutional, community, and public policy factors. This approach adds to educational activities "advocacy, organizational change efforts, policy development, economic supports, environmental change, and multi-method programs" (Glanz & Rimer, 1995, p. 15). Other social work concepts effective in this work include "enabling," "empowerment," and "community organization."

FUTURE SOCIAL WORK ROLES IN ILLNESS PREVENTION AND HEALTH PROMOTION

In Chapter 3, we discussed the *lack of resources* jeopardizing the ability of state and local public health departments to perform effectively even their basic functions. The Institute of Medicine study on the future of public health (1988a) found that "public health functions are handicapped by reductions in federal support; economic problems in particular states and localities; the appearance of new, expensive problems like AIDS and toxic waste; and the diversion of resources from community wide maintenance functions to individual patient care" (p. 156) and recommended the following: (a) Federal support of state-level health programs should help balance disparities in revenue-generating capacities through "core" funding, as well as funds targeted for specific uses; and (b) state support of local-level health services should balance local revenue-generating disparity through "core" funding. In the next century, the wellness movement will gradually improve the legitimacy of the claim of public health departments for a greater share of resources, but the claim will not automatically translate into the availability of more resources.

> Without major health reform in the interim, projections of the Health Care Financing Administration, based on continued inflation of costs, indicate a national expenditure by 2030 of 15,969 trillion dollars, with 206 billion dollars remaining for preventive programs. This will represent a further reduction in the public health share of expenditures to 1.29%, or about half of the current proportion. (Koplin, 1993, p. 400)

Even if a greater share of the national dollar for health activity is allowed for illness prevention and health promotion, public health departments will be competing with many other public and private entities providing illness prevention and wellness services.

In the 21st century, more and more hospitals will expand their activities to include illness prevention and health promotion work, and most of them will expect that work to generate profit or at least be self-sustaining financially. Similarly, other agencies involved in such work are likely to need greater financial resources to improve the extent and quality of their efforts.

Besides the paucity of funds, one major hurdle to the effectiveness of the local health department is organizational. Most such departments are too small to have adequate resources for effectiveness and efficiency; they lack the necessary infrastructure. The large number of local departments can be traced to a necessity that was valid in the horse-and-buggy days of transportation. Even 50 years ago, Emerson (1945) saw the small size of local health units as a problem and proposed their restructuring, but the then prevailing local home-rule philosophy would not allow for any sacrifice of the local unit's autonomy (Koplin, 1993). The consensus about the core functions of public health departments is sufficient, and the Institute of Medicine study (1988a) suggested a number of significant attainable courses of action for public health units at all levels. The focus of planning must be on the removal of barriers to the effective and efficient functioning of these units. Creating greater resources and convincing politicians of the need for reorganization would break most of those barriers.

Beyond that, *planning* community-based health promotion and illness prevention programs would involve a bifocal approach that considers and provides for activities that help modify health-risk behaviors *and* the conditions and environments that support those behaviors. These activities include communitywide health education, risk-factor interventions, and efforts to change laws and regulations in areas that affect health (Wickizer et al., 1993). Planning for a hospital's illness prevention and health promotion program would involve deciding on the "what," "where," and "how" of its activities. Planning in agencies devoted to the prevention of a specific illness or problem would involve the same process but be much more focused. At the national level of these organizations, planning would also be guided by the particular focus/foci of the agency's activity. Ganikos et al. (1994) identified the following four roles that a national health education and promotion organization can take: (a) a broker of knowledge, information, and communication strategies and skills; (b) a producer of educational strategies, messages, and materials; (c) an energizer, through sponsorship of market research, educational model development, and demonstration programs; and (d) a catalyst, serving as the consensus builder and coordinator of a national strategy.

Even *service provision* activities in the area of illness prevention and health promotion must be bifocal—individuals and groups, as well as the community at large. Individuals must be educated and encouraged to change their health-related behaviors directly, as well as through the community's reinforcing atmosphere, pressure, and sanction. This would be true whether the agency is the public health department, a hospital, or a voluntary nonprofit organization. While recognizing that the two important components of a public health program are enforcement and education, even the public health department would rather convince than coerce people.

> Even though police power exists and can be used as necessary, public health workers recognize their inability to be in all places at all times to enforce good health practice in public and private sectors. It is necessary, therefore, to concurrently emphasize health education to enhance voluntary compliance with recommended health practices. (Brecken, Harvey, & Lancaster, 1985, p. 37)

In the future, in every illness prevention and health promotion organization—public health departments, hospitals, and disease-specific agencies such as the American Cancer Society—social workers will be able to assume roles that have relevance to the organization's major needs. In different combinations, these needs are (a) generation of financial resources, (b) planning of appropriate service programs, and (c) provision of effective services.

Social Work Role in Creating and Mobilizing Financial Resources

Social workers can make significant contributions to all agencies engaged in illness prevention and health promotion in exploring and generating financial resources. Despite the commitment to the idea of general welfare, as a nation the United States has generally been reluctant to provide for those with special needs—the disabled, disadvantaged, distressed, defeated, dependent, and deviant—people of special concern for social workers. Social workers have, therefore, been forced to be creative and skillful in generating and mobilizing resources. Generating future funds for the three types of agencies will require different approaches. For augmenting the resources of state and local public health departments, applying for grants from the federal government will be the major strategy. For hospitals, marketing their wellness activities both as part of their health maintenance package and as an independent program will be the preferred approach. For other organizations, streamlining their fund-raising efforts will be the focus of the social worker's contributions. Social workers will play the role of the *creator and mobilizer of financial resources.*

Social Work Role in Program Planning

Planning involves specifying objectives, evaluating the means for achieving them, and making deliberate choices about the appropriate courses of action (*Social Work Dictionary,* 1991). This process is applicable at all levels and is relatively easy for social workers to practice and perfect because of their understanding and expertise in problem solving. The different needs of the three types of agencies will dictate differential emphasis on the various steps of the planning process.

The possibilities of "what" activities to include in a health promotion program are countless. For example, Longe and Wolf (1983) listed six categories of health promotion activities offered by hospitals: (a) *community patient education* in such areas as living with arthritis, management of asthma, and parenting a child with diabetes; (b) *behavior change* for smoking cessation, stress reduction, and weight control; (c) *wellness and lifestyle* involving aerobic exercises and walking, communication and conflict resolution, and low-calorie, low-sodium, and low-fat cooking; (d) *medical self-care,* providing knowledge and skills about choosing a physician and understanding medications; (e) *lifesavers,* including baby-sitting certification, cardiac crisis program, cardiopulmonary resuscitation (CPR), and first aid; and (f) *workplace-related activities* such as employee assistance programs, organizational safety or hazard assessments, safety education, and work-site chronic disease control programs. The question of "where" a hospital's health promotion activities should be offered can also have numerous possible answers. These activities can be offered at the hospital, its clinics in the community, community centers, churches, libraries, recreational sites, schools, workplaces, and conferences and fairs. Similarly, the "how" of these activities is limited only by the imagination and resources that can be devoted to them. Basic social work skills, with some focus and refinement, are relevant for these functions. Social workers can easily play the role of *program planner* in all agencies engaged in illness prevention and health promotion work.

Social Work Role in Program Implementation
and Service Provision

Illness prevention and health promotion agencies will offer social workers opportunities also in areas other than resource generation and program planning. Social workers can significantly contribute to the implementation of an agency's program and provision of its services. Their major roles will be as *educator* and *community activator.* Community activation is a means to public education. These roles involve planning, conducting, and evaluating the necessary activities.

Other Social Work Roles in Illness
Prevention and Health Promotion

Social workers have special sensitivity for, understanding of, and expertise in the problems of child abuse, AIDS, and old age. They should therefore take on leadership roles appropriate for illness prevention and health promotion in these areas. Also, illness prevention and health promotion organizations will be required by policymakers and third-party payers to show that their efforts lead to the desired health status outcome and are cost-effective. Social workers will be able to contribute to the needed research activities pertaining to this requirement.

SOCIAL WORK KNOWLEDGE AND SKILLS

As in earlier chapters, our discussion of social work knowledge and skills necessary for illness prevention and health promotion work is organized in relation to the roles identified above.

Social Worker as a Generator of
Financial Resources

The social worker should know that the possible resources of funds for illness prevention and health promotion programs are likely to be different for different agencies. On the one hand, for most local public health departments, the local government is not likely to be a resource beyond the minimal funds it already allocates for public health activities. Social workers must seek more resources from the federal and state governments. Similarly, state public health departments must look to the federal government and the state legislature for extra resources.

On the other hand, voluntary organizations engaged in illness prevention and health promotion work must raise funds from the general public and supplement those with grants from government and charitable foundations. Social workers can bring their skills for grant writing, fund-raising, and political advocacy to bear on the agency's efforts to increase its financial resources. They will find the following information and suggestions helpful in enriching and refining those skills.

Grant Writing

The federal government makes money available to local governments and nongovernmental agencies by contract and by grant. By contract, the government buys the effort of someone to do specifically what the government wants done. A grant provides the money for the recipient to do something it wants that also is in the government's area of interest. Thus, a grantee has much more freedom of action than a contractor. The various kinds of grants can be broadly grouped as formula grant and project grant:

> A *formula grant* is money distributed to a class of entitled agencies (e.g., state or local governments, universities). All members of the class are entitled to receive a portion of the total sum appropriated as long as they meet the conditions governing entitlement to the money. The money is distributed on approval of the application on the basis of some mathematical formula, which, with state government, typically is weighted according to population and per capita income. . . . *Project grants* are not entitlement. These are grants awarded on a competitive basis. The applicant develops a plan or proposal stating what is to be done if money is awarded. The applications are reviewed competitively, though, in fact, the government is sensitive to the need to spread the awards around. (Raffel & Raffel, 1989, p. 308)

Block grants and capitation grants are kinds of formula grants. Some grants, both formula and project grants, require that the applicant match the government grant. Local and state public health departments should seek formula grants and insist that these grants be based on need. "Project grants and those requiring matching local funds are not recommended because they favor the better-established entities, and are therefore disadvantageous for the poorer, rural, and otherwise underserved areas" (Koplin, 1993, p. 396). Project grants can supplement the resources of local and state public health departments. Similarly, hospitals and other voluntary organizations should seek project grants to add to their funds from other sources.

Other sources of grants include foundations of various kinds—community trusts (e.g., Cleveland Foundation), special-purpose foundations, corporations (e.g., General Electric Foundation), family foundations, and general-purpose foundations (e.g., Rockefeller Foundation). A foundation may fall into more than one category. The appropriate foundation can be located from the latest edition of the *Foundation Directory,* which has a double listing—alphabetical by state and by field of interest. Foundations are likely to fund demonstration projects more easily than ongoing programs. All federal invitations/requests for grant applications are published in the *Federal Register.* Another source of information about federal funds is the *Catalog of Federal Domestic Assistance.* The following suggestions about grant writing are based on workshops on fiscal resource development that I have attended over the years and on my experience as a grant reviewer for the U.S. Department of Health and Human Services.

Elements of grant proposals submitted to the government or private foundations are essentially the same although foundation requests are generally shorter. A summary of the proposal is followed by the following detailed sections: (a) introduction, (b) problem statement or assessment of need, (c) project/program objectives, (d) methodology, (e) evaluation, (f) budget, and (g) future support for the project/program. While writing a grant proposal, the social worker should give special attention to the following suggestions:

- Learn as much as possible about the funding source and its expectations of the grant seeker; study the material about the grant, call and talk with the appropriate officer in the funding department of the government or contact the grantmaker at the foundation, "discover what that source is interested in supporting, and figure out how your organization can help the source meet its funding priority" (Nickelsberg, 1988, p. 126). In the proposal, address what the funding organization wants to fund.

- In the introduction, build the agency's credibility as one that deserves to be supported.

- Be specific about the problem and the target population; document the need for the project/program. Be truthful about the population being served by the agency or the number of potential beneficiaries of the project.

- Do not mix project objectives and methodology; list specific objectives that are realistic and measurable.

- Be innovative in the approach to the problem but justify the proposed methodology; do not make assumptions that cannot be backed; describe the "how" of the methods; and show how the agency has the capacity to carry out the project/program, particularly in terms of the experience and skills of its personnel. Most funding sources are also interested in the replicability of the projects they fund. Show how yours can be easily replicated.

- Build in an evaluation design for ongoing and final evaluation, both in terms of the project implementation process and its impact on those served.

- Make sure the proposed budget is appropriate, reasonable, and adequately justified; describe the fiscal control and accounting procedures to be used.

- Present a plan for the continuation of the program beyond the grant period.

- Overall, be clear, concise, and logical; avoid unsupported assumptions and the use of jargon; and package the proposal so as to make it attractive in terms of proper typing, spacing, margins, tabs, as well as correctness of spellings.

- Read, review, and rewrite the proposal as many times as necessary to make it as good and strong as possible. Have someone who knows nothing about the project read the proposal and point out which parts are confusing or unclear. Also in this process of refining the document, consult the appropriate officer in the government or the grantmaker at the foundation, if needed.

- Mail the proposal in plenty of time; let your proposal be among the first to arrive, and after a week or so, call your contact and ask whether any other information is needed.

- Do try to know the people who make decisions about funding proposals or those who influence the decision makers. Some authors are of the opinion that, in the case of an application for a federal grant, copies of the proposal should be sent to one's congressperson and senators. "Get to know either the members themselves or, more important, one of their key staff people who might be interested. That staff person could go with you to your interview with the grantmaker or could help his or her boss follow up with letters and phone calls" (Nickelsberg, 1988, p. 129).

Fund-Raising

Social workers in voluntary organizations are likely to be involved in all major functions of the agency, including fund-raising. With their professional expertise, particularly communication and problem-solving skills, they can easily assume leadership in this activity as well. The literature on different aspects of the "how" of fund-raising is vast and rich. For example, Bakal (1979) described at length the various techniques of fund-raising.[1] Most of these require elaborate planning in terms of "what," "where," "when," and "how." The "how" part invariably involves skills appropriate for communication, persuasion, and motivation.

Social workers should realize that their basic communication skills are as applicable in approaching people for charity as they are in problem-oriented assessment and intervention with individuals, groups, and larger entities. Persuasion strategies involve giving information that influences the recipient to feel, think, and act in a new way. The attributes of successful persuaders are expertise, trustworthiness, and likability. An effective persuader is perceived as possessing one or more of these (Simon & Aigner, 1985). The social worker should make conscious efforts to conduct him- or herself as well as come across as an expert and trustworthy. This task can be accomplished by (a) a thorough grasp of the agency's mission, programs, and activities and the material being shared with people; and (b) an unwavering commitment to social work values. Likability depends on many factors, and the individual may have no control over some of these. However, "Individuals are more likely to like, or be attracted to, workers whom they view as genuine, understanding, and accepting" (Simon & Aigner, 1985, p. 120). People have differing reasons for giving; they are guided by their philosophies, upbringing, religious attitudes, and social desirability of the people giving, as well as their experience with the particular cause. In general, giving is considered more blessed than receiving, and giving may also enhance an individual's self- and social esteem.

For motivating people to give, the approach must be both generalized and special. The generalized approach is based on answers to the question, "What does everyone need to know about us and our cause?" The special approach builds on assumptions about "what the particular person needs to know about us and our cause." Nickelsberg (1988) is of the opinion that making people feel good about giving would stimulate them to give. Appreciate their giving by giving them something tangible—a little gift (with your logo on it) that people cannot get any other way, something they can show off. This possibility would make them feel good about it. His other advice: "Set up categories of support to make people feel they are joining an elite club. Finally, always publish lists of joiners because it's nice to have personal recognition—and testimonials encourage joiners" (Nickelsberg, quoted in N. M. Davis, 1988, p. 125).

For motivating organizations to give, the approach should be directed at appealing to their self-interest, pride, and social values. With his focus on large corporations, Nickelsberg (1988) proposed several tenets of fund-raising: (a) People only give to people; (b) people only give to people they know; (c) people who give want visibility; (d) people love to support a winner; and (e) people want to invest in the future.

These tenets can be turned into techniques for fund-raising. "People only give to people, the people they know" suggests that fund-raisers should be people-people and that they should try to know the prospective givers before approaching them. Social workers are people-people by training and can thus provide one basic ingredient of a successful fund-raising program. Knowing the potential corporate giver may require talking with the agency's board members (who are generally businesspersons with contacts and connections) and requesting one of them to accompany the worker while approaching for funds. The worker should approach corporate givers with the aim of establishing common interest between them and his or her agency, showing them how the agency's programs are likely to bring about improvement in the community, and explaining how contributing to the cause is an investment in the community's future. Therefore, the worker should be armed with facts when approaching a corporate executive.

Most social workers are creative and resourceful. They should let those qualities inform their fund-raising work as well. Just be themselves. A social worker with the Salvation Army in a large Midwestern town conceived the idea of approaching the corporate office of the area's largest chain of food stores and suggesting that the chain give its shoppers the option of donating to the Salvation Army any change due them that was less than a dollar. The corporation agreed and thereby became a proud partner in the raising of thousands of dollars on a regular basis for a local charity.

Social workers should always remember and remind others in their organization that accountability is an absolute necessity for fund-raising. They all can learn an important lesson from Canada. A recent poll of Ontario hospital foundations showed that 96% of them published audited financial statements and made these available to their donors and community. Members of the Association for Healthcare Philanthropy made presentations to an Ontario government committee in support of legislation requiring disclosure (Locke, 1993).

Political Advocacy

In Chapter 5, we discussed the concept of "advocacy" and its application at the case and class levels—that is, advocacy in micro as well as macro social work practice. Here are a few suggestions that social workers will find helpful in sharpening their political advocacy skills. More are presented later in the section on community organizing.

1. *Be proactive.* Proactivity involves being on top of the issues pertaining to the cause one is advocating. It requires gathering facts and formulating a clear position on the issues. "It means generating a social view of oneself as someone who is prepared and has to be dealt with, rather than as someone who is reactionary and who comes to confront well after the fact of a decision having been made or action having been taken" (Flynn, 1995, p. 2177). Proactivity creates credibility with those who have authority, influence, and power.

2. *Know the local, state, and federal legislative systems and understand the legislative processes.* To influence legislation appropriately, besides expert knowledge of the issues, one must know how the system works and keep abreast of changes in policy-making bodies—for example, the membership of various legislative committees.

3. *Remember that influence can result from several approaches, such as provision of information on the issues, personal persuasion, negotiation, and constituency support* (Checkoway, 1995). Lawmakers and their staffs welcome valid information on issues, but persuasion has limits. It is often wiser to concentrate on reinforcing the opinions of those who are in basic agreement with one's stance. Negotiation and compromise go hand in hand. Politicians are very sensitive to the support of their constituents. Combining these and other approaches in a systematic and pragmatic strategy would yield greater results.

4. *Build on basic social work communication skills for approaching and educating policymakers and program administrators, mobilizing clients and community groups, and forming alliances with other groups and organizations.* Many human service organizations and groups have tried and tested different approaches to influencing sources of power. Their examples (see Douglass & Winterfeld, 1995; McFarland, 1995; Myers, 1995) can also guide advocacy work.

Social Worker as a Program Planner

The term *planning* refers to both a process and an outcome. The planning *process* deals with the movement from problem definition to problem solution along the various stages between the two points. The planning *outcome* is a plan, a design for action that specifies the essential elements of the program. It spells out *what the objectives* of the program (short-term as well as long-term) will be; *what targets* will be influenced or changed; *how the change* will be brought about in terms of the tasks, tactics, and procedures to be used; *who will perform* the required tasks and procedures; *where and when* the services will be provided in terms of the facilities and timing for the use of personnel and their procedures; *what fiscal and other resources* will be needed to implement the program; and *how the program will be monitored and evaluated.*

There are several planning models. The PRECEDE-PROCEED model (Green & Kreuter, 1991) is a noteworthy one. It has nine phases, the first five of which are diagnostic: (a) *social diagnosis* of the self-determined needs, wants, resources, and barriers in a community; (b) *epidemiological diagnosis* of health problems; (c) *behavioral and environmental diagnosis* of specific behaviors and environmental factors for the program to address; (d) *educational and organizational diagnosis* of the behavior-related predisposing, enabling, and reinforcing conditions; and (e) *administrative and policy diagnosis* of the resources and barriers within the organization and community. The remaining four phases pertain to implementation and evaluation: (f) *implementation,* (g) *process evaluation,* (h) *impact evaluation,* and (i) *outcome evaluation.* Process evaluation begins as soon as the program implementation starts, and impact evaluation begins as the implementation proceeds. The impact evaluation is done when enough time as specified in the program objectives has passed. Rainey and Lindsay (1994) divided the community health promotion program planning process into eight stages: (a) epidemiologic assessment, (b) needs assessment, (c) analysis of behavior, (d) working through social institutions, (e) goals and objectives, (f) political groundwork, (g) implementation, and (h) evaluation. They listed 101 questions that a planner should ask to ensure that nothing of importance has been left out. The planning-related suggestions given below elaborate on some of these stages. Social workers can enrich their knowledge and skills by taking these suggestions to heart:

1. *Take the task of developing program objectives seriously.* This may be the single most important part of the job as a planner. Many plans fail because the objectives are too loose, too subjective, too narrow, or too difficult to measure. Build the objectives on a thorough analysis of all relevant factors, such as the problem, policy, program, and environment. An understanding of the nature, origin, and scope of the problem or need is an absolute necessity.

2. *Know the various approaches to problem analysis and needs assessment.* The major strategies include (a) review of the literature; (b) interviews with key informants—the people with special knowledge or expertise about the problem or the people with the problem; (c) use of focus groups made up of agency staff members and potential program beneficiaries, with the aim of learning people's preferences regarding community health promotion and the reasons for their choices (Longe & Wolf, 1983); (d) study of statistical documents on the problem and the people affected by it, as well as reports of the local and regional health planning agencies; (e) surveys of prospective program participants; and (f) community forums where interested community members can express their opinions about the proposed program. Similarly, an analysis of the policy relevant to the problem and the proposed program is important for specifying program objectives.

3. *Know the various models of policy analysis.* Policies determine major approaches, priorities, and funding for programs. Various models of *policy analysis* learned in basic social work courses are appropriate for this purpose. A *program analysis* either of the agency's past efforts regarding the problem or of similar other programs would help in developing the appropriate objectives. Particular attention should be paid to the organizational, budgetary, and cost-benefit aspects of the programs being analyzed. For example, the design and implementation of a hospital's community health promotion program would depend on the hospital's mission, scope of the program, and decision about where the program would fit into its organization and what kind of personnel and resources would be allowed for it. Longe and Wolf (1983) discussed three organizational structures for hospital-based health promotion programs. Such a program can be operated as a function of an existing department or division, as a department in itself, or as a separate corporate entity. All of these can be either for-profit or not-for-profit. In cases of multi-institutional hospital systems, again there are several possibilities. Each hospital may have its own health promotion program, one hospital may have the program that provides health promotion

services for the entire system, or the program may be part of the corporate management entity separate from individual hospitals (Longe & Wolf, 1983).

4. *Include in an environmental analysis the study of factors likely to help and hinder the program being planned, as well as the major trends that may affect it positively or negatively.* A hospital that wants its illness prevention and health promotion program to make a profit or at least pay for itself may also need a market analysis along with a needs assessment. A *market analysis* shows who the actual and potential consumers of community health promotion activities will be, which offerings they will participate in, and how they will determine their satisfaction with an offering (Longe & Wolf, 1983).

5. *Let the carefully selected realistic objectives lead to the specifica- tion of other elements of the program, such as the appropriate tech- nologies, staff functions, personnel policies, and procedures.* Make sure the program will have the necessary tools for its implementation; these are economic, informational, management, legal, and political. For health promotion, make sure the program allows for multilevel in- tegrated interventions. Elder, Schmid, Dower, and Hedlund (1993) categorized a community heart-health program's interventions as (a) social marketing; (b) direct behavior change efforts that include health education, skills training, and contingency management; (c) screening; and (d) environmental change efforts that include changes in policy, as well as in physical environment.

6. *Build into the program a strong evaluation element with the appropriate needed information system.* Evaluation of the program— ongoing, periodic, and final—is as important as its implementation. In this age of accountability and scarce resources, an agency's ability to document the effectiveness and efficiency of its program determines the program's continued existence. All kinds of designs—preexperimental, quasi-experimental, and experimental (Campbell & Stanley, 1966)— can be used for evaluating programs. Similarly, an evaluation can have many foci, such as the program's acceptability, accessibility, adequacy, comprehensiveness, continuity, cost-effectiveness, efficiency, effort, impact, integration of services, performance, and process (Attkisson & Broskowski, 1978; Suchman, 1967). Choose a design and the focus according to the purpose of the program and to the need and resources of the agency. Select evaluation measures that quantify the extent to which the program objectives would be met and even capture the qualitative aspects of the program consequences.

Social Worker as an Educator and Community Activator

The social work educator role involves giving new information and helping in the acquisition and practice of new behaviors and skills. It is one of the oldest professional roles, sometimes standing out as the major thrust of social work activity and very often embedded in a worker's total practice. Social workers have played this role not only in their work with individual clients but also in community programs, in family life and consumer education, and in the training of volunteers for community service (Siporin, 1975). In the words of Connaway and Gentry (1988),

> Social workers helped Asian and European wives of returning servicemen to learn how to shop, cook, and negotiate social institutions in their adopted country. We taught budgeting and food commodity preparation to financially struggling families. We taught members of youth clubs how to make decisions. We assisted immigrants to learn how a democratic society works. We helped unemployed persons practice filling out job applications. We designed learning opportunities for persons with specific developmental lags and disabilities to acquire skills to master environmental tasks. (p. 114)

Social workers have traditionally engaged in the educator role in two contexts: with one person at a time and with groups of persons. Most social workers today come out of their training programs adept at playing this role. Social workers in illness prevention and health promotion will be expected to play this role not only with individuals and groups but also at the larger community level. The importance of the community cannot be minimized. I agree with the view of Green and Raeburn (1990):

> The most effective vehicle for health promotion activity, whether it be directed at policy, environmental change, institutional change, or personal skills development, is the human group, a coalition with all its aspects of social support and organizational power. Community groups can exist to set priorities in health promotion, to run programs, to advise public officials, and to help each other in a wide variety of ways. These groups are perfect vehicles for an enabling approach. (p. 41)

Community organization has been an area of social work practice throughout its history, and social work has made significant contributions to the development of the theory and technology of community organization. Earlier, I alluded to the role of social workers in public health who functioned both as case workers and community organizers. The significance of their contributions is reflected in the judgment of Rosen (1974) that "the roots of social medicine are to be found in organized social work" (p. 112).

Before suggesting effective approaches to individual-, group-, and community-level illness prevention and health promotion work, I discuss the concepts of "enabling," "empowerment," and "community organization" relevant for this work.

Enabling is to make able, to provide the means or opportunity, and to help in the improvement of capacity. Enabling has traditionally been viewed as a social work role. As an enabler, a social worker helps individuals, groups, and communities articulate their needs; identify and clarify their problems; explore, select, and apply strategies to resolve those problems; and develop their capacities to deal with their problems more effectively (Zastrow, 1985). WHO's Ottawa Charter defined *health promotion* as "the process of enabling people to increase control over and improve their health" (WHO, 1986). To be effective, illness prevention and health promotion work has to be bifocal. Green and Raeburn (1990) called these foci theoretical and ideological perspectives:

> The first emphasizes political and sociological or "system" factors in health. The second emphasizes personal and small group decision making, psychological factors, and health education methods. An integration of these viewpoints appears to prevail in actual policies and practice, though some advocates and practitioners continue to defend or push for one of the more polar views on the health promotion spectrum. (p. 30)

The principle of "enabling" is not only applicable at both these levels but also can be used to merge the two perspectives into an integrated, total, person-environment approach in which the responsibility for health is shared between individuals and systems. This enabling approach involves "returning power, knowledge, skills, and other resources in a range of health areas to the community—to individuals, families, and whole populations" (Green & Raeburn, 1990, p. 38).

Empowerment refers to the process of gaining, developing, facilitating, or giving power. Because the history of social work is essentially the history of its work with the poor and the powerless, empowerment has been a part of the social work approach to serving its clients. Simon

(1994) identified the following five components of the empowerment approach that have existed across every period of social work history since 1893: (a) the construction of collaborative partnerships with clients, (b) the emphasis on their strengths rather than their weaknesses, (c) the focus on both individuals and their social and physical environments, (d) the recognition of the clients' rights, responsibilities, and needs, and (e) the direction of professional energies toward helping historically disempowered individuals and groups. Despite this history, although some question the ability of social workers to empower their clients because of their own powerlessness, others consider power to be a central theme in social work practice and want client empowerment to be made the cornerstone of social work theory and practice (e.g., see Calista, 1989; Hasenfeld, 1987; Heger & Hunzeker, 1988). Social workers are making significant contributions to the development of a theory of empowerment and are formulating empowerment-related practice principles and techniques (e.g., Gutierrez, 1992; Hasenfeld, 1987; Kieffer, 1984; Parsons, 1988; Pinderhughes, 1983; Staples, 1990). Others (for our purpose, those in the fields of health, education, and community psychology) are also recognizing the importance of empowerment and are exploring this concept and ways of operationalizing it (e.g., Bernstein et al., 1994; Flynn, Ray, & Rider, 1994; Israel, Checkoway, Schulz, & Zimmerman, 1994). Neighbors, Braithwaite, and Thompson (1995) hold that empowerment operates on multiple levels and suggest that personal empowerment and community action must go together. Social workers should keep themselves abreast of new empowerment-related knowledge and skills.

   Community organizing means mobilizing people to solve their problems and to form organizations that enhance their power (Rubin & Rubin, 1986). Community can be defined in many ways: It can refer to geopolitical, geocultural, or interest communities. There are several models of community organization practice. For example, Rothman (1970) proposed three models: locality development, social planning, and social action. *Locality development* seeks to bring about community change through broad participation of citizens in identifying goals and selecting actions. The emphasis here is on the process of generating self-help and improving community capacity and integration. *Social planning* emphasizes the use of technical processes to solve substantive community problems by rational, deliberate, and controlled efforts. *Social action* seeks basic changes in the institutions and/or community practices by shifting power relationships and resources. The strategies and techniques of these models can be mixed and matched for different purposes.

Bracht and Kingsbury (1990) proposed an extensive 5-stage model of community organizing for health promotion. They discussed the key elements of each of the stages: (a) community analysis, (b) design initiation, (c) implementation, (d) maintenance-consolidation, and (e) dissemination-reassessment. On the basis of experience from the community heart-health programs, Elder et al. (1993) offered helpful ideas that can serve as practice principles: (a) Community participation in planning, designing, and evaluating the program promotes its adoption by the community; (b) feedback to the community is essential; (c) primary prevention should be given priority over secondary prevention; (d) interventions using multiple strategies and promoted through multiple channels are more effective; and (e) policy and environmental interventions should be preferred over direct behavioral change efforts.

Different approaches to education may be taken when the target is an individual or small group rather than the community. For their role as educator of individuals and groups, social workers would find the following suggestions helpful.

1. *Strive for a match between the educational strategy and the characteristics of the system (individual, group, or community) to be worked with in terms of its composition, demographics, and culture.* Answers to the question, "Given what is to be learned and the characteristics of the system, how best can it learn the needed information and skills?" would guide in ensuring the needed communication fit.

2. *Remember that different people learn in different ways.* Some learn primarily by doing (enactive learner); others by summarizing, visualizing, and organizing perceptions into patterns and images (iconic learners); and still others by abstracting and conceptualizing (symbolic learners) (Jerome Brunner, as mentioned by Gitterman, 1988). Social workers should try to respond to different learning styles by using the appropriate teaching methods, which may include (a) the didactic method, which involves sharing information and ideas; (b) the discussion method, which allows for much more interaction between the worker and the client system; (c) the visual method, which uses graphs, diagrams, pictures, films, and other aids to learning and understanding; and (d) the action method, which emphasizes learning through experiencing and allows for role modeling and coaching.

Beyond the above general educational methods, Gitterman (1988) listed the following specific educational skills and strategies for social workers in health care: (a) providing relevant information, (b) clarifying misinformation, (c) offering advice, (d) offering interpretations, (e) providing feedback, (f) inviting feedback, (g) specifying action tasks, and (h) preparing and planning for task completion.

3. In choosing an educational strategy, *be sensitive to such system characteristics as intelligence, verbal ability, and self-respect.* "In general, the most effective strategies are those that partialize information and tasks into manageable units applied to real problems or tasks. Some system members who do not tolerate stress well can benefit from learning opportunities arranged in a clear, step-by-step manner to fit their needs" (Connaway & Gentry, 1988, p. 123). For health promotion aimed at behavioral change, the educational strategy must include skills training and contingency management. The components of skills training are "instruction, modeling, practice during training sessions, feedback, reinforcement, and practice between sessions," and "contingency management involves altering consequences for behavior to change the probability of the behavior in the future" (Elder et al., 1993, p. 470).

4. *Carefully select the context of educational activity.* Again, an understanding of the system's characteristics would help in selecting the context that promises a high degree of success. Any context has room for mixing and matching the various educational approaches and techniques mentioned above. Similarly, the social worker should determine the degree of structure for the educational activity, with an eye toward maximizing the impact of that education.

> Degree of structure is the extent to which a technique determines what information is presented and how persons interact about this information. We determine degree of structure imposed by examining precisely what the technique requires people to do. A paper and pencil test has different behavioral requirements than watching a film or participating in a discussion or role playing. (Connaway & Gentry, 1988, p. 126)

Social workers are able to engage in the educational role at the larger community level without much difficulty. Nolte and Wilcox (1984) considered two sets of abilities essential for success in reaching the public: personal characteristics and skills. Their list of personal characteristics includes awareness, courage, creativity, curiosity, diplomacy, empathy, judgment, speed, and thoroughness; these are not at all uncommon in social workers. The required skills are essentially the same as the problem-solving skills that all social workers have learned and practiced. In organizing community-level educational activities, social workers will be able to benefit from the following suggestions.

- *Supplement their knowledge and skills with ideas and strategies from the literature on health education and social marketing.* Social marketing is a new methodology that applies profit-sector marketing techniques to the task of increasing the acceptance of social ideas and practices and thereby changing people's attitudes and behaviors (e.g., see Kotler, 1982).

- *Use existing resources in the community.* Various disease-specific organizations, such as the American Heart Association, American Lung Association, and National Kidney Foundation, are doing impressive illness prevention and health promotion work. "They have produced publications, public service announcement, and programs which have frequently been both sustained and effective" (McGinnis, 1982, p. 413). Other groups are engaged in more generic wellness activities. Social workers should reach out to these organizations, collaborate with them, and coordinate their own educational activities with theirs.

- *Target specific groups and populations for intensive education and use audience-appropriate educational strategies.* A multipronged approach involving several strategies is likely to produce the maximum impact. Social workers should remember that the goal of their activities is not merely imparting information, but being instrumental in bringing about behavioral changes.

- *Let their knowledge of the target population and its need, their agency's resources, other resources in the community that can be mobilized, and their imagination create a package of appropriate strategies.* (This suggestion is given because there is no standard list of educational strategies for illness prevention and health promotion work.)

- *Treat the local mass media—both print and electronic—as a special resource.* Attract their attention, gain their support, and cultivate an ongoing positive relationship with them. The media are moving toward what Joslyn-Scherer (1980) called "therapeutic journalism"; that is, besides being sources of information, they want to become active shapers of helping trends. Helping the media with their need would serve the social worker's public education purpose well. Flora and Cassady (1990) defined three roles that media organizations can play in community-based health promotion: (a) media organization as news producer, (b) media organization as equal partner, and (c) media organization as health promotion leader. These authors discussed ways of integrating those media functions into the health promotion process. Several books on how to make the media work for you (e.g., Brawley, 1983; Klein & Danzig, 1985) can help in improving workers' know-how.

In the literature on health education, *media advocacy* refers to the use of mass media (including paid advertising) for influencing individual behavior, stimulating community action, and changing public policies. Wallack (1994) considered it a strategy for empowering people and communities. According to him, whereas the traditional media approaches seek to fill the "knowledge gap," media advocacy addresses the "power gap." "Social, economic, and political determinants of health have been largely ignored by the most pervasive media. Media advocacy tries to change this by emphasizing the social and economic, rather than individual and behavioral, roots of the problem" (Wallack, 1994, p. 421). The primary strategy is to work with individuals and groups to claim power of the media for changing the environment in which health problems occur.

Much planning goes into media advocacy. The major steps are (a) establishing the policy goal; (b) deciding the target; (c) framing the issue and constructing the message; (d) delivering the message and creating pressure for change; and (e) evaluating the process and its outcome. Social workers, well-versed in the problem-solving process, should not have much difficulty in mastering the media advocacy approach. Wallack, Dorfman, Jernigan, and Themba (1993) provide several examples of media advocacy works.

Emerging technologies, such as CD-ROM, interactive videodiscs, and virtual reality programs, are providing newer media with tremendous possibilities for illness prevention and health promotion programs. "Enter-education" or "edu-tainment" is a concept that combines entertainment and education for changing attitudes and behaviors. Its operationalization as an approach to health promotion has great potential for success because "the entertainment media are pervasive, popular, personal, and persuasive" (Steckler et al., 1995, p. 320). Social workers should stay abreast of the technological advancements and of how to enrich their activities and programs from the same.

The social work educational role may need to be directed toward educating politicians and policymakers. Social workers should sharpen their class advocacy skills, which are appropriate for educating and influencing policymakers. There are many time-honored methods, "including one-to-one lobbying; collecting and presenting signed petitions; initiating and managing letter writing, telephone call, and telegram campaigns; mobilizing groups to appear at public hearings; preparing and presenting statements at public hearings; and suggesting the wording of the proposed law" (Dhooper, 1994a, p. 159). They should make sure that their cause and point of view are presented in a forceful, dignified, and polite manner.

Facts, arguments, and demonstrations of power are the tools for influencing policymakers. Therefore, social workers should use a strategy that includes presentation to the policymakers and their staffs of accurate and unbiased information on their cause; rational and non-emotional argument in favor of that cause; and subtle hints about the backing of an organized voting block whenever possible.

Social workers should keep in mind that all politicians want to stay popular, desire to be viewed as sensitive and responsive to the needs and situations of their constituents, and need to give the impression of being tough-minded and responsible public servants. Social workers should try to meet these needs by keeping in touch with them, providing them information and opinions on important issues, sending them reports of their agency's work, inviting them to its events, and being involved with their offices.

This section ends with a list of principles of health education that Freudenberg and his associates (1995) drew from relevant theories, practice, and research. Although presented as hypotheses, these can guide social work activities:

- Effective health education interventions should be tailored to a specific population within a particular setting.
- Effective interventions involve the participants in planning, implementation, and evaluation.
- Effective interventions integrate efforts aimed at changing individuals, social and physical environments, communities, and policies.
- Effective interventions link participants' concerns about health to broader life concerns and to a vision of a better society.
- Effective interventions use existing resources within the environment.
- Effective interventions build on the strengths found among participants and their communities.
- Effective interventions advocate for the resource and policy changes needed to achieve the desired health objectives.
- Effective interventions prepare participants to become leaders.
- Effective interventions support the diffusion of innovation to a wider population.

- Effective interventions seek to institutionalize successful components and to replicate them in other settings.

Social Work Role in Work With Special Populations/Problems

In this section, we discuss the knowledge and skills appropriate for social work with problems and populations that social workers are likely to be looked to for leadership. These problems include (a) health promotion for AIDS prevention, (b) prevention of child abuse, and (c) illness prevention and health promotion among the elderly. Involvement in these will require social workers to assume several professional roles simultaneously.

Health Promotion for AIDS Prevention

AIDS will continue as a major health and public health concern for at least the first few decades of the 21st century. Despite the high rates of prevalence and incidence of the disease, society has been reluctant to respond to it. Because the majority of those affected by AIDS have belonged to groups (e.g., gay men, intravenous [IV] drug users, Hispanics, and blacks) viewed as socially marginal, society has let bigotry, racism, homophobia, and elitism dictate its responses. On the one hand, these attitudes have promoted ignorance and antipathy, delayed recognition of the disease, and obstructed development of effective prevention efforts (Altman, 1987); on the other hand, they have allowed most U.S. citizens to believe that they are not at risk of contracting HIV (House & Walker, 1993).

As mentioned earlier, social workers have been among the pioneers in creating programs and activities to serve AIDS patients. They have much to offer to the prevention efforts as well. Some impressive medically oriented preventive work is being done—for example, the use of zidovudine for the prevention of HIV transmission from mother to infant. An estimated 7,000 births occur each year to HIV-infected women in the United States; the result is approximately 1,500 HIV-infected infants (Goedert & Cote, 1994). All efforts to prevent the infection of children are welcome; however, prevention of infection of women is still the ideal strategy (Stein, 1993), and that will require combining and integrating birth control, family planning, HIV testing, and counseling services. Social workers engaged in AIDS prevention programs would find the following information and suggestions helpful.

1. *Most people at risk of AIDS are not a cohesive community.* Despite the decline in the incidence of the disease among gay men, they, particularly rural gays and younger gays who do not see themselves at risk, must be given special attention. Men who have sex with other men and do not openly identify themselves as gay are another hidden population. Similarly, most IV drug users are at high risk for AIDS, but they are an invisible minority because "U.S. citizens do not want to recognize the existence of so many drug users in our society" (House & Walker, 1993, p. 283). Adolescents are at great risk for the spread of HIV (Hein, 1990). Other populations of growing concern are runaways, prostitutes, the homeless, older persons, and those with disabilities. Racially, Hispanics and blacks continue to be at greater risk.

2. *Identifying and reaching out to most of these groups is difficult.* Even after they are identified, each of these groups poses special problems in reaching out to, educating, and influencing them. It is difficult to educate those under the influence of drugs. Adolescence is characterized by a sense of immortality and invulnerability, experimentation, confusion, and challenging of authority (Gray & House, 1989). Merely giving adolescents information is not sufficient to change their behaviors. Cultural and religious factors discourage Hispanics from being open about sex and drugs. The belief that it is wrong to touch their own bodies and that spermicides may hurt them is widespread (Lewis, Das, Hopper, & Jencks, 1991). The taboo against homosexuality is strong in the black population. Dalton (1989) listed reasons why blacks resist AIDS education, including their reaction to larger society's blaming of race as a reason for the origin and spread of the disease, their general mistrust and suspicion of whites, and their resentment about being dictated to once again.

3. Overall, as the major element of prevention, *AIDS education has been underfunded, erratic, uncoordinated, confusing, and timid* (Levine, 1991). Numerous AIDS education programs, many of them quite innovative and targeted to specific at-risk populations, have been tried with varying degrees of success, but they have often been implemented without community input or formal planning (House & Walker, 1993).

Social workers should use their community organizational skills for designing a top-down community AIDS-prevention program. They should refine and validate those skills with ideas and suggestions from the literature on community assessment, coalition building, community involvement, and service coordination (e.g., see Barker et al., 1994; Bracht & Gleason, 1990; Bracht & Kingsbury, 1990; Haglund, Weisbrod, & Bracht, 1990; Luepker & Rastam, 1990; Myers, Pfeiffle, & Hinsdale, 1994) and tailor these to the specific task in hand. House and Walker (1993) suggested the following design as a blueprint for organizing an HIV education program:

1. Obtain political commitment from community members.
2. Establish a community education task force.
3. Review existing education information and materials.
4. Identify the high-risk groups targeted for education in your community.
5. Develop, implement, and evaluate a short-term plan of action.
6. Develop and implement a long-term plan of action.
7. Evaluate the program results. (House & Walker, 1993, p. 286)

4. *AIDS prevention work involves challenging and changing social norms and, therefore, community institutions must be made a part of the effort.* As Wolfred (1991) put it, "AIDS educators must be prepared to push social norms and community leaders to new limits in order to stop the spread of HIV infection" (p. 135). Most institutions can be somehow involved directly or indirectly in some aspect of the effort. Social workers should try to make the task force (item 2 in the above list) as broad-based as possible.

The workers should educate the task force about what has been learned from past efforts in this area. The major lessons are as follows:

- A long-term commitment to inform and motivate people to change behavior is needed.
- Programs must be designed to reach all at-risk populations with their specific needs.
- It is necessary to slant messages toward members of specific high-risk groups.
- All AIDS education programs must be culturally and community sensitive.
- Educational programs that merely provide information are not likely to be effective.
- Programs that provide specific tools and techniques for behavioral change are most effective.

- Peers teaching peers will have positive results in both attainment of knowledge and behavioral change (Ostrow, 1989).

The planning of an AIDS prevention and control program will involve the same skills and steps we discussed earlier. Its elements will be as follows:

1. Establishing goals; these may be (a) to prevent HIV infection, (b) to reduce the personal and social impact of HIV infection, or (c) to reduce the AIDS-related fear and stigma.
2. Doing an initial assessment of people's AIDS-related knowledge, behavior, culture, and sources of information.
3. Defining the target audiences by demographic indicators, reference groups, organizations, or risk-prone behaviors.
4. Setting objectives and performance targets on the basis of information from the assessment.
5. Developing (a) messages and materials appropriate for target audiences and (b) channels of communication, institutional networks, and activities that can best attract the attention of target audiences.
6. Promoting and ensuring support services such as counseling, HIV testing, promotion of condoms and spermicide, development and distribution of educational materials, and training of health educators.
7. Deciding monitoring and evaluation procedures and process.
8. Establishing a schedule and budget for the different components of the plan.
9. Reassessing on the basis of any new data on changes in the program, audiences, program impact, and so on. (WHO, 1989)

5. *The importance of assessing, mobilizing, and creating the needed resources cannot be minimized.* The local mass media are a vital resource for any educational endeavor. Social workers should keep in mind that awareness and education also create expectation for services. A health promotion program for AIDS prevention, for example, cannot simply educate people about the risk of unsafe sex. It must ensure that people have access to the wherewithal for safe sex, that testing services are available, and that those who are HIV-seropositive but asymptomatic, those who have AIDS-related complex symptoms, and those who have full-blown AIDS have the necessary counseling, health, and social services. In providing services, targeting the setting should also be considered important. Latkin and associates (1994) examined

the relationships between HIV-related injection practices of drug users and injection settings. They found that injecting at a friend's residence, in shooting galleries, and in semipublic areas and the frequency of injecting with others were significantly associated with the frequency of sharing unclean needles. Social workers' grant-writing skills would be helpful in exploring financial resources. Myers et al. (1994) described the building of a community-based consortium for obtaining federal funds for the treatment of AIDS patients.

Social workers should understand the psychosocial barriers to behavioral change. The relevant barriers include (a) a person's perceived vulnerability for HIV infection, (b) perceived benefits of changing behavior, and (c) self-efficacy (Hayes, 1991). Workers' efforts should address these barriers by convincing the targets of the efforts that they are vulnerable, highlighting for them the benefits of change, and helping them become competent and comfortable in trying new behaviors. Similarly, given the significance of cultural and religious values pertaining to sex-related behaviors, workers should try to understand and work with those values.

In keeping with social work values, the strategy should eschew scare tactics and even hints of moral condemnation. It should incorporate techniques of education, motivation, and enabling for responsible behavior. While working with adolescents for education and behavioral change, the social worker should treat them as grown-ups and at the same time use their propensity for influence by their peers to reinforce their learning and efforts to change. Treating them as responsible grown-ups would demand that, beyond giving them information and facts, they are engaged and encouraged to discuss those facts and to learn about the "what" and "how" of the desired behavioral change.

Social workers as health promoters for AIDS prevention should observe the following "do's" that WHO (1989) called the health promotor's responsibility:

- *Be informed:* Remain abreast of fresh knowledge.
- *Be bold:* Challenge their assumptions about sexuality, find new resources, and work with people previously considered unimportant.
- *Be clear:* Speak plainly, honestly, and directly and avoid ambiguous language, half-truths, and technical jargon.
- *Avoid stereotyping and blaming:* HIV is a virus with no racial, ethnic, or sexual preference.
- *Concentrate efforts on changing the behavior of target groups.*

- *Act on a broad front:* Under people's reasons for maintaining their behavior find acceptable alternatives and provide the resources and support required to introduce the alternatives.

Child Abuse Prevention

The problem of child abuse will persist in the next century, both as part of the overall violence in society and because of changes in the family. Families will become more complex and unstable in their structure and weaker in their social supports and other resources. Both these sets of factors will likely increase the risk of children for abuse and neglect, and the need for efforts to deal with the problem will continue. The U.S. Advisory Board on Child Abuse and Neglect concluded that child abuse and neglect in the United States now represents a national emergency and that the country's lack of an effective response is a moral disaster. It presented 31 recommendations organized into the following eight areas: (a) recognizing the national emergency, (b) providing leadership, (c) coordinating efforts, (d) generating knowledge, (e) diffusing knowledge, (f) increasing human resources, (g) providing and improving programs, and (h) planning for the future (U.S. Department of Health and Human Services, 1990). The validity of these recommendations is not likely to diminish in the 21st century. Social workers have always been a significant part of the efforts to deal with the problem of child abuse and will continue to contribute to all the above areas of activity.

Earlier, I introduced the concepts of "primary prevention," "secondary prevention," and "tertiary prevention."

> In the area of child maltreatment, primary intervention efforts aim to completely avoid the onset of parenting dysfunction; secondary intervention efforts attempt early detection of parenting problems so remediation procedures can be applied; and tertiary interventions are treatment-oriented services designed to rehabilitate maltreating parents. (Kaufman & Zigler, 1992, p. 271)

The primary prevention of child abuse has been the overlooked dimension of the work done in the field of child abuse and neglect. From the beginning, the focus has been on "child rescue," preventing child abuse from recurring. "Although the definitive intellectual history of child abuse has yet to be written, it appears to have taken nearly fifty years before primary prevention was actually embedded in child abuse and neglect program designs" (Rodwell & Chambers, 1992, p. 160). Given the enormity and complexity of the problem, interventions at all levels will continue to be needed, and prevention of recurrence through secondary and tertiary interventions is also of vital importance.

Gordon (1993) proposed a different system of classifying preventive interventions in behavioral/mental health problems, with the focus on who receives the intervention. According to his system, interventions are "universal," "selected," and "indicated," with universal interventions targeted to all segments of the population, selected interventions targeted at high-risk populations, and indicated interventions directed at those already affected by the disorder. The following discussion of social work contributions to the prevention of child abuse includes primary and secondary or universal and selected interventions.

How can the social worker intervene at the primary prevention level? The first requirement is knowledge of the predictors of child abuse. That knowledge does not exist at present. On the basis of an extensive review of the relevant literature, Rodwell and Chambers (1992) concluded that "no set of variables, or combination, does a good enough job of early identification to allow those committed to child protection to speak thoroughly about the efficacy of primary prevention because accurate targeting is practically impossible" (p. 173). They recommended that priority be given to secondary prevention or treatment programs that are effective in limiting the damage of the first abuse incident and/or preventing recurrence.

Although it is true that social work does not have and is not likely to have an empirically validated grand theory of child abuse, considerable work has been done in studying its etiology, and various conceptual frameworks and models have been presented. Belsky's (1980) ecological framework is the most comprehensive and akin to the social work perspective. It conceptualizes child maltreatment as a psychosocial phenomenon determined by multiple forces across four levels: the individual (ontogenetic development), the family (the microsystem), the community (the exosystem), and the culture (the macrosystem).

On the ontogenetic level, Belsky gave characteristics of parents who mistreat their children, such as a history of abuse or experience of stress. On the microsystem level, he discussed aspects of the family environment that increase the likelihood of abuse, such as having a poor marital relationship or a premature or unhealthy child. On the exosystem level, he included work and social factors, such as unemployment and isolation; and on the macrosystem level, he depicted cultural determinants of abuse, such as society's acceptance of corporal punishment as a legitimate form of discipline. (Kaufman & Zigler, 1992, p. 269)

Kaufman and Zigler (1992) extensively reviewed the literature on intervention programs and delineated strategies appropriate for each of the four levels in the Belsky model. The *ontogenetic level* strategies include (a) psychotherapeutic intervention for abusive parents, (b) treatment for abused children, (c) alcohol and drug rehabilitation, (d) stress management skills training, and (e) job search assistance programs. The *microsystems level* strategies include (a) marital counseling, (b) home safety training, (c) health visiting, (d) parent-infant interaction enhancement, (e) parents' aids, (f) education for parenthood, and (g) parenting skills training programs. The *exosystem level* strategies involve the development/establishment or facilitation of (a) community social and health services, (b) crisis hotlines, (c) training for professionals to identify abuse, (d) foster and adoptive homes, (e) informal community supports, (f) family planning centers, (g) Parents Anonymous groups, (h) respite child care facilities, and (i) a coordinating agency for child abuse services. Included in the *macrosystem level* strategies are (a) public awareness campaigns; (b) formation of National Commission on Child Abuse and Neglect (NCCAN) grants for research; (c) establishment of a National Commission on Child Abuse and Neglect; (d) the requirement that states adopt procedures for the prevention, treatment, and identification of maltreatment; (e) a legislative effort to combat poverty; (f) establishment of laws against corporal punishment in schools; and (g) research on incidence of maltreatment and effectiveness of prevention and treatment.

Despite the complexity and multidimensionality of the problem, comprehensive child abuse prevention programs can become a reality with an extensive coordination among health and human service agencies such as hospitals, clinics, child protective services, schools, and public health departments. Their training makes social workers superbly qualified to take the lead in this work. Depending on their work setting, they can contribute to primary and secondary prevention. Those working in hospitals can exploit the special advantage that hospitals have in this respect. As Kaufman, Johnson, Cohn, and McCleery (1992) put it,

The hospital's influence can be viewed at a number of levels. Educational efforts, such as prenatal classes, postnatal instruction and parental skills workshops, are directed towards the community as a whole. In-service trainings provide medical and psychological updates necessary for com-

munity physicians and community mental health providers to offer high
quality educational, diagnostic, and treatment-oriented services. Finally,
prenatal visits, well child visits, annual physicals, and specialty clinics
for chronically ill children represent opportunities for hospital personnel
to intervene at the individual level. (p. 193)

Despite their emphasis on tertiary care, hospitals have been involved
in primary and secondary prevention activities, and these can be further
strengthened. Altepeter and Walker (1992) mentioned several relatively
short-term parent-training programs that can be made available to
parents of all socioeconomic levels. Social workers can be instrumental
in institutionalizing such programs. They can easily help other health
care professionals sharpen their basic interviewing skills to screen
parents of infants and children seen in the hospital outpatient departments by using criteria across the four areas included in the Belsky
model. Belsky (1980) conceptualized child abuse as a psychosocial
phenomenon determined by many forces at work across the four levels
mentioned above. He drew from diverse theories, including psychological disturbance in parents, abuse-eliciting characteristics of children,
dysfunctional patterns of family interaction, stress-inducing social forces, and abuse-promoting cultural values. A system of follow-up of
families at high risk can be built into outpatient services. These
programs should be directed at meeting parent-child needs.

Social workers, whether based in hospitals or as a part of other
agencies, should take a lead or significantly collaborate with others in
building a systematic evaluation of program outcomes into child abuse
prevention efforts. A strong commitment to program evaluation is
needed for improvement and innovation in the field.

There are strong reasons for targeting school-age children and their
families for child abuse prevention work. The developmental period
spanning the ages of 6 through 12 represents the highest risk period for
at least one type of abuse: sexual abuse (Finkelhor & Baron, 1986).
Moreover, most abused or potentially abused children come to the
attention of authorities when they start school. Planning preventive
interventions at this time also takes advantage of the child's (and
thereby the family's) expanding connection with the community. "Even
the most isolated families will need to contend with the myriad changes
brought on by the their child's increased involvement with school and
other community settings" (Rosenberg & Sonkin, 1992, p. 79). Social
workers in public health and those in hospitals with strong community-
oriented health promotion programs can organize school-based child-

abuse prevention programs. Although school-based programs are only part of the answer, and parents, other adults, and potential abusers must also be the focus of preventive efforts, these programs have been found to be helpful. They clearly prompt many victimized children to disclose their abuse. On the basis of a review of evaluation studies of sexual abuse prevention education programs, Finkelhor and Strapko (1992) said that "they certainly rescue many children, who would not have otherwise been rescued, from extremely troublesome situations, and they short-circuit situations which might otherwise have continued for an extended period of time at much greater ultimate cost to the child's mental health" (pp. 164-165).

The prevention and treatment of abuse of adolescents has been a particularly neglected area. "Adolescent maltreatment tends to be associated with problematic acting-out behavior of the teenager or dysfunction with the family, and tends to be dealt with as such by agencies other than protective services" (Garbarino, 1992, p. 105). Garbarino (1992) proposed several hypotheses about adolescent maltreatment and found support of them in the available research literature:

- Prevention programs should target adolescents because the incidence of adolescent abuse equals or exceeds the incidence of child maltreatment.
- These programs should give special attention to female adolescents and the issues they face.
- Some adolescent abuse is the continuation of abuse and neglect begun in childhood; other abuse represents the deterioration of unwise childhood patterns or the family's inability to meet new challenges of adolescence. Programs should take account of these different etiologies.
- Programs in general should reach families across the board regardless of their socioeconomic resources.
- Families with stepparents should be a special target.
- Less socially competent adolescents are at high risk and should be given special attention.
- Programs should adopt a broadly based approach to supporting and redirecting families that tend to be at high risk on the dimensions of adaptability, cohesion, support, discipline, and interpersonal conflict.

These recommendations can be woven into family preservation approaches that are being tried all over the country and are likely to become more popular in the future. Social workers can also help in incorporating these recommendations into school health programs.

The area of child sexual abuse is particularly difficult for preventive work. Determining targets for intervention is all the more difficult because sexual abuse is not strongly linked to demographic factors and because knowledge about the characteristics of offenders is insufficient (Melton, 1992). Finkelhor (1979) conceptualized four preconditions—individual and societal level—for sexual abuse: I. Factors related to motivation to abuse sexually; II. Factors predisposing to overcoming internal inhibitors; III. Factors predisposing to overcoming external inhibitors; and IV. Factors predisposing to overcoming a child's resistance. Most prevention efforts so far have focused on precondition IV. Social workers should keep themselves abreast of the latest research and programmatic work in the field and enrich their interventions with lessons from that.

Whatever setting they are working in, social workers should engage in larger systemic change efforts aimed at effective coordinated involvement of the various societal systems in child abuse prevention. That would require the use of their lobbying skills.

Illness Prevention and Health
Promotion Among the Elderly

In the next century, the elderly will constitute a substantial proportion of the population, and their health care needs will demand special attention. Social workers will realize more and more the importance of preventive work with the elderly as well. Illness prevention and health promotion work focused on the elderly is quite new. For example, public health has turned its attention to older persons only lately. "The Gerontological Health section of Aging and Public Health Association was founded in 1978" (Kane, 1994, p. 1214). Several reasons have been proposed for the past neglect of this work,[2] including the following: (a) The focus of health promotion programs is on extending life, and the elderly are not perceived as having a future; (b) the goal is usually prevention of premature death, and the elderly are considered to be beyond that point; (c) the programs often promote looking youthful and preventing signs of aging; and (d) their focus is on avoidance of chronic disease, which is irrelevant for older adults because almost 85% of them have one chronic disease (Minkler & Pasick, 1986).

This picture is slowly changing. Realization is increasing that people of all ages can benefit form health promotion activities although the progress of illness prevention and health promotion activities for the elderly is impaired by a lack of scientific data. The need for health promotion in the elderly is, however, obvious. The circular pattern of unhappy and unhealthy aging that results *in* and *from* poor nutritional intake, lack of physical and social activity, depression, and chronic disease (Fallcreek, Warner-Reitz, & Mettler, 1986) needs to be broken. Social workers have the skills to create and implement illness prevention and health promotion programs, as well as to contribute to the generation of much-needed knowledge.

Arnold, Kane, and Kane (1986) divided the preventive strategies into two groups: those focused on conditions or disease states, and those focused on specific behaviors that are likely to have beneficial or adverse effects on the disease states. They showed that the elderly have generally been excluded from studies of both these types of preventive strategies.

In planning illness prevention and health promotion programs for the elderly, social workers should do the following:

- Realize that needs of the elderly are manifold and that no agency's own resources are likely to be adequate to meet all needs. Take stock of what and how much their own agency can do.
- Design the program to meet the unique needs of the target population. For identifying and specifying the target population and its needs, do a systematic assessment. I have elsewhere discussed the various approaches to needs assessment. These efforts should be aimed at a twofold purpose: (a) an assessment of the needs and (b) a survey of the relevant community resources. In looking for resources, include both the current and potential resources and define the concept of "resources" broadly. These should include (a) funders, service providers, and volunteers; (b) use of space and facilities and other in-kind contributions; (c) special interest groups such as the Heart Association, Cancer Society, and service clubs such as the Lions Club; (d) local newspapers and other mass media; and (e) experience, skills, and knowledge of the target population itself (Fallcreek et al., 1986).
- Take advantage of existing programs for the elderly. For example, nutrition programs have become a central and permanent part of services under the Older Americans Act. These provide hot, nutritious meals to millions of elderly on a daily basis. These can be used for surveying the needs of the elderly, imparting information about illness prevention and health promotion programs, and motivating them for participation.
- Strive for the best possible match between the identified needs and available resources. Within the overall goals of the program, involve the participants in setting its specific objectives that reflect their existing health status and motivation for change.

- Mix and match the preventive strategies and, in general, aim at the prevention or minimization of functional impairment, rather than at the cure of particular ailments. Select general health promotion activities on the basis of an assessment of the realistically achievable improvements. A multifaceted health promotion program may address physical fitness, safety, nutrition, appropriate use of medication, stress management, and communication skills. Choose a mix of educational approaches and strategies. I discussed several of those earlier in this chapter. Again, try to match the educational strategies to the audiences.

- Use imagination and creativity in planning illness prevention and health maintenance and promotion activities. In Japan, "health notebooks" have been used to aid the aged in managing their health (Gotou et al., 1994). The elderly are given notebooks in which are recorded their concerns, questions, and health data, as well as health professionals' advice, recommendations, and suggestions.

- Make sure that appropriate measures have been taken to legally protect the agency's assets and employees, as well as program participants. These measures include screening participants (through such tools as preprogram health-screening examination), having appropriate liability insurance, and using appropriate release forms. "All participants are required to sign a program release-from-liability form; physician release forms are obtained when possible. Although such measures are not always legally binding, they demonstrate that care and precaution have been taken to provide for participants' safety" (Fallcreek et al., 1986, p. 232).

- Build into the program a strong evaluation component that captures its process, as well as its impact, so that the experience gained adds to the knowledge and skills of the service community.

Social Worker as a Researcher

Evaluation of illness prevention and health promotion programs for their effectiveness and efficiency on a continuing basis will become an absolute necessity in the future. In Chapter 7, I discuss at some length social work's contribution to the various approaches to quality assurance. Here, I briefly discuss areas of health promotion work that should be subjected to systematic research not only for quality assurance purposes but also for building theories and testing intervention models.

Health promotion approaches and strategies can be categorized by the level of intervention—individual, community, and policy. These are based on different theoretical assumptions and models. At the individual level, strategies that deal with both intrapersonal and interpersonal dimensions are based on theories of *social learning and self-efficacy* (Bandura, 1986), *learned helplessness* (Seligman, 1975), *coping* (Lazarus & Folkman, 1984), *social support* (Cassel, 1976), and *consumer information processing* (Bettman, 1979), as well as models such as the *stages of change model* (Prochaska, DiClemente, & Norcross, 1992) and the *health belief model* (Rosenstock, Strecher, & Becker, 1988). Some quite impressive work has been done on individual-level strategies, but much more needs to be learned.

Steckler and his colleagues (1995) suggested that future research should further explore the role of social support and the mechanism of its action; most effective combinations of strategies in comprehensive interventions; approaches to long-term adherence to changed health behaviors; ways of adapting what we already know works to the needs of new and diverse groups; and the impact of emerging learning technologies on individuals.

At the community level, strategies have been built on ideas from theories of *community organization, organizational change,* and *diffusion of innovation,* and interventions have included mediating social structures (e.g., through community coalition building), linking agents (e.g., through network interventions), empowerment, and ecological approaches (Steckler et al., 1995). More research is needed to discover the effectiveness of these strategies in various combinations for health promotion.

At the policy level, there is an obvious neglect of research into effects of the sociopolitical environment on health behavior and health status. As Wallack (1994) put it, "Even though 30% of all cancer deaths and 87% of lung cancer deaths are attributed to tobacco use, the main focus of cancer research is not on the behavior of the tobacco industry, but on the biochemical and genetic interactions of cells" (p. 429). Even researchers in health education, while acknowledging the importance of sociopolitical environmental factors for health-related behaviors, have focused most of their work on factors at the individual level. Future research should be aimed at enhancing the understanding of the nature of social, economic, and political power and ways of influencing the policy processes.

In this work, social workers would use their research-related knowledge and skills to contribute to this dimension of their agency's work. They should strive to design research studies that not only evaluate the efficacy and effectiveness of particular strategies but also test the validity of the underlying theoretical assumptions.

NOTES

1. These techniques include (a) advertising appeals, (b) street and door-to-door collections, (c) silent salespeople (coin-collecting devices in stores and restaurants), (d) "something" for the money: special events, (e) selling services and things (e.g., Girl Scout cookies), (f) secondhand chic (charity-run thrift shops), (g) auctions: live and televised, (h) art shows, (i) fashion shows, (j) other people's homes (showing outstanding homes with such treasures as rare paintings), (k) movie and theater benefits, (l) fun and games, (m) gambling: leaving charity to chance, and (n) walk-a-thon and other "thons" (Bakal, 1979).

2. Reasons given by Arnold et al. (1986) include (a) difficulty in applying the traditional taxonomy of prevention—primary, secondary, and tertiary prevention—to the chronic diseases that the elderly suffer (a condition may be at once a preventable disease and a risk factor for another disease); (b) lack of adequate understanding of the propensity of the elderly to change their behavior for reducing the risk factor; (c) uncertainty of effectiveness of an altered risk factor for preventing the disease; (d) issues of cost and efficacy, which are often hard to demonstrate; (e) the long past-time horizon of the elderly posing questions such as when to intervene, especially when time of exposure to risk is a significant factor; and (f) difficulty in distinguishing between the possibilities of doing good and doing harm.

Chapter 7

SOCIAL WORK IN LONG-TERM CARE

Long-term care, as the term suggests, is care provided over a sustained period of time. It may be continuous or intermittent. Besides the length, the name does not reflect other characteristics of this type of care. It is generally understood, however, that long-term care is not of an acute nature. It differs from acute care not only in its duration but also in the intensity and expected outcome of service. It is not concerned with curing disease or preventing mortality (Weiner, 1994).

Long-term care is concerned with individuals' functional incapacity for self-care, and this incapacity may never be completely overcome. The functional incapacity or impairment might have resulted from any combination of physical, cognitive, emotional, and social factors (Kane & Kane, 1981). Therefore, the need for this type of care cannot be predicted by the presence or absence of a particular medical problem (Malone-Rising, 1994). The care is aimed at reducing the degree of functional impairment and enabling the person to attain the highest level of health and well-being by improving his or her functional ability.

Functional ability is defined in several ways. The general areas of function are physical, cognitive, emotional, and social. *Physical functioning* is frequently viewed as a person's ability to perform activities of daily living (ADL) and instrumental activities of daily living (IADL). Basic ADL include ambulating, bathing, dressing, toileting, and eating; IADL are those necessary to maintain independent living, such as preparing meals, shopping, housekeeping, telephoning, and managing finances. A person's ability to perform these functions is rated as either full, partial, minimal, or nil. It is affected by physical, mental, and social conditions and economic status. The person may be (a) independent, (b) requiring mechanical assistance, (c) requiring personal assistance, or (d) unable to do specific activities (Evashwick & Branch, 1987). Measures of the ability to perform these activities are diverse.

Recipients of long-term care are both the old and the young. They can be categorized into three groups: the elderly, non-elderly adults, and children. The elderly, being at greatest risk of functional disability, form the majority of the users of long-term care. Non-elderly adults needing this type of care are those with long-term disabilities resulting from (a) accidents such as spinal-cord injury, (b) heart attacks and strokes, (c) multiple sclerosis, (d) cerebral palsy, (e) developmental disabilities, and (f) chronic mental illness. Most children requiring long-term care are those with developmental disabilities.

It is difficult to determine precise numbers of those who need long-term care; different sources of data have used different definitions of functional disability and have employed different data collection methodologies. Here, I mention the rising number of the elderly in the United States, most of whom live in non-institutional settings. Depending on the number of functional disabilities they experience, however, the number of elderly needing community-based long-term care would vary. For example, in 1989, 2.7% (848,000) of community-dwelling persons over age 65 were unable to function independently in five or six ADL; 3.5% (1,079,000) had three or four ADL deficits; and 6.5% (1,993,000) had one or two such deficits. Five and one half percent of the total population over age 65 (1,685,000) were in institutional settings (Manton, Corder, & Stallard, 1993).

Disability for non-elderly adults is generally defined in terms of their ability to perform income-producing work. In 1989, an estimated 13.3 million adults (8.6% of the working-age population) were disabled thus defined. The exact percentage of this group needing long-term care is not known. According to Batavia, DeJong, and McKnew (1991), 5% of all adults with disabilities need personal assistance to maintain independence. More than 3.2 million (5.1% of all) children have some type of activity limitation (Kraus & Stoddard, 1989).

The settings for long-term care are numerous and varied: institutions such as nursing homes, "quasi institutions" such as boarding homes, community-based ambulatory program sites, and various other kinds of living arrangements, including foster homes, shared housing, Older Cottage Housing Opportunity (ECHO) units, and the care recipient's own apartment in retirement villages and life care communities, as well as his or her own home within the regular community. It is unclear what even the institutional long-term care settings are and how they differ from each other. As Brody (1977) put it,

> Distinctions are blurred, and different institutional names mean different things to different people in different places at different times. A few of the names used in referring to institutions that provide long-term care are homes for aged, homes or hospitals for chronically ill, nursing homes, geriatric centers, rehabilitation hospitals, county homes, veterans' homes, and psychiatric hospitals. (p. 29)

On the other extreme, ambulatory sites for long-term care include physicians' offices; outpatient clinics; comprehensive assessment clinics—both pediatric and geriatric; day care centers for adults and children with disabilities; day hospitals; mental health clinics; alcohol and substance abuse rehabilitation centers; and senior centers providing wellness, informational, educational, recreational, and social group programs, transportation, and congregate meals. In-home care may include home health; homemaker and personal care services; high-technology home therapy (e.g., kidney dialysis, respiratory care, tube feeding); use of durable medical equipment; hospice, home visiting, and telephone contact services; respite and attendant services; and home-delivered meals. A set of financial programs such as home equity conversion, reverse annuity mortgage, and sale/lease-back programs make more cash available to elderly homeowners and thereby allow them to continue living in their communities.

As is evident from the above discussion, long-term care includes health and social services. Experts do not agree about the boundaries between this type of care and many other service sectors, such as primary health care, mental health, and adult social services (Kane, 1987). This type of care, however, differs from acute care in that it involves such "life choices" as where to live and how to live (Merrill, 1992). Other than one's own home, living arrangements may include retirement communities, senior housing, congregate care facilities, and adult family homes.

HISTORY OF SOCIAL WORK
IN LONG-TERM CARE SETTINGS

As pointed out earlier, long-term care is provided in many settings—institutions, quasi-institutions, outpatient centers, and clients' own homes. The history of social work involvement in long-term care is different in different settings. Because we have focused on the care provided through nursing homes, community residential care settings, and home-based/near home-based programs, we look at the history of social work in these separately.

Social Work in Nursing Homes

The history of social work in nursing homes is not very long. Social workers, like other health care professionals, were rarely involved in nursing homes prior to 1965. The Social Security Act amendments of 1965 led to many changes. The law required hospitals to enter into transfer agreements with extended care facilities, and the provision of social services was included as a requirement for certification for an extended care facility (Clark, 1971). Nevertheless, nursing homes continued to be on the periphery of the medical establishment. Not only did the health care provided to nursing home residents remain of questionable quality, but the psychosocial needs of those residents also continued to be given minimal attention. Legal requirements were met in many ways. Some nursing homes valued social work education and employed social workers with appropriate professional degrees; others hired a "social work designee," someone often without any social work training and experience. These nursing homes contracted with a professionally trained social work consultant to guide the social work designee in attending to the psychosocial needs of the residents. Many nonprofit sectarian nursing homes have employed qualified social workers, even those with master's degrees, whereas many private for-profit nursing homes have tried to do without them (Greene, 1982).

Social work roles and functions in nursing homes have varied vastly. At the one extreme, nursing home social workers may deal mainly with admission-related financial arrangements and coordination of services, organization of recreational activities for residents, and attendance to a resident's very obvious social needs. At the other extreme, social workers' professional skills may significantly affect most dimensions of the nursing home's functioning. They may provide services to the (a) residents, (b) families of residents, (c) nursing home staff, (d) nursing home policymakers, and (e) community in relationship to the nursing home. In the nursing home industry as a whole, social workers in the latter group have been more an exception than the rule. In their study of skilled nursing facilities, Pearman and Searles (1978) identified the above five areas of unmet social service needs. As a conceptual road map for exploring the social work territory in the nursing home world, their findings have as much relevance today as they did 20 years ago. Since then, the psychosocial needs of nursing home residents have been reviewed as part of the quality-of-life issue.

Nursing home reform legislation (Omnibus Budget Reconciliation Act [OBRA] of 1987 [P.L. 100-203]) made the goal of enhancing the quality of life of nursing home residents a part of the national policy. Regulations under that law, implemented in October 1990, require all nursing homes to identify the medically related social and emotional needs of their residents to assist them in the adjustment to the social and emotional aspects of their illness, treatment, and stay in the facility. Every nursing home of more than 120 beds is also required to provide social work services. Variance in the degree and nature of social work as practiced in nursing homes, however, persists.

Social Work in Community Residential Care Settings

Most information about the involvement of social work in community residential care settings comes from the Department of Veterans Affairs' residential care programs; community residential arrangements for deinstitutionalized persons with mental illness, mental retardation, and developmental disability; and foster care for children who cannot live with their natural families. Social workers have played many roles and performed many functions in these programs. On the one hand, they have identified, trained, supervised, and monitored foster care providers. On the other hand, they have created, organized, and supervised foster care and other living arrangements. They are also involved in the working of group homes, sheltered residential facilities, and life care communities in different capacities.

Social Work in Home-Based/ Near Home-Based Care

Given the complexity of home-based/near home-based care, it is difficult to talk definitively about the extent of social work involvement. It has varied considerably. In some settings and programs, social workers have occupied center stage; in others, they have been on the periphery; and in still others, they have been hardly visible. In social service programs for the elderly, social workers have functioned as program planners and organizers; case workers and case managers; and supervisors and pace-setters for paraprofessional and volunteer service providers. In health clinics and mental health centers, they have functioned as psychosocial therapists and service coordinators. In agencies serving people with disabilities, they have provided such services as psychosocial assessment and intervention; case management and coordination; environmental manipulation; and protection from physical abuse, neglect, and financial exploitation. They have helped families of people with disabilities deal with the physical, emotional, and social stress of caring. They have worked with multidisciplinary teams serving people with disabilities and the community at large on their behalf.

Social workers have played these varied professional roles despite the constraints on social work activities imposed by reimbursement rules of various funding sources. In home health care agencies, the social work role has been secondary. Although Medicare conditions for home health agencies mandate that social services be made available to patients, they do not require that a social worker see these patients or be involved in the planning for their care. A nurse usually determines the need for social work intervention. Medicaid-funded programs are even less clear about the role of social workers. There is no uniform requirement that social work services be available to patients, and even when needed, these are not reimbursed by the program (Cox, 1992).

Social workers currently play many professional roles and perform important functions in long-term care. Some roles and functions are likely to persist although they may have to be reemphasized and asserted. Others will have to be assumed in view of the changing situation and needs of long-term care facilities.

FUTURE SOCIAL WORK ROLES
IN LONG-TERM CARE SETTINGS

Chapter 3 identified major needs of the long-term care sector as (a) nursing homes improving their public image, becoming a part of an integrated continuum of services, and extending themselves into the community; (b) community residential care settings increasing their visibility, increasing their resources, and improving their service performance; and (c) home-based/near home-based program agencies improving the overall quality of their care so that their services are appropriate, comprehensive, well-coordinated, and sensitive to the unique situations of their clients. In this chapter, we discuss social work roles geared to meeting these needs.

Social Work Roles in Nursing Homes

It is very likely that as more and more educated, assertive, and hitherto politically active elderly enter nursing homes, emphasis on quality of life will increase. These elderly will demand improvements in services. Hubbard, Werner, Cohen-Mansfield, and Shusterman (1992) described the development of "seniors for justice," a political and social action group of nursing home residents in the greater Washington, D.C., area, and how this not only has given a group of cognitively intact nursing home residents a sense of empowerment and enhanced self-esteem but also has resulted in many other positive changes. In the future, nursing homes will realize the importance of social work skills for dealing with the psychosocial needs of their residents, as well as for intervening at the system level for positive changes. Social workers' involvement with the community on behalf of their nursing home will be like icing on the cake. That involvement will enable them to use their professional skills for, on the one hand, more comprehensive and meaningful work with and on behalf of their clients and, on the other hand, a more effective integration of the nursing home with community health and human services. That integration would enhance the public image of the nursing home. Hence, social workers will play many roles vital for nursing homes in the future.

Social Work Role in Helping Residents
Adjust to the Nursing Home Environment

Even now, most nursing home social workers view helping residents adjust to the nursing home as one of their most important roles although the time devoted to it is inadequate for the residents' psychosocial needs and the workers' professional satisfaction. They know that the decision about placement and the actual entry into a nursing home are difficult experiences for most people. Feelings of loss with the potential for depression, helplessness, and hopelessness are common (Solomon, 1983).

Vourlekis, Gelfand, and Greene (1992) compared the views of nursing home social workers and administrators on (a) psychosocial needs of residents and families and (b) functions performed and expected to be performed by the social worker. Both groups agreed on three of the five top-ranked needs. These three needs were for support/help with (a) transition to the home, (b) feelings of loss throughout the stay in the home, and (c) relatedness and intimacy issues. This finding may reflect the beginning of convergence of different opinions on the appropriate roles and functions of nursing home social workers. In the future, adjustment to the nursing home environment will have many more implications with more end points of placement than is the case currently. Nursing home residents move back and forth between nursing homes and acute care hospitals until they die either in the nursing home or at the hospital. In the future, they will have many more options. Mitchell and Braddock (1990) pointed out that, of the approximately 51,000 persons with developmental disabilities who resided in nursing homes in 1989, 40% needed to be relocated under P.L. 100-203.

Social Work Role in Improving Residents' Relationship With Their Families

The warmth and meaningfulness of human relationships are among the ingredients of quality of life. As the enhancement of the quality of life of their residents becomes an important goal of nursing homes, social workers will assume this role with the aim of increasing meaningful involvement of families in the lives of nursing home residents. It is being realized that families do not abandon their members who are old and disabled when they can no longer care for them at home. The decision regarding the placement of a family member in a nursing home is often as painful for the family as it is for the member him- or herself. Even if the nursing home placement is not abandonment by the family, feelings of abandonment are part of the reality of institutionalization. Beyond the initial crisis of placement, families need help in staying involved in the lives of their institutionalized members. Families in the 21st century will become increasingly more diverse structurally and weaker in their emotional and social resources. Consequently, they will need more assistance, encouragement, and professional direction in sustaining mutually fulfilling relationships with their loved ones in nursing homes.

Social Worker Role in Making the Nursing Home a Therapeutic Community

For maximum impact of social work presence in nursing homes, social workers should go beyond the work with individual residents and their families and contribute to the conversion of the nursing home into what Jones (1953) called a therapeutic community. Social workers are generally involved in dealing with "difficult" residents and families, admissions and discharges, and institutional "crises" and are able to use their professional skills effectively in the resolution of these problems. They can easily add another dimension to that role and make significant contributions to the organizational health of nursing homes and the quality of their services so that these homes do not breed difficult residents and problem situations. This contribution would require addressing three sets of variables: (a) the organizational policies, procedures, and routines; (b) staff attitudes, opinions, relations, and perception of organizational climate; and (c) meaningful involvement of residents and their families.

Social Work Role in Improving the Nursing Home-Community Relationship

For nursing homes to become important elements in the coordinated and comprehensive continuity of health care in the next century and also to improve their public image, they must do some creative and proactive reaching-out work in the community. No other nursing home professional is as well acquainted with the community's health and human services network and as used to coordinating services as the social worker. Besides knowledge of the community's formal and informal resources and of case management skills, he or she also possesses basic community organizational know-how. With little extra imagination and creativity, nursing home social workers can take on this role and make significant contributions to the field of long-term care, as well as to the viability and healthier public image of their institutions.

Social Work Roles in Community Residential Care Settings

In view of our earlier discussion of the needs of community residential care settings, the following social work roles will attain prominence in the future.

Social Work Role in Recruiting Community Residential Care Providers

The search for noninstitutional approaches to the needs of people requiring long-term care will continue and likely will become more essential as families are less able emotionally and financially to take care of their aged members with disabilities. Identification, recruitment, and retention of individuals and families willing to provide this type of care will become an important social work function. With the advantage of their experience in the fields of child welfare and mental health, social workers will be able to take on this role with creativity.

Social Work Role in Training Community
Residential Care Providers

Appropriate training, supervision, and support of those caring for children, adults with emotional, mental, and physical disability, and the elderly is a necessity for the success of community residential care programs. Most care providers have the desire to serve their fellow human beings and the ability to relate to them warmly, but they often lack an understanding of the (a) needs and problems, general as well as specific, of those under their care; (b) appropriate responses to those needs and problems; (c) community resources relevant to those needs and problems; and (d) approaches to accessing those resources.

Social Work Role in Supporting and
Monitoring Community Residential Care

The technical knowledge and know-how of community residential care is important for effective service, but care providers also need appreciation, encouragement, and support from their sponsors, organizers, and employers. Very often, those they serve cannot show their appreciation for the services provided. This is particularly essential in view of the fact that society generally tends to value and reward the least, those who perform the most difficult and unpleasant tasks. Social workers will be able to fill that important gap.

Social Work Roles in Home-
Based/Near Home-Based Care

Social workers will have opportunities to demonstrate their unique skills in response to the needs of the in-home and near-home health care organizations identified earlier. No other professionals are more suited by their training, philosophy, and experience to make significant contributions to the quality-of-care efforts or to deal with such problems as the (a) lack of a holistic view of human problems, (b) inability to devise comprehensive approaches to those problems, and (c) difficulty in providing coordinated services. The following are some ways that social workers can serve these organizations.

Social Work Role in the Organization's Continuous Quality Improvement

The total quality management (TQM) philosophy demands total organizational commitment to continuous improvement in quality of care; an organizational culture that encourages participation by all who use the organization's services; and ongoing feedback from patients, families, and health care practitioners. This patient-inclusive approach, when compared with traditional provider-centered approaches, is one of the greatest challenges presented by the Agenda for Change of the Joint Commission on Accreditation of Healthcare Organizations (Lehr & Strosberg, 1991). The challenge becomes awesome when one considers the nature and structure of in-home care (which make monitoring of quality difficult); the lack of regional, state, or national norms for such care; and the problems encountered in in-home care agencies. The problems include unprofessional conduct on the part of service providers, taking the form of disregard for dignity, autonomy, and independence of the client; tardiness and absenteeism; inappropriate service and inadequate records; drug and alcohol abuse; and theft and fraud. Social workers will be able to contribute positively to the efforts for quality improvement.

Social Work Role in Case Management and Service Coordination

In the future, the recipients of health and human services will be more educated and avid consumers of health care information, aware of their rights, and vocal in their demands. They will not tolerate services that are not appropriate, adequate, comprehensive, and culturally sensitive and proper. That stance will increase the importance of case management and service coordination. Their professional philosophy and training give social workers a holistic view of human problems and comprehensive approaches to those problems. They will have opportunities to demonstrate their superior abilities to perform this role.

SOCIAL WORK
KNOWLEDGE AND SKILLS

Before I discuss the knowledge and skills needed for social work practice in long-term care in relation to the roles identified earlier, I make a few general observations. Earlier, I referred to the person-in-environment as the unique social work perspective and to systems theory as providing a useful model for conceptualizing this perspective. Similarly, the concepts of "enabling" and "empowerment" are operationalized as important elements of social work practice. These are useful for practice in long-term care settings as well. The helping world is discovering the validity of the social work perspective and practice principles. A comprehensive perspective on the client's reality, encompassing both the person and the environment as well as a life span view, is becoming popular. The social work client-worker relationship marked by equality is being adopted by other professionals as the principle of equal partnership between clients and helpers.

Because the major recipients of long-term care services are the elderly and the disabled, social workers should understand the laws—federal, state, and local—that reflect the various policies and service programs for these populations. They should judge these policies and programs by the underlying value that people have a right to services designed to maximize their capacities to meet basic human needs (Brody, 1977). Maslow's conceptualization of human needs can be used to determine, for example, the extent of a nursing home's work toward the improvement of its residents' quality of life in compliance with OBRA of 1987 (Umoren, 1992).

Social workers should recognize that despite the fundamental rights that the elderly and the disabled have as citizens and the policies addressing their special needs, society tends to view and treat these people as less than equal. Often, society's negative view of the aged and the disabled is accepted and believed by the aged and the disabled themselves. They need to be treated as populations at risk.

Within the overall needs resulting from their old age or disability, there are tremendous variations among individuals. Old age or disability does not affect all individuals and their families in a standard way. Numerous variables in myriad ways result in peculiar reactions, situations, and needs of these people. Social workers should be sensitive to the universal as well as the unique elements of their realities and build those into plans for intervention whether in the form of case-level therapeutic work or class-level advocacy.

Although disability affects an individual in many ways, it does not define his or her total being. Social workers should consciously desist from making or accepting such assumptions as the following: (a) Disability is located solely in the biology of persons with disabilities; (b) when a person with a disability faces problems, the impairment causes the problems; (c) the person with a disability is a "victim"; (d) disability is central to the self-concept, self-definition, social comparisons, and reference group of the person with the disability; and (e) having a disability is synonymous with needing help and social support (Fine & Asch, 1988).

Social workers should also be in tune with major developments and philosophical shifts in the fields of chronic physical disabilities, chronic mental illness, and developmental disabilities. Overall, movement has been away from the traditional psychotherapeutic models in favor of educational models (Hirschwald, 1984).

Social Worker as a Helper With Adjustment to the Nursing Home

The nursing home reform law (P.L. 100-203) requires, among other things, that nursing homes assist their residents in adjusting to the social and emotional aspects of their illness, treatment, and stay in the facility. Because improving their public image is the major need of nursing homes, meeting the needs of residents well and acquiring a reputation for that will simultaneously benefit both clients and the institutions. Social work skills are superbly appropriate for both purposes. Here are a few suggestions for social work with new residents in their adjustment to their new environment.

1. *Anticipate the possibility that the cognitively intact elder or person with a disability entering the nursing home has a negative image of the place as a setting for long-term care.* Whether the resident comes from a hospital or from home, the decision about placement in a nursing home is always painful. He or she may also experience a sense of being abandoned by the family.

The decision to enter can trigger feelings of loss, which without intervention often result in depression with concomitants of helplessness and hopelessness. This can happen so easily because the decision to enter is an acknowledgment to self and others of diminished capacity to care for oneself. (Solomon, 1983, pp. 86-87)

2. *View this as a stressful event for the individual and plan on reducing the stress.* Because most nursing home social workers are involved in preadmission planning, it will be comparatively easy to build some stress reduction elements into the preadmission and postadmission protocol. These elements can include a preadmission visit to the family member with a twofold purpose: (a) giving information about the institution, answering questions, giving the person a good feel for the institution in terms of both its pluses and minuses, and suggesting ways of preparing the individual for the move; and (b) obtaining information about the individual and his or her modes of functioning.

3. *Use the information about the person to develop creative ways of making the institutional environment congruent with his or her previous modes of functioning* (Solomon, 1983). Use crisis intervention skills in dealing with the person's transition to the nursing home. Make sure that attention is given to such issues as privacy, possessions, display of family pictures, and decorations in the room. This will give the individual a sense of control. A general demonstration of warmth, interest, and concern on the part of the staff will convey the message that he or she is welcome and is among caring and concerned people. These simple and inexpensive gestures will yield positive results in assisting the person's adjustment.

4. The mastery of adjustment is dependent on the person's ability to mobilize his or her aggressive feelings and to remain active (Solomon, 1983). *Stimulate or support aggressive mobilization of psychological resources so that he or she does not withdraw and fall prey to depression.* The "how" of this stimulation will depend on an assessment of the person's personality, style, and resources. Therefore, do a thorough psychosocial assessment.

5. *Encourage family and friends to visit often and spend more time with the newly placed individual, at least during the first few days and weeks.* Explore family conflict, guilt, feelings of abandonment, and other effects of placement on the family; help them deal with these; and encourage open communication between them and the resident. The aim of this extra effort is to remove psychological hurdles from the path of

the institutionalized member's adjustment, to sustain the family's positive involvement in that member's life, and to win allies in the nursing home's efforts at improving its public image.

6. *Encourage the resident to join group activities.* It is very likely that the nursing home already has some organized group work going on. If not, be instrumental in starting groups that can benefit residents. The therapeutic effects of group experiences are being increasingly realized, and group approaches will become even more popular in the future. Groups are believed to be particularly suitable for work with the elderly because of the advantages of economy, socialization, and emotional validation. Nursing homes can be appropriate settings for innovation in group modalities of social work intervention. Dhooper, Green, Huff, and Austin-Murphy (1993) tested the efficacy of an eclectic group approach to reducing depression in nursing home elderly residents and found the approach effective. Other models have been tried with different groups of nursing home residents. For example, Hyer and associates (1990) applied a cognitive behavioral model to two groups of older people with stress-related problems: recent (adjustment reaction or grief) and remote (post-traumatic stress disorder). Capuzzi, Gross, and Friel (1990) discussed five types of groups: (a) reality orientation, (b) remotivation therapy, (c) reminiscing, (d) psychotherapy, and (e) topic-specific and support groups. Group approaches are being tried even with those who are cognitively impaired, the goal being reminiscence, reorientation, and rehabilitation (Salamon, 1986). The gerontological literature is becoming richer in ideas and suggestions for effective group work (e.g., see Abramson & Mendis, 1990; Fernie & Fernie, 1990; Stones, Rattenbury, Taichman, Kozma, & Stones, 1990).

Here we reiterate the age-old social work practice principles. Social work activity guided by these principles will effectively help a resident in dealing with the transition and adjustment to the nursing home environment:

- *Be honest and open* with the client; people respond to authenticity and genuineness.
- *Start where the client is;* begin with the client's definition of the problem.
- *Maximize the client's choices and options;* there is always room for reducing the "institutional effects" of nursing homes—increasing the degree of privacy, independence, and convenience and decreasing the rigidity of schedules and controls and the extent of isolation from the outside world.

Social Worker as
a Sustainer of
Resident-Family Relationships

Although the family in the future will change in its structure and resources, its meaningfulness for its members will not diminish. Variations based on ethnic, racial, and regional differences will occur in that meaning, however. For most elderly, the family will continue to be a crucial reference point. We have discussed admission into a nursing home as a stressful event for the person concerned. It is also a serious and painful crisis for the family (Dobrof & Litwak, 1977). Even when care for the person at home was stressful and draining emotionally, physically, financially, and socially (Dhooper, 1991), many familial caregivers continue to experience considerable emotional stress and subjective burden after the loved one's institutional placement (Colerick & George, 1986; Pratt, Schmall, Wright, & Hare, 1987; Townsend, 1990; Zarit & Zarit, 1982). Families need help in dealing with the emotional and other consequences of placement of a loved one and in sustaining mutually fulfilling relationship with him or her. Social workers may benefit from the following suggestions:

1. *Keep in mind that, in general, the visibility and concern of the family have a positive effect not only on the mental health of the institutionalized person but also on the quality of care he or she receives.*

2. *Be instrumental in establishing and supporting institutional practices/facilities that encourage family visits.* These may include open visiting hours, coffee shops and lounges for family members to spend time with the resident, encouragement for bringing special food treats, and many open channels of communication between nursing home staff and families (Solomon, 1983).

3. *View the admission of the person as a crisis for his or her family.* Explore the crisis and provide necessary assistance. "The developmental task which accompanies the crisis of admission is that of maintaining close family ties while feeling angry, hurt, afraid of rejection and abandonment, and most of all feeling deeply sorrowful" (Solomon, 1983, p. 90). Depending on a host of factors, the nature and extent of the crisis for each family varies. For families with a history of severe relationship problems, maintaining closeness may be complex and chal-

lenging. Such families are becoming more the rule than the exception, partly because people are living longer and having more time for experiences that are sources of conflicts and alienation.

> In some cases, they [schisms] are about property disputes, with the elderly believing they have been financially mistreated in some business arrangement with their children or grandchildren. In other cases, the conflicts may result from disapproval either by the parents or their children of the other's marriages, divorces, child-rearing practices, career pursuits, smoking, alcohol and other substance abuse, religious choices—the lists are endless. (Harbert & Ginsberg, 1990, p. 136)

In general, family members may feel an element of guilt, whereas the reactions of the person being placed may reflect anger, rejection, and separation.

4. *While assessing the family's situation, reactions, coping style, and resources for adjustment, look for their potential and capacity for sustaining ongoing family relationships* (Greene, 1982). At the same time, acknowledge and validate the enormity of the task before them. Provide and/or procure for family members the needed help from within the nursing home or from outside in the community. The help the social worker him- or herself can provide may include brief casework, education and consultation, mediation between family members and the resident, and an offer of membership in an ongoing family support group, if available.

Families of patients with dementing illnesses such as Alzheimer's disease have special problems of transition when the patient must be placed in a nursing home. Most families have cared for their member at home for 5 to 7 years after the diagnosis (Cheek, 1987) and experienced and adjusted to numerous burdens caused by the member's progressively worsening condition. Morgan and Zimmerman (1990) identified the factors that made the transition from in-home care to institutional care less stressful for spousal caregivers. They clustered these factors into five categories: (a) emotional support, (b) control of situation, (c) acceptability of nursing home, (d) acceptance of situation, and (e) permission/command by an authority figure. Build ideas from such findings into the intervention with these families.

5. *Encourage the family to reminisce together.* Since Butler (1963) first described the therapeutic value of reminiscing, life review therapy has been found to be a viable approach to helping the elderly maintain self-esteem, reaffirm a sense of identity, and work through personal losses. Family reminiscing can also be a powerful method of bringing families together. As Solomon (1983) put it,

> The elderly relative is given the opportunity to be valued in her entirety with strengths as well as weaknesses and dependencies. Younger people are given the chance to learn from the struggles of the past and to preserve those struggles. And for the family, reminiscence becomes the family legacy; it can ensure family continuity; it is the preservation of the past which ensures the future. (p. 94)

Reminiscence is particularly helpful if family members seem not to know what to talk about during their visits.

6. *Take on the responsibility for coordinating activities of all the staff and for helping them incorporate family involvement into the resident's care.* This involvement will add another meaningful dimension to the family's visits. This can be done by regular participation in patient care conferences and sharing the family's needs and concerns, interpreting the behavior of family and resident, and suggesting ways of involving the family in the life of the resident (Dobrof & Litwak, 1977; Greene, 1982).

If the resident is becoming disoriented and confused, the family may find it increasingly more difficult to maintain its interest in visiting. Such families can be taught basic reality orientation techniques. Families thus trained can make their visits with the resident meaningful and also supplement the nursing home staff's efforts to keep the patient alert and oriented. Explore and assist in this form of family involvement.

Family members whose relative is severely disoriented need help. If they come to visit, they experience emotional frustration, pain, and upset, and if they do not come to visit, they feel guilty. On the one hand, they need to know that their visits are important and to hear that keeping their visits short or less frequent is OK. On the other hand, family members visiting the demanding, talkative relative can use help in setting limits without feeling guilty (Greene, 1982).

Social Worker as a Contributor to the Nursing Home as a Therapeutic Community

Helping the nursing home provide a therapeutic environment essential for the optimal quality of life and independent functioning of the residents is one of the social work responsibilities under NASW standards. This can be done through a multipronged approach that includes (a) advocating on behalf of all residents, with the aim of easing stringent organizational routines, policies, and procedures; (b) advocating for and helping residents create and maintain a mechanism for their active involvement in the working of the institution, with the aim of ensuring that their voice influences the organizational policies and practices; and (c) educating staff and administrators, with the following goals:

Sensitizing them to the importance of the residents' cultures for their well-being, with the aim of incorporating aspects of their culture into care

Making them aware of the rights of residents and their social and emotional needs, with the aim of individualizing planned programs for residents

Training them, with the aim of improving their (a) attitudes toward residents, (b) knowledge of the needs of residents, (c) understanding of roles of all involved in caregiving, (d) cooperation and communication, and (e) integration of care of residents (Pearman & Searles, 1978).

The following suggestions are likely to be helpful to social workers in operationalizing the above approach:

1. *Consider themselves as most suited for this role of contributor to the nursing home as a therapeutic community because of the social work belief system and training.* Social workers believe in the people's right to self-determination and self-direction. They have learned how to clearly communicate that belief and to generate a desire to exercise that right. They have been trained to offer people choices, encourage decision making, and stimulate active participation in problem solving. Hence, they should take the responsibility for providing leadership to the facility's efforts to become a therapeutic community.

2. *Share with administrators the emerging literature on the benefits of changing the nursing home's milieu for the residents, staff, and the institutional image in the community.* Residents who are involved in decisions about their care and care-giving policies and procedures reveal healthier and happier attitudes (Blair, 1994-1995). When residents are a part of the decisions concerning themselves, their autonomy

and self-worth are upheld (Lindgren & Linton, 1991), and that has a positive effect on their motivation. That, in turn, makes the work of the staff also worthwhile. It is very satisfying to work with those who are actively involved in their care, are motivated to benefit from the service, appreciate the work being done, and are intent on drawing the best out of the service provider. The residents' participation in the running of the institution further benefits the staff because it leads to a more smoothly run facility (Grover, 1982). Similarly, the interest and energies of families can be a tremendous resource if these are channeled as help in the care of their institutionalized members and for the needs of the nursing home.

3. *Use advocacy skills to motivate or reinforce the administrator and staff in favor of changes.* Share with them the relevant principles and approaches, seek ideas and input, and neutralize resistance. The following are a few examples of strategies:

The hospice ideology has a special appeal for those who work with the dying, and nursing home staff also often experience death. The hospice approach is based on principles that include a *total needs emphasis, increased resident autonomy, a community ideology,* and a *multidisciplinary team orientation* that cuts across levels of staff hierarchy. These principles can be relevant for humanizing nursing home environments (Munley, Powers, & Williamson, 1982).

The health promotion movement has generated principles and techniques that can be applied to the task of motivating and involving the nursing home residents in their care and the life of their "home." Health promotion emphasizes the residents' responsibilities and incorporates their abilities into the management of their disabilities. The social work concepts of "enabling" and "empowerment" have significant relevance for health promotion work.

Resident councils or committees are a popular approach to encouraging the involvement of residents and the creation of a community spirit in a nursing home. Helpful information about how to form these councils and to encourage reluctant residents is becoming available (e.g., see Blair, 1994-1995; Grover, 1982; Miller, 1986).

Group work is used not only for therapeutic purposes with nursing home residents but also for converting nursing homes into therapeutic communities. Whereas therapeutics may be the main purpose of many groups such as activity, art therapy, exercise, humor, movement therapy, music therapy, poetry therapy, reality orientation, reminiscence, and psychodrama groups, these also enrich the lives of residents and thereby change the atmosphere of the place. Various types of discussion, governing, and activities groups can also be organized to create an integrated therapeutic milieu. Johnson, Agresti, Jacob, and Nies (1990) described the history of group work in a nursing home unit of a VA medical center that culminated in an ongoing weekly video program. That program, over time, created *therapeutic persona*—characters that are "outrageous, funny, and ridiculous, yet which represent some unacknowledged common experience of the residents. These characters then serve as the basis for an ongoing series of video skits" (Johnson et al., 1990, p. 209). These authors hold that "the collective awareness of these characters provides an endless source of jokes and kidding during the week and serves to support an environment of intimacy among staff and residents" (p. 216), and that contributes to the building of a therapeutic community.

Adelman, Frey, and Budz (1994) described the process of creating and maintaining the community spirit in a residential facility for persons with AIDS. During the entry phase, the newcomer is assisted through several formal strategies, including a buddy system, an orientation packet, support group meetings, and postentry interviews. The full participation of residents is facilitated through such strategies as weekly house meetings, a three-member elected residents' council, private meetings between residents and the director of the facility, support group meetings, in-house seminars, cultural events, assigned house duties, and the availability of counselors for substance abuse problems and pastoral care. During the last phase, the resident is offered practical, psychological, and spiritual assistance in preparing for death, and others (residents and staff) go through elaborate community coping rituals.

4. *For encouraging families as active members of the lives of residents, a multifold approach is effective.* I earlier discussed approaches to involving families in the planning and implementation of individual care programs, as well as to helping them in sustaining meaningful relationship with their institutionalized member. Family members can also function as volunteers performing important chores within the nursing home or in the community on behalf of the nursing home. It is not uncommon for family members to offer assistance, for example, in such group activities as outings and trips for residents. Volunteers add an important element to the community spirit of the facility. Maximize communication between families and the nursing home. This should be done both formally and informally. One nursing home created a family information center in its main lobby (Conroy, 1994) where official

communications, notices of upcoming events, health and welfare service announcements, and appeals for volunteers were displayed. Orientation and ongoing support groups serve several purposes. These enable
family members to know the place, get acquainted with the staff,
contribute to the care of their member, and understand how they can add
to the quality of the place and its services. Devise arrangements
whereby the contributions of families as volunteers are publicly recognized and appreciated.

Wildon (1994) discussed going beyond "home" and creating a
hometown for generating a sense of community in the facility. Her
nursing homes participate in July 4th festivities. Their efforts yield
impressive results. "More than 20,000 fellow community service members take part in an old fashioned Independence Day complete with car
shows, kid games, local radio and television personalities and dig-
nitaries and fireworks—all on our campus" (p. 9). They also have an
elaborate holiday gift-giving program and other Christmastime activities. Their presents-for-patients program matches residents without
families with people in the community who visit them at Christmastime
and bring gifts ("Conference," 1994). These activities give nursing
home residents and their families a touch of the holidays to which the
whole community has contributed.

There are also other ways of involving the community and expanding
the world of nursing home residents. Identify the community ties that
existed before their admission and reestablish those ties. "Many residents had group associations such as church or synagogue, veterans'
organizations, Golden Age Clubs, fraternal orders, and charitable or
service organizations. Identifying those links to the community can lead
to invitations for them to visit or to arrange for the resident to attend
their meetings" (Brody, 1977, p. 268).

Social Worker as a Community Liaison
and Community Organizer

The strategies of community work that we discussed in Chapter 4 are
equally applicable for assisting nursing homes to extend themselves
into the community. Here, we focus on the social worker's role in
helping the nursing home improve its image in the community. Starting
with the assumption that a good image of an entity depends on its doing
good, looking good, and letting the world know that it is good, the social
worker as a nursing home's liaison with the community can adopt a

multipronged approach. The following are a few suggestions on the "what" and "how" of that approach.

1. *Help the nursing home in the provision of the best possible care that is resident-centered, family-involved, and community-conscious.* I have already discussed some ways of incorporating into their care the wishes and preferences of residents and involvement of their families. Attending to the total needs of residents, understanding and accommodating the needs of families, and involving families meaningfully in the care of their loved one impresses the families, who carry their positive impression into the community.

2. *Mix and match the various strategies to make families believe that the nursing home cares about them and their need to maintain family integrity despite the placement of a member.* Mintz (1994) recommended assessing needs, establishing a "buddy system," starting a support group, establishing a caregiver resource center, inviting families to social events, suggesting a family council, encouraging family involvement with other residents/activities, designating family-staff liaisons, involving families in care planning, and making visiting easier. Build into the admission protocol a requirement for (a) asking every family about its greatest need and expectation for help, (b) processing that information, and (c) planning an appropriate intervention. The answers to most families' needs lie in the already existing services or arrangements.

3. *Survey families of nursing home residents semiannually about their satisfaction with the nursing home services and their suggestions for improvement.* Sample survey forms are available from the American Health Care Association "Quest for Quality" program (Wood, 1994). Also, institute a program for regular follow-up of discharged residents to see how they are doing and whether they are getting the needed community-based services. This follow-up can be done through an arrangement for telephone calls by volunteers. Share the findings of these family surveys and follow-up contacts with care providers at all levels, seek their reactions and suggestions for improvement, and urge management to take the same seriously.

3. *Identify the unmet community needs for which the nursing home has the resources and initiate activities to meet those needs.* The identification of needs can be accomplished informally through ongoing contacts with human services professionals and organizations—contacts regarding the coordination of services for specific clients, or

regarding problems and issues of interest to the local professional community, or through formal needs assessment. In Chapter 4, we discussed approaches to needs assessment. Several areas of need can be explored. Not long ago, the combined efforts of the American Association of Homes for the Aging and the Catholic Health Association of the United States produced a document, *Social Accountability Program: Continuing the Community Benefit Tradition of Not-for-Profit Homes and Services,* that suggests a number of activities for responding to community needs (Trocchio, 1993):

- *Services that can improve quality of life,* such as offering intergenerational recreation programs, providing respite care, becoming part of a communitywide recycling program, and encouraging residents to volunteer in community charitable projects.

- *Services that can improve health status,* such as screening blood pressure and other health conditions and teaching sessions on health promotion and disease prevention at health fairs, providing immunization services, helping with meals-on-wheels programs, and making space available for various self-help and support groups.

- *Services that can improve accessibility to needed services,* such as providing information and referral services for such vulnerable groups as AIDS patients and the elderly, opening an adult day care, offering comprehensive assessment services to the elderly, initiating a physician referral program for physicians who participate in Medicaid, and working with other community groups to provide primary care for the homeless.

- *Services to help contain the cost of health care services,* such as offering free or discounted services to those unable to pay for them, donating unneeded equipment or food to homeless shelters and other programs, and becoming a part of telephone reassurance programs for shut-ins or latch-key children.

- *Services that reach out to minorities, the poor, persons with disabilities, and other underserved persons,* such as opening child care programs for families unable to pay full cost, teaming up with community schools in developing self-esteem programs for children with learning disabilities, providing internships for persons with disabilities from sheltered workshops, making facility vans available to disability groups, establishing an "adopt a grandchild" program with children of single-parent families, and operating a legal clinic for the community elderly.

- *Services that demonstrate leadership and the role of the facility,* such as offering rotations for medical, nursing, and other health professionals; participating in research on innovative ways of caring for patients; participating in efforts to reduce such problems as overmedication among the elderly; sponsoring radio and television talk shows on important issues; and sponsoring such events as a volunteer opportunities fair.

5. *Share with the nursing home administration the information about community needs, their extent, and the potential for the home to extend itself into the community.* The initiation of a new program requires a consideration of many variables, including its financial viability and marketing. Provide meaningful input on many of these variables. Impressive literature is becoming available on the establishment of long-term care services. For example, Henry (1993) described some important do's and don'ts of opening an adult day care center.

Wood (1994) is of the opinion that, for enhancing their image, nursing homes should choose one or two charity groups (e.g., Alzheimer's Association, Arthritis Foundation, feeding the homeless) and assist them by raising money or donating staff time. Many such groups can use the services of social work professionals and the resources of local human service agencies. Be instrumental in the nursing home's involvement in such groups.

6. *Let the public know about the agency's efforts and accomplishments.* This can be done by (a) developing and distributing an annual community benefit report; (b) incorporating community benefit efforts in all the facility's communication tools—newsletters, calendar of events, advertisement, bulletin boards, speeches to community groups, and other reports to the board and the public (Trocchio, 1994); and (c) taking advantage, for publicity, of opportunities that make the facility newsworthy and cultivating an ongoing relationship with the local media. Its innovative programs, community involvement, human interest stories, and special celebrations make a nursing home newsworthy. Make the staff mindful of events that may be of interest to the general public and the media ("Conference," 1994). Create an information file that lists the media (all newspapers, magazines, radio stations, television stations), appropriate contact persons, and requirements (e.g., formats for news releases, preferred type of stories, length restrictions, lead times, and deadlines for submitting items). Invite reporters to cover events or send news items and stories followed by notes of appreciation, provide them with accurate information in usable format, and help them meet their deadlines (Chapman, 1989).

7. *Undertake outreach educational programs targeted at families of potential nursing home residents.* Since the passage of the Patient Self-Determination Act of 1991, nursing home residents (and their

families) are playing a larger role in decisions about their care. By encouraging the use of advance directives, the 1991 act extends the autonomy of patients into the period when they can no longer communicate. In most places, social workers are responsible for giving patients information about the law, telling them about advance directives, inquiring about their choices, and having them sign the necessary papers. However, this is done at the time of admission. "Unfortunately the sheer volume of paperwork involved in an admission meant that patients and family members often may not devote enough attention to such crucial question as who could serve as proxy decision-makers if the resident cannot communicate" (Stoil, 1994, p. 8). Although social workers implement this law, the community education part of its provisions is neglected. The lack of public education and inadequate attention given to this issue at the time of admission results in the family being forced into making a difficult decision in a crisis situation and experiencing conflict with the nursing home. Social workers can minimize these problems and enhance the image of the nursing home by undertaking outreach educational programs targeted at families of potential nursing home residents.

Social Worker as a Recruiter of Community Residential Care Providers

Community residential care facilities are the best solution for those who have no families or whose families can no longer care for them at home and who do not belong in a hospital or a nursing home. The availability of these facilities can also be reassuring to elderly parents unable to continue to care for their middle-aged child with mental retardation. "The knowledge that family life and a sense of stability will go on without a need for institutionalization can also alleviate fears held by the disabled person" (Sherman & Newman, 1988, p. 171). The prospect of going to a familylike environment is also reassuring to the elderly who are ready for discharge from a hospital but who cannot go home and would not want to go to a nursing home. For many old and disabled persons, foster care can at least postpone, if not prevent, nursing home placement. In view of the advantages of this type of care, there is the need for creating more foster care settings for the frail elderly and persons with mental illness, mental retardation, and developmental disability. Although foster care has a long history, the general public does not know of adult foster care. Social workers in hospitals, social service departments, and agencies serving the elderly and persons with mental illness and mental retardation must consider the development and promotion of this type of care as an essential part of their professional responsibilities. Here are a few helpful suggestions.

1. *Explore ways of educating the public about the need for families and individuals willing to provide this type of care and to receive the satisfaction of providing care.* Approaches to public education can range from mass media communication to word of mouth. Discussing New York State, Sherman and Newman (1988) stated that recruitment is primarily by television and radio public service announcements (PSAs), newspaper advertisements, transit cards on subways and buses, and word of mouth. Lawrance and Volland (1988) recruited foster home caregivers through advertisements placed in the classified sections of city and suburban newspapers.

Although newspaper advertisements are not very expensive, PSAs on radio and television are free of cost, and the audience reached is very large. Under the Communications Act of 1934, radio and television stations licensed by the Federal Communications Commission were required to give free time to PSAs, and the time devoted to this public service was taken into consideration when their licenses came up for renewal. During the Reagan administration, that requirement was changed so that radio and television stations are no longer required to air PSAs. Most stations, however, still provide this service. If their agency does not have a public relations department, social workers can take on the job of preparing and having a PSA aired. This involves a twofold action: (a) preparing a statement, rehearsing it, and tape-recording it; and (b) calling the radio station newsroom, identifying oneself, and giving the statement. If the station airs the announcement, send a letter of thanks. If it does not, write and ask why (Klein & Danzig, 1985).

Besides the use of mass media, selling the idea of adult foster care and recruiting of foster families can be done through talks and presentations at churches, offices for the aging, and parent-teacher association meetings (Talmadge & Murphy, 1983). Use creativity and imagination in deciding the "what" and "how" of these presentations so that they are audience appropriate. Stress the benefits of such care for both the provider and the receiver. "Foster family care doesn't require extensive outlays of money for bricks and mortar; rather, it takes advantage of the spare bedrooms of empty-nesters, widows and widowers, and others who can so usefully contribute to the lives of the less fortunate, and in the process enhance their own" (Heckler, 1984).

2. In response to the PSA, newspaper advertisement, or talk given at a meeting or from an acquaintance, some potential care providers will contact the worker's agency for more information. *Express an appreciation for their interest and arrange for an in-person interview with them at their home.* Use the visit to their home for a threefold purpose: (a) giving information about foster care and expectations from the caregiver, (b) assessing the person's values and nurturing skills, and (c) determining the appropriateness and adequacy of the home for accommodating persons with special needs. Give them information about the range of people needing care, the needs of these people in general, the efforts made to match persons needing care and the care-giving family, and the type of support that will be available from the worker's organization and what can be expected from other local health and human service agencies.

The general consensus is that no particular set of demographic variables combines to make an ideal foster care provider. Therefore, look for indicators of such intangible qualities as concern for others, desire to help, urge to give, empathy, and ability to nurture. These may be reflected in the interactions of the potential care provider with children and family members and the responses to questions about the motivation for the new role. With his focus on family foster care for persons with chronic mental illness, Carling (1984) listed the following among those who are usually screened out as care providers: (a) people who depend on foster care for their principal source of income, (b) people with criminal convictions, (c) current service providers (because of potential conflicts of interest), (d) people with other family members not supportive of family foster care, (e) people with grossly inappropriate or unhelpful beliefs, and (f) people who want to be "therapists." Similarly, look for the adequacy of the physical environment and setup of the place, with an eye to its potential for becoming a home for a stranger.

Social Worker as a Trainer of Community Residential Care Providers

Despite their importance, the desire and willingness to take on the role of a caregiver for a vulnerable stranger are not enough for the effective performance of that role to the satisfaction of all concerned.

Training becomes an important variable that can make caregiving a satisfying and successful endeavor. As the professional responsible for training of care providers, the social worker should consider the following suggestions.

1. *Make the training a multipurpose activity.* Training can be used as an extension of the recruitment effort for screening potential caregivers. It should be used for creating and maintaining a positive relationship with the care provider. It should be so structured that various foster care providers are encouraged to get to know each other and to form an informal peer support system. The formal coming together and informal ongoing contacts among care providers thus generated can lead to their organizing themselves as advocates for their needs and for greater recognition of their contribution to the field of health care.

2. *Let the principle of flexibility guide their choice of the "when" and "where" of training sessions.* Make it convenient for care providers to attend as many as possible and also give them incentives to do so. The incentives may be in the form of assistance with transportation, recognition for their service, and coverage of care during their absence from home (Carling, 1984).

3. *Make the content of the training appropriate for the care-giving role.* Important variables that should be considered include the needs of the residents whom these care providers are or will be caring for, their educational background, their health-related knowledge, and their caregiving experience. It is wise to do a simple needs assessment and make that the basis for topic selection. The topics generally considered essential for such training can be clustered into the following groups:

- *Safety and crisis care:* home hazards and accident prevention, first aid and emergency assistance
- *Drug management and medical treatment:* administration of medication, effects and side effects of medications, common diseases (e.g., in the elderly), signs of illness, infection control, and medical follow-up
- *Food and nutrition:* basic nutrition and special diets
- *Activities of daily living:* basic personal care, use of adaptive equipment and aids, client independence, and realistic expectations
- *Issues related to chronic illness and aging:* experience of losses (sensory and social), depression, mental confusion, aging process, behavioral aspects of mental illness, and death and dying

- *Caregiving and help seeking:* stresses of caregiving, effects of caring on the family, dealing with stress, problem solving, and using community resources (Carling, 1984; Oktay & Volland, 1981; Sherman & Newman, 1988; Sylvester & Sheppard, 1988)

In the foster care program for the frail elderly developed by the Johns Hopkins Hospital, the training lasted a week, and at the end of the training course, "potential caregivers were tested on items such as patient's personal care, diet, common illnesses, CPR, psychosocial and emotional needs. Those who passed the test were ready to be matched with an appropriate patient" (Lawrance & Volland, 1988, p. 28).

4. *Involve professionals with knowledge and expertise in the areas to be covered in the training.* For hospital-based social workers, it is not likely to be difficult because all professionals are directly or indirectly interested in early and appropriate discharges of patients and will be willing to contribute to the development of new residential care facilities. Social workers not associated with hospitals will need to use their contacts with human services professionals in the community to stretch the resources of their agency for training.

Social Worker as a Provider of Support and Monitor of Quality of Care

Provision of ongoing support is a necessity for the success of long-term care. When a family begins taking on this responsibility, the need for support is extensive. Vandivort, Kurren, and Braun (1984) considered the first three months crucial. During this period, the caregiver is adjusting to a new role, and the resident is adjusting to a new environment. This support can take the form of (a) the worker's frequent visits (at least once a month), (b) easy availability between visits, (c) help in identifying and articulating the resident's needs, (d) assistance with designing a plan for care, (e) linking the caregiver with other sources of services for the resident, (f) quick and appropriate response to crisis situations, (g) aid in organizing and keeping the minimal record of care expected or required by the state certifying or licensing agency if applicable, (h) arrangements for respite and backup care, and (i) periodic retraining or refresher programs.

1. *Mix and match the various forms of support to address the specific needs of care providers.* Let the principle of individualization of people,

their needs, and circumstances guide the selection and combination of the various modes of support.

2. *Handle the crisis situations carefully so that the crisis becomes a source of new insight, strength, and positive change.* View the client, other residents, and the care provider as all in "crisis" during an emergency and conduct a "postincidence" evaluation to identify what could have predicted the crisis and what could be alternative responses (Carling, 1984).

3. *Remember that quality of support is often more meaningful and helpful than its quantity.* Try to convey the message that staff are there to strengthen the care provider's commitment and ability to care and that the caregiver, the resident, and the worker are a team bent on deriving the best results from the joint effort.

4. *The quality of care will depend on the combined effect of training, support, and other factors,* such as matching of residents and caregivers and continuous monitoring of the care arrangement. Matching is a difficult task, particularly in the beginning, when there is no good intuitive feeling for the care provider and his or her home. Until the social workers get to the stage in their relationship with the care provider that they know what type of resident would fit into that provider's home, it will be helpful to (a) solicit from the care provider information about what type of resident would be ideally desirable; (b) share with the care provider as much information about the prospective resident as possible, while protecting the need for privacy and confidentiality; (c) give the prospective resident a clear picture of the foster home; (d) arrange for the care provider to meet the client/patient in the hospital; (e) arrange, whenever possible, for the visit of the prospective resident to the caregiver's home to give both a chance to decide whether the arrangement is suitable (Sherman & Newman, 1988); and (f) consider as many as possible of the following prospective resident's characters and preferences:

Personality characteristics
Social interests
Personal habits
Gender
Race
Religion
Cultural factors

Smoking
Pets
Children
Location
Medical needs
Mental health needs
Rehabilitation needs
Support service needs
Alcohol/drug problems
Wheelchair accessibility (Carling, 1984)

Assurance of quality of care in a safe and healthy environment will result from several efforts. Use follow-up visits to the foster home for providing support and giving necessary direction and supervision to the caregiver. In one study, Sherman and Newman (1988) found that about two thirds of care providers considered personal follow-ups beneficial to both residents and provider. The visits should be scheduled as well as unscheduled.

Review the resident's progress and care plan periodically and modify it in view of his or her changing condition and needs, if needed.

Get to know the residents well enough for them to talk candidly. They can add to the validity of impressions about the quality of care and the success of placement.

Most residents are likely to have health care needs requiring the services and involvement of several agencies and professionals. Act as the case manager and use the opportunities provided by that role to monitor the effectiveness and efficiency of the foster home as part of the total package of care.

5. Because adult foster care has no uniform licensing standards (Oktay, 1987), *push for the certification of family foster care in the state if it does not license or certify this type of care.* Most presenters at a workshop on family foster care favored "a 'certification' approach in which States or local agencies had flexibility in decertifying providers, viewing the certification as a privilege, rather than a right" (Carling, 1984, p. 15).

6. *Encourage the caregiver to join a professional group,* such as the National Association of Residential Care Facilities. Membership in an organized group can be a source of heightened morale, pride and

professionalism, support and strength, and training. Professionalism provides a self-propelling force for commitment to providing for high-quality care.

Social Worker as a Contributor to the Agency's Continuous Quality Improvement

Before we discuss the knowledge and skills necessary for social workers to assume this contributor role, let us briefly look at the concept of "continuous quality improvement" (CQI) and its methodology. This concept was developed in the 1930s by W. Edwards Deming and Joseph M. Juran and was originally implemented in manufacturing. In the late 1980s, its relevance to the health care industry began being realized (Balinsky, 1994), and as O'Leary (1991b) explained, "American industry is *a,* if not *the,* major purchaser of health care. And like any good American group, they are quickly deciding that what is good for them is good for you as well. In this case, I would suggest that they are right" (p. 72). *Quality assurance* (QA), the approach to quality in health care until then, was punitive in its mind-set, outlier oriented, inefficient, and frustrating. In contrast with QA as a "blame-fixing" activity, CQI is seen as an organizationwide way of life (O'Leary, 1991b). QA separated *production* (the service-providing unit) from *inspection* (the QA department), and *responsibility* for quality (the QA committee) from *authority* (the service). This separation (a) undermined teamwork, (b) delayed feedback, (c) increased cost of data collection, and (d) communicated a less than total organizational commitment to quality (Eskildson & Yates, 1991).

Quality in health care is a multifaceted and multidimensional phenomenon. Dimensions include accessibility, appropriateness, effectiveness, continuity, efficacy, and efficiency of care. Quality is also the safety of the care environment, acceptability of care as judged by the patient and family, as well as the qualitative interactions between patient/family and care providers (Balinsky, 1994; O'Leary, 1991a). It is believed that CQI will positively affect all facets and dimensions of quality. Eskildson and Yates (1991) considered TQM a new paradigm:

> Important components of the new paradigm include commitment to an unrelenting focus on customer satisfaction, continuous improvement, employee involvement, "management by fact" (including the use of statistical process control), effective internal and external teamwork,

emphasis on prevention (rather than inspection), cycle-time reduction, and widespread staff training in multiple areas affecting quality. (p. 38)

The basic principles of TQM according to Deming (1986) are as follows:

1. Create constancy of purpose for improvement of product and service.
2. Adopt the new philosophy of doing things right the first time.
3. Cease dependency on inspection to achieve quality.
4. End the practice of awarding business on price tag alone.
5. Improve constantly and forever the system of production and service.
6. Institute training on the job.
7. Begin leadership for system improvement.
8. Drive out fear; create trust.
9. Break down barriers between staff areas.
10. Eliminate slogans, exhortations, and targets for the workforce.
11. Eliminate numerical quotas for production; institute methods for improvement.
12. Remove barriers to pride of workmanship.
13. Institute a vigorous program of education and self-improvement for everyone.
14. Put everyone to work to accomplish this transformation.

The technology of CQI involves the use of the following:

1. *Teams*—these are of three types: (a) cross-functional improvement teams, (b) quality circles, and (c) process improvement teams (Keys, 1995).
2. *Methods* such as Plan-Do-Check-Act or Plan-Do-Study-Adjust cycle and benchmarking involve identifying the best practices, studying their application, and applying them (McCabe, 1992).
3. *Supportive infrastructure*, which is created through vertical alignment, horizontal process management, and independent assessment (McCabe, 1992).
4. *Statistical tools* such as a flow chart, cause-and-effect diagram, control chart, and Pareto diagram (Burr, 1990; Sarazan, 1990; Shainin, 1990).

Social workers in home-based and near home-based long-term care agencies should seize the opportunity offered by the need of these agencies to move toward CQI and provide leadership to their efforts. They have an edge over professionals from many other disciplines.

Applying their existing skills or building on them will ensure their readiness for the job. Their basic team-building and teamwork approaches can easily be adapted for CQI. The Plan-Do-Check-Act cycle is similar to the problem-solving process that they have thoroughly grasped and practiced. Their understanding and skills for organizational work can help their agency become supportive of the CQI philosophy through structural and procedural changes. Methods of vertical alignment and horizontal process management can be incorporated into their organizational skills. Brushing up on their knowledge of statistical data display techniques would enable them to use the appropriate statistical tools for CQI. The following are some helpful suggestions.

1. *Consider the patient in the same way as a customer is in industry.* The application of the TQM approach to health care requires this, with regard to quality.

> Quality is a customer determination, not a engineer's determination, not a marketing determination or a general management determination. It is based on the customer's actual experience with the product or service, measured against his or her requirements—stated or unstated, conscious or merely sensed, technically operational or entirely subjective—and always representing a moving target in a competitive market. (Feigenbaum, 1983, p. 7)

2. *View and involve clients as active partners in the quality improvement work.* This task is difficult in health care because, traditionally, quality is defined by the provider. A distinction is made between the technical and interpersonal aspects of health care to limit the patient's involvement in quality assessment. It is assumed that the patient is unable to understand the technical aspects of care (Lehr & Strosberg, 1991). This situation will gradually change as, on the one hand, clients become better educated consumers of health care services, more informed of health care techniques and procedures, more demanding of choices and options, and more conscious of their rights, and on the other hand, health care providers start acknowledging and appreciating the role that patients, their families, and other informal helpers play in the recovery and/or management of patients. Social workers should realize the advantage they have over other professionals. They have been trained to treat their clients as equals, and educating and empowering them are the major social work approaches to enabling clients to exercise self-determination, solve their problems, and manage their lives.

3. *Help agencies institute a threefold approach to involving clients in the continuous quality improvement endeavor:* (a) service protocols that require client input into all aspects of care; (b) continuing education for professional and paraprofessional service providers on techniques of encouragement, involvement, and empowerment of clients; and (c) ongoing supervision and support for service providers in the field. Besides these organization-level contributions, social workers should monitor their clients as part of the quality improvement work of the agency.

4. *Recognize that, for CQI, all parts of the organization—service management, as well as maintenance management—are equally important.* The spirit of quality not only should be visible in the clinical and technical services but also should pervade the total organization. Studies by Bowen (1985) found that (a) a strong correlation exists between customer and employee views of service quality and the internal climate for service; (b) when employees view favorably an organization's human resource policies, customers view favorably the quality of service they receive; (c) a positive work climate directly affects customer service for the better; and (d) human resources is an excellent vehicle for satisfying both employee and customer needs.

The concept of "customer" is much broader in TQM philosophy. It applies internally as well as externally. External customers for a home care agency include patients, families, payers, volunteers, and the community. All employees of the agency are its internal customers. All persons and units function as both "producers" and "customers" at every level and in every process of an organization (Re & Krousel-Wood, 1990). Involvement of both external and internal customers is necessary for CQI. Feedback mechanisms should be developed for different groups of external customers. Constant effort should be made not only to involve the internal customers but also to develop their full potential. This can be facilitated by such enabling principles as (a) setting clear expectations; (b) maintaining skills and providing resources; (c) providing feedback as a learning tool; (d) granting authority to act; and (e) providing encouragement, support, and recognition (McCabe, 1992).

The creation of a culture of quality and a supportive infrastructure is extremely important for CQI. Social workers can contribute to this task as advisers, technical experts, and team players. The following are a few helpful strategies.

1. *The agency must develop a definition of quality that is meaningful for and is understood by everyone.* Management must emphasize that quality improvement is an ongoing effort and look for opportunities to demonstrate its full support for quality (Sahney & Warden, 1991). Although TQM is a participatory and decentralized approach to quality, the involvement of management must be intense and in detail in top-down priority setting and modeling (Eskildson & Yates, 1991; Kaluzny & McLaughin, 1992).

2. *Identification of problems should be considered an opportunity for improvement and not a means for laying blame.* "Long-range thinking and planning should replace the focus on short-term results" (Sahney & Warden, 1991, p. 9).

3. *Vertical alignment will aid in the creation of a supportive infrastructure for quality.* Vertical alignment means that everyone in the agency from top to bottom understands what the agency is trying to accomplish and how he or she fits into the big picture. This shared understanding becomes possible through the linking of goals, plans, and responsibilities from the top through all departments to each individual (McCabe, 1992). All goals, plans, policies, and procedures should aim at supporting the agency's mission. Constant efforts should be made for improving communication throughout all levels of the organization and increasing opportunities for meaningful involvement of all employees.

4. *It is better to focus on important processes involved in the agency's work than on the people in those processes.* Horizontal process management is aimed at improving the processes. As processes cut across departmental boundaries, this is best accomplished by a team of process implementers. "The team must be given the responsibility and authority to define and control its processes, to assess performance of the processes, and to modify the processes based on assessment findings" (McCabe, 1992, p. 137). This strategy has been presented as a 9-step methodology:

1. Find a process to improve.
2. Organize a team that knows the process.
3. Clarify current knowledge of the process.
4. Understand source of process variation.
5. Select the process improvement.
6. Plan a change or test.
7. Carry out the change.

8. Check and observe the effects of the change.

9. Accept, adopt, or modify the plan (James, 1989).

5. *Keep abreast of the literature on the implementation of CQI in the health care field.* Many hospitals and other health care organizations are making impressive efforts in this regard (e.g., Dimant, 1991; Graves & MacDowell, 1994-95; Re & Krousel-Wood, 1990; Sahney & Warden, 1991). It would be wise to learn from their experience.

Social Worker as a Case Manager and Service Coordinator

Case management is likely to continue to expand in a variety of delivery systems. Social workers should seek jobs in home-based care agencies, as well as in near home-based service agencies. In the former, they will be able to take on case management responsibilities; in the latter, they should apply their case management skills to such jobs as agency director, program planner, and direct service provider. They should keep themselves abreast of the emerging literature on the "what," "why," and "how" of long-term care case management. For example, Gerson and Chassler (1995) described a 15-month project to develop case management practice guidelines. A national advisory committee was created that formulated several basic principles of case management.[1] Some case management strategies were presented in Chapter 5. Here, we discuss more ideas regarding case management that are likely to be helpful.

Despite its popularity, case management lacks precise definition. There is no consensus on its exact nature and purpose. It can be viewed narrowly or widely. "It can be a gatekeeping mechanism to control costs and access; it can be an advocacy function to increase access to services and navigate a confusing array of services; or it can serve a diagnostic and prescriptive function" (Williams, 1993, p. 7).

Starting with the assumption that the underlying structure of a program's financing has a fundamental impact on its services, Applebaum and Austin (1990) identified three models of case management: (a) the broker model, (b) the service management model, and (c) the managed care model. Case managers under the *broker model* do not have service dollars to spend on behalf of their clients. They develop care plans and make referrals for services from the existing service system. Under the *service management model,* case managers have access to funds, develop care plans, and authorize services within the predetermined cost caps. The *managed care model* is based on prospective financing that creates "provider risk": Financial responsibility and liability for expenditures are shifted to provider agencies. This puts pressure on the care planning process, creating incentives for the provider to control cost. Social workers should make their understanding of these models of case management serve their agency's mission and program objectives. We have discussed social work role in managed care in Chapter 8. Here, we focus on the broker model of case management.

The most generally accepted components of case management are (a) eligibility determination—financial, medical, and other; (b) level of care determination; (c) assessment of needs, including medical, physical, functional, and psychosocial; (d) place of care determination; (e) care plan development; (f) service prescription or arrangement; (g) coordination of services from multiple providers; (h) budget planning for service units, time periods, or episodes; (i) reassessment of needs; (j) monitoring of delivery and quality of service; and (k) support to family (Williams, 1993). Not all programs incorporate all these functions. In home care programs, for example, the typically covered functions are assessment of needs, planning of appropriate services, ordering or provision of services, monitoring and evaluation of services, and reassessment of the need situation.

Home care programs are offered by many agencies—home health agencies, multiple service health care providers, free-standing case management agencies, and Area Agencies on Aging. Home health agencies provide nursing and other skilled services, such as physical, occupational, and speech therapy and home health aide services. On the one hand, they have historically used a community health nursing model, in which the nurse goes into the home and family setting and performs the assessment, care planning, advocacy, and other roles. On the other hand, Area Agencies on Aging have traditionally focused on social services, meals-on-wheels, senior activities, and advocacy to the exclusion of health services (Williams, 1993). Social workers should recognize the inherent deficiencies of these models. They should make concerted efforts to move toward a model that combines and coordinates a wide array of health and social services. The integrated health/social service model (Brody, 1977) can be a good guide. That model includes the following services:

- *Maintenance services* include income maintenance and personal maintenance. Income maintenance is secured through such programs as Supplemental Security Income, Social Security, Veterans' Benefits, Workers Compensation, and Food Stamps. Homemaker service, home-delivered and congregate meals, and chore services constitute the personal maintenance services.
- *Personal care* is provided through the services of home-health aides representing many public and private health care agencies.
- *Supportive medical services* include nursing; physical, occupational, and speech therapy services generally provided by hospitals; health clinics; public health departments; and visiting nurse organizations.
- *Personal planning* includes counseling, advocacy, community resources mobilization, and protection services provided by social workers through family service agencies, state social services organizations, community mental health centers, and home health care and vocational rehabilitation agencies.
- *Linkages* include such services as information and referral, transportation, outreach, telephone alert, and friendly visiting services.

Even single agencies can offer packages of the needed health and social services. In some areas, the Area Agencies on Aging are capable of running comprehensive long-term care programs, and some home health agencies have broadened their scope by including services unrelated to health.

Social workers should consider the following principles of case management proposed by Williams (1993):

- *Only certain individuals should be case managed.* This service should be offered only to those who need it. Possible criteria for selection are (a) high risk because of physical and cognitive impairments and lack of family supports; (b) eligibility for nursing home level of care but electing community-based care; (c) complex care needs; (d) short-term posthospital care needs; (e) high-cost care needs; and (f) high risk for repeat hospitalization.
- *Assessment of service needs and case management are related.* Separating assessment from case management functions is likely to create confusion, delays, and duplication.
- *Case management has multidimensional requirements.* An interdisciplinary approach to staffing is needed. At a minimum, medical and social services must be available; other consultant services could be contracted for.

- *Case management is a team effort.* Links with many types of community agencies, including hospitals, housing providers, meal providers, and others, must be forged.
- *Equity assurance is important in case management.* Services must be distributed equitably among similar clients. "A major goal of case management should be to serve the neediest and spread available resources to do so in a judicious way" (p. 27).
- *Cost control is part of case management.* Incentives for controlling costs must be built into the system.
- *Quality assurance is essential.* Quality assurance mechanisms should be made an integral part of both case management and services. These may include the use of standardized, specific, and generally understood criteria, supervision, and quality reviews.

The broker models of case management, which emphasize referrals and linkage, generally within one service sector, are most common in long-term care settings. Even these models are very often provider-driven, rather than client-driven. Rose and Moore (1995) brought out the differences between the client-driven and provider-driven approaches. Whereas one (client-driven approach) views clients as subjects, the other (provider-driven approach) views them as objects; one looks for strengths to develop, the other identifies problems and pathology to manage; one seeks active participation, the other encourages compliance; the goals of the one are positive direction and self-confidence, and those of the other are improved patterns of service consumption and patient role behavior; the needs assessment is derived in one from the client's direction, plan, and goals, in the other from the service provider's definitions and outputs; resources to be linked are seen in one as the total community with all its formal and informal networks, and in the other as existing formal service providers; monitoring in one involves mutual evaluation of process in relation to direction plan, and in the other compliance with treatment plan; and evaluation in one emphasizes increasing autonomy, growing self-confidence, and involvement with informal networks, and in the other increased units of service consumed, use of fewer inpatient days, and improved compliance. Because of their philosophical orientation and as a result of their professional training, social workers are most suited to practice client-driven approaches to case management. They should make sure they are seen as the model, as well as a source of formal and informal training, for client-centered and client-driven approach in the agency.

In Chapter 5, we discussed strategies and techniques of brokering. Here, we reemphasize that social workers should (a) keep an updated directory of all the formal and informal resources in their community; (b) know the agency eligibility criteria for benefits and services from all the formal sources of assistance; (c) keep themselves abreast of legislation and regulations that are likely to affect policies and procedures of major agencies and programs; (d) develop an awareness of such characteristics of major agencies as the degree of flexibility in accommodating client problems (some agencies are extremely formal and rule-bound, whereas others are willing to bend the rules); (e) get to know the contact persons in as many resource agencies as possible; and (f) become involved in the community.

> Join a service club, participate in community meetings, sit in on city council meetings, or attend major community events (pancake day, fireman's chicken dinner, Fourth of July celebration, etc.). These activities will increase your knowledge of community resources and enlarge the circle of people you can call upon in times of need. (Kirst-Ashman & Hull, 1993, p. 497)

Although the case manager's role involves brokering, case management is more than brokering. The client's needs may require more services than are brokered for. The case manager must ensure that those needs are met effectively and efficiently. A commitment to the following principles articulated by Gerhart (1990) would be helpful.

- *Individualization of services* requires that services be developed or designed specifically to meet the identified needs.
- *Comprehensiveness of services* means that the services address needs in all areas of the client's life.
- *Parsimonious services* means services that are well-coordinated, unduplicated, and cost-effective.
- *Fostering autonomy* requires that services and the way they are provided encourage maximum client self-determination.
- *Continuity of care* demands that case management services monitor the client's needs as he or she moves through different settings of care—institutional and community.

Social workers as case managers should show special sensitivity to the needs and situations of families that care for the elderly and the disabled—the focus of case management. Family caregivers live 24 hours a day, 7 days a week with their caregiving responsibilities, struggling to balance their own needs and those of the ones they care for. Caring for a chronically ill person takes its toll in the form of such problems as family disruptions, psychological stress, physical fatigue, social isolation, financial and at times legal difficulties (Dhooper, 1991), as well as intrafamilial conflict. With her focus on the effects of Alzheimer's disease, Gwyther (1995) described four types of family caregiving conflicts: (a) normative conflicts around the limits of family solidarity; (b) conflicts arising from family members' disapproval of other members' action or attitude toward the patient; (c) conflicts from disagreement over the nature and seriousness of the patient's impairment and the most appropriate care; and (d) conflicts from perceptions that less involved family members either do not appreciate the extent of demands on the primary caregiver or disapprove of the quality of care being given. They should assess the total familial situation and appropriately address the conflicts, problems, and stresses that a family may experience.

NOTE

1. The National Advisory Committee identified the following principles:

   Case management is a consumer-centered service that respects consumers' rights, values, and preferences.

   Case management coordinates all and any type of assistance to meet identified consumer needs.

   Case management requires clinical skills and competencies.

   Case management promotes the quality of services provided.

   Case management strives to use resources efficiently (Gerson & Chassler, 1995).

Chapter 8

THRIVING IN HEALTH CARE

In this chapter, I present strategies, based on an extensive review of the literature, that are helpful in enhancing social worker effectiveness and efficiency. Most social workers can easily acquire and refine these strategies. As in any host setting, social work in health care is strenuous. It involves not only providing social work services to clients but also constantly educating others and demonstrating how social work contributes to the setting's overall function, helps fill the gaps in its services, and enriches the quality of those services. "Whether the practice domain be a hospital, a clinic, the legislative or public health district, an HMO or a shelter, the health social worker is constantly moving on a moment's notice between potentially conflicting roles, statuses, functions, and contexts" (Dillon, 1990, p. 91). The strategies for thriving in health care have been clustered into two groups: worker-focused strategies and other strategies.

WORKER-FOCUSED STRATEGIES

Stress Management

The stressfulness of social work in health care settings is a major reality that must be acknowledged and dealt with. Otherwise, this stress tends to result in burnout. Stress is influenced by a host of factors, including genes, events, lifestyle, and attitudes. Whereas one may not have much control of the genetic factors, one can alter one's lifestyle and attitudes and can similarly change the stressful events and/or modify one's perception of them. Various models for understanding and management of stress have been proposed. For example, Meichenbaum and Jaremko (1983) hold that stress lies neither in the individual nor in the situation, but rather depends on the transaction of the individual in the situation. It occurs when the demands of the situation exceed the needed resources of the individual for dealing with the situation.

A manifold approach to stress management would yield the best results. It should include an assessment of the stressful situation and one's resources and should aim at developing skills appropriate for preventing, preparing for, and responding to stress. The following are a few helpful suggestions. Social workers should:

- *Take an inventory of their attitudes and consciously work on modifying the ones that are unhealthy, unhelpful, and dysfunctional.*
- *Look at their lifestyle critically and incorporate into it on a regular basis (a) some exercise, (b) some recreation, (c) some relaxation, and (d) an appropriate, nutritious diet.* These strategies have significant preventive and preparatory stress management relevance. The literature—both popular and professional—on the "how" of these strategies is enormous and rich. Techniques abound. For example, relaxation techniques include deep breathing, progressive muscle relaxation, imagery, meditation, self-hypnosis, and biofeedback.
- *Leave their work at the office and not let work-related stuff clutter their personal life.* At the same time, they should attend to the potential or present stresses in their personal lives because these tend to deplete their energy and adversely affect their ability to deal with work-related stress. Improving interpersonal communication, problem solving, using social skills, and seeking professional help, if needed, are appropriate measures.
- *Identify major situational factors that cause stress and devise appropriate strategies to deal with them.* Dillon (1990) listed several of these, including (a) existential stressors, (b) team stressors, (c) sex role stressors, (d) membership stressors, (e) family influences as stressors, and (f) vulnerability (because of the relative unimportance of psychosocial functions) as a stressor. Some of these require renewed commitment to social work mission and values, others the improved professional skills, others the creation or strengthening of formal and informal support systems, and still others organizational work aimed at improving the status of the social work department or unit.
- *Build a support group of colleagues or friends who can understand and relate to their frustrations.* Mix some enjoyable activity with the sharing, ventilation, and problem solving within the group.
- *Consciously try to recognize how they respond to stress.* The beliefs people hold about themselves and the world around them also affect their responses to stress. De-emphasize beliefs that are unrealistic and that have the

potential for creating or adding to stress. Klarreich (quoted in DiNitto & McNeece, 1990) identified 13 such beliefs, including (a) something terrible will happen if I make a mistake; (b) it is awful to be criticized; (c) people in authority should not be challenged; (d) life must be fair and just; (e) I must be in control all the time; (f) I must anticipate everything; (g) I must feel perfect all the time; and (h) I was promised a rose garden.

- *Convince themselves that positive thinking provides a positive view of people, problems, and possibilities and generates hope and optimism.* Positive thinking is likely to lead to positive actions with desirable consequences. Social workers should form the habit of thinking positively and thereby looking for the positive side of things.

- *Recognize that most work-related tasks do not require perfection;* even with the best of intentions, planning, and problem-solving skills, mistakes are likely to be made. Social workers should think of their previous accomplishments, put the situation in the proper perspective, and try to recover from their mistake.

- *Try not to be immobilized by fears, whether real or imagined.* "As a technique for handling your fears, try exaggerating them all out of proportion. For example, if you fear being embarrassed, visualize yourself blushing to the point of turning beet red, sweating buckets, and shaking so hard your watch vibrates off your wrist. Exaggerating your fears to the point of being ludicrous may help you laugh at yourself and put your fear into perspective" (Sheafor et al., 1988, p. 174).

- *Develop and maintain a sense of humor.* Humor helps diffuse potentially unpleasant situations, put things in perspective, reduce negative feelings, and relax us. Social workers may find "Saving Face in the Status Race" by Winkler (1980) humorously interesting.

Time Management

Lack of time management can add to the loss of control over one's situation and to a sense of being overwhelmed. In busy health care settings, time is always a scarce resource. Some research has been done on the place of time in medical settings (e.g., see Finley, Mutran, Zeitler, & Randall, 1990; Frankenberg, 1992; Yoel & Clair, 1994; Zerubavel, 1979). Mizrahi (1986) found that medical residents at a major medical center tried to control the workflow through a number of strategies that she termed "GROP"—getting rid of patients—reflecting an attitude of distancing from and depersonalizing patients. Yoel and Clair (1994) studied how medical residents learned to manage time over the course of their residency and found that controlling time was an ongoing concern and a central dimension of their subculture. This controlling is influenced by the structural constraints of the residency program, such as the year of residency, and patient care loads as well as time management strategies. The latter included learning to work quickly, focusing on only bodily symptoms (to the neglect of the psychosocial realm), making themselves scarce (by not being visible, not wearing lab coats so that patients would not remember the resident's name), manipulating the appointment schedule, deflecting time complaints onto nurses, and using other residents for shortcuts (e.g., asking others for advice, rather than reading journal articles).

Lack of adequate time to do a job well has the potential for forcing one to let the quality of one's work suffer, to experience burnout, or both. Hence, to guard against damage of the quality of their work and/or burnout, social workers should master time management strategies. They have some advantages over many other health care professionals. Their work is not unidimensional; it has much variety, involving as it does interventions with individual clients and their families, interventions on behalf of those clients within the agency and outside, work with other professionals, and organization- and community-level activities. Most social workers are female, and most females with outside-the-home jobs are used to accommodating work-related and household demands. Recently, Hessing (1994) studied how women employed in clerical and related office positions manage their time and coordinate their work and household responsibilities. She found that time use was not simply dictated by external demands, but rather was mediated through an innovative time management process. The methods they used included conformity to and prioritization of the office schedule, manipulation of time use (especially in household schedules), routinization of activities (both in the office and at home), synchronization of events, and preparation for any contingency. These methods highlight the importance of thorough assessment and planning as the basis of time management. The following are a few helpful time management strategies. Social workers should:

- *Understand their job requirements and become clear about their responsibilities.* Analyze the different dimensions of the job either by roles or by major activities. Learn about the priorities of the agency and the order of those priorities and examine how their roles or activities relate to those priorities.

- *Work for a convergence of the agency's goals and objectives and their roles and responsibilities.* Have a clear understanding of how their roles and responsibilities fit into the larger picture. Negotiate, if necessary, with their supervisor or the agency boss for reaching that understanding and clarity.

- *Convince themselves that planning their work and setting priorities are absolute necessities.* "Don't hide behind the claim that you are too busy to get organized" (Sheafor et al., 1988, p. 123).

- *Spend a few minutes at the end of each workday to plan for the next day.* List all the tasks to be accomplished and prioritize the list. Setting priorities has several approaches. Lakein (1973) suggested the ABC priority system, in which one assigns an A to all those tasks that are the most important, a B to those tasks that are less important, and a C to those that are the least important. Next, one looks at the tasks within each of these groups and prioritizes them according to their importance or urgency. The result will be a list of tasks that have been labeled A-1, A-2, A-3; B-1, B-2, B-3; C-1, C-2, C-3; and so on. Another approach is to divide the work into such categories as (a) routine work, (b) regular job duties, (c) special assignments, and (d) creative work and to assign importance and allot time to the tasks in each category. Still another approach is to create a list of "things-to-do" for each day, with an estimate of time required to do each thing. One can divide a things-to-do list not only by priority but also by persons involved, so that one over-the-telephone or in-person contact can cover several items of business (Sheridan, 1988).

- *Let the priority list or the list of things to do guide their task performance each day, starting with the most important task.* Although unforeseen situations and crises would, at times, claim immediate attention and accommodation on the priority list or push a low-priority task up into a high-priority position, these do not minimize the importance of establishing priorities as an approach to controlling and managing time.

- *Allow time for emergencies.* Social workers should look for a pattern in emergencies, however, and plan accordingly. If uncovered areas or hours of service generate emergencies, improved coverage may be the answer. Similarly, they should analyze why and when situations tend to escalate into crises. Answers to the following questions will help in preventing emergencies: Who is truly experiencing the crisis—the patient, another staff member, or the social worker? Could the crisis have been prevented, as by more thorough work ahead of time? Does an individual emergency actually represent a chronic problem? Procrastination causes matters to become more urgent priorities and usually generates far more anxiety than relief (Sheridan, 1988, p. 98).

- In noncrisis situations, *attend to more difficult and more time-consuming tasks first.* "It is usually best to tackle lengthy tasks before those that can be done in a short period of time. It is also best to schedule work on the most difficult tasks when your energy level is highest (e.g., first thing in the morning)" (Sheafor et al., 1988, p. 124).

- *Keep handy an updated information file on the "who," "what," and "how" of the frequently used resources.* That will prevent the wasting of precious time in locating resources. Similarly, keep the needed forms, handouts, and telephone numbers within easy reach. It will save time.

- *Look for ways of saving time while making referrals to outside resources.* "Community inquiries and referrals can be made in the presence of the patient concerned so that needed information can be exchanged on the spot and the sometimes lengthy process of reporting back is eliminated" (Sheridan, 1988, p. 97).

- *As much as possible, try to do one thing at a time.* Tackling several things at once is often at the cost of both efficiency and quality. Social workers should look around their workplaces and creatively work out ways of reducing interruptions. It may be as simple as closing the door when they are working in the office or gracefully saying no to avoidable demands on their time. It is best to give an unqualified no, lest the requester interpret it as a conditional refusal (Gillies, 1989).

- *Wherever possible, delegate to others those tasks that do not require professional decision-making skills.* Spending less time performing low-priority items allows more time for important tasks (Pagana, 1995).

- *Learn the use of computers.* The use of computers for communication and documentation will be commonplace in the future. There will be room for individual discretion in the use of computers, however, from the minimal required to the maximum possible. Social workers should go for the maximum, master the various software, and use the computer as a powerful time-saving and management aid.

- *Limit time spent in meetings.* Meetings are often the source of time loss. For limiting the time spent on meetings, Sheafor et al. (1988) provided the following helpful recommendations:

Consider alternatives to a meeting, such as telephone calls.
Choose the location and time for the meeting that would ensure the most efficient use of time.
Attend the meeting for the time needed for one's contribution.
Define the purpose of the meeting clearly so that everyone comes prepared.
Prepare an agenda and follow it.
Stay on the task.
Start on time and end on time.
Control interruptions.

*Evaluate the success of the meeting and make that the basis for
improvements in the future.*

- *From time to time, analyze how they spend their time on different dimensions of the work, the degree of control they have over their time, and the time management strategies they use.* Let that analysis help them discover their mistakes and guide their future planning and organizing. A comparison of time actually spent with time estimated for specific tasks can be particularly helpful. Social workers can identify their most productive hours for high-priority tasks or activities requiring high concentration (Sheridan, 1988).

Self-Empowerment

Working in host settings dominated by high-power professionals who may not fully realize the significance of one's professional contributions has the possibility of creating a sense of powerlessness. Although the client's self-determination has always been a basic value of social work practice, during the past three or four decades the profession has emphasized the importance of empowerment as a fundamental practice principle. Empowerment-based practice is strength oriented so that social workers look for strengths in their clients and clients' situations and environments, as well as help them acquire new strengths in the form of problem-solving skills and resources. The same workers, however, do not always use their professional skills for self-empowerment. The perception is that power is bad. Assuming that a powerless worker cannot be an optimum source of empowerment for others, I discuss below the concepts of "power" and "empowerment" and approaches to self-empowerment.

Power is the ability to carry out one's will. It manifests itself in the form of authority, as well as influence. *Authority* lies in the position and not the occupier of the position, whereas *influence* comes more from the individual than from his or her position (Berger, 1990). Power has several bases. Building on the work of French and Raven (1959), Bisno (1988) identified the following:

Reward power is based on the ability to provide rewards.
Coercive power is based on the ability to punish.
Expert power is contingent on the desired knowledge and skills.
Positional power is derived from filling an "official" position.

Informational power lies in the capacity to control the flow of information.

Exchange power comes from the ability to create an imbalance in exchange relationships (e.g., "calling in" a political IOU).

Mobilizational power is based on the capacity to mobilize other people's support for desired goals.

Moral power lies in the capacity to gain one's objectives by invoking moral commitments of others.

Personal power is contingent on personal characteristics (e.g., attractiveness, persuasiveness, charisma) that enables one to affect the behavior of others.

Positional or legitimate power is based on the formal delegation of rights and responsibilities. This comes from the formal authority designated by the structure of the organization. It is, however, only one of several sources of power. "Individuals in the organization can acquire some degree of power regardless of their location in the hierarchical structure, professional training, or status" (Berger, 1990, p. 80). Power is dynamic and relative. This discussion of self-empowerment emphasizes strategies for increasing one's influence irrespective of one's official position in the organization. The strategies are divided into two groups: one focused on attitudes, and the other on skills.

Social workers should consciously develop and cultivate attitudes that reflect a brighter and positive view of the world and their ability to affect it. They will find the following suggestions helpful.

1. *Carefully study the situations that seem "impossible" and look for the presence of hope howsoever feeble.* A simple apostrophe has the power to turn *Impossible* into *I'mpossible*. Substitute "something" for "nothing"; instead of assuming that nothing can be done about the situation, shift to the stance that "something can be done about the situation." That leads to exploring "what can be done" and moving on to "this is what can be done" about the situation. This idea of the possible is impressively conveyed by a cartoon accompanying a paper by Lawrence (1980). It shows, on the one end, a man looking at a flying bird and wondering whether he could do likewise and, on the other, a flying jet. Underneath are written the words spoken by an ancient philosopher, "Anything the human mind can conceive it can one day consider; anything the human mind can consider long enough it can one day accept; anything the human mind can accept it can one day believe; and anything the human mind can believe it can act upon."

2. *Consciously guard against acquiring a victim mentality.* Settings dominated by more powerful professionals and social workers' identification with weak and powerless clients tend to encourage such a mentality. Although very appealing, it is not helpful. Anyone who has choices is not a victim; social workers have choices and the ability to make and increase choices. The notion of choices is applicable to the realm of feelings as well. John Wax, a social worker with the VA medical system for years, advised that to increase their choices, social workers should practice controlling their first response to a stimulus. "Feel your response but do not go with it, process your experience and multiply your responses, then use the best response. That allows you to ensure that others do not control your emotions and you are able to make it the other party's problem" (Wax, 1982).

3. *High self-esteem is a must for self-empowerment.* High self-esteem comes from many sources, over some of which one has control. Social workers can build strong attitudinal views of their capabilities, and "the world largely accepts us at our own estimate of ourselves. There is a good reason: It is because we almost always live up to our own estimate of ourselves" (Lawrence, 1980, p. 19). Programming their thinking positively will help improve their self-image. The programming tool is the subconscious mind. It is always moved by a positive suggestion. It will respond to the direction of the conscious mind, and it will not consider whether the suggestion of the conscious mind is right or wrong. The subconscious simply accepts. If one says, "I am angry" or "I am afraid," the subconscious mind will accept the dictate of the conscious mind and create the characteristics of fear or anger in the body. It is important to realize that a statement such as "I am not afraid" or "I am not angry" has no impact on the subconscious. The subconscious does not understand the word *not.* Therefore, the suggestion must be positive: "I am calm" . . . "I am courageous" (Lawrence, 1980, p. 19).

4. *Labeling one's experiences determines the meaning one gives to those experiences, and one's ability to give meaning to one's experiences is the most powerful thing going for a person* (Wax, 1982). This ability can be developed and enhanced. Social workers should work on assigning positive labels to stressful and unpleasant experiences. Adverse situations can thus be turned into opportunities for learning and growth.

5. *Recognize one's strengths and the relevance of those strengths to the mission and purpose of one's organization.* For example, social work's holistic approach to people and their problems, and workers' comprehensive understanding of clients and their ability to intervene at

different levels are some of the unique strengths they bring to their work.

6. *Learn to be assertive but not aggressive.* Assertiveness is a learned attribute. Assertive statements start with *I,* whereas aggressive statements start with *You.* Social workers should use their professional and interpersonal communication skills for self-empowerment.

7. *Treat one's job as the gateway to power.* Social workers should take responsibility for their job, take it seriously, and do it so well that they acquire a high reputation for their knowledge, skills, wisdom, integrity, and credibility. They should cultivate dependency in others, professionally and otherwise.

8. *Remember that the approaches and strategies that are effective with clients are equally effective with other people as well.* The relevant practice principles are as follows: (a) Start where the other person is; (b) recognize his or her needs; (c) affirm his or her strengths; (d) understand his or her point of view or let him or her know that you really want to understand that point of view; (e) respect differences; (f) use all the channels of communication—verbal, extraverbal, and nonverbal; and (g) give credit for his or her situation-related efforts and accomplishments.

9. *Use the problem-solving process learned and mastered as social workers.* Every situation lends itself to the use of that process.

10. *Wherever possible, use group work skills.* Monitoring and careful handling of the group process can make social workers significant contributors to group problem solving. Fighting in groups is a time-limited phenomenon; people get tired. Keeping out of the conflict, looking for the first sign of the desire for reconciliation, and introducing a new idea or a solution will save the situation (Wax, 1982).

11. *Similarly, put one's understanding of the crisis theory and crisis intervention skills to use in dealing with other professionals and the organization in crisis situations.* In crises, people and organizations are much more open to suggestions and amenable to change.

12. *Look for other sources of power and borrow it from those sources.* Building and strengthening coalitions and alliances with others increases one's power base and provides opportunities to influence those in the alliances and others through those alliances.

13. *Understand that power can be derived also from structural sources.* Resource control and network centrality are among the major structural sources. Those who secure or control the supply of essential

resources for the organization acquire power (Astley & Sachdeva, 1984; Jansson & Simmons, 1984). Similarly, those who are in the center of the network of relationships among the many positions essential for the organization's workflow gain power (Gummer, 1985). Social workers should explore ways of encroaching on both these sources of power individually or as a unit. In earlier chapters, we discussed ideas for social work contributions to creating new resources for their organizations. In the words of Berger (1990),

> For example, social work departments are creating fiscally sound plans for the development and management within the hospital home health care programs, revenue producing counseling services, case management for a variety of clinical groups (elderly, maternal-child health, AIDS and transplant patients), and bio-feedback programs within the hospital setting. (p. 88)

14. *Realize that making one's activities essential to the organization's workflow will bring one into the network.* The role of a case manager is potentially powerful because all service providers depend on the case manager for the maximum effectiveness of their interventions. With her focus on hospital-based social work, Berger (1990) said, "Social work is often at the central point or node in the network for discharge planning by virtue of its skills in helping individuals in crisis, its counseling skills as well as its knowledge of community resources" (p. 89).

In short, social workers should be alert to "the potential power opportunities residing in the multiple sources of power that exist in every organization, including both individual and structural sources" (Berger, 1990, p. 91).

Using Research Skills

Social workers should view their knowledge of research methodology and their research-related skills as essential parts of their professional repertoire. Throughout its history, social work has appreciated the importance of systematic research for strengthening the scientific base of the profession. Examples of early research work include the study of deserted wives reported by Mary Richmond in 1895 and the 1907 Pittsburgh survey that was an elaborate social investigation of the conditions of that city (Task Force on Social Work Research, 1991). Reid (1995) divided social work research literature into four categories: "studies of (1) behaviors, personality, problems, and other characteristics of individuals, families, and small groups; (2) characteristics, utilization, and outcome of services; (3) attitudes, orientations, and training of social workers, the profession, or interdisciplinary concerns; and (4) organizations, communities, and social policy" (p. 2044).

At the level of social work practitioners as well as social work agencies and programs, however, attitudes toward research have varied widely. These attitudes have reflected varying degrees of commitment to systematically creating and testing practice knowledge and skills, as well as incorporating research-based knowledge into social work practice and programs with the result that "a hundred years of effort to construct a base of scientific knowledge for the profession has fallen far short of the enthusiastic hope of the pioneers" (Reid, 1995, p. 2041). Here are a few suggestions for ensuring that the future of the profession in this regard will be brighter than its past.

1. All social workers should view themselves as practitioner/researcher (Grinnell, 1985) and consciously incorporate elements of research into their everyday professional activities. This task may require their convincing themselves that it is necessary and possible to be a practitioner and a researcher at once. Attitudinal barriers are often more difficult than logistical and methodological difficulties. The ability to contribute to the strength and prestige of their profession, improvement in their professional skills and strategies, and enhanced respect from other professionals and society at large are benefits of operating on the practitioner/researcher model. They should keep such benefits in mind.

2. Every setting can lend itself to being imbued with the desire for improved service approaches and systematic data collection. "Social workers would do well to seek out opportunities for knowledge building by participating and collaborating in existing efforts, proposing and undertaking new projects themselves, building elements of research into their service activities, and systematically evaluating the effectiveness and efficiency of their programs, roles and tasks" (Dhooper, 1994b, p. 189). In health care settings, the atmosphere is generally much more congenial for research-oriented thinking and practice than in many social work agencies. Talking about hospitals, Holden and Rosenberg (1991) said, "The range of potential research topics seems infinite. The possibilities for inter-disciplinary collaboration are many" (p. 2). Social workers should take advantage of that atmosphere.

3. With most health care agencies subscribing to the concept of continuous quality improvement (CQI) in all dimensions of their work,

there will be room for innovative approaches to CQI and its measurement. Social workers should creatively mix and match the quantitative and qualitative methodologies and the various data collection approaches they have learned as part of their professional training. These include (a) survey approach, (b) interview approach, (c) observational approach, (d) experimental approach, and (e) program evaluation approaches.

4. The availability of computers in health and social service agencies will be universal in the next century. Computers will do much more than make client records and agency-generated data easily accessible to professionals. Computer-assisted practice using various kinds of expert systems will become common. "An expert system is a computer program designed to give advice on decisions" (Mullen & Schuerman, 1990, p. 67). Computers will also put within easy reach of professionals the resources of libraries, consultation of research experts, and tools for data processing and analysis. Social workers should master computer technology and take advantage of these possibilities for enriching the research dimension of their practice.

5. Coulton (1985) reviewed the impact of several social work research studies on different aspects of social work practice in health care and saw in the cumulative effects of that research a movement toward what Kane (1984) called "science of health care social work." She also identified general trends about the types of social work research. These included movements toward (a) a greater focus on specialty areas, (b) interdisciplinary research, and (c) greater emphasis on analysis and evaluation rather than simple description, and (d) a concern over health care cost. The themes reflected in these trends will continue in importance and will be joined by others. The concern over health care costs will definitely persist. Social workers should take note of these and contribute to the related efforts.

6. Other areas for ongoing research will include quality of care in terms of access, comprehensiveness, and sensitivity to the characteristics and needs of clients and communities and the impact of quality of care on the quality of life. Social workers should view these as areas of their special knowledge and expertise and take initiative in researching these. Setting-specific areas that can benefit from a research-oriented look abound.

7. Social workers should also initiate, encourage, and collaborate in interdisciplinary research endeavors. These endeavors carry more clout;

command more resources; are richer in their design; and have greater impact on agency policies, programs, and procedures. They will find physicians willing partners. The nursing profession also urges its members to view research as an important professional activity. Martin (1995) suggested a number of ways for nurses to find time for research.

8. For disciplinary research, social workers can benefit from the experience of Adler et al. (1993), who as social work practitioners in a VA medical center, overcame barriers to research and publication activity. They formed themselves into a support group that emphasized "peer involvement, acceptance and trust, combined with a commitment to measurable progress on an ongoing basis" (Adler et al., 1993, p. 125). Their efforts resulted in the publication of seven articles and submission for publication of five articles over a period of a few years.

9. Social workers should help their agencies/departments create a climate supportive of research and research-oriented activities. This can be done in many ways: (a) encouraging intellectual discussion about practice issues and treatment techniques, participation in case conference presentations and grand rounds, and program evaluation as a means of developing interest in research; (b) providing tangible support such as time for specific research-related activities, access to library resources, consultation regarding methodological issues and statistical data analysis, and clerical assistance; (c) matching those practitioners who are experienced or are better at combining the practitioner and researcher roles with those who are just starting; and (d) providing a "clear understanding between administration and clinical researchers about what research is allowed, how resources are to be allocated, and what avenues of appeal exist when conflict develops" (Adler et al., 1993, p. 125).

10. Social workers should also seek the assistance and collaboration of faculties of local or nearby social work programs. University-based teachers and researchers are always looking for ways to stay connected with the field. Rathbone-McCuan (1995) listed reasons for this linkage, including (a) the need to field-test instruments and practice models developed in nonagency settings; (b) the need to reach specific client populations as research subjects; (c) the need to test methodological validity through an agency's database; (d) the need for an agency willing to cooperate in a research project or a grant application; (e) the need to create research opportunities for students in the agency; (f) the need to reconnect with the field to update professional knowledge about practice, programs, and policies; (g) the need to learn the perspectives of

different age, ethnic, racial, and socioeconomic groups; and (h) the need to supplement income by providing consultation or doing research on a contractual basis.

OTHER STRATEGIES

Conflict Resolution

Conflict is inevitable, it is a universal part of life. Whatever its causes, conflict appears at various levels—internal, interpersonal, and intergroup. Internally, it represents the mental struggle of two or more mutually exclusive impulses, motives, drives, or social demands; and at other levels it reflects the striving by two or more parties to achieve opposing or mutually exclusive goals (*Social Work Dictionary,* 1991). Costs of conflict are huge. Conflict, even within a group, uses up energy, wastes time, weakens the group bond, saps the group's morale, lowers the self-esteem of its members and accelerates their burnout, and diverts attention away from the group's purpose (Wax, 1982).

Major causes of social conflict are (a) relationship issues, (b) value conflicts, (c) inconsistencies in data, (d) structural problems, and (e) conflicts about interests (Moore, 1986). Some or all of these elements may be involved in a particular conflict. Brill (1976), with her focus on conflicts in teams, traced those conflicts to (a) different and incompatible goals that arise out of different values, (b) struggles over allocations of resources and rewards, and (c) threats to one's identity and rights seen in the existence or actions of another person or group.

Elaborating on the definition of conflict as two or more parties believing they have incompatible objectives (Kriesberg, 1982), Mayer (1995) pointed out two essential elements of conflict: (a) the perception of being in conflict and the feelings that accompany it and (b) the objective differences in the expected outcomes of conflict. The first requires attention to the emotions and tensions created by the conflict; the second demands that the issues and interests of the parties be addressed.

The various possible causes of conflict must be acknowledged and understood for conflict resolution. The different issues involved in a conflict make it harder or easier to resolve it. In general, issues about facts are easier to resolve than those about methods. Conflicts about methods are easier to resolve than those about goals. Conflicts about values are the hardest to resolve.

In their therapeutic roles as case workers, counselors, and case managers, social workers help their clients deal with conflicts in the personal and interpersonal realm, as well as in their relations with human service organizations. In conflict situations at the interpersonal and person-organizational levels, they function as mediators. Mediation as a social work approach to serving its clients is particularly useful in marital problems, child custody and divorce disputes, adoption disputes, child protection conflicts, conflicts between adolescents and their families, care of the elderly, victim-offender situations, equal employment opportunity disputes, and conflictual relationships among the various elements of the mental health system (Mayer, 1995). The National Association of Social Workers has recently established standards of practice for social work mediators (National Association of Social Workers, 1991). The negotiation skills that social workers use in dealing with involuntary clients are also helpful in conflict resolution.

Health care organizations are no different from others in breeding conflict. By building on their client-related conflict resolution skills involving both mediation and negotiation, social workers can become a significant resource for conflict resolution in health care settings. This will add another dimension to their position. With our focus on conflict resolution within and between organizations, the following are a few helpful suggestions.

1. Social workers should apply to conflict resolution the problem-solving framework that they are well-versed in. This can simply be a 4-step process: (a) recognizing the conflict, (b) assessing the conflict, (c) choosing a strategy, and (d) intervening (Friesen, 1987). *Recognizing the conflict* is not difficult; its existence is generally obvious. For *assessing the conflict,* it will help to know something about (a) the characteristics of the parties in conflict, such as their values and motivations, beliefs about the conflict, and resources for waging or resolving it; (b) the prior relationship of those parties to one another, particularly attitudes, beliefs, and expectations; (c) the nature of the issue giving rise to the conflict in terms of its scope, rigidity, and motivational significance; (d) the social environment within which the conflict occurs; (e) the interested audiences to the conflict and their relationships to the parties in the conflict and their interest in the conflict and its outcomes; (f) the strategy and tactics employed by the parties in the conflict; and (g) the consequences of the conflict to each of the participants and to other interested parties (Deutsch, 1973). They should gather as much information from as many sources about the parties in

conflict or their opponent if they are a party to a conflict and are negotiating for themselves. *Choosing and using the appropriate strategy* for intervention should be given careful consideration. This should be done with the following things in mind: an overall philosophy of conflict resolution, a set of general principles, an assessment of the level of the conflict, and a preference for a win-win approach.

2. The philosophy of how to resolve conflict should remind social workers that (a) the relationship must not be sacrificed—the issue will pass but the relationship must go on; (b) the issue must not be personalized; (c) they have nothing to gain by undermining the other party—they must not get into win-lose situations; (d) the issue must not be defined as "you against me," but rather as "we against the problem"; (e) they must take responsibility for their feelings and behavior; and (f) they have the power to give meaning to their experience (Wax, 1982).

3. The general principles they should observe are as follows:

- Maintain fairness and objectivity.
- Do not criticize a participant in front of others.
- Do not be critical of the other relationships of the adversary.
- Do not attack the opponent's motives.
- Do not indicate "concern" or doubts about the adversary's emotional well-being.
- Do not attribute the divergent views of the opponent to personality or personal factors.
- Do not depreciate another participant behind his or her back.
- Reciprocate debts, favors, and compliments.
- Keep confidences.
- Demonstrate a caring concern and be emotionally supportive, even in respect to an adversary.
- Take into account the opponent's desire for recognition and self-esteem and other matters of "face."
- Avoid blatant or subtle manifestation of arrogance (Bisno, 1988, p. 57).

4. Understand the level of the conflict. Levels of conflict include: (a) survival, (b) basic values, (c) resources, (d) turf, (e) priorities, (f) communication, and (g) semantics (Wax, 1982). Social workers should try to go up or down the scale to stay in control.

5. Realize the importance of framing and labeling as significant techniques. "One of the subtlest and most powerful ways in which conflict can be exacerbated or reduced is the framing of the conflict

itself" (Mayer, 1995, p. 617). Labeling a problem as a communication problem defuses the issue.

6. Use the win-win approach, which attempts to satisfy mutual needs by building trust, personalizing the situation, and making concessions on both sides (H. A. Cohen, 1980). This approach involves the use of negotiation. The following are a few helpful guidelines.

- Listen carefully to what the other party is saying and where he or she is coming from.
- Allow the other party to be right too.
- Do not try to prove the other party "wrong."
- Do not move from being right to becoming righteous.
- Stay out of the blame game; it weakens your creativity, initiative, and control.
- Try to know how much authority/power the other party has and what is the range of bargaining.
- Challenge the other party's data and assumptions, if needed, but never attack his or her motives.
- Make a clear statement of your need that the other party can understand.
- Let your total being—your oral and body language—convey the message, "I am entitled to what I am asking."
- Give the other party several options regarding your need.
- Do not make a threat unless absolutely necessary, and even then make a veiled threat. Do not remove the threat from the other party's threat.
- Be prepared to make concessions for what you get (Wax, 1982).

Coalition Building

Health problems with profound social dimensions, such as AIDS and alcohol and drug abuse, as well as social problems with powerful health consequences, such as poverty, homelessness, and violence in homes and on the streets, will persist in the 21st century. These problems cross professional and organizational boundaries and require comprehensive, multipronged approaches that demand multiprofessional and multiorganizational involvement. To retain their prominence in the community, health care organizations will feel compelled to go beyond the narrow scope of their traditional involvement and become partners with others in dealing with major social problems. Social workers can be instrumental in helping these organizations take on this added social responsibility. With their professional knowledge and skills, as well as their ongoing relationships within the wider human services community, social workers should be able not only to represent their organizations on the various community efforts but also assume leadership roles in generating those efforts. Coalition building is an important approach to dealing with social issues and problems.

A coalition represents a time-limited organization in which there is a convergence of interests of a number of actors, both individuals and organizations, and interactions around furthering those common interests (Warren, 1977). The goals of a coalition may be both political and nonpolitical (Dluhy, 1990). Coalitions have a special appeal for organizations. They allow individual organizations to become involved in broader issues without total responsibility for managing those issues. "Thus coalitions give organizations greater power and influence over an issue than any single organization would have working alone. They enable the mobilization of greater number of resources, and they bring a wider variety of effective strategies to bear on an issue" (Dluhy, 1990, p.12).

For improving their ability to build coalitions on behalf of their organizations, social workers will find the following suggestions helpful.

1. They should familiarize themselves with the various theoretical explanations of the coalition phenomenon and models of coalition building. Hill (1973) identified three major theoretical models: (a) the mathematical-normative model, based on game theory, which uses mathematical analysis to discover rational outcomes for conflict situations; (b) the economic or cost-benefit model, which is also related to game theory and seeks to maximize the net payoff (gross payoff minus the cost of making the decision and living with its consequences); and (c) the sociopsychological model, which endeavors to explain "coalition forming behavior as a result of specific modes of cognitive processing (psychological) or as the result of the interaction of group behaviors and individual cognitions (sociological)" (Hill, 1973, pp. 13-14).

Similarly, social workers should keep themselves abreast of the relevant emerging research- and practice-based knowledge on coalitions. For example, Dluhy (1990) studied coalitions in terms of a number of their characteristics, such as selection and recruitment of members, ideology, resources, staff, communications, longevity, issues, and organizational structure. He developed a typology of coalitions that include bread-and-butter, consciousness raising, network, preassociation, prefederation, and presocial movement coalitions. The first three are more short-term ad hoc coalitions formed around a single issue. These tend to disband either after the issue has been resolved or when interest in the issue has dissipated. The other three have a longer life and tend to move beyond a single issue.

Social workers should visualize the type of coalition they would like to build. With their focus on relationship building, Tucker and Mc-Nerney (1992) viewed coalition building as an opportunity for organizing a team of opinion leaders to build public trust and supportive behavior. They identified four types of coalitions: (a) representatives of stakeholder groups that are tired of expensive confrontation and need to create consensus on an active issue, (b) representatives of stakeholders who find themselves on the same side of the fence on an issue, (c) multidisciplined groups brought together by their "sensitivity or empathy to a point of view on an emerging issue" (p. 28), and (d) representatives of stakeholders who share a position on an issue that already enjoys widespread acceptance. Their advice is that coalition building should result from a systematic process of issues management. Miner and Jacobsen (1990) described the process of building a rural human services coalition in New York State, and Stone and Olson (1989) described the organization of a coalition for cost-effective discharge planning in Eastern Massachusetts.

Whatever the type of coalition, its purpose, and degree of existing agreement on the issue among the coalition members, success is dependent on the strategy and tactics and the ability to mobilize those members. Tucker and McNerney (1992) suggested a fivefold approach: (a) manage the issue, (b) identify coalition participants, (c) conduct research, (d) organize meeting design, and (e) develop messages and tactics.

Managing the issue is very important. It involves developing a position and creating a strategy to pursue that position. Social workers should help their organization develop its position on the issue around which a coalition should be built. This task will require a thorough analysis of all the forces affecting the issue: those driving the issue, those working for and against it, those likely to be affected by it, and those who may perceive themselves to be affected by it. They should try to ensure that the position that is developed is beneficial to their organization, as well as to others who are likely to be affected by the issue.

Social workers should look at their analysis of the stakeholders in the issue for help in identifying candidates for participation in the coalition. Criteria for selecting coalition participants can include credibility with peers and broader audiences, interest in the issue, moderate (vs. extreme) point of view, receptivity to the organizer's position or willingness to seek common ground, ability to work in a group seeking consensus, and availability of avenues to reach out to peers and broader audiences (Tucker & McNerney, 1992, p. 29). They can either approach stakeholder organizations for recommending participants or start with a core group that generates a list of people to be approached for participation. In recruiting (and retaining) members, the key is a shared goal "that does not require members to give up their individual, professional, or organizational or agency goals" (Dluhy, 1990, p. 52).

The first meeting of a coalition is crucial. Its goal should be to establish an organizational framework, elect temporary leadership, and plan organizational action (Staples, 1987). The "temporary governance committee," as Dluhy (1990) termed this leadership, should determine the formal process of electing the coalition's leaders and provide a forum for discussing its strategy and tactics. This meeting should also clarify the extent to which "the coalition should remain narrow or be broadened. Because there may not be a specific answer to this question, making this tentative or approaching the issue as a preliminary discussion may take some of the edge off of disagreement" (Dluhy, 1990, p. 52). Such decisions can always be reviewed.

Coalitions can have many organizational structures, depending on the scope of their work and the geographic area they cover. A coalition can be organized into committees or work groups. Dluhy (1990) proposed an organizational model of a statewide coalition that provides for seven committees: (a) long-range planning, (b) talent and recruitment, (c) communications, (d) special events, (e) monitoring and oversight, (f) medical and public relations, and (g) advocacy strategy. The advocacy strategy committee is at the core of the structure. He recommended that this committee be composed of five to seven people who are able to devote considerable time and effort to the coalition work and can meet regularly. This committee would be responsible for the overall plan of action, coordination of the various activities, and continuous evaluation of the plan of action.

Having adequate professional staff for the coalition's work is extremely important. Explore all possible avenues for this. These include (a) the coalition's own fiscal resources that can be used for hiring needed staff, (b) the member organizations that may be willing either to share the cost of hiring staff or to lend the services of their employees with appropriate skills, (c) people involved with the coalition who have professional qualifications and skills, and (d) student interns from various professional programs of the local educational institutions.

Continuous careful attention is needed for maintaining coalitions. Members' willingness to continue involvement in and to remain committed to the coalition depends on several factors. Dluhy (1990) listed principal incentives for participation in a coalition, including (a) ideological or symbolic benefits, (b) tangible benefits for the member's agency or profession, (c) tangible benefits for the person, (d) social benefits for the person, (e) enhancement of agency or professional reputation, (f) improvement of client situation, (g) civic duty or pride, and (h) critical up-to-date information and knowledge about clients, services, or the broader field (pp. 60-61). Let these incentives guide them in the management of the coalition.

To summarize, for ongoing successful coalition work, social workers should:

- From time to time, remind the members of the benefits of membership.
- Give equal importance to the needs of the members and the tasks of the organization.
- Maintain an effective communication network within the coalition and not let the organization become too formal and rigid.
- Make sure that everyone has a place in the coalition and is matched with the tasks he or she enjoys.
- Keep issues in front of the members and highlight even small successes.
- Take advantage of external events or crises, whenever possible, to validate the coalition and energize its members.
- Stress organizational and professional credibility above all else.
- Develop internal decision-making processes that keep members coming together.
- Design strategies that require maximum participation and interaction among members.
- Use periodic retreats and other self-assessment techniques (Dluhy, 1990; Friesen, 1987; Hasenfeld, 1983).
- Manage and resolve conflict as it emerges. (We discussed several approaches to conflict resolution earlier.)

Community Work

In Chapters 4, 5, and 7, we discussed some community work-related knowledge and skills relevant for social workers in different health care settings. The purpose of adding more material on social workers' community work on behalf of their agencies is to emphasize the importance of that work as a strategy for thriving in health care. Social workers' skills related to community work will set them apart from many other professionals and not only give them an edge over others but also provide them opportunities for leadership.

In our earlier discussion, we presented models of community social work (e.g., the Bracht & Kingsbury, 1990, community organizational model for health promotion) appropriate for the needs of particular health care settings. Here, we present a view of the larger picture, highlighting the basic similarities among the various modes of social work practice—clinical-, organizational-, and community-level work—and offer helpful ideas/suggestions.

The history of community organizing in the United States is closely tied to the development of social work theory and practice (Kahn, 1995). The roots of community practice can be traced to the settlement house and charity organization movements (Weil & Gamble, 1995). Knowledge of community variables has always been an important part of social workers' professional assets.

> In spite of the influences of the scientific charity movement of the early 20th century and of Freudian psychology and its intrapsychic corollaries, social work never totally removed itself from its early roots in the community. Social work practice, regardless of the context or specialty, requires an understanding of the ties that bind the individual, the family, or the group to larger societal networks. Further, as resources dwindle, social workers increasingly fill the role of mobilizer of community resources to resolve personal problems or address public issues. (Martinez-Brawley, 1995, pp. 545-546)

There is more to community work than knowing and mobilizing the community resources, however. Some social workers trained as specialists in clinical work might not have acquired adequate skills for effective community-level work.

On the basis of an extensive review of the community practice literature, Weil and Gamble (1995) identified eight models of community work.[1] They discussed these models in terms of the desired outcome, system targeted for change, primary constituency, scope of concern, and social work roles. These models illustrate the types of community organizations existing in the 1990s that are likely to persist in the future. According to Weil and Gamble, the 21st century will witness a resurgence of community practice aimed at supporting these trends.

> Ideologies, theories, and practice methods that support these trends will expand, with particular focus on applied democratic development, consumer participation, neopopulist ideology, feminist theory and practice, and theory and practice for sustainable development. The knowledge and research base for community practice will continue to grow and use more-sophisticated quantitative and qualitative methodologies to assess the outcomes of service reforms and planning and development efforts. (Weil & Gamble, 1995, p. 591)

Other models will appear in response to these trends. An example of such future work is the community management approach proposed by Smith, Loppnow, and Davis (1995), which blends selected elements of traditional community social work concepts and methods with mainstream modern corporate leadership and management concepts and methods.

Similarly, models for integrating social work practice at different levels (micro, mezzo, and macro) have started appearing in the literature. One such model is the community intervention model of clinical social workers (CIM) proposed by Frankel (1989). This model presents parallel steps involved in the clinical, community, and agency-organizational work.[2] Social workers in clinical practice positions venturing into community work often must do extensive work within their own agency as a precondition for effective community work.

While discussing her approach to integrating micro, mezzo, and macro practice perspectives, Kirst-Ashman (1994) proposed two process-oriented tools, one with the acronym PREPARE for assessing organizational change potential, and the other called IMAGINE for intervention. The steps included in PREPARE are (a) identify PROBLEMS to be addressed, (b) assess one's macro REALITY, (c) ESTABLISH primary goals, (d) identify relevant PEOPLE of influence, (e) ASSESS potential costs and benefits to clients and the agency, (f) evaluate professional and personal RISK, and (g) EVALUATE the potential success. The process represented by IMAGINE includes the following steps: (a) Start with an innovative IDEA, (b) MUSTER support, (c) identify ASSETS, (d) specify GOALS, (e) IMPLEMENT the plan, (f) NEUTRALIZE opposition, and (g) EVALUATE progress.

Given below are some suggestions that social workers in health care settings, embarking on community organizational projects, will find helpful.

1. *Study the various models of community work and determine how mixing and matching elements of those models will help in creating an approach peculiarly suitable for their purpose.* The actual work in any community will require the combining of different aspects of the various models, depending on the purpose of that work and a host of other factors.

2. *Remain familiar with other emerging practice models that propose newer approaches to community work or ways of integrating clinical and community social work.* Social workers should consciously try to incorporate into their practice, strategies for integrating micro, organizational, and macro modalities.

3. *Sharpen skills pertaining to such social work roles as advocate, mediator, negotiator, planner, and facilitator.* We have discussed strategies and techniques appropriate for these roles in earlier chapters. It is important to have the appropriate skills because most models of community work involve these roles.

4. *Use several methods of needs assessment.* We have discussed various approaches to community needs assessments in an earlier chapter. These are as diverse as analyzing the existing secondary data and contacting people—both key informants and lay. To the extent possible, several methods of needs assessment should be used. If several methods yield the same results, the reliability of those findings is much higher. The process of a community needs assessment itself, when several methods are used, creates the involvement of many community people. This is essential for going beyond the assessment.

5. *Remember that there is a political aspect of needs assessment.* Involvement of those affected by the need should be treated an important principle of needs assessment. "Any needs assessment involves making some judgments about the adequacy (or inadequacy) of existing institutional or organizational arrangements. Such judgments can be threatening to the guardians of those institutions and may lead to inappropriate criticism of the assessor" (Tropman, 1995, p. 568). Therefore, social workers should strive for a balance between the technical and the political aspects of community needs assessment.

6. *Develop a community profile that highlights the various dimensions of the community's life.* For effective work at the community level, a community analysis is essential. The important dimensions include (a) its identification—how the community identifies itself; (b) its location in terms of major geographic characteristics, and accessibility to the different forms of transportation; (c) its history, major events, traditions, and values; (d) its population and the population's characteristics; (e) its economic base and employment and income characteristics of its people; (f) its housing characteristics in terms of the type, ownership, and conditions; (g) its educational facilities, their level and characteristics; (h) its health and human service resources; (i) its major problems; and (j) an assessment of the community's strengths and liabilities (Devore & Schlesinger, 1981; Siporin, 1975)

7. *Offer their community-related expertise and help their agencies either start new community-level programs or undertake joint projects with other agencies.* The importance of interagency collaboration in different ways will increase in the future. Coordination of interagency activities is an absolute necessity in joint ventures. Social workers should remember that interagency coordination can be of different types and can take different forms. The possibilities include the following:

- *Administrative fiscal integration* encompassing (a) purchase of service, (b) joint budgeting, and (c) joint funding.
- *Administrative support services* such as (a) conducting studies; (b) information processing, dissemination, and exchange; (c) record keeping; (d) grants management and technical assistance; (e) publicity and public relations; (f) procedural integration; (g) joint program or project evaluation; and (h) standards and guidelines.
- *Administrative and programmatic linkages involving agency personnel* through (a) loaner staff; (b) outstationing; (c) liaison teams and joint use of staff; (d) staff training and development; (e) screening, employment counseling, and placement; (f) volunteer bureaus; and (g) ombudsmen.
- *Programmatic linkages* through development of centralized services such as (a) information and outreach, (b) intake, (c) diagnosis, (d) referral, (e) transportation, (f) follow-up, and (g) grievance machinery.
- *Programmatic coordination* through service integration taking the form of (a) case management, (b) ad hoc case coordination, (c) case conferences, (d) joint program development, and (e) joint projects (Lauffer, 1978).

8. *Ensure that a common mission and a shared view of the problem and its solution are reflected in formal contracts and protocols spelling out the responsibilities of the collaborating parties and the operationalization of those responsibilities.*

The essential requisites of interagency coordination are mutual benefits, similarity or complementarity of goals, and mutual respect and communication. "All [collaborations] require certain conditions, commitment, contributions, and competence, and all inherently experience dynamic tensions, which must be expected and managed" (Abramson & Rosenthal, 1995, p. 1481). Social workers' group work knowledge and skills would enable them to make significant contributions to the building and maintaining of interagency collaboration. We have discussed other skills earlier under coalition building.

Culturally Sensitive Practice

In the next century, the current minorities will constitute a majority of the U.S. population, and public policy will support cultural diversity. The need of health care organizations to deliver their services in culturally sensitive and culturally appropriate ways will be ever-present. Social work has a history of concern for such issues as prejudice and discrimination, intergroup relations, and social justice. "Since the 1960s, social work has strongly supported cultural pluralism and diversity. Social work was one of the first and most consistent supporters of civil rights activity and built the commitment to oppose prejudice and discrimination into its organizational structure and code of ethics" (Guzzetta, 1995, p. 2515). The Council on Social Work Education standards for accreditation of social work programs also mandate that every program make specific and continuous efforts to enrich students' educational experience by content on diverse racial, ethnic, and cultural perspectives. The aim is to prepare culturally competent social work practitioners. An impressive body of social work literature on understanding and working with ethnic and cultural minorities has grown over the past two decades. In the words of Lum (1992),

Social work educators have addressed a number of crucial themes: race, ethnicity and power; therapy for ethnic minority families; approaches to minority youth intervention; race, gender, and class practice guidelines for individuals, families, and groups; social work perspectives on the mental health of ethnic minority groups; and minority perspectives on human behavior in the social environment. (p. 4)

Social workers' professional commitment and training for culturally competent practice should give them an edge over many other health care providers. This is another area with opportunities for their assuming leadership positions. Those positions may involve teaching others through example and orientation, as well as becoming the link between patients and communities on the one hand and other health care providers and organizations on the other. The following suggestions for social workers are likely to enhance culturally sensitive and effective practice.

1. *Keep abreast of the newly emerging literature on culturally sensitive and multicultural practice modalities and stay aware of the barriers to multicultural practice.* Kirst-Ashman and Hull (1993) listed a number of barriers.[3]

2. *Know the various conceptualizations of culturally sensitive practice.* For example, Schlesinger and Devore (1995) conceptualized ethnic-sensitive practice as made up of three components: a professional perspective based on layers of understanding, a series of assumptions, and some practice principles.

The layers of understanding include (a) social work values, (b) knowledge of human behavior, (c) knowledge of social welfare policies and services, (d) self-awareness, (e) knowledge of the impact of ethnic reality, (f) the route to the social worker, and (g) the adaptation and modification of strategies and skills. The impact of ethnic reality determines not only the need for services but also service-related attitudes and abilities. The route to the social worker can be viewed as the path to health care services. Differential approaches are needed for clients taking different paths—those coming on their own and those who are forced, required, or encouraged to come. Regular practice strategies often require rethinking and adaptation for ethnically and culturally effective intervention.

The assumptions of ethnic-sensitive practice include "(1) Individual and collective history have a bearing on the generation and solution of problems; (2) the present is the most important; (3) unconscious phenomena affect individual functioning; and (4) ethnicity is a source of cohesion, identity, and strengths, as well as of strain, discordance, and strife" (Schlesinger & Devore, 1995, p. 905).

The practice principles include (a) give simultaneous attention to individual and systemic concerns and (b) modify the social work cognitive, affective, and behavioral skills in view of the understanding of the client's ethnic reality.

3. *Give attention to both the etic and emic characteristics of the client.* Etic and emic refer to cultural commonality and cultural specificity, respectively. Lum (1992) proposed a process-stage approach to social work with members of minority communities that delineates practice process stages, worker-system practice issues, client-system practice issues, and worker-client tasks. "In a real sense, the worker communicates the message that the client is a human being with basic needs and aspirations (etic perspective) and is also a part of a particular cultural and ethnic group (emic perspective). Moving between these two points of reference is a creative experience for both worker and client" (p. 90).

4. *Apply the following strategies, which can be used for assessment across all cultural groups:*

- Consider all clients as individuals first, as members of minority status next, and as members of a specific ethnic group last. This will prevent overgeneralization.
- Never assume that a person's ethnic identity tells you anything about his or her cultural values and patterns of behavior. There can be vast within-culture differences.
- Treat all "facts" about cultural values and traits as hypotheses to be tested anew with each client.
- Remember that all minority groups in this society are at least bicultural, living in two cultures—their own and the majority culture. The difficulty of surviving in a bicultural environment may be more important than their cultural background.
- Remember that not all aspects of a client's cultural history, values, and lifestyle are relevant to social work. Only the client can identify which aspects are important.
- Identify and build on the strengths in the client's cultural orientation.
- Be aware of one's own attitude about cultural pluralism.
- Engage the client in the process of learning what cultural content— beliefs, values, and experiences—is relevant for the work together.
- Keep in mind that there is no substitute for professional skills.

5. *With a focus on multicultural counseling, use Dillard's (1983) recommendations for effective interventions:*

- Being aware that the nonverbal component constitutes more of the communication than its verbal component.
- Recognizing that eye contact can be a problem for many ethnic groups.

- Using both open-ended and closed-ended questions as they are almost universally acceptable.
- Remembering that reflection of feelings does not work with all cultures.
- Recalling that paraphrasing is a generally acceptable technique in most cultures.
- Using self-disclosure judiciously.
- Giving interpretations and advice in cultures expecting a directive helper.
- Summarizing from time to time.
- Using confrontation carefully with certain racial groups.
- Remembering that openness, authenticity, and genuineness are respected in all cultures.

6. *Be aware of the following skills for culturally competent practice,* which Rogers (1995) considers essential for case management:

- *Ability to be self-aware:* This challenges one's self-image as an unbiased person and tunes into one's stereotypical thinking.
- *Ability to identify difference as an issue:* This helps in recognizing that both the worker and the client have cultures that cause differential perceptions and possibility of miscommunication.
- *Ability to accept others:* This makes the worker comfortable with a wide range of people and acknowledges that values and behaviors can be understood in relation to a person's culture.
- *Ability to individualize and generalize:* This helps in the application of a generalizable model to any given situation and then the search for its unique elements.
- *Ability to advocate:* This provides for the extra help needed by disadvantaged and nonmainstream clients.

Dealing With Managed Care

For the next several decades, managed care will continue to be the country's major approach to improving access, controlling cost, and ensuring quality of health care. No health care setting—inpatient or outpatient, short-term or long-term—will stay outside the purview of managed care. Already about 65% of those insured through their employers are under some form of managed care, and HMO penetration hit 50 million in 1994 ("How Psychotherapists," 1994). More than 40 states have filed waivers with the Health Care Finance Administration for introducing managed care practices into their Medicaid systems (Sullivan, 1995). On the one hand, social workers are increasingly occupying important positions in managed care companies as owners, administrators, supervisors, clinical directors, and case managers (Edinburg & Cottler, 1995). They perform utilization management, network development and management, and operations management functions (Lopez et al., 1993). On the other hand, they will continue to provide social work services in all types of health care settings and must deal with insurance companies' case managers on behalf of individual clients. By understanding the "what" and "how" of the managed care approach, social workers will be able to make significant contributions to the health care field, their agencies, and their clients.

As pointed out earlier, *managed care* is a term that represents many different ideas about health care delivery and resource management. Those ideas have found expression in many different programs. The entities providing managed care have proliferated over the past few years. These have grown out of utilization review companies, provider groups, insurance companies, employee assistance programs, and independent ventures. They vary on a number of dimensions.

> The variations include their primary corporate client (for example, HMO, commercial insurance, large corporations), the primary service they provide (for example, utilization review, EAPs, direct service delivery), and their use of providers (for example, group practices and solo practitioners). Most of the major companies are now subsidiaries of insurance companies or other corporate health conglomerates. (NASW, 1994a, p. 3)

The manner of their operation is influenced by their origin.

> First-generation managed care firms limit access to costly services by lowering utilization. Second-generation firms lower costs through benefit redesign, instituting service caps and larger consumer co-payments. Third-generation organizations allegedly truly manage care through careful case management on a case-by-case basis. Advanced generation firms are now moving from controlling networks to purchasing private practice groups. (Vandivort, 1994, p. 1)

Much variance also occurs in the degree of regulation of managed care companies. They may be regulated by such agencies as insurance, health, or other departments of the local, state, or federal government, or care may not be regulated at all except as profit-making corporations (NASW, 1994b). Social workers will find the following suggestions helpful.

1. *Look for changes in the current form of managed care.* Schreter (1993) forecast several trends, including (a) the emergence of selective contracting and networks of providers, (b) an increase in fiscal management of care at the expense of clinical management, (c) a shift of control from provider to payer, and (d) a change in the basic concept of what constitutes treatment and outcome resulting in a lower level of care. This looking for changes will enable social workers to take a proactive stance.

2. As part of managed care programs, *not only function within the framework of professional values and standards but also enrich the perspective of others in the agency with the essentials of social work values and practice principles.* Social workers should become instrumental in managed care programs working toward the best interest of the consumer of care and not saving costs at the expense of quality of care.

3. *Help in the development and implementation of innovative service delivery models that improve options and quality of care.* In that work, social workers should be guided by the basic values of the social work profession that emphasize the primacy of the individual and a just and equitable social order, its "person-in-environment" perspective, and such concepts as "continuum of care," "optimal functioning of the patient/client," and "least restrictive environment."

4. *Use advocacy skills against detrimental policies and practices both at the larger systems and individual case levels.* Most managed care programs operate on a "medical model," with its focus primarily on eliminating symptoms of the problem rather than on a "social health model," which views the patient from a biopsychosocial perspective (NASW, 1994b). Thus, there is wide room for denying patients comprehensive needed services. Similarly, efforts to control health care costs can take the form of limiting access to and quality of services. Social workers should work against such policies and practices.

5. *Use these helpful approaches for the larger level social work advocacy:* lobbying for legislation to regulate managed care, making alliances with other health care providers, and using research and analysis of data generated by their practice. For case-level advocacy, social workers should "use every contact with case managers [of managed care companies] to express their priority, that is, meeting the needs of the client" (Cornelius, 1994, p. 59).

6. *Sensitize the managed care establishment to the needs of Medicaid populations and the necessity for adapting services to those populations.* Edinburg and Cottler (1995) forecast that, by 1997, 90% of private health insurance plans will be managed care plans. More and more of the publicly insured also will be covered under managed care. Fifteen percent of all Medicaid recipients are already covered under managed care, and almost all states have at least one managed care product under Medicaid (Vandivort, 1994). "Successful programs include educating clients about utilizing the health care system, linking clients to a primary case manager or primary care provider, facilitating transportation, and offering more flexible hours of service" (Vandivort, 1994, p. 3).

7. *Strive to ensure that the following standards are observed.* The National Association of Social Workers has formulated this set of standards for managed care plans: (a) a full range of readily available services from emergency to primary care to subspecialty services; (b) clearly maintained safeguards for confidentiality; (c) access to services that meet the needs of families, working people, older people, and people with disabilities; (d) clear agreements with specialty care providers, hospital pharmacies, home care, and other services agencies; (e) appropriate transitions for clients who have to change their health care plans or who have exhausted their benefits; (f) access to social work services such as crisis intervention, assessment, prevention, health education, rehabilitation, and continuity of care; (g) specialized mental health services provided by social workers, such as psychotherapy and counseling for individuals, families, and groups, and substance abuse prevention and treatment; (h) easy-to-use and readily available complaint and appeal mechanisms; and (i) advisory boards that include consumers and that participate in policy and program development decisions (NASW, 1994b).

8. *Use professional knowledge, skills, and value commitments to ensure that managed care serves appropriate ends.* Managed care has the potential of becoming the strategy for a more equitable distribution of health care resources. There is much about the stated intent of managed care that social workers may wish to support: (a) the control of the use of health care resources for treatments that are efficacious and necessary, (b) the need to control the proportion of private and public resources spent on health care at the expense of other social needs and problems, (c) the use of public monies to improve and maintain the health of the poor and the disabled, rather than an emphasis on treatment

of illness alone, and (d) the opportunity to educate the public about the proportionate use of health care services and the distinction between medical need and personal want (Cornelius, 1994, p. 60).

This chapter concludes our discussion of the anticipated changes in the health care system and how social work can continue making significant contributions to the health and progress of that system. The generic strategies suggested in this chapter are not difficult to master and are likely to be helpful to future social work professionals in any work setting. It is hoped that these strategies, combined with basic social work skills and the use of the material presented in preceding chapters, will enable social workers to navigate the waters of the health care system with competence and confidence.

NOTES

1. These models are (a) neighborhood and community organizing, (b) organizing functional communities, (c) community social and economic development, (d) social planning, (e) program development and community liaison, (f) political and social action, (g) coalitions, and (h) social movements.

2. In the CIM, the steps included in clinical intervention are (a) assessment, (b) diagnosis—problem specification, (c) current status of the problem—baseline, (d) goal setting, (e) controlling conditions—problem causation/the working hypothesis, (f) developing intervention strategies/plans, (g) intervention, (h) evaluation, and (i) maintenance.

Corresponding to these, the steps in the community-level intervention are (a) community needs assessment, (b) identification of community resources, (c) identification of target populations, (d) goal setting, (e) controlling conditions, (f) program planning, (g) program implementation, (h) evaluation of the program impact, and (i) maintenance of the program in the community.

The necessary within-the-agency work involves a process with similar steps, which include (a) needs assessment, including the identification of power bases in the agency; (b) identification of formal and informal rules and norms; (c) building an informal coalition; (d) development of the agency's goals for the community program; (e) modification of the intervention plan in view of the agency goals; (f) development of the final community program plan and its presentation to the agency administration; (g) formalization of agency support; (h) implementation of the community program; (i) evaluation of the program impact on the agency; and (j) maintenance of the program in the agency.

3. These barrier are as follows:

Continued acceptance of the melting pot theory; that can result in blaming people of color for failing to "melt."

The assumption that everyone who immigrates to this country is overjoyed to be here; that can lead to ignoring/minimizing clients' losses, fears, and anxieties.

The tendency to explain a person's behavior by reference to his or her culture; that
ignores the diversity within a culture and the person's uniqueness.

An attempt to be color-blind and thereby treat everyone alike; this ignores the
importance of the person's culture and experience.

A tendency to assume that words carry the same meaning for everyone.

The assumption that clients think as we do; this ignores the fact that everyone has
a different frame of reference for viewing the reality.

The expectation that clients understand the social worker's role; their understanding is likely to be conditioned by their experience.

Insufficient self-awareness; this lets the worker's own values, beliefs, and biases
color the reality of the client.

The lack of knowledge of the culture and experiences of particular client groups
and an absence of a repertoire of appropriate, effective intervention techniques.

REFERENCES

AAMC policy on the generalist physician. (1993). *Academic Medicine, 68,* 1-5.

Aaron, H. J. (1991). *Serious and unstable condition: Financing America's health care.* Washington, DC: Brookings Institution.

Aaronson, W. E., Zinn, J. S., & Rosko, M. D. (1994). Do for-profit and not-for-profit nursing homes behave differently? *Gerontologist, 34,* 775-786.

Abdul Hamid, W., Wykes, T., & Stansfeld, S. (1993). The homeless mentally ill: Myths and realities. *International Journal of Social Psychiatry, 39*(4), 237-254.

Abramson, J. S., & Rosenthal, B. B. (1995). Interdisciplinary and interorganizational collaboration. In *Encyclopedia of Social Work* (19th ed.). Washington, DC: National Association of Social Workers.

Abramson, M. (1983). A model for organizing an ethical analysis of the discharge planning process. *Social Work in Health Care, 9*(1), 45-51.

Abramson, M. (1984). Collective responsibility in interdisciplinary collaboration: An ethical perspective for social workers. *Social Work in Health Care, 10*(1), 35-43.

Abramson, M. (1990). Ethics and technological advances: Contributions of social work practice. *Social Work in Health Care, 15*(2), 5-17.

Abramson, T. A., & Mendis, K. P. (1990). The organizational logistics of running a dementia group in a skilled nursing facility. *Clinical Gerontologist, 9*(3/4), 111-122.

Adelman, M. B., Frey, L. R., & Budz, T. J. (1994). Keeping the community spirit alive. *Journal of Long-Term Care Administration, 22*(2), 4-7.

Adler, G., Alfs, D., Greeman, M., Manske, J., McClellan, T., O'Brien, N., & Quam, J. (1993). Social work practitioners as researchers: Is it possible? *Social Work in Health Care, 19*(2), 115-127.

Ahlburg, D. A., & De Vita, C. J. (1992, August). New realities of the American family. *Population Bulletin, 47,* 2-44.

Alper, P. R. (1984). The new language of hospital management. *New England Journal of Medicine, 311,* 1249-1251.

Altepeter, T. S., & Walker, C. E. (1992). Prevention of physical abuse of children through parent training. In D. J. Willis, E. W. Holden, & M. Rosenberg (Eds.), *Prevention of child maltreatment: Developmental and ecological perspectives* (pp. 226-248). New York: John Wiley.

Altman, D. (1987). *AIDS in the mind of America.* New York: Anchor.

Altman, D. (1995). The 1995 health policy debate. *Journal of the American Medical Association, 273*(3), 247-248.

Altman, S. H., & Henderson, M. G. (1989). Introduction. In S. H. Altman, C. Brecher, M. G. Henderson, & K. E. Thorpe (Eds.), *Competition and compassion.* Ann Arbor, MI: Health Administration Press.

American Hospital Association (AHA). (1989). *Hospitals and older adults: Meeting the challenge.* Chicago: Author.

American Hospital Association (AHA). (1990). *Hospitals and physicians in the year 2000.* Chicago: Author.

Amputees get back on their feet. (1990, September-October). *The Futurist,* p. 5.

Anderson, E. A. (1988). AIDS public policy: Implications for families. *New England Journal of Public Policy, 4,* 411-427.

Andrews, F. M., & Withey, S. B. (1976). *Social indicators of well-being: America's perception of life quality.* New York: Plenum.

Andrews, K. (1986). Relevance of readmission of elderly patients discharged from a geriatric unit. *Journal of the American Geriatric Society, 33,* 422-428.

Anti-aging research. (1989, January-February). *The Futurist,* p. 6.

Antonucci, T. C., & Israel, B. A. (1986). Veridicality of social support: A comparison of principal and network members' responses. *Journal of Consulting Clinical Psychology, 54,* 432-437.

Applebaum, R., & Austin, C. (1990). *Long-term care case management: Design and evaluation.* New York: Springer.

Applebaum, R., & Phillips, P. (1990). Assuring the quality of in-home care: The "other" challenge for long-term care. *The Gerontologist, 30,* 444-450.

Archer, J., Probert, B. S., & Gage, L. (1987). College students' attitudes toward wellness. *Journal of College Student Personnel, 28,* 311-317.

Ardell, D. B. (1988). The history and future of the wellness movement. In J. P. Opatz (Ed.), *Wellness promotion strategies: Selected proceedings of the Eighth Annual National Wellness Conference.* Dubuque, IA: Kendall/Hunt.

Arnold, S., Kane, R. L., & Kane, R. A. (1986). Health promotion and the elderly: Evaluating the research. In K. Dychtwald & J. MacLean (Eds.), *Wellness and health promotion for the elderly* (pp. 327-344). Gaithersburg, MD: Aspen.

Aromacology: The psychic effects of fragrances. (1990, September-October). *The Futurist,* pp. 49-50.

Arthritis cases to soar in the 21st century. (1994, June 24). *Lexington Herald Leader,* p. A3.

Artificial chromosome. (1988, January-February). *The Futurist,* p. 5.

Astley, W. G., & Sachdeva, P. S. (1984). Structural sources of intraorganizational power: A theoretical synthesis. *Academy of Management Review, 91,* 104-113.

Attkisson, C. C., & Broskowski, A. (1978). Evaluation and the emerging human service concept. In C. C. Attkisson, W. A. Hargreaves, M. J. Horowitz, & J. E. Sorensen (Eds.), *Evaluation of human service programs* (pp. 3-26). San Diego: Academic Press.

Bakal, C. (1979). *Charity U.S.A.* New York: Times Books.

Balinsky, W. (1994). *Home care: Current problems and future solutions.* San Francisco: Jossey-Bass.

Bandura, A. (1986). *Social foundations of thought and action.* Upper Saddle River, NJ: Prentice Hall.

Barber, W. H. (1990). Induction of tolerance to human renal allografts with bone marrow and antilymphocyte globulin. *Transplant Review, 4,* 68.

Barker, J. B., Bayne, T., Higgs, Z. R., Jenkin, S. A., Murphy, D., & Synoground, G. (1994). Community analysis: A collaborative community practice project. *Public Health Nursing, 11,* 113-118.

Barzansky, B., Friedman, C. P., Arnold, L., Davis, W. K., Jonas, H. S., Littlefield, J. H., & Martini, C. J. M. (1993). A view of medical practice in 2020 and its implications for medical school admission. *Academic Medicine, 68,* 31-34.

Bass, S. A., Kutza, E. A., & Torres-Gil, F. M. (Eds.). (1990). *Diversity in aging: Challenges facing planners and policymakers in the 1990s.* Glenview, IL: Scott, Foreman.

Batavia, A. I., DeJong, G., & McKnew, L. B. (1991). Toward a national personal assistance program: The independent living model of long-term care for persons with disabilities. *Journal of Health Policy, Politics and Law, 16,* 523-545.

Baumann, L. J., Young, C. J., & Egan, J. J. (1992). Living with a heart transplant: Long-term adjustment. *Transplant International, 5*(1), 1-8.

Bayles, J. (1979). Ambulatory care options: Home care programs. In M. M. Melum (Ed.), *The changing role of the hospital: Options for the future.* Chicago: American Hospital Association.

Beauchamp, D. (1976). Public health as social justice. *Inquiry, 13,* 3-14.

Behrens, R. A., & Longe, M. K. (1987). *Hospital-based health promotion programs for children and youth.* Chicago: American Hospital Association.

Bellin, L. E. (1982). The politics of ambulatory care. In E. F. Pascarelli (Ed.), *Hospital-based ambulatory care* (pp. 95-109). Norwalk, CT: Appleton-Century-Crofts.

Belsky, J. (1980). Child maltreatment: An ecological integration. *American Psychologist, 35,* 320-335.

Bennett, C. (1988). A social worker comments: Some implications for social work practice in health care settings. *Social Work in Health Care, 13*(4), 15-18.

Benton, D., & Marshall, C. (1991). Elder abuse. *Clinical Geriatric Medicine, 7*(4), 831-845.

Berger, C. S. (1990). Enhancing social work influence in the hospital: Identifying sources of power. *Social Work in Health Care, 15*(2), 77-93.

Bergman, A., et al. (1993). High-risk indicators for family involvement in social work in health care: A review of the literature. *Social Work, 38,* 281-288.

Berkman, B., Bedell, D., Parker, E., McCarthy, L., & Rosenbaum, C. (1988). Pre-admission screening: A efficacy study. *Social Work in Health Care, 13*(3), 35-50.

Berkman, B. J., & Sampson, S. E. (1993). Psychological effects of cancer economics on patients and their families. *Cancer, 72*(9 Suppl.), 2846-2849.

Berkowitz, G., Halfon, N., & Klee, L. (1992). Improving access to health care: Case management for vulnerable children. *Social Work in Health Care, 17*(1), 101-123.

Bernard, L. D. (1977). Education for social work. In *Encyclopedia of social work* (17th ed., pp. 290-300). Washington, DC: National Association of Social Workers.

Bernstein, E., Wallerstein, N., Braithwaite, R., Gutierrez, L., Labonte, R., & Zimmerman, M. (1994). Empowerment forum: A dialogue between guest editorial board members. *Health Education Quarterly, 21,* 281-294.

Best-Sigford, B., Bruininks, R. H., Lakin, K. C., Hill, B. K., & Heal, L. W. (1982). Resident release patterns in a national sample of public residential facilities. *American Journal of Mental Deficiency, 87,* 130-140.

Bettman, J. R. (1979). *An information processing theory of consumer choice.* Reading, MA: Addison-Wesley.

Biegel, D. E., Tracy, E. M., & Corvo, K. N. (1994). Strengthening social networks: Intervention strategies for mental health case managers. *Health & Social Work, 19,* 206-216.

Bisno, H. (1988). *Managing conflict.* Newbury Park, CA: Sage.

Blair, C. E. (1994-1995). Residents who make decisions reveal healthier, happier attitudes. *Journal of Long-term Care Administration, 22,* 37-39.

Blaisdell, F. W. (1994). Development of the city-county (public) hospital. *Archives of Surgery, 129,* 760-764.

Blanton, T., & Balch, D. C. (1995, September-October). Telemedicine: The health system of tomorrow. *The Futurist,* pp. 14-17.

Blaustein, M., & Veik, C. (1987). Problems and needs of operators of board and care homes: A survey. *Hospital and Community Psychiatry, 38,* 750-754.

Blazyk, S., & Canavan, M. M. (1985). Therapeutic aspects of discharge planning. *Social Work, 30,* 489-496.

Blazyk, S., & Canavan, M. M. (1986). Managing the discharge crisis following catastrophic illness or injury. *Social Work in Health Care, 11*(4), 19-32.

Blendon, R. J., Brodie, M., & Benson, J. (1995). What should be done now that national health system reform is dead? *Journal of the American Medical Association, 273*(3), 243-244.

Bloom, M. (1981). *Primary prevention: The possible science.* Upper Saddle River, NJ: Prentice Hall.

Bloom, M. (1987). Prevention. In *Encyclopedia of social work* (18th ed.). Silver Spring, MD: National Association of Social Workers.

Blumenfield, S. (1986). Discharge planning: Changes for hospital social work in a new health care climate. *Quality Review Bulletin, 12*(2), 51-54.

Blumenfield, S., & Lowe, J. I. (1987). A template for analyzing ethical dilemmas in discharge planning. *Health and Social Work, 12,* 41-56.

Blumenfield, S., & Rosenberg, G. (1988). Toward a network of social health services: Redefining discharge planning and expanding the social work domain. *Social Work in Health Care, 13,* 31-48.

Bond, A. F., & Duffle, D. (1995). Forming productive mutually challenging inter-agency relationships. In J. B. Rauch (Ed.), *Community-based, family-centered services in a changing health care environment.* Arlington, VA: National Maternal and Child Health Clearinghouse.

Bond, G., Miller, L., Krumwied, R., & Ward, R. (1988). Assertive case management in three CMHCs: A controlled study. *Hospital and Community Psychiatry, 39,* 411-417.

Bone substitute. (1994, January-February). *The Futurist,* p. 6.

Bonuck, K. A. (1993). AIDS and families: Cultural, psychological, and functional impacts. *Social Work in Health Care, 18*(2), 75-89.

Borden, W. (1989). Life review as a therapeutic frame in the treatment of young adults with AIDS. *Health and Social Work, 14,* 253-259.

Borenstein, D. B. (1990). Managed care: A means to rationalizing psychiatric treatment. *Hospital and Community Psychiatry, 41,* 1095-1098.

Bowen, D. E. (1985, November). Taking care of human relations equals taking care of the business. *Human Resources Reporter.*

Bower, B. (1994, January 22). Mental disorders strike about half of U.S. *Science News, 145,* 55.

Boyd, D. R. (1982). Emergency medical services systems. In E. F. Pascarelli (Ed.), *Hospital-based ambulatory care* (pp. 113-140). Norwalk, CT: Appleton-Century-Crofts.

Bracht, N. (1987). Preventive health care and wellness. In *Encyclopedia of social work* (18th ed.). Silver Spring, MD: National Association of Social Workers.

Bracht, N. (Ed.). (1990). *Health promotion at the community level.* Newbury Park, CA: Sage.

Bracht, N., & Gleason, J. (1990). Strategies and structures for citizen participation. In N. Bracht (Ed.), *Health promotion at the community level* (pp. 109-124). Newbury Park, CA: Sage.

Bracht, N., & Kingsbury, L. (1990). Community organization principles in health promotion. In N. Bracht (Ed.), *Health promotion at the community level* (pp. 66-88). Newbury Park, CA: Sage.

Bracht, N. F. (1978). *Social work in health care: A guide to professional practice.* New York: Haworth.

Brack, G., Jones, E. S., Smith, R. M., White, J., & Brack, C. J. (1993). A primer on consultation theory: Building a flexible worldview. *Journal of Counseling & Development, 71,* 619-628.

Bradshaw, B. R., Vonderharr, W. P., Keeney, V. T., Tyler, L. S., & Harris, S. (1976). Community-based residential care for the minimally impaired elderly: A survey analysis. *Journal of the American Geriatric Society, 24,* 423-428.

Brawley, E. A. (1983). *Mass media and human services: Getting the message across.* Beverly Hills, CA: Sage.

Brecken, D. J., Harvey, J. R., & Lancaster, R. B. (1985). *Community health education: Settings, roles, and skills.* Gaithersburg, MD: Aspen.

Brickner, P. W. (1978). *Home health care for the aged.* Norwalk, CT: Appleton-Century-Crofts.

Brill, N. I. (1976). *Teamwork: Working together in the human services.* Philadelphia: J.B. Lippincott.

Brockett, R. G. (1981). The use of reality orientation in adult foster care homes: A rationale. *Journal of Gerontological Social Work, 3,* 3-13.

Brockington, C. F. (1975). The history of public health. In W. Hobson (Ed.), *The theory and practice of public health.* London, UK: Oxford University Press.

Brody, E. M. (1977). *Long-term care of older people: A practical guide.* New York: Human Sciences Press.

Brown, B. B. (1978). Social and psychological correlates of help-seeking behavior among urban adults. *American Journal of Community Psychology, 6,* 425-439.

Brown, D., Pryzwansky, W. B., & Schultz, A. C. (1987). *Psychological consultation: Introduction to theory and practice.* Needham Heights, MA: Allyn & Bacon.

Brown, J. S. T., & Furstenberg, A. (1992). Restoring control: Empowering older patients and their families during health crisis. *Social Work in Health Care, 17*(4), 81-101.

Brown, T. M. (1982). A historical view of health care teams. In G. J. Agich (Ed.), *Responsibility in health care.* Boston: D. Reidel.

Buada, L., Pomeranz, W., & Rosenberg, S. (1986). *Developing long-term care services: Product lines for the rural elderly* (Rural hospitals: Strategies for survival monograph series). Kansas City, MO: National Rural Health Care Association.

Burling, T., Lentz, E. M., & Wilson, R. N. (1956). *The give and take in hospitals: A study of human organization in hospitals.* New York: G. P. Putnam.

Burr, J. T. (1990, November). The tools of quality: Part VI. Pareto charts. *Quality Progress,* pp. 59-61.

Butcher, S. (1995). Promoting maternal and child health social work in a changing health care environment. In J. B. Rauch (Ed.), *Community-based, family-centered services in a changing health care environment.* Arlington, VA: National Maternal and Child Health Clearinghouse.

Butler, R. N. (1963). The life review: An interpretation of reminiscence in the aged. *Psychiatry, 26*(3), 65-76.

Byrd, W. M., & Clayton, L. A. (1993). The African-American cancer crisis: Part II. A prescription. *Journal of Health Care for the Poor and Underserved, 4*(2), 102-116.

Cable, E. P., & Mayers, S. P. (1983). Discharge planning effect on length of hospital stay. *Archives of Physical Medicine and Rehabilitation, 64*(2), 57-60.

Cabot, R. C. (1915). *Social service and the art of healing.* New York: Moffat, Yard.

Cahalan, D. (1987). *Understanding America's drinking problem: How to combat the hazards of alcohol.* San Francisco: Jossey-Bass.

Calista, M. R. (1989). *Implications of empowerment concept and strategies for social work education and practice.* Paper presented at the Annual Program Meeting of the Council on Social Work Education, Chicago.

Callahan, J. J., & Wallack, S. S. (1981). *Reforming the long-term care system.* Lexington, MA: D. C. Heath.

Campbell, D. T., & Stanley, J. C. (1966). *Experimental and quasi-experimental designs for research.* Chicago: Rand McNally.

Cannon, I. M. (1913). *Social work in hospitals.* New York: Russell Sage.

Cannon, I. M. (1952). *On the social frontier of medicine: Pioneering in medical social service.* Cambridge, MA: Harvard University Press.

Cantor, M., & Chichin, E. (1990). *Stress and strain among home care workers of the frail elderly.* New York: Fordham University, Third Age Center, Brookdale Research Institute on Aging.

Caplan, G., & Caplan, R. (1993). *Mental health consultation and collaboration.* San Francisco: Jossey-Bass.

Cappo, J. (1990). *FutureScope: Success strategies for the 1990s and beyond.* Chicago, IL: Longman Financial Services.

Capuzzi, D., Gross, D., & Friel, S. E. (1990, Winter). Recent trends in group work with elders. *Generations,* 43-48.

Carlett, C. (1993). Teams and teamwork. *ASHA, 35,* 30-31.

Carling, P. J. (1984). *Developing family foster care programs in mental health: A resource guide.* Boston: Boston University, Center for Rehabilitation Research & Training in Mental Health.

Carlton, T. O. (1984). *Clinical social work in health settings: A guide to professional practice with exemplars.* New York: Springer.

Carlton, T. O. (1989). Stand up and cheer. *Health and Social Work, 14,* 227-230.

Caro, F. G. (1990). The world of home care: What does it look like? In C. Zuckerman, N. N. Dubler, & B. Collopy (Eds.), *Home health care options: A guide for older persons and concerned families.* New York: Plenum.

Caroff, P. (1988). Clinical social work: Present role and future challenge. *Social Work in Health Care, 13*(3), 21-33.

Caroff, P., & Mailick, M. D. (1985). The patient has a family: Reaffirming social work's domain. *Social Work in Health Care, 10*(4), 17-34.

Cassata, D. M., & Kirkman-Liff, B. L. (1981). Mental health activities of family physicians. *Journal of Family Practice, 12,* 683-692.

Cassel, J. (1976). The contribution of social environment to host resistance. *American Journal of Epidemiology, 104,* 107-123.

Cetron, M. J., Rocha, W., & Lucken R. (1988, September-October). The future of American business firms. *The Futurist,* pp. 9-15.

Chapman, M. (1989, Spring). Making peace with the media. *Public Welfare,* pp. 35-36.

Checkoway, B. (1995). Six strategies of community change. *Community Development Journal, 30,* 220.

Cheek, L. B. (1987). Alzheimer's families. *Aging, 335,* 17-19.

Chell, B. (1988). But murderers can have all the children they want: Surrogacy and public policy. *Theoretical Medicine, 9,* 3-21.

Childless families. (1989, January-February). *The Futurist,* p. 6.

Children and heart disease. (1994, July-August). *The Futurist,* p. 6.

Children's Defense Fund. (1991). *The state of America's children.* Washington, DC: Author.

Christen, A. G., & Christen, J. A. (1994). Why is cigarette smoking so addicting? An overview of smoking as a chemical and process addiction. *Health Values: The Journal of Health Behavior, Education & Promotion, 18,* 17-24.

Ciotti, M., & Watt, S. (1992). Discharge planning and the role of the social worker. In M. J. Holosko & P. A. Taylor (Eds.), *Social work practice in health care settings.* Toronto: Canadian Scholars' Press.

Clapp, R. L. (1993, November/December). Health care continuum. *Nursing Homes,* pp. 7-9.

Clark, D., & Connelly, T. (1979). *Developing interdisciplinary education in allied health programs: Issues and decisions.* Atlanta: Southern Regional Education Board.

Clark, E. (1971). Nursing homes. *Encyclopedia of social work* (16th ed., pp. 886-890). New York: National Association of Social Workers.

Clark, R. E., & LaBeff, E. E. (1982). Death telling: Managing and delivery of bad news. *Journal of Health and Social Behavior, 23,* 366-380.

Clement, J. L., & Durgin, J. S. (1987). Emergency health services. *Encyclopedia of social work* (18th ed.). Silver Spring, MD: National Association of Social Workers.

Cloarec, A., Rivault, C., Fontaine, F., & Le Guyader, A. (1992). Cockroaches as carriers of bacteria in multifamily dwellings. *Epidemiology and Infection, 109*(3), 483-490.

Coates, J. (1994, July-August). The highly probable future: 83 assumptions about the year 2025. *The Futurist,* pp. 1-7.

COBRA: The Emergency Medical Treatment and Active Labor Act, 42 USC 1395 (1986). (Pub. No. 99-272, 9121, 1986). GPO.

Cohen, H. A. (1980, September). The fine art of negotiating. *Leadership,* pp. 27-31.

Cohen, J. (1980). Nature of clinical social work. In P. L. Ewalt (Ed.), *Toward a definition of clinical social work.* Washington, DC: National Association of Social Workers.

Cohen, J. J. (1995). Academic medicine: Facing change. *Journal of the American Medical Association, 273*(3), 245-246.

Coile, R. C., Jr. (1990). *The new medicine: Reshaping medical practice and health care management.* Gaithersburg, MD: Aspen.

Colerick, E. J., & George, L. K. (1986). Predictors of institutionalization among care-givers of patients with Alzheimer's disease. *Journal of the American Geriatrics Society, 34,* 493-498.

Collins, A., Pancoast, D., & Dunn, J. (1977). *Consultation workbook.* Portland, OR: Portland State University.

Committee on Aging of the Group for the Advancement of Psychiatry. (1971). *The aged and community mental health: A guide to program development* (Report No. 80). New York: Group for the Advancement of Psychiatry.

Committee on Cost of Medical Care. (1932). *Medical care for the American people: The final report of the committee.* Chicago: University of Chicago Press.

Committee on Nutrition in Medical Education. (1985). *Nutrition education in United States medical schools.* Washington, DC: National Academy Press.

Conference. (1994, November/December). *Nursing Homes,* pp. 10-15.

Conger, S. A., & Moore, K. D. (1988). Chronic illness and the quality of life: The social worker's role. In J. S. McNeil & S. E. Weinstein (Eds.), *Innovations in health care practice* (pp. 102-115). Washington, DC: National Association of Social Workers.

Connaway, R. S., & Gentry, M. E. (1988). *Social work practice.* Upper Saddle River, NJ: Prentice Hall.

Conroy, A. M. (1994). Bringing family members into the community. *Journal of Long-term Care Administration, 22*(2), 8.

Cornelius, D. S. (1994). Managed care and social work: Constructing a context and a response. *Social Work in Health Care, 20*(1), 47-63.

Cornish, E. (1994, May-June). Responsibility for the future. *The Futurist,* p. 60.

Coulton, C. J. (1985). Research and practice: An ongoing relationship. *Health & Social Work, 10,* 282-291.

Cox, C. (1992). Expanding social work's role in home care: An ecological perspective. *Social Work, 37,* 97-192.

Crossman, L. (1992, August). *A history of rape in American society prior to 1990.* Paper presented at the Annual Meeting of the American Psychological Association, Washington, DC.

Crouch, D. J., Birky, M. M., Gust, S. W., Rollins, D. E., Walsh, J. M., Moulden, J. V., Quilan, K. E., & Beckel, R. W. (1993). The prevalence of drugs and alcohol in fatally injured truck drivers. *Journal of Forensic Science, 38*(6), 1342-1353.

Cunningham, P. J., & Monheit, A. C. (1990). Insuring the children: A decade of change. *Health Affairs, 9*(4), 76-90.

Currie, B. F., & Beasley, J. W. (1982). Health promotion in medical encounter. In R. B. Taylor, J. R. Ureda, & J. W. Denham (Eds.), *Health promotion: Principles and clinical applications* (pp. 143-160). Norwalk, CT: Appleton-Century-Crofts.

Czeizel, A. E., Kodaj, I., & Lenz, W. (1994). Smoking during pregnancy and congenital limb deficiency. *British Medical Journal, 308*(6942), 1473-1476.

Dalton, H. L. (1989). AIDS in black face. *Daedalus, 118,* 205-227.

Daro, D., & McCurdy, K. (1991). *Current trends in child abuse reporting and fatalities: The results of the 1989 annual fifty state survey.* Chicago: National Center on Child Abuse Prevention Research, National Committee for Prevention of Child Abuse.

Davidson, K. W. (1978). Evolving social work roles in health care: The case of discharge planning. *Social Work in Health Care, 4*(1), 43-54.

Davis, E. M., & Millman, M. L. (1983). *Health care for the urban poor: Directions for policy.* Totowa, NJ: Rowman & Allanheld.

Davis, M. A. (1991). On nursing home quality: A review and analysis. *Medical Care Review, 48,* 129-166.

Davis, N. J. (1988). Shelters for battered women: Social policy response to interpersonal violence. *Social Science Journal, 25,* 401-419.

Davis, N. M. (1988, November). Fund-raising success: Knowing why people give. *Association Management,* pp. 120-127.

Day, J. C. (1993). *Population projections of the United States, by age, sex, race, and Hispanic origin: 1993-2050.* Washington, DC: Government Printing Office.

Deming, E. W. (1986). *Out of the crisis.* Cambridge: Massachusetts Institute of Technology, Center for Advanced Engineering Study.

DeSpiegler, G. (1979). The South Dakota experimental swing-bed program. In M. M. Melum (Ed.), *The changing role of the hospital: Options for the future.* Chicago: American Hospital Association.

Deutsch, M. (1973). *The resolution of conflict: Constructive and destructive processes.* New Haven, CT: Yale University Press.

Devore, W., & Schlesinger, E. G. (1981). *Ethnic-sensitive social work practice.* St. Louis, MO: C. V. Mosby.

Dhooper, S. S. (1983). Coping with the crisis of heart attack. *Social Work in Health Care, 9*(1), 1531.

Dhooper, S. S. (1984). Social networks and support during the crisis of heart attack. *Health and Social Work, 9,* 294-303.

Dhooper, S. S. (1990). Identifying and mobilizing social supports for the cardiac patient's family. *Journal of Cardiovascular Nursing, 5*(1), 6573.

Dhooper, S. S. (1991). Caregivers of Alzheimer's disease patients: A review of the literature. *Journal of Gerontological Social Work, 18,* 19-37.

Dhooper, S. S. (1994a). *Social work and transplantation of human organs.* New York: Praeger.

Dhooper, S. S. (1994b, May). *Social work contributions to interdisciplinary teamwork in the field of disabilities.* Paper presented at the Conference on Social Work and Disabilities, Young Adult Institute, New York.

Dhooper, S. S., Green, S. M., Huff, M. B., & Austin-Murphy, J. (1993). Efficacy of a group approach to reducing depression in nursing home elderly residents. *Journal of Gerontological Social Work, 20,* 87-100.

Dhooper, S. S., Royse, D. D., & Rihm, S. J. (1989). Adults with mental retardation in community residential settings: An exploratory study. *Adult Residential Care Journal, 3,* 33-51.

DiBlasio, F. A., Belcher, J. R., & Connors, K. A. (1993). The employed homeless: A crisis in public policy. *Journal of Sociology & Social Work, 20,* 51-58.

Diebold, J. (1994, May-June). The next revolution in computers. *The Futurist,* pp. 34-37.

Dillard, J. M. (1983). *Multicultural counseling.* Chicago: Nelson-Hall.

Dillon, C. (1985). Families, transitions, and health: Another look. *Social Work in Health Care, 10*(4), 35-44.

Dillon, C. (1990). Managing stress in health social work roles today. *Social Work in Health Care, 14*(4), 91-108.

Dimant, J. (1991). From quality assurance to quality management in long-term care. *Quality Review Bulletin, 17,* 207-215.

DiNitto, D. M., & McNeece, C. A. (1990). *Social work: Issues and opportunities in a changing profession.* Upper Saddle River, NJ: Prentice Hall.

Dluhy, M. J. (1990). *Building coalitions in the human services.* Newbury Park, CA: Sage.

Dobrof, R., & Litwak, E. (1977). *Maintenance of family ties of long-term care patients: Theory and guide to practice.* Rockville, MD: National Institute of Mental Health.

Doner, K. (1994). Why violence is a health-care priority. *Social Policy, 24*(3), 58-62.

Doss-Martin, L., & Stokes, D. J. (1989). Historical development of social work in primary care. In M. L. Henk (Ed.), *Social work in primary care* (pp. 17-30). Newbury Park, CA: Sage.

Douglass, A., & Winterfeld, A. (1995). *Helping children and families through legislative activism: A guide to the legislative process.* Englewood, CO: American Humane Association.

Drew, J. A. (1979). A Connecticut hospital's experience with satellite clinics. In M. M. Melum (Ed.), *The changing role of the hospital: Options for the future* (pp. 107-14). Chicago: American Hospital Association.

Drubach, D. A., Kelly, M. P., Winslow, M. M., & Flynn, J. P. (1993). Substance abuse as a factor in the causality, severity, and recurrence rate of traumatic brain injury. *Maryland Medical Journal, 42,* 989-993.

Dukakis, M. S. (1995). Health care reform: Where do we go from here? *Journal of Health Politics, Policy and Law, 20*(3), 787-794.

Dunkel, J., & Hatfield, S. (1986). Countertransference issues in working with persons with AIDS. *Social Work, 31,* 114-117.

Durkin, M. S., Davidson, L. L., Kuhn, L., O'Connor, P., & Barlow, B. (1994). Low-income neighborhoods and the risk of severe pediatric injury: A small-area analysis in northern Manhattan. *American Journal of Public Health, 84,* 587-592.

Dworkin, S. H., & Pincu, L. (1993). Counseling in the era of AIDS. *Journal of Counseling & Development, 71,* 275-281.

Edelman, M., & Mihaly, L. (1989). Homeless families and the housing crisis in the United States. *Children and Youth Services Review, 11,* 91-108.

Edelman, M. W. (1991). Introduction. *The state of America's children, 1991.* Washington, DC: Children's Defense Fund.

Edinburg, G. M., & Cottler, J. M. (1995). Managed care. In *Encyclopedia of social work* (19th ed.). Washington, DC: National Association of Social Workers.

Edlis, N. (1993). Rape crisis: Development of a center in an Israeli hospital. *Social Work in Health Care, 18*(3/4), 169-178.

Egan, G. (1990). *The skilled helper: A systematic approach to effective helping.* Pacific Grove, CA: Brooks/Cole.

Ehrlich, P., & Anetzberger, G. (1991). Survey of state public health departments on procedures for reporting elder abuse. *Public Health Reports, 106*(2), 151-154.

Eisdorfer, C., & Maddox, G. L. (1988). A distinctive role for hospitals in caring for older adults: Issues and opinions. In C. Eisdorfer & G. L. Maddox (Eds.), *The role of hospitals in geriatric care* (pp. 1-18). New York: Springer.

Elder, J. P., Schmid, T. L., Dower, P., & Hedlund, S. (1993, Winter). Community heart health programs: Components, rationale, and strategies for effective interventions. *Journal of Public Health Policy, 14,* 463-479.

Ellis, L. (1991). A synthesized (biosocial) theory of rape. *Journal of Consulting and Clinical Psychology, 59,* 631-42.

Emerson, H. (1945). *Local health units for the nation.* New York: Commonwealth Fund.

Encyclopedia of social work (16th ed.). (1971). New York: National Association of Social Workers.

Ethnoven, A. C., & Singer, S. J. (1995, Spring). Market-based reform: What to regulate and by whom. *Health Affairs,* pp. 105-119.

Erdmann, E., & Stover, D. (1993, September-October). Drowning in preconceptions. *The Futurist,* p. 60.

Erickson, R., & Erickson, G. (1992). An overview of social work practice in health settings. In M. J. Holosko & P. A. Taylor (Eds.), *Social work in health care settings.* Toronto: Canadian Scholars' Press.

Eskildson, L., & Yates, G. R. (1991). Lessons from industry: Revising organizational structure to improve health care quality assurance. *Quality Review Bulletin, 17,* 38-41.

Eustis, N. N., Kane, R. A., & Fischer, L. R. (1993). Home care quality and the home care worker: Beyond quality assurance as usual. *The Gerontologist, 33,* 64-73.

Evans, R. W. (1990). The private sector vis-à-vis government in future funding of organ transplantation. *Transplantation Proceedings, 22,* 975-979.

Evans, R. W. (1991). Quality of life assessment and the treatment of end-stage renal disease. In R. W. Evans, D. L. Manninen, & F. B. Dong (Eds.), *The National Cooperative Transplantation Study: Final report* (BHARC-100-91-020). Seattle, WA: Battelle-Seattle Research Center.

Evans, R. W., Manninen, D. L., & Dong, F. B. (1991). *Executive summary: The National Cooperative Transplantation Study* (BHARC-100-91-020). Seattle, WA: Battelle-Seattle Research Center.

Evashwick, C. J., & Branch, L. G. (1987). Clients of the continuum of care. In C. J. Evashwick & L. J. Weiss (Eds.), *Managing the continuum of care* (pp. 45-56). Gaithersburg, MD: Aspen.

Ewing, R. S. (1979). Future of the trustee. In M. M. Melum (Ed.), *The changing role of the hospital: Options for the future* (pp. 11-14). Chicago: American Hospital Association.

Fallcreek, S., Warner-Reitz, A., & Mettler, M. H. (1986). Designing health promotion programs for elders. In K. Dychtwald (Ed.), *Wellness and health promotion for the elderly* (pp. 219-233). Gaithersburg, MD: Aspen.

Fat meter. (1988, May-June). *The Futurist,* p. 3.

Feather, J. (1993). Factors in perceived hospital discharge planning effectiveness. *Social Work in Health Care, 19*(1), 1-14.

Feder, J., & Levitt, L. (1995, Spring). Steps toward universal coverage. *Health Affairs,* pp. 140-149.

Federal Task Force on Homelessness and Severe Mental Illness. (1992). *Outcasts on Main Street.* Washington, DC: Interagency Council on the Homeless.

Feigenbaum, A. V. (1983). *Total quality control.* New York: McGraw-Hill.

Fenske, V., & Roecker, M. (1971). Finding foster homes for adults. *Public Welfare, 29,* 404-410.

Ferguson, T. (1992, January-February). Patient, heal thyself: Health in the information age. *The Futurist,* pp. 9-13.

Fergusson, D. M., Horwood, J., & Lynskey, M. T. (1993). Maternal smoking before and after pregnancy: Effects on behavioral outcomes in middle childhood. *Pediatrics, 92,* 815-822.

Fernie, B., & Fernie, G. (1990). Organizing group programs for cognitively impaired elderly residents of nursing homes. *Clinical Gerontologist,* pp. 123-134.

Field, D. M. (1993, January-February). Highlights from "Creating the 21st Century." *The Futurist,* p. 35.

Fields, G. (1978). Editorial. *Social Work in Health Care, 4*(1), 5-6.

Fine, M., & Asch, A. (1988). Disability beyond stigma: Social interaction, discrimination, and activism. *Journal of Social Issues, 44,* 3-21.

Finkelhor, D. (1979). *Sexually victimized children.* New York: Free Press.

Finkelhor, D., & Baron, L. (1986). High-risk children. In D. Finkelhor (Ed.), *A sourcebook on child sexual abuse* (pp. 60-88). Beverly Hills, CA: Sage.

Finkelhor, D., & Strapko, N. (1992). Sexual abuse prevention education: A review of evaluation studies. In *Prevention of child maltreatment: Developmental and ecological perspectives* (pp. 150-167). New York: John Wiley.

Finley, W., Mutran, E., Zeitler, R., & Randall, C. (1990). Queues and care: How medical residents organize their work in a busy clinic. *Journal of Health and Social Behavior, 31,* 292-305.

First, R. J., Rife, J. C., & Toomey, B. G. (1994). Homeless in rural areas: Causes, patterns, and trends. *Social Work, 39,* 97-108.

Fisher, J. A. (1992). *Rx 2000: Breakthroughs in health, medicine, and longevity in the next five to forty years.* New York: Simon & Schuster.

Flora, J. A., & Cassady, D. (1990). Role of media in community-based health promotion. In N. Bracht (Ed.), *Health promotion at the community level* (pp. 143-157). Newbury Park, CA: Sage.

Flynn, B. C., Ray, D. W., & Rider, M. S. (1994). Empowering communities: Action research through health cities. *Health Education Quarterly, 21,* 395-405.

Flynn, J. P. (1995). Social justice in social agencies. In *Encyclopedia of social work* (19th ed., pp. 2173-2179). Washington, DC: National Association of Social Workers.

Foods that bring better health. (1991, September-October). *The Futurist,* pp. 52-53.

Forecasts for the 1990s. (1989, July-August). *The Futurist,* p. 43.

Foreman, M. D., Theis, S. L., & Anderson, M. A. (1993). Adverse events in the hospitalized elderly. *Clinical Nursing Research, 2*(3), 360-370.

Frankel, A. J. (1989, March). *Clinical social work and community organization: A re-marriage made in heaven.* Paper presented at the 35th Annual Program Meeting, Council on Social Work Education, Chicago.

Frankenberg, R. (Ed.). (1992). *Time, health, and medicine.* Newbury Park, CA: Sage.

Frazier, P. A., & Cohen, B. B. (1992). Research on the sexual victimization of women: Implications for counselor training. *Counseling Psychologist, 20,* 141-158.

French, J. R. P., & Raven, B. (1959). The bases of social power. In D. Cartwright (Ed.), *Studies in social power.* Ann Arbor: University of Michigan, Institute for Social Research.

Freudenberg, N., Eng, E., Flay, B., Parcel, G., Rogers, T., & Wallerstein, N. (1995). Strengthening individual and community capacity to prevent disease and promote health: In search of relevant theories and principles. *Health Education Quarterly, 22,* 290-306.

Friedman, E. (1991). Patients as partners: The changing health care environment. *Social Work in Health Care, 17,* 31-46.

Friesen, B. (1987). Administration: Interpersonal aspects. In *Encyclopedia of social work* (18th ed.). Silver Spring, MD: National Association of Social Workers.

Friesen, B. J. (1993). Overview: Advances in child mental health. In H. C. Johnson (Ed.), *Child mental health in the 1990s: Curricula for graduate and undergraduate professional education.* Washington, DC: Government Printing Office.

Fulmer, T. T. (1984). Elder abuse assessment tool. *Dimensions of Critical Care Nursing, 10*(12), 16-20.

Fuqua, D. R., & Kurpius, D. J. (1993). Conceptual models in organizational consultation. *Journal of Counseling & Development, 71*, 607-618.

Furlong, R. M. (1986). The social worker's role on the institutional ethics committee. *Social Work in Health Care, 11*(4), 93-100.

Furstenberg, A. (1984). Social work in medical care settings. In R. J. Estes (Ed.), *Health care and the social services: Social work practice in health care* (pp. 23-77). St. Louis, MO: Warren H. Green.

Furstenberg, A., & Mezey, M. D. (1987). Mental impairment of elderly hospitalized hip fracture patients. *Comprehensive Gerontology, 1*, 80-85.

Furstenberg, A., & Olson, M. M. (1984). Social work and AIDS. *Social Work in Health Care, 9*(4), 45-62.

Galanter, M., Egelko, S., & Edwards, H. (1993). Rational recovery: Alternative to AA for addiction? *American Journal of Alcohol Abuse, 19*, 499-510.

Gallo-Silver, L., Raveis, V. H., & Moynihan, R. (1993). Psychosocial issues in adults with transfusion-related HIV infection and their families. *Social Work in Health Care, 18*(2), 63-74.

Ganikos, M. L., et al. (1994). A case study in planning for public health education: The organ and tissue donation experience. *Public Health Reports, 109*, 626-631.

Garbarino, J. (1992). Preventing adolescent maltreatment. In D. J. Willis, E. W. Holden, & M. Rosenberg (Eds.), *Prevention of child maltreatment: Developmental and ecological perspectives* (pp. 94-114). New York: John Wiley.

Gelberg, L., & Leake, B. D. (1993). Substance use among impoverished medical patients: The effect of housing status and other factors. *Medical Care, 31*, 757-766.

Gellert, G. A. (1993). U.S. health care reform and the economy of prevention. *Archives of Family Medicine, 2*, 563-567.

Gerhart, U. C. (1990). *Caring for the chronically mentally ill.* Itasca, IL: F. E. Peacock.

Germain, C. B. (1984). *Social work practice in health care: An ecological perspective.* New York: Free Press.

Germain, C. B., & Gitterman, A. (1980). *The life model of social work practice.* New York: Columbia University Press.

Gerson, S. M., & Chassler, D. (1995). Advancing the state of the art: Establishing guidelines for long-term care case management. *Journal of Case Management, 4*(1), 9-13.

Getzel, G. S. (1992). AIDS and social work: A decade later. *Social Work in Health Care, 17*(2), 1-9.

Gillies, D. A. (1989). *Nursing management: A systems approach.* Philadelphia: W. B. Saunders.

Gitterman, A. (1988). The social worker as educator: An educator's view. In *Health care practice today: The social worker as educator* (Conference proceedings). New York: Columbia University School of Social Work.

Glanz, K., & Rimer, B. K. (1995). *Theory at a glance: A guide for health promotion practice.* Washington, DC: U.S. Public Health Service, National Institute of Health.

Gleick, J. (1987). *Chaos: Making a new science.* New York: Viking.

Goedert, J. J., & Cote, T. R. (1994). Editorial: Public health interventions to reduce pediatric AIDS. *American Journal of Public Health, 84*, 1065-1066.

Goering, P., Wasylenki, D., Farkas, M., & Ballantyne, R. (1988). What difference does case management make? *Hospital and Community Psychiatry, 39,* 272-276.

Golan, N. (1969). When is a client in crisis? *Social Casework, 50,* 389-394.

Goldbeck, W. B. (1988, March-April). AIDS and the workplace: Business fights the epidemic. *The Futurist,* pp. 18-19.

Goldberger, A. L., Rigney, R. D., & West, B. J. (1990). Chaos and fractals in human physiology. *Scientific American,* pp. 43-49.

Goldfrank, L. R. (1995). Health care reform or a return to social Darwinism? *Annals of Emergency Medicine, 25*(5), 692-693.

Goldstein, H. (1987). The neglected moral link in social work practice. *Social Work, 32,* 181-186.

Goldwater, S. S. (1943). Concerning hospital origins. In A. C. Bachmeyer & G. Hartman (Eds.), *The hospital in modern society.* New York: Commonwealth Fund.

Gordon, L. (1993). Public health is more important than health care [Guest Editorial]. *Journal of Public Policy, 14,* 261-264.

Gotou, J., et al. (1994). Evaluation of the effective use of the "health notebook." *Nippon Koshu Eisei Zasshi, 41,* 1090-1098.

Gottlieb, B. (1995). *New choices in natural healing: Over 1,800 of the best self-help remedies from the world of alternative medicine.* Emmaus, PA: Rodale.

Gottlieb, B. H. (1985). Assessing and strengthening the impact of social support on mental health. *Social Work, 30,* 293-300.

Goudsblom, J. (1986). Public health and the civilizing process. *Milbank Quarterly, 64,* 161-188.

Grant, L. A., & Harrington, C. (1989). Quality of care in licensed and unlicensed home care agencies: A California case study. *Home Health Care Services Quarterly, 10,* 115-138.

Grant, M. (1987). *Handbook of community health.* Philadelphia: Lea & Febiger.

Graves, J. R., & MacDowell, N. M. (1994-1995, Winter). Mapping out the road to quality. *Journal of Long-term Care Administration,* 12-17.

Gray, B. H. (1991). *The profit motive and patient care.* Cambridge, MA: Harvard University Press.

Gray, L. A., & House, R. M. (1989). AIDS and adolescents. In D. Capuzzi & D. Gross (Eds.), *Working with at-risk youth: Issues and interventions* (pp. 231-270). Alexandria, VA: American Association for Counseling and Development.

Gray, N. L. (1993). The relationship of cigarette smoking and other substance use among college students. *Journal of Drug Education, 23,* 117-124.

Green, A. (1993, March-April). The fragrance revolution: The nose goes to new lengths. *The Futurist,* pp. 13-17.

Green, L. W., & Kreuter, M. W. (1991). *Health promotion planning: An educational and environmental approach.* Mountain View, CA: Mayfield.

Green, L. W., & Raeburn, J. (1990). Contemporary developments in health promotion: Definitions and challenges. In N. Bracht (Ed.), *Health promotion at the community level* (pp. 2944). Newbury Park, CA: Sage.

Greenberg, M., Schneider, D., & Martell, J. (1995). Health promotion priorities of economically stressed cities. *Journal of Health Care for the Poor and Underserved, 6*(1), 10-22.

Greene, G., Kruse, K. A., & Arthurs, R. J. (1985). Family practice social work: A new area of specialization. *Social Work in Health Care, 10*(3), 53-73.

Greene, R. R. (1982). Families and the nursing home social worker. *Social Work in Health Care, 7*(3), 57-67.

Greer, D. S., Bhak, K. N., & Zenker, B. M. (1994). Comments on the AAMC policy statement recommending strategies for increasing the production of generalist physicians. *Academic Medicine, 69,* 245-260.

Grinnell, R. M., Jr. (1985). *Social work research and evaluation.* Itasca, IL: F. E. Peacock.

Grover, R. M. (1982). The impact of resident councils. *Journal of Long-term Care Administration, 10,* 2-6.

Gummer, B. (1985). Power, power—who's got the power. *Administration in Social Work, 9*(2), 99-111.

Gutierrez, L. (1992, October). *Macro practice for the 21st century: An empowerment perspective.* Paper presented at the First Annual Conference on the Integration of Social Work and Social Science, School of Social Work, University of Michigan, Ann Arbor.

Guzzetta, C. (1995). White ethnic groups. In *Encyclopedia of social work* (19th ed.). Washington, DC: National Association of Social Workers.

Gwyther, L. P. (1995). When "the family" is not one voice: Conflict in caregiving families. *Journal of Case Management, 4*(4), 150-155.

Haber, P. A. (1983). The Veterans Administration community care setting. *Psychiatry Quarterly, 55,* 187-191.

Haggard, W. K. (1991). The feminist theory of rape: Implications for prevention programming targeted at male college students. *College Student Affairs Journal, 11,* 13-20.

Haglund, B., Weisbrod, R. R., & Bracht, N. (1990). Assessing the community: Its services, needs, leadership, and readiness. In N. Bracht (Ed.), *Health promotion at the community level* (pp. 91-107). Newbury Park, CA: Sage.

Hahn, B., & Flood, A. B. (1995). No insurance, public insurance, and private insurance: Do these options contribute to differences in general health? *Journal of Health Care for the Poor and Underserved, 6*(1), 41-59.

Hall, H. D. (1985). Historical perspective: Legislative and regulatory aspects of discharge planning. In E. McClellan, K. Kelly, & K. C. Buckwalter (Eds.), *Continuity of care: Advancing the concept of discharge planning* (pp. 11-20). New York: Grune & Stratton.

Halper, A. S. (1993). Teams and teamwork: Health care settings. *ASHA, 35,* 34-35, 48.

Handy, J. (1995). Alternative organizational models in home care. *Journal of Gerontological Social Work, 24*(3/4), 49-65.

Haney, P. (1988). Providing empowerment to the person with AIDS. *Social Work, 33,* 251-253.

Hanlon, J., & Pickett, G. (1984). *Public health administration and practice.* St. Louis, MO: Times Mirror/Mosby.

Harbert, A. S., & Ginsberg, L. H. (1990). *Human services for older adults: Concepts and skills.* Columbia: University of South Carolina Press.

Harden, W. G. (1979). Family-centered care. In M. M. Melum (Ed.), *The changing role of the hospital: Options for the future* (pp. 93-98). Chicago: American Hospital Association.

Harrington, M. (1987). *Who are the poor?* Washington, DC: Justice for All National Office.

Harris, L. I. (1919). The epidemic of influenza. *Hospital Social Service Quarterly, 1,* 1-14.

Harris, S. N., Mowbray, C. T., & Solarz, A. (1994). Physical health, mental health, and substance abuse problems of shelter users. *Social Work, 19,* 37-45.

Hasenfeld, Y. (1983). *Human service organizations.* Upper Saddle River, NJ: Prentice Hall.

Hasenfeld, Y. (1987). Power in social work. *Social Service Review, 61,* 469-483.

Haughton, J. G. (1972). Federal government and the poor: Why has it failed? In L. C. Corey, S. E. Saltman, & M. F. Epstein (Eds.), *Medicine in a changing society.* St. Louis, MO: C. V. Mosby.

Hay, D., & Oken, D. (1972). The psychological stresses of intensive care unit nursing. *Psychosomatic Medicine, 34*(2), 109-118.

Hayes, J. A. (1991). Psychosocial barriers to behavior change in preventing human immunodeficiency virus (HIV) infection. *Counseling Psychologist, 19,* 585-602.

Healthy children 2000: National health promotion and disease prevention objectives related to mothers, infants, children, adolescents, and youth (DHHS Publication No. HRSA-M-CH 91-2). (1991). Washington, DC: U.S. Department of Health and Human Services.

Heckler, M. M. (1984). Preface. In P. J. Carling, *Developing family foster care programs in mental health: A resource guide.* Boston: Boston University, Center for Rehabilitation Research and Training in Mental Health.

Heger, R. L., & Hunzeker, J. M. (1988). Moving toward empowerment-based practice in public child welfare. *Social Work, 33,* 499-502.

Hein, K. (1990). Adolescent acquired immunodeficiency syndrome. *American Journal of Diseases in Children, 144,* 46-48.

Helms, C. M., & Damiano, P. C. (1995, January). Health care system reform and public health: Protecting the safety net. *Archives of Family Medicine, 4,* 12-13.

Henry, R. S. (1993, November/December). Considerations in opening an adult day center. *Nursing Homes,* pp. 16-17.

Hepworth, D. H., & Larsen, J. A. (1986). *Direct social work practice: Theory and practice.* Belmont, CA: Dorsey.

Herman, S. P. (1990, November). Special issues in child custody evaluations. *Journal of the American Academy of Child and Adolescent Psychiatry, 29,* 969-974.

Hess, P. M. (1994). Supporting foster families in their support of families. *Journal of Emotional and Behavioral Problems, 2*(4), 24-27.

Hessing, M. (1994). More than clockwork: Women's time management in their combined workloads. *Sociological Perspective, 37,* 611-633.

Hettler, B. (1984). Wellness: Encouraging a lifetime pursuit of excellence. *Health Values, 8*(4), 13-17.

Hill, P. (1973). *A theory of political coalitions in simple and policy making situations.* Beverly Hills, CA: Sage.

Hirschfeld, M. J. (1988). Nursing and care of the elderly: A view from Israel. In C. Eisdorfer & G. L. Maddox (Eds.), *The role of hospitals in geriatric care.* New York: Springer.

Hirschwald, J. F. (1984). Social work in physical rehabilitation. In R. J. Estes (Ed.), *Health care and the social services: Social work practice in health care* (pp. 165-205). St. Louis, MO: Warren H. Green.

Hoffman, L. (1988). The family life cycle and discontinuous change. In B. Carter & M. McGoldrick (Eds.), *The changing family life cycle: A framework for family therapy* (pp. 91-106). New York: Gardner.

Hogue, C. J., & Hargraves, M. A. (1993). Class, race, and infant mortality in the United States. *American Journal of Public Health, 83*(1), 9-12.

Holden, G., & Rosenberg, G. (1991). Research challenges for social workers in health. *Social Work in Health Care, 16*(1), 1-4.

Holosko, M. J. (1992). Social work practice roles in health care: Daring to be different. In M. J. Holosko & P. A. Taylor (Eds.), *Social work practice in health care settings.* Toronto: Canadian Scholars' Press.

Hospital of the future. (1990, November-December). *The Futurist,* pp. 46-47.

House, R. M., & Walker, C. M. (1993). Preventing AIDS via education. *Journal of Counseling & Development, 71,* 282-289.

How psychotherapists rate managed care firms. (1994). *Psychotherapy Finances, 17*(7), 6-7.

Howard, G., Burke, G. L., Szklo, M., Tell, G. S., Eckfeldt, J., Evans, G., & Heiss, G. (1994). Active and passive smoking are associated with increased carotid wall thickness: The Atherosclerosis Risk in Communities Study. *Archives of Internal Medicine, 154,* 1277-1282.

Howell, M. (1987). Clients who are mentally retarded and also old: Developmental, emotional, and medical needs. In S. F. Gilson, T. L. Goldsbury, & E. H. Faulkner (Eds.), *Three populations of primary focus: Persons with mental retardation and mental illness, persons with mental retardation who are elderly, persons with mental retardation and complex medical needs* (pp. 95-102). Omaha: University of Nebraska Medical Center.

Hubbard, P., Werner, P., Cohen-Mansfield, A., & Shusterman, R. (1992). Seniors for justice: A political and social action group for nursing home residents. *The Gerontologist, 32,* 856-858.

Hudson, R. B. (1990). Home care policy: Loved by all, feared by many. In C. Zuckerman, N. N. Dubler, & B. Collopy (Eds.), *Home health care options: A guide for older persons and concerned families* (pp. 271-301). New York: Plenum.

Hughes, S. (1992). Home care: Where we are and where we need to go. In M. Ory & A. Duncker (Eds.), *Home care for older people.* Newbury Park, CA: Sage.

Huntington, J. (1986). The proper contributions of social workers in health practice. *Social Science and Medicine, 22,* 1151-1160.

Hutchins, V. L. (1985). Celebrating a partnership: Social work and maternal and child health. In A. Gitterman, R. B. Black, & F. Stein (Eds.), *Public health social work in maternal and child health: A forward plan* (Report of the Working Conference of the Public Health Social Work Advisory Committee for the Bureau of Health Care Delivery and Assistance). New York: Columbia University School of Social Work.

Hydrogel: A versatile new material. (1989, July-August). *The Futurist,* p. 6.

Hyer, L., Swanson, G., Lefkowitz, R., Hillesland, D., Davis, H., & Woods, M. G. (1990). The application of the cognitive behavioral model to two older stressor groups. *Clinical Gerontologist, 9*(3/4), 145-189.

Ignagni, K. (1995, Spring). Navigating the health care marketplace. *Health Affairs,* pp. 221-225.

Iles, P., & Auluck, R. (1990). Team building, interagency team development, and social work practice. *British Journal of Social Work, 20,* 151-164.

Infertility services boom. (1988, November-December). *The Futurist,* p. 40.

Institute of Medicine. (1978). *Report of a study: A manpower policy for primary health care.* Washington, DC: National Academy of Sciences.

Institute of Medicine. (1986). *Improving the quality of care in nursing homes.* Washington, DC: National Academy Press.

Institute of Medicine. (1988a). *The future of public health.* Washington, DC: National Academy Press.

Institute of Medicine. (1988b). *Homelessness, health, and human needs.* Washington, DC: National Academy Press.   •

Institute of Medicine. (1989). *Prevention and treatment of alcohol problems: Research opportunities.* Washington, DC: National Academy Press.

Institute of Medicine. (1990). *Broadening the base of treatment for alcohol problems.* Washington, DC: National Academy Press.

Invisible scalpel. (1989, September-October). *The Futurist,* p. 5.

Israel, B. A., Checkoway, B., Schulz, A., & Zimmerman, M. (1994). Health education and community empowerment: Conceptualizing and measuring perceptions of individual, organizational, and community control. *Health Education Quarterly, 21,* 149-170.

James, B. C. (1989). *Quality management for health care delivery.* Chicago: American Hospital Association.

Jansson, B. S., & Simmons, J. (1984). Building departmental or unit power within human service organizations: Empirical findings and theory building. *Administration in Social Work, 8*(3), 41-56.

Jaynes, G. D., & Williams, R. M., Jr. (1989). *Common destiny: Blacks and American society.* Washington, DC: National Academy Press.

Johnson, D. L., et al. (1993, March). *Tobacco smoke in the home and child intelligence.* Paper presented at the 60th Biennial Meeting of the Society for Research in Child Development, New Orleans.

Johnson, D. R., Agresti, A., Jacob, M. C., & Nies K. (1990). Building a therapeutic community through specialized groups in a nursing home. *Clinical Gerontologist, 9*(3/4), 203-217.

Johnson, K. A. (1990). Medical technology and public meaning: The case of viable organ transplantation. In J. Shanteau & R. J. Harris (Eds.), *Organ donation and transplantation: Psychological and behavioral factors.* Washington, DC: American Psychological Association.

Johnson, L. C. (1989). *Social work practice: A generalist approach.* Needham Heights, MA: Allyn & Bacon.

Johnson, M. (1991). Why the nation doesn't have attendant services. *Disability Rag, 12,* 1-10.

Johnston, W. B., & Hopkins, K. R. (1990). *The catastrophe ahead: AIDS and the case for a new public policy.* New York: Praeger.

Jolly, P. (1988, September). Medical education in the United States, 1960-1987. *Health Affairs,* pp. 144-157.

Jones, M. (1953). *The therapeutic community.* New York: Basic Books.

Jones, W. J. (1979). Selecting and implementing specific role options. In M. M. Melum (Ed.), *The changing role of the hospital: Options for the future* (pp. 31-42). Chicago: American Hospital Association.

Joslyn-Scherer, M. S. (1980). Communication in the human services: A guide to therapeutic journalism. Beverly Hill, CA: Sage.

Justins, D. (1994). Hospital pain clinics: An invaluable resource. *Practitioner, 238,* 278, 281-282.

Kagan, R., & Schlossberg, S. (1989). *Families in perpetual crisis.* New York: Norton.

Kahn, S. (1995). Community organization. In *Encyclopedia of social work* (19th ed.). Washington DC: National Association of Social Workers.

Kaluzny, A. D., & McLaughlin, C. P. (1992). Managing transitions: Assuring the adoption and impact of TQM. *Quality Review Bulletin, 18,* 380-384.

Kane, R. A. (1984). Toward a science of hospital social work. In T. O. Carlton, *Clinical social work in health settings: A guide to professional practice with exemplars.* New York: Springer.

Kane, R. A. (1987). Long-term care. *Encyclopedia of social work* (18th ed.). Silver Spring, MD: National Association of Social Workers.

Kane, R. A., & Kane, R. L. (1981). *Assessing the elderly: A practical guide to measurement.* Lexington, MA: D. C. Heath.

Kane, R. A., & Kane, R. L. (1987). *Long-term care: Principles, programs, and policies.* New York: Springer.

Kane, R. L. (1988). The hospital and geriatrics: Can a medical center be happy at the periphery? In C. Eisdorfer & G. L. Maddox (Eds.), *The role of hospitals in geriatric care* (pp. 19-34). New York: Springer.

Kane, R. L. (1994). Making aging a public health priority. *American Journal of Public Health, 84,* 1213-1214.

Kapp, M. B. (1990). Home care service deliverers: Options for consumers. In C. Zukerman, N. N. Dubler, & B. Collopy (Eds.), *Home health care options: A guide for older persons and concerned families.* New York: Plenum.

Kapust, L. R. (1982). Living with dementia: The ongoing funeral. *Social Work in Health Care, 7*(4), 82.

Karinch, M. (1994). *Telemedicine: What the future holds when you're ill.* Far Hills, NJ: New Horizon.

Katz, S., & Committee on Nursing Home Regulation, Institute of Medicine. (1986). *Improving the quality of care in nursing homes.* Washington, DC: National Academy Press.

Kaufman, K. L., Johnson, C. F., Cohn, D., & McCleery, J. (1992). Child maltreatment prevention in the health care and social service system. In D. J. Willis, E. W. Holden, & M. Rosenberg (Eds.), *Prevention of child maltreatment: Developmental and ecological perspectives* (pp. 193-225). New York: John Wiley.

Kaufman, K. L., & Zigler, E. (1992). The prevention of child maltreatment: Programming, research, and policy. In D. J. Willis, E. W. Holden, & M. Rosenberg (Eds.), *Prevention of child maltreatment: Developmental and ecological perspectives* (pp. 269-296). New York: John Wiley.

Kelly, M. P., Charlton, B. G., & Hanlon, P. (1993). The four levels of health promotion: An integrated approach. *Public Health, 107,* 319-326.

Kemler, B. (1985). Family treatment in the health setting: The need for innovation. *Social Work in Health Care, 10*(4), 45-53.

Kenny, J. J. (1990). Social work management in emerging health care system. *Health and Social Work, 15,* 22-31.

Kermis, M. D. (1986). *Mental health in late life: The adaptive process.* Boston: Jones & Bartlett.

Kerson, T. S. (1979). Sixty years ago: Hospital social work in 1918. *Social Work in Health Care, 4*(3), 331-343.

Kerson, T. S. (1985). Responsiveness to need: Social work's impact on health care. *Health and Social Work, 10,* 300-307.

Kerson, T. S., DuChainey, D., & Schmid, W. W. (1989). Maternal and child health: Teen mother-well baby clinic. In T. S. Kerson & Associates, *Social work in health settings: Practice in context* (pp. 215-230). New York: Haworth.

Keys, P. R. (1995). Quality management. *Encyclopedia of social work* (19th ed.). Washington, DC: National Association of Social Work.

Kieffer, C. (1984). Citizen empowerment: A developmental perspective. In J. Rappaport, C. Swift, & R. Hess (Eds.), *Studies in empowerment: Steps toward understanding and action.* New York: Haworth.

Kirsch, A., & Donovan, S. (1992, August). Quality issues: The journey to quality improvement in health care. *Caring,* pp. 46-51.

Kirst-Ashman, K. K. (1994, March). *A generalist approach to macro practice: Integrating micro, mezzo, and macro perspectives.* Paper presented at the 40th Annual Program Meeting of the Council on Social Work Education, Atlanta, GA.

Kirst-Ashman, K. K., & Hull, G. H., Jr. (1993). *Understanding generalist practice.* Chicago: Nelson-Hall.

Klein, T., & Danzig, F. (1985). *Publicity: How to make the media work for you.* New York: Scribner.

Klima, D. E. (1992). Incremental change: Community hospital reaction. In B. J. Jaeger (Ed.), *Hospitals in the year 2000: Three scenarios* (Report of the 1991 National Forum on Hospital and Health Affairs held in Durham, NC, May 15-17; pp. 49-56). Durham, NC: Duke University.

Kokkinos, J., & Levine, S. R. (1993). Stroke. *Neurology Clinician, 11*(3), 577-590.

Koplin, A. N. (1993). A national program to restructure local public health agencies in the United States. *Journal of Public Health Policy, 14,* 393-402.

Kotler, P. (1982). *Marketing for nonprofit organizations.* Upper Saddle River, NJ: Prentice Hall.

Kramer, A. M., Fox, P. D., & Morgenstern, N. (1992). Geriatric care approaches in health maintenance organizations. *Journal of the American Geriatrics Society, 40,* 1055-1067.

Kraus, L. E., & Stoddard, S. (1989). *Chartbook on disability in the United States.* Washington, DC: National Institute of Disability and Rehabilitation Research.

Kraus, W. A. (1980). *Collaboration in organizations: Alternatives to hierarchy.* New York: Human Sciences Press.

Kriesberg, L. (1982). *Social conflict.* Upper Saddle River, NJ: Prentice Hall.

Kurlowicz, L. H. (1994). Depression in hospitalized medically ill elders: Evolution of the concept. *Archives of Psychiatric Nursing, 3*(2), 124-136.

Kurpius, D. J. (1978). Consultation theory and process: An integrated model. *Personnel and Guidance Psychologist, 13,* 368-389.

Kurpius, D. J., & Fuqua, D. R. (1993). Fundamental issues in defining consultation. *Journal of Counseling & Development, 71,* 598-600.

Kurpius, D. J., Fuqua, D. R., & Rozecki, T. (1993). The consulting process: A multidimensional approach. *Journal of Counseling & Development, 71,* 601-606.

Lakein, A. (1973). *How to get control of your time and your life.* New York: New American Library.

Lakey, J. F. (1992). Myth information and bizarre beliefs of male juvenile sex offenders. *Journal of Addictions and Offender Counseling, 13*(1), 2-10.

Lamm, R. D. (1989). Columbus and Copernicus: New wine in old wineskins. *Mount Sinai Journal of Medicine, 56,* 1-10.

Latinos on the rise. (1993, January-February). *The Futurist,* pp. 48-49.

Latkin, C., Mandell, W., Vlahov, D., Oziemkowska, M., Knowlton, A., & Celentano, D. (1994). My place, your place, and no place: Behavior settings as a risk factor for HIV-related injection practices of drug users in Baltimore, Maryland. *American Journal of Community Psychology, 22,* 415-430.

Lauffer, A. (1978). *Social planning at the community level.* Upper Saddle River, NJ: Prentice Hall.

Law, S. (1976). *Blue Cross: What went wrong?* New Haven, CT: Yale University Press.

Lawrance, F., & Volland, P. J. (1988). The community care program: Description and administration. *Adult Foster Care Journal, 2,* 26-37.

Lawrence, T. (1980, September). Your self-image determines your success as a leader. *Leadership,* pp. 17-19.

Lawton, M. P. (1986). Functional assessment. In L. Teri & P. M. Lewinson (Eds.), *Geropsychological assessment and treatment.* New York: Springer.

Lazarus, R. S., & Folkman, S. (1984). *Stress, appraisal, and coping.* New York: Springer.

Lazes, P. (1977). Health education project guides outpatients to active self-care. *Hospitals, 51.*

Leavell, H. R., & Clark, E. G. (1965). *Preventive medicine for the doctor in his community.* New York: McGraw-Hill.

Lee, P. R. (1994). Reinventing the Public Health Service: A look in a 50-year-old mirror [Editorial]. *Public Health Reports, 109,* 466-467.

Lee, P. R. (1995). Advancing America's health. *Journal of the American Medical Association, 273*(3), 248-249.

Lee, P. R., & Toomey, K. E. (1994). Epidemiology in public health in the era of health care reform. *Public Health Reports, 109,* 1-3.

Lehman, D. R., Ellard, J. H., & Wortman, C. B. (1986). Social support for the bereaved: Recipients' and providers' perspectives on what is helpful. *Journal of Consulting and Clinical Psychology, 54,* 438-446.

Lehr, H., & Strosberg, M. (1991). Quality improvement in health care: Is the patient still left out? *Quality Review Bulletin, 17,* 326-329.

Lehrmann, E.I. (1994). It's time to take back our streets. *Modern Maturity, 37,* 4-5.

Leukefeld, C. G., & Welsh, R. (1995). Health care systems policy. In *Encyclopedia of social work* (19th ed.). Washington, DC: National Association of Social Workers.

Levine, C. (1984). Questions and (some very tentative) answers about hospital ethics committees. *Hastings Center Report, 14*(3), 9-12.

Levine, C. (1991). Commentary: AIDS prevention and education: Reframing the message. *AIDS Education and Prevention, 3,* 147-163.

Levine, S. (1987). The changing terrains of medical sociology: Emergent concern with quality of life. *Journal of Health and Social Behavior, 28,* 1-6.

Levitas, A. S., & Gilson, S. F. (1987). Emotional and developmental needs of mentally retarded people. In S. F. Gilson, T. L. Goldsbury, & E. H. Faulkner (Eds.), *Three populations of primary focus* (pp. 139-140). Omaha: University of Nebraska & Creighton University.

Lewis, D., Das, N. K., Hopper, C. L., & Jencks, M. (1991). A program of support for AIDS research in the social/behavioral sciences. *Quarterly Journal of Minority Community AIDS Research, 5*(3), 2-5.

Lewis, V. S. (1971). Charity organization society. In *Encyclopedia of social work* (16th ed., pp. 94-98). New York: National Association of Social Workers.

Lewit, E. M. (1993). Child indicators: Why is poverty increasing among children? *Future of Children, 3*(2), 198-207.

Lindgren, C. L., & Linton, A. D. (1991). Problems of nursing home residents: Nurse and resident perceptions. *Applied Nursing Research, 4,* 113-121.

Linn, M. W., Caffey, E. M., Klett, J., & Hogarty, G. (1977). Hospital vs. community (foster) care for psychiatric patients. *Archives of General Psychiatry, 34,* 78-83.

Lippitt, R., & Lippitt, G. (1978). *The consulting process in action.* La Jolla, CA: University Associates.

Litwak, E., & Meyer, H. F. (1966). A balanced theory of coordination between bureaucratic organizations and community primary groups. *Administrative Science Quarterly, 11,* 31-58.

Litwak, E., & Meyer, H. J. (1974). *School, family, and neighborhood: The theory and practice of school-community relations.* New York: Columbia University Press.

Locke, N. H. (1993). Hospitals and raising funds. *Canadian Medical Association Journal, 149*(3), 260.

Lockhart, L. L., & Wodarski, J. S. (1989). Facing the unknown: Children and adolescents with AIDS. *Social Work, 34,* 215-222.

London, H. I. (1988, July-August). The phenomenon of change. *The Futurist,* p. 64.

Long, C. E., et al. (1993). The hospital: An important site for family-centered early intervention. *Topics in Early Childhood Special Education, 13*(1), 106-119.

Longe, M. E., & Wolf, A. (1983). *Promoting community health through innovative hospital-based programs.* Chicago: American Hospital Association.

Longer-lived artificial hips. (1994, July-August). *The Futurist,* p. 5.

Loomis, J. (1988). Case management in health care. *Health and Social Work, 13,* 219-225.

Lopez, S. A., et al. (1993). *The social work perspective on managed care for mental health and substance abuse treatment.* Washington, DC: National Association of Social Workers.

Lorber, J. (1975). Good patients and problem patients: Conformity and deviance in a general hospital. *Journal of Health and Social Behavior, 16,* 213-225.

Louria, D. B. (1989). *Your body, your healthy life: How to take control of your medical destiny.* New York: Master Media Limited.

Lowe, J. I., & Harranen, M. (1981). Understanding teamwork: Another look at the concepts. *Social Work in Health Care, 7*(2), 1-11.

Luepker, R. V., & Rastam, L. (1990). Involving community health professionals and systems. In N. Bracht (Ed.), *Health promotion at the community level* (pp. 185-198). Newbury Park, CA: Sage.

Lum, D. (1992). *Social work practice and people of color: A process-stage approach.* Pacific Grove, CA: Brooks/Cole.

Lundberg, G. D. (1994). United States health care system reform: An era for shared sacrifice and responsibility begins. *Journal of the American Medical Association, 271,* 1530-1533.

Lundberg, G. D. (1995). How to approach universal access to basic medical care without our government doing it. *Journal of the American Medical Association, 273*(3), 242.

MacAdam, M., & Yee, D. (1990). *Providing high-quality services to the frail elderly: A study of homemaker services in greater Boston.* Boston: Brandeis University, Bigel Institute for Health Policy.

Macias, C., Kinney, R., Farley, O. W., Jackson, R., & Vos, B. (1994). The role of case management with a community support system: Partnership with psychosocial rehabilitation. *Community Mental Health Journal, 30,* 323-339.

Maguire, L. (1983). *Understanding social networks.* Beverly Hills, CA: Sage.

Mainstream takes new look at alternative medicine. (1994, September 22). *Lexington Herald-Leader,* pp. A3, A8.

Malamuth, N. M. (1991). Characteristics of aggressors against women: Testing a model using a national sample of college students. *Journal of Consulting and Clinical Psychology, 59,* 670-681.

Malone-Rising, D. (1994). The changing face of long-term care. *Nursing Clinics of North America, 29,* 417-429.

Mandel, I. (1994). Smoke signals: An alert for oral disease. *Journal of American Dental Association, 125,* 872-878.

Man-made materials save life and limb. (1988, November-December). *The Futurist,* p. 59.

Mantell, J. E. (1984). Social work in public health. In R. J. Estes (Ed.), *Health care and the social services: Social work practice in health care* (pp. 207-259). St. Louis, MO: Warren H. Green.

Manton, K. G., Corder, L. S., & Stallard, E. (1993). Estimates of change in chronic disability and institutional incidence and prevalence rate in the U.S. elderly population from 1982, 1984, and 1989 National Long-Term Care Survey. *Journal of Gerontology, 48,* S153-S166.

Many clues, few conclusions on AIDS. (1994). *Journal of the American Medical Association, 272*(10), 753-756.

Maple, M. F. (1992). STEAMWORK: An effective approach to team building. *Journal of Specialists in Group Work, 17,* 144-150.

Marcenko, M. O., & Smith, L. K. (1992). The impact of a family-centered case management approach. *Social Work in Health Care, 17*(1), 87-99.

Martin, P. A. (1995). Finding time for research. *Applied Nursing Research, 8*(3), 151-153.

Martin, P. Y., & O'Connor, G. (1988). *The social environment: Open systems applications.* New York: Longman.

Martinez-Brawley, E. E. (1995). Community. In *Encyclopedia of social work* (19th ed.). Washington, DC: National Association of Social Workers.

Martino, J. P. (1993, July-August). Technological forecasting: An introduction. *The Futurist,* pp. 13-16.

Marx, J. (1993). Up in smoke: The effects of secondhand smoke on children's health. *PTA Today, 19*(2), 10-11.

Mayer, B. S. (1995). Conflict resolution. In *Encyclopedia of social work* (19th ed.). Washington, DC: National Association of Social Workers.

McCabe, W. J. (1992). Total quality management in a hospital. *Quality Review Bulletin, 18,* 134-140.

McCoin, J. M. (1983). *Adult foster homes.* New York: Human Sciences Press.

McCoin, J. M. (1995). Editorial observations: What is adult residential care? *Adult Residential Care Journal, 9,* 1-11.

McCubbin, H., & Patterson, J. M. (1981). *Systematic assessment of family stress, resources, and coping: Tools for research, education, and clinical practice.* St. Paul, MN: Family Social Science.

McDonnell, J. R., Abell, N., & Miller, J. (1991). Family members' willingness to care for people with AIDS: A psychosocial assessment model. *Social Work, 35,* 43-53.

McFarland, S. (1995, April). *Government by special interest: The Children's Defense Fund lobby.* Paper presented at the Annual Meeting of the Central States Communication Association, Indianapolis, IN.

McGinnis, J. M. (1982). Future directions of health promotion. In R. B. Yaylor, J. R. Ureda, & J. W. Denham (Eds.), *Health promotion: Principles and clinical applications.* Norwalk, CT: Appleton-Century-Crofts.

McGowan, B. G. (1987). Advocacy. In *Encyclopedia of social work* (18th ed.). Silver Spring, MD: National Association of Social Workers.

McInerney, S. L. (1979). Inpatient options: Summary of hospice. In M. M. Melum (Ed.), *The changing role of the hospital: Options for the future* (pp. 43-60). Chicago: American Hospital Association.

McMahon, B. (1993). Time for a change in direction: Effects of poverty on ill health and service provision. *Professional Nurse, 8,* 610-613.

McNally, P. C. (1990). Expanding the public mind. *Justice Horizons, II*(2).

Mechanic, D. (1980). The management of psychosocial problems in primary care: A potential role for social work. *Journal of Human Stress, 6,* 16-21.

Medicaid Access Study Group. (1994). Access of Medicaid recipients to outpatient care. *New England Journal of Medicine, 330,* 1426-1430.

Meichenbaum, D., & Jaremko M. E. (1983). *Stress reduction and prevention.* New York: Plenum.

Melton, G. B. (1992). The improbability of prevention of sexual abuse. In D. J. Willis, E. W. Holden, & M. Rosenberg (Eds.), *Prevention of child maltreatment: Developmental and ecological perspectives* (pp. 168-192). New York: John Wiley.

Merrill, J. (1992). A test of our society: How and for whom we finance long-term care. *Inquiry, 29,* 176-187.

Merrill, J. C. (1994). *The road to health care reform: Designing a system that works.* New York: Plenum.

Meyer, C. H. (1984). The perils and promises of the health practice domain. *Social Work in Health Care, 10*(2), 1-11.

Mezey, M., & Knapp, M. (1993). Nurse staffing in nursing facilities. In P. R. Katz, R. L. Kane, & M. D. Mezey (Eds.), *Advances in long-term care* (pp. 130-149). New York: Springer.

Mihaly, L. (1991). Beyond the numbers: Homeless families with children. In J. Kryder-Coe, L. Salamon, & M. Molnar (Eds.), *Homeless children and youth: A new American dilemma* (pp. 11-31). New Brunswick, NJ: Transaction Publishing.

Miller, C. A., Brooks, E. F., DeFriese, G. H., Gilbert, B., Jain, S. C., & Kavaler, F. (1977). A survey of local public health departments and their directors. *American Journal of Public Health, 67,* 931-939.

Miller, L. (1986). The making of a home. *Nursing Times, 82,* 40-41.

Miller, R. H., & Luft, H. S. (1994). Managed care plan performance since 1980: A literature analysis. *Journal of the American Medical Association, 271,* 1512-1519.

Milton, T. (1983). What is primary care? *Journal of Public Health Policy, 4,* 129-130.

Miner, E. J., & Jacobsen, M. (1990). Coalition building in human services: Enhancing rural identity in the shadow of the Big Apple. *Human Services in the Rural Environment, 14,* 5-9.

Minkler, M., & Pasick, R. J. (1986). Health promotion and the elderly: A critical perspective on the past and future. In K. Dychtwald (Ed.), *Wellness and health promotion for the elderly* (pp. 39-54). Gaithersburg, MD: Aspen.

Mintz, S. G. (1994, November/December). Family outreach: Image upgrade. *Nursing Homes,* pp. 22-24.

Mishel, M. M., & Murdaugh, C. L. (1987). Family adjustment to heart transplantation: Redesigning the dream. *Nursing Research, 36*(6), 332-338.

Mitchell, D., & Braddock, D. (1990). Historical and contemporary issues in nursing home reform. *Mental Retardation, 28,* 201-210.

Mizrahi, T. (1986). *Getting rid of patients: Contradictions in the socialization of physicians.* New Brunswick, NJ: Rutgers University Press.

Mizrahi, T. (1993). Managed care and managed competition: A primer for social work. *Health & Social Work, 18,* 86-91.

Mongan, J. J. (1995, Spring). Anatomy and physiology of health reform's failure. *Health Affairs,* pp. 99-101.

Monk, A. (1981). Social work with the aged: Principles of practice. *Social Work, 26,* 61-68.

Moonilal, J. M. (1982). Trauma centers: A new dimension for hospital social work. *Social Work in Health Care, 7*(4), 15-25.

Moore, C. W. (1986). *The mediation process: Practical strategies for resolving conflict.* San Francisco: Jossey-Bass.

Morey, M. A., & Friedman, L. S. (1993). Health care needs of homeless adolescents. *Current Opinion in Pediatrics, 5*(4), 395-399.

Morgado, P. B., Chen, H. C., Patel, V., Herbert, L., & Kohner, E. M. (1994). The acute effect of smoking on retinal blood flow in subjects with and without diabetes. *Ophthalmology, 101, 1220-1226.*

Morgan, A., & Zimmerman, M. (1990). Easing transition to nursing homes: Identifying the needs of spousal caregivers at the time of institutionalization. *Clinical Gerontologist, 9*(3/4), 1-17.

Morrice, J. K. W. (1976). *Crisis intervention: Studies in community care.* Elmsford, NY: Pergamon.

Morrow-Howell, N., Proctor, E., & Mui, A. (1991). Adequacy of discharge plans for elderly patients. *Social Work Research and Abstracts, 27,* 6-13.

Morton, C. J. (1985). Public health social work priorities in maternal and child health. In A. Gitterman, R. B. Black, & F. Stein (Eds.), *Public health social work in maternal and child health: A forward plan* (Report of the Working Conference of the Public Health Social Work Advisory Committee for the Bureau of Health Care Delivery and Assistance). New York: Columbia University School of Social Work.

Moynihan, R., Christ, G., & Gallo-Silver, L. (1988). AIDS and terminal illness. *Social Casework, 6,* 380-387.

Mullaney, J. W., & Andrews, B. J. (1983). Legal problems and principles in discharge planning: Implications for social work. *Social Work in Health Care, 9*(1), 53-62.

Mullen, E. J., & Schuerman, J. R. (1990). Expert systems and the development of knowledge in social welfare. In L. Videka-Sherman & W. J. Reid (Eds.), *Advances in clinical social work research* (pp. 67-83). Silver Spring, MD: National Association of Social Workers.

Munley, A., Powers, C., & Williamson, J. B. (1982). Humanizing nursing home environments: The relevance of hospice principles. *International Journal of Aging and Human Development, 15,* 263-284.

Myers, A. M., Pfeiffle, P., & Hinsdale, K. (1994). Building a community-based consortium for AIDS patient services. *Public Health Reports, 109,* 555-562.

Myers, V. (1995, April). *Offering a pragmatic approach to State Speech Association involvement in advocacy efforts—Or lessons learned, unlearned, and relearned the hard way in seeking to influence education policy in Texas.* Paper presented at the Annual Meeting of the Central State Speech Communication Association, Oklahoma City.

Nacman, M. (1977). Social work in health settings: A historical review. *Social Work in Health Care, 2*(4), 407-418.

Nadel, V. (1993). *Emergency departments: Unevenly affected by growth and change in patient use* (Pub. No. 93-4). Washington, DC: General Accounting Office, Human Resources Division.

Naisbitt, J., & Aburdene, P. (1990). *Megatrends 2000: Ten new directions for the 1990s.* New York: William Morrow.

Nason, F. (1983). Diagnosing the hospital team. *Social Work in Health Care, 9*(2), 25-45.

National Academy of Sciences. (1966). *Accidental death and disability: The neglected disease of modern society.* Washington, DC: U.S. Department of Health, Education & Welfare.

National Association for Home Care. (1994). *Basic statistics about home care 1994.* Washington, DC: Author.

National Association of County Health Officials. (1990). *National profile of local public health departments.* Washington, DC: Author.

National Association of Social Workers (NASW). (1981). *Guidelines for the selection and use of social workers.* Silver Spring, MD: Author.

National Association of Social Workers (NASW). (1991). *Standards of practice for social work mediators.* Silver Spring, MD: Author.

National Association of Social Workers (NASW). (1994a). *A brief look at managed mental health care.* Washington, DC: Author.

National Association of Social Workers (NASW). (1994b). Managed care. In *Social work speaks* (pp. 169-174). Washington, DC: Author.

National Coalition for the Homeless. (1989). *Over the edge: Homeless families and the welfare system.* Washington, DC: Author.

National Committee for Prevention of Child Abuse (NCPCA). (1989). *Fact sheet: Substance abuse and child abuse.* Chicago: Author.

Neighbors, H. W., Braithwaite, R. L., & Thompson, E. (1995). Health promotion and African Americans: From personal empowerment to community action. *American Journal of Health Promotion, 9,* 281-286.

Neville, K., Bromberg, A., Ronk, S., Hanna, B. A., & Rom, W. N. (1994). The third epidemic: Multidrug-resistent tuberculosis. *Chest, 105*(1), 45-48.

New laser for eyes. (1990, May-June). *The Futurist,* p. 5.

Nickelsberg, B. (1988, November). Getting a grant. *Association Management,* pp. 126-129.

Nolte, W. W., & Wilcox, D. L. (1984). *Effective publicity: How to reach people.* New York: John Wiley.

Norris, F. H. (1992). Epimediology of trauma: Frequency and impact of different potentially traumatic events on different demographic groups. *Journal of Consulting and Clinical Psychology, 60,* 409-418.

No-scalpel vasectomy. (1988, March-April). *The Futurist,* p. 4.

O'Brien, J., Saxberg, B., & Smith, H. (1983). For-profit or not-for-profit: Does it matter? *The Gerontologist, 23,* 229-248.

O'Donovan, T. R. (1976). *Ambulatory surgical centers: Development and management.* Gaithersburg, MD: Aspen.

Office of Technology Assessment. (1987). *Life-sustaining technologies and the elderly.* Washington, DC: U.S. Congress, GPO.

Office of Technology Assessment. (1990). *Confused minds, burdened families.* Washington, DC: U.S. Congress, GPO.

O'Hare, P. A., Malone, D., Lusk, E., & McCorkle, R. (1993). Unmet needs of black patients with cancer posthospitalization: A descriptive study. *Oncology Nurses Forum, 20*(4), 659-664.

Oktay, J. S. (1987). Foster care for adults. *Encyclopedia of social work* (18th ed., pp. 634-638). Silver Spring, MD: National Association of Social Workers.

Oktay, J. S., & Palley, H. A. (1988). The frail elderly and the promise of foster care. *Adult Foster Care Journal, 2,* 8-25.

Oktay, J. S., & Volland, P. J. (1981). Community care programs for the elderly. *Health & Social Work, 6,* 41-47.

Oktay, J. S., & Volland, P. J. (1987). Foster home care for the frail elderly as an alternative to nursing home care: An experimental evaluation. *American Journal of Public Health, 77,* 1505-1510.

Olds, D. L., Henderson, C., & Tatelbaum, R. (1994). Intellectual impairment in children of women who smoke cigarettes during pregnancy. *Pediatrics, 93,* 221-227.

O'Leary, D. S. (1991a). Accreditation in the quality improvement mold: A vision for tomorrow. *Quality Review Bulletin, 17,* 72-77.

O'Leary, D. S. (1991b). CQI: A step beyond QA. *Quality Review Bulletin, 17,* 4-5.

Olesen, D. E. (1995, September-October). The top 10 technologies for the next 10 years. *The Futurist,* pp. 9-13.

Olson, D. H. (1989). Circumplex model of family systems: Part VIII. Family assessment and intervention. In D. H. Olson, C. S. Russell, & D. H. Sprenkle (Eds.), *Circumplex model: Systemic assessment and treatment of families* (pp. 7-50). New York: Haworth.

Olson, D. H., & Hanson, M.K. (1990). *2001: Preparing families for the future.* Minneapolis, MN: National Council on Family Relations.

Olson, D. H., McCubbin, H., Barnes, H., Larsen, A., Muxen, M., & Wilson, M. (1982). *Family inventories: Inventories used in a national survey of families across the family life cycle.* St. Paul: University of Minnesota Family Social Science.

Organ regeneration. (1989, November-December). *The Futurist,* p. 5.

Osgood, N. J., Brant, B. A., & Lipman, A. (1991). *Suicide among the elderly in long-term care facilities.* Westport, CT: Greenwood.

Osman, L. M., Abdalla, M. I., Beattie, J. A., Ross, S. J., Russell, I. T., Friend, J. A., Legge, J. S., & Douglas, J. G. (1994). Reducing hospital admission through computer supported education for asthma patients. *British Medical Journal, 308*(6928), 568-571.

Oss, M. (1994). Managed care and industry analysis: Behavioral health providers in a changing health care landscape. *Treatment Today, 6*(1), 28-30.

Ostrow, D. G. (1989). AIDS prevention through effective education. *Daedalus, 118,* 229-253.

Owens, A. (1988, September). How much did your earnings grow last year? *Medical Economics, 65,* 159-180.

Pagana, K. D. (1995). Teaching students time management strategies. *Journal of Nursing Education, 33*(8), 381-383.

Pagelow, M. D. (1981). *Woman-battering: Victims and their experiences.* Beverly Hills, CA: Sage.

Pagelow, M. D. (1992). Adult victims of domestic violence: Battered women. *Journal of Interpersonal Violence, 7,* 87-120.

Parsons, R. J. (1988). Empowerment for role alternatives for low-income minority girls: A group work approach. *Social Work with Groups, 11*(4), 27-45.

Pascarelli, E. F. (Ed.). (1982). *Hospital-based ambulatory care.* Norwalk, CT: Appleton-Century-Crofts.

Patterson, J. (1995). Pediatric and maternal HIV/AIDS: Social work intervention. In J. B. Rauch (Ed.), *Community-based, family-centered services in a changing health care environment.* Arlington, VA: National Maternal and Child Health Clearinghouse.

Pearman, L. U., & Searles, J. (1978). Unmet social service needs in skilled nursing facilities. In N. F. Bracht (Ed.), *Social work in health care: A guide to professional practice* (pp. 184-197). New York: Haworth.

Pepper, C. (1986). *Statement at the hearings before the Subcommittee on Health and Long-Term Care of the Select Committee on Aging, House of Representatives, 99th Congress on September 18, 1985* (Comm. Pub. No. 99-543). Washington, DC: Government Printing Office.

Petersdorf, R. G. (1993). The doctor is in. *Academic Medicine, 68,* 113-117.

Pietgen, H. O., & Richter, P. H. (1986). *The beauty of fractals: Images of complex dynamical systems.* New York: Springer.

Piliavin, I., Westerfelt, A., Yin-Ling, I., & Afflerbach, A. (1994). Health status and health-care utilization among the homeless. *Social Service Review, 68*(2), 236-253.

Pinderhughes, E. B. (1983). Empowerment for our clients and for ourselves. *Social Casework, 64,* 331-338.

Pizer, H. F., & the Massachusetts General Hospital Organ Transplant Team. (1991). *Organ transplants: A patient's guide.* Cambridge, MA: Harvard University Press.

Plichta, S. (1992). The effects of woman abuse on health care utilization and health status: A literature review. *Women's Health Issues, 2*(3), 154-163.

Pope, A. M., & Tarlov, A. R. (1991). *Disability in America: Toward a national agenda.* Washington, DC: National Academy Press.

Pratt, C., Schmall, V., Wright, S., & Hare, J. (1987). The forgotten client: Family caregivers to institutionalized dementia patients. In T. Brubaker (Ed.), *Aging, health, and family: Long-term care* (pp. 197-285). Newbury Park, CA: Sage.

Prentky, R. A., & Knight, R. A. (1991). Identifying critical dimensions for discriminating among rapists. *Journal of Consulting and Clinical Psychology, 59,* 643-661.

President's Commission for the Study of Ethical Problems in Medicine and Biomedical and Behavioral Research. (1983). *Deciding to forego life-sustaining treatment: A report of the ethical, medical, and moral issues in treatment decisions.* Washington, DC: Government Printing Office.

Preventing birth defects. (1986, November-December). *The Futurist,* p. 47.

Preventing sudden cardiac death. (1990, July-August). *The Futurist,* p. 6.

Prochaska, J. O., DiClemente, B., & Norcross, J. C. (1992). In search of how people change: Applications to addictive behaviors. *American Psychologist, 47,* 1102-1114.

Proctor, E., & Morrow-Howell, N. (1990). Complications in charge planning with Medicare patients. *Health and Social Work, 8,* 45-54.

Proton therapy. (1989, November-December). *The Futurist,* p. 5.

Public Health Foundation. (1991). *Public health agencies 1991: An inventory of programs and block grant expenditures.* Washington, DC: Author.

Public Health Service. (1979). *Healthy people: The Surgeon General's report on health promotion and disease prevention.* Washington, DC: Government Printing Office.

Public Health Service. (1980). *Promoting health/preventing disease: Objectives for the nation.* Washington, DC: Government Printing Office.

Public Health Service. (1992). *Healthy people 2000 consortium action.* Washington, DC: Author.

Public Health Service. (1993). *Health promotion goes to work: Programs with an impact.* Washington, DC: Author.

Quinn, J., Segal, J., Raisz, H., & Johnson, C. (Eds.). (1982). *Coordinating community services for the elderly: The triage experience.* New York: Springer.

Raffel, M. W., & Raffel N. K. (1989). *The U.S. health system: Origin and functions.* New York: John Wiley.

Rainey, J., & Lindsay, G. (1994). 101 questions for community health promotion program planning. *Journal of Health Education, 25,* 309-312.

Randall, T. (1990). Domestic violence intervention calls for more than treating injuries. *Journal of the American Medical Association, 264,* 939-940.

Randall, V. R. (1994). Impact of managed care organizations on ethnic Americans and underserved populations. *Journal of Health Care for the Poor and the Underserved, 5*(3), 224-236.

Rapaport, L. (1967). Crisis-oriented short-term casework. *Social Service Review, 41,* 31-43.

Rathbone-McCuan, E. (1995). Agency-based research. In *Encyclopedia of social work* (19th ed., pp. 136-142). Washington, DC: National Association of Social Workers.

Rauch, J. B. (1988). Social work and the genetics revolution: Genetic services. *Social Work, 33,* 389-394.

Ray, J. (1993). Survival methods of young street mothers. *Child and Adolescent Social Work Journal, 10*(3), 189-205.

Re, R. N., & Krousel-Wood, M. A. (1990). How to use continuous quality improvement theory and statistical quality control tools in a multispecialty clinic. *Quality Review Bulletin, 16,* 391-97.

Reamer, F. G. (1991). The emergence of bioethics in social work. *Health and Social Work, 10,* 271-281.

Reardon, G. T., Blumenfield, S., Weissman, A. L., & Rosenberg, G. (1988). Findings and implications from preadmission screening of elderly patients waiting for elective surgery. *Social Work in Health Care, 13*(3), 51-63.

Rehr, H. (1986). Discharge planning: An ongoing function of quality care. *Quality Review Bulletin, 12*(2), 47-50.

Rehr, H. (1991). Introduction: The changing context of social-health care. *Social Work in Health Care, 17,* 3-16.

Rehr, H., & Rosenberg, G. (1991). Social health care: Problems and predictions. *Social Work in Health Care, 15*(4), 97-120.

Reid, W. J. (1995). Research overview. *Encyclopedia of social work* (19th ed.). Washington, DC: National Association of Social Workers.

Report of the ASM Task Force on Antibiotic Resistance. (1995). *Antimicrobial Agents and Chemotherapy*(Suppl.), 1-23.

Reynolds, R. E. (1975). Primary care, ambulatory care, and family medicine: Overlapping but not synonymous. *Journal of Medical Education, 50*(9), 893-895.

Rice, E. P. (1957, November). *Social work in public health.* Paper presented at National Association of Social Workers meeting, Cleveland Chapter, Cleveland, OH.

Richman, D. (1987, June 5). PPOs outstripped HMOs last year in number of locations and enrollment. *Modern Health Care*, pp. 130-136.

Riessman, F. (1994). Alternative health movements. *Social Policy, 24*(3), 53-57.

Roberts, C. S., Severinsen, C., Kuehn, C., Straker, D., & Fritz, C. J. (1992). Obstacles to effective case management with AIDS patients: The clinician's perspective. *Social Work in Health Care, 17*(2), 27-40.

Roberts, M. C. (1994). Prevention/promotion in America: Still spitting on the sidewalk. *Journal of Pediatric Psychology, 19*, 267-281.

Robinson, J. C. (1994). The changing boundaries of the American hospital. *Milbank Quarterly, 72*, 259-275.

Robinson, M. A. (1982). Telephone notification of relatives of emergency and critical care patients. *Annals of Emergency Medicine, 11*, 616-618.

Rock, B. D., Haymes, E., Auerbach, C., & Beckerman, A. (1992). Helping patients in the supportive milieu of a community residence program for the chronically mentally ill: Conceptual model and initial evaluation. *Social Work in Health Care, 16*(3), 97-114.

Rockwood, G. F. (1993). Edgar Schein's process versus content consultation models. *Journal of Counseling & Development, 71*, 636-638.

Rodwell, M. K., & Chambers, D. E. (1992). Primary prevention of child abuse: Is it really possible? *Journal of Sociology and Social Welfare, 19*(3), 159-176.

Roemer, M. I. (1986). *Introduction to the health care system.* New York: Springer.

Roessler, R. T., & Rubin, S. (1982). *Case management and rehabilitation counseling.* Baltimore, MD: University Park Press.

Rogers, G. (1995). Educating case managers for culturally competent practice. *Journal of Case Management, 4*(2), 60-65.

Role of the social worker in discharge planning: Position statement of the Society for Hospital Social Work Directors of the American Hospital Association. (1986). *Quality Review Bulletin, 12*(2), 76.

Rose, S. M., & Moore, V. L. (1995). Case management. *Encyclopedia of social work* (19th ed.). Washington, DC: National Association of Social Workers.

Rosen, B., Locke, B., Goldberg, I., & Babigian, H. (1972). Identification of emotional disturbance in patients seen in general medical clinics. *Hospital and Community Psychiatry, 23*, 12.

Rosen, G. (1974). *From medical police to social medicine: Essays on the history of health care* (pp. 112-116). New York: Science History Publications.

Rosenberg, C. E. (1989). *Caring for the working man: The rise and fall of the dispensary—An anthology of sources.* New York: Garland.

Rosenberg, G., & Clarke, S. (Eds.). (1987). [Special issue]. *Social Work in Health Care, 12*(3).

Rosenberg, M. S., & Sonkin, D. J. (1992). The prevention of child maltreatment in school-aged children. In D. J. Willis, E. W. Holden, & M. Rosenberg (Eds.), *Prevention of child maltreatment: Developmental and ecological perspectives* (pp. 78-93). New York: John Wiley.

Rosenfeld, L. S. (1971). *Ambulatory care: Planning and organization*. Rockville, MD: U.S. Department of Health, Education and Welfare, Health Services and Mental Health Administration.

Rosenkrantz, B. G. (1972). *Public health and the state*. Cambridge, MA: Harvard University Press.

Rosenstock, I. M., Strecher, V. J., & Becker, M. H. (1988). Social learning theory and health belief model. *Health Education Quarterly, 15,* 175-183.

Ross, A., & Williams, S. J. (1991). In A. Ross, S. J. Williams, & E. L. Schafer (Eds.), *Ambulatory care administration*. Albany, NY: Delmar.

Ross, J. W. (1993). Taking responsibility. *Health and Social Work, 16,* 3-5.

Rothman, J. (1970). Three models of community organization practice. In F. M. Cox, J. L. Erlich, J. Rothman, & J. E. Tropman (Eds.), *Strategies of community organization* (pp. 20-36). Beverly Hills, CA: Sage.

Rubin, A., & Babbie, E. (1993). *Research methods for social work*. Pacific Grove, CA: Brooks/Cole

Rubin, F. H., & Black, J. S. (1992). Health care and consumer control: Pittsburgh's town meeting for seniors. *The Gerontologist, 32,* 853-855.

Rubin, H. J., & Rubin, I. (1986). *Community organizing and development*. Upper Saddle River, NJ: Merrill/Prentice Hall.

Sahney, V. K., & Warden, G. L. (1991). The quest for quality and productivity in health service. *Frontiers of Health Services Management, 7*(4), 2-40.

Salamon, M. J. (1986). *A basic guide to working with elders*. New York: Springer.

Sanborn, C. J. (Ed.). (1983). *Case management in mental health services*. New York: Haworth.

Sarazan, S. J. (1990, July). The tools of quality: Part II. Cause-and-effect diagrams. *Quality Progress*, pp. 59-62.

Schlesinger, E. G., & Devore, W. (1995). Ethnic-sensitive practice. *Encyclopedia of social work* (19th ed.). Washington, DC: National Association of Social Workers.

Schreter, R. (1993). Ten trends in managed care and their impact on the biopsychosocial model. *Hospital and Community Psychiatry, 44,* 325-327.

Schroeder, S. A. (1993). Training an appropriate mix of physicians to meet the nation's needs. *Academic Medicine, 68,* 118-122.

Self-help groups. (1988, January-February). *The Futurist*, pp. 51-52.

Seligman, M. E. P. (1975). *Helplessness: On depression, development, and death*. New York: Freeman.

Seward, P. J., & Todd, J. S. (1995). Health system reform: Whither or whether? *Journal of the American Medical Association, 273*(3), 246-247.

Shachter, B., & Seinfeld, J. (1994). Personal violence and the culture of violence. *Social Work, 39,* 347-350.

Shainin, P. D. (1990, August). The tools of quality: Part III. Control charts. *Quality Progress*, pp. 79-82.

Sharara, F. I., Beatse, S. N., Leonardi, M. R., Navot, D., & Scott, R. T., Jr. (1994). Cigarette smoking accelerates the development of diminished ovarian reserve as evidenced by the clomiphene citrate challenge test. *Fertility and Sterility, 62,* 257-262.

Sheafor, B. W., Horejsi, C. R., & Horejsi, G. A. (1988). *Techniques and guidelines for social work practice*. Needham Heights, MA: Allyn & Bacon.

Shelton, T. L., Jeppson, E. S., & Johnson, B. H. (1987). *Family-centered care for children with special health care needs.* Washington, DC: Association for the Care of Children's Health.

Sheridan, J. E., White, J., & Fairchild, T. J. (1992). Ineffective staff, ineffective supervision, or ineffective administration? Why some nursing homes fail to provide adequate care. *The Gerontologist, 32,* 334-341.

Sheridan, M. S. (1988). Time management in health care social work. *Social Work in Health Care, 13*(3), 91-99.

Sherman, S. R., & Newman, E. S. (1988). *Foster families for adults: A community alternative in long-term care.* New York: Columbia University Press.

Shevlin, K. M. (1983). Why a social service department in a hospital? In I. Hubschman (Ed.), *Hospital social work practice* (pp. 1-14). New York: Praeger.

Shine, K. I. (1995). Quality of health and health care. *Journal of the American Medical Association, 273*(3), 244-245.

Sickman, J. N., & Dhooper, S. S. (1991). Characteristics and competence of care providers in a Veterans Affairs community residential care home program. *Adult Residential Care Journal, 5,* 171-184.

Siefert, K. (1983). An exemplar of primary prevention in social work: The Sheppard-Towner Act of 1921. *Social Work in Health Care, 9*(1), 87-103.

Siegel, K., & Krauss, B. (1991). Living with HIV infection: Adaptive tasks of seropositive gay men. *Journal of Health and Social Behavior, 32,* 17-32.

Siegel, L. M., Attkisson, C. C., & Carlson, L. G. (1995). Need identification and program planning in the community context. In J. E. Tropman, J. Erlich, & J. Rothman (Eds.), *Tactics and techniques of community intervention* (3rd ed.). Itasca, IL: F. E. Peacock.

Sigerist, H. E. (1946). *The university at the crossroads.* New York: Henry Schuman.

Silverman, E. (1986). The social worker's role in shock-trauma units. *Social Work, 31,* 311-313.

Simmons, L., & Wolff, H. (1954). *Social science and medicine.* New York: Russell Sage.

Simmons, R. J., & Abress, L. (1990). Quality-of-life issues for end-stage renal disease patients. *American Journal of Kidney Diseases, 15,* 311-308.

Simon, B. L. (1994). *The empowerment tradition in American social work: A history.* New York: Columbia University Press.

Simon, R. L., & Aigner, S. M. (1985). *Practice principles: A problem-solving approach to social work.* New York: Macmillan.

Siporin, M. (1975). *Introduction to social work practice.* New York: Macmillan.

Skin scan. (1989, January-February). *The Futurist,* p. 5.

Smirnow, V. (1994, June). News and commentary from the nation's capital. *Dialysis & Transplantation.*

Smith, D. R. (1979). Hospice: Lessons of a Wisconsin hospital. In M. M. Melum (Ed.), *The changing role of the hospital: Options for the future* (pp. 61-64). Chicago: American Hospital Association.

Smith, H. Y., Loppnow, D. M., & Davis, L. E. (1995, March). *Community management: A postmodern response to traditional social work education and practice.* Paper presented at the 41st Annual Program Meeting of the Council on Social Work Education, San Diego, CA.

Smith, L. L. (1977). Crisis intervention theory and practice. *Community Mental Health Review, 2,* 4-13.

Smith, M. D., Alman, D. E., Leitmen, R., et al. (1992, Summer). Taking the public's pulse on health system reform. *Health Affairs*, pp. 125-133.

Snow, D. L., & Gordon, J. B. (1980). Social network analysis and intervention with the elderly. *The Gerontologist, 20,* 463-467.

Social work dictionary (2nd ed.). (1991). Silver Spring, MD: National Association of Social Workers.

Social work speaks (NASW policy statements, 3rd ed.). (1994). Washington, DC: National Association of Social Workers.

Solomon, R. (1983). Serving families of the institutionalized aged: The four crises. In G. S. Getzel & M. J. Mellor (Eds.), *Gerontological social work practice in long-term care.* New York: Haworth.

Sosin, M., & Caulum, S. (1983). Advocacy: A conceptualization for social work practice. *Social Work, 28,* 12-17.

Soskis, C. W. (1980). Emergency room on weekends: The only game in town. *Health and Social Work, 5*(3), 37-43.

Soskis, C. W. (1985). *Social work in the emergency room.* New York: Springer.

Space age computing aimed at damaged hearts. (1988, Summer). In *Cardiovascular Research Report.* Dallas, TX: American Heart Association.

Spiegal, A. D. (1987). *Home health care.* Owings Mills, MD: National Health Publishing.

Spitzer, W. J., & Neely, K. (1992). Critical incident stress: The role of hospital-based social work in developing a statewide intervention system for first-responders delivering emergency services. *Social Work in Health Care, 18*(1), 39-58.

A spoonful of hydrogel? (1991, January-February). *The Futurist,* p. 6.

Spotlight. (1992). *Dialysis and Transplantation, 21,* 618.

Staples, L. (1987). Can't ya hear me knocking: An organizing model. In F. M. Cox, J. L. Erlich, J. Rothman, & J. E. Tropman (Eds.), *Strategies of community organization.* Itasca, IL: F. E. Peacock.

Staples, L. H. (1990). Powerful ideas about empowerment. *Administration in Social Work, 14,* 29-42.

Stark, E., Flitcraft, A., Zuckerman, D., Gray, A., Robinson, J., & Frazier, W. (1981). *Wife abuse in the medical setting: An introduction for health personnel* (Domestic Violence Monograph Series No. 7). Washington, DC: National Clearinghouse on Domestic Violence, Government Printing Office.

Statistical abstract of the United States. (1993). Washington, DC: Government Printing Office.

Steckler, A., Allegrante, J. P., Altman, D., Brown, R., Burdine, J. N., Goodman, R. M., & Jorgensen, C. (1995). Health education intervention strategies: Recommendations for future research. *Health Education Quarterly, 22,* 307-328.

Steckler, A., Dawson, L., Goodman, R. M., & Epstein, N. (1987). Policy advocacy: Three emerging roles for health education. In W. Ward (Ed.), *Advances in health education and promotion* (Vol. 2, pp. 5-27). Greenwich, CT: JAI.

Stein, Z. (1993). HIV prevention: An update on the status of methods women can use. *American Journal of Public Health, 83,* 1379-1382.

Steinberg, R. M., & Carter, G. W. (1983). *Case management and the elderly.* Lexington, MA: Lexington Books.

Steinberg, T. N. (1991). Rape on college campuses: Reform through Title IX. *Journal of College and University Law, 18,* 39-71.

Stephens, G. (1994, July-August). The global crime wave: And what we can do about it. *The Futurist*, pp. 22-28.

Stevens, R. (1989). *In sickness and in wealth: American hospitals in the twentieth century.* New York: Basic Books.

Stewart, V. (1990). *The David solution.* Brookfield, VT: Gower.

Stoddard, J. J., St. Peter, R. F., & Newachech, P. W. (1994). Health insurance status and ambulatory care for children. *New England Journal of Medicine, 330,* 1421-1425.

Stoil, M. J. (1994, November/December). Patient self-determination: A good idea that needs work. *Nursing Homes,* pp. 8-9.

Stone, J. P., & Olson, J. F. (1989). A coalition to influence public policy. *Social Work in Health Care, 14*(1), 107-112.

Stones, M. J., Rattenbury, C., Taichman, B., Kozma, A., & Stones, L. (1990). Effective selection of participants for group discussion intervention. *Clinical Gerontologist, 9*(3/4), 135-143.

Strait, H. S. (1979). Wellness. In M. M. Melum (Ed.), *The changing role of the hospital: Options for the future* (pp. 139-144). Chicago: American Hospital Association.

Suchman, E. (1967). *Evaluative research.* New York: Russell Sage.

Suddenly breathless. (1990, July-August). *The Futurist,* p. 6.

Sullivan, M. J. (1995). Medicaid's quiet revolution: Merging the public and private sectors of care. *Professional Psychology: Research and Practice, 26*(3), 229-234.

Sutherland, B. S., & Oktay, J. S. (1987). Adult foster programs: Different strokes for different folks? *Adult Foster Care Journal, 1,* 226-237.

Sylvester, C., & Sheppard, F. (1988). Health and social services in the community care program. *Adult Foster Care Journal, 2,* 38-51.

Tabone, C., et al. (1992, April). *Why do women accept the rape myth?* Paper presented at the 63rd Annual Meeting of the Eastern Psychological Association, Boston.

Talmadge, H., & Murphy, D. F. (1983). Innovative home care program offers appropriate alternative for elderly. *Hospital Progress, 64,* 50-51, 72.

Tampons with vitamins. (1988, May-June). *The Futurist,* p. 3.

Task Force on Social Work Research. (1991). *Building social work knowledge for effective service and policies: A plan for research development* (Report). Austin, TX: Capital.

Taylor, R. B., Denham, J. W., & Ureda, J. R. (1982). Health promotion: A perspective. In R. B. Taylor, J. R. Ureda, & J. W. Denham (Eds.), *Health promotion: Principle and clinical applications.* Norwalk, CT: Appleton-Century-Crofts.

Teltsch, K. (1991, August 27). Mothers dying of AIDS get help with custody. *New York Times,* pp. B1, B2.

Terris, M. (1975). Approaches to an epidemiology of health. *American Journal of Public Health, 65,* 1037-1044.

Terris, M. (1983). The cost-effective national health program. *Journal of Public Health Policy, 5*(3).

Thomas, J. (1992). *Protecting children and animals: Agenda for a non-violent future.* Summary of the American Humane Association Conference, September 14-15, Herndon, VA.

Thompson, D. H., Fawley-Huss, K., Miller, C., Modrzynski, J., Morrison, M., Pieh, M., Pierson, T., Schmude, S., Stewart-York, J., Stiles, D., & Vanderschel, C. (1989). *Adult foster care in Michigan: A descriptive study.* Kalamazoo: Western Michigan University, School of Social Work.

Tiny hearing aid developed. (1995, January-February). *The Futurist,* p. 5.

Tiny pumps for drugs. (1988, March-April). *The Futurist*, p. 4.

Torabi, M. R., Bailey, W. J., & Majd-Jabbari, M. (1993). Cigarette smoking as a predictor of alcohol and other drug use by children and adolescents: Evidence of the "gateway drug effect." *Journal of School Health, 63*, 302-306.

Townsend, A. L. (1990). Nursing home care and family caregiver's stress. In M. A. P. Stephens, J. H. Crowther, S. E. Hobfoll, & D. L. Tennenbaum (Eds.), *Stress and coping in later-life families* (pp. 267-215). New York: Hemisphere.

Tracy, E. M., & Biegel, D. E. (1994). Preparing social workers for social network interventions in mental health practice. *Journal of Teaching in Social Work, 10*(1/2), 19-41.

Trocchio, J. (1993, November/December). Community partnerships for nursing homes. *Nursing Homes*, pp. 18-19, 24.

Trocchio, J. (1994). Oldest and newest promise is responding to community needs. *Journal of Long-term Care Administration, 22*(3), 22-24.

Tropman, J. E. (1995). Community needs assessment. In *Encyclopedia of social work* (19th ed.). Washington, DC: National Association of Social Workers.

Tucker, K., & McNerney, S. L. (1992, January). Building coalitions to initiate change. *Public Relations Journal*, 28-30.

Turnock, B. J., Handler, A., Hall, W., Potsic, S., Nalluri, R., & Vaughn, E. H. (1994). Local health department effectiveness in addressing the core functions of public health. *Public Health Reports, 109*, 653-658.

Ullman, D. (1988, July-August). Homeopathy: Medicine for the 21st century. *The Futurist*, pp. 43-47.

Umoren, J. A. (1992). Maslow's hierarchy of needs and OBRA 1987: Toward need satisfaction by nursing home residents. *Educational Gerontology, 18*, 657-670.

Underwood, S. M., Hoskins, D., Cummins, T., & Williams, A. (1994). Obstacles to cancer care: Focus on the economically disadvantaged. *Oncology Nurses Forum, 21*(1), 47-52.

Uniform crime reports for the United States. (1992). Washington, DC: Government Printing Office.

United Network for Organ Sharing (UNOS). (1993). *UNOS update.* Richmond, VA: Author.

United Network for Organ Sharing (UNOS). (n.d.). *Facts everyone should know about organ donation and transplantation.* Richmond, VA: Author.

U.S. Bureau of the Census. (1994). *Statistical brief 94-28.* Washington, DC: Author.

U.S. Department of Health and Human Services (DHHS). (1990). *Child abuse and neglect: Critical first steps in response to a national emergency.* Washington, DC: Government Printing Office.

U.S. Department of Health, Education and Welfare (DHEW). (1975). *Emergency medical services systems program guidelines* (DHEW Pub. No. [HSA] 75-2013). Hyattsville, MD: Author.

U.S. House Select Committee on Aging. (1986, August). *The "black box" of home care quality* (Report prepared by the American Bar Association, Comm. Pub. No. 99-573). Washington, DC: Government Printing Office.

U.S. Senate Special Committee on Aging. (1991). *Aging America: Trends and projections.* Washington, DC: Government Printing Office.

Usatine, R. P., Geldberg, L., Smith, M. H., & Lesser, J. (1994). Health care for the homeless: A family medicine perspective. *American Family Physician, 49*, 139-146.

Vandivort, R. E. (1994). Advanced social work practice update paper: Report of the 1994 National Managed Care Congress. In *Social work practice update*. Washington, DC: National Association of Social Workers.

Vandivort, R., Kurren, G. M., & Braun, K. (1984). Foster family care for frail elderly: A cost-effective quality care alternative. *Journal of Gerontological Social Work, 7*, 101-114.

Velleman, R. A. (1990). *Meeting the needs of people with disabilities: A guide for librarians, educators, and other service professionals.* Phoenix, AZ: Oryx.

Viney, L. L., & Westbrook, M. T. (1981). Psychological reactions to chronic illness-related disability as a function of its severity and type. *Journal of Psychosomatic Research, 25,* 513-523.

Vladeck, B. C. (1980). *Unloving care: The nursing home tragedy.* New York: Basic Books.

Vladeck, B. C. (1988). Hospitals, the elderly, and comprehensive care. In C. Eisdorfer & G. L. Maddox (Eds.), *The role of hospitals in geriatric care* (pp. 35-48). New York: Springer.

Vourlekis, B. S., Gelfand, D. E., & Greene, R. R. (1992). Psychosocial needs and care in nursing homes: Comparison of views of social workers and home administrators. *The Gerontologist, 32,* 113-119.

Wallace, S. R., Goldberg, R. J., & Slaby, A. E. (1984). *Clinical social work in health care: New biopsychosocial approaches.* New York: Praeger.

Wallack, L. (1994, Winter). Media advocacy: A strategy for empowering people and communities. *Journal of Public Health Policy,* 421-436.

Wallack, L., Dorfman, L., Jernigan, D., & Themba, M. (1993). *Media advocacy and public health: Power of prevention.* Newbury Park, CA: Sage.

Warren, R. (1977). *Social change and human purpose.* Chicago: Rand McNally.

Watkins, E. L. (1985). The conceptual base for public health social work. In A. Gitterman, R. B. Black, & F. Stein (Eds.), *Public health social work in maternal and child health* (Report of the Working Conference of the Public Health Social Work Advisory Committee for the Bureau of Health Care Delivery and Assistance). New York: Columbia University School of Social Work.

Watters, F. (1961). Group Health Association Inc. Washington, DC. *Group Practice, 10,* 661-674.

Wax, J. (1982, August). *Workshop on social work power and conflict negotiation* (Sponsored by Mid-Northern Ohio Society of Hospital Social Work Directors, Akron, OH.

Weick, A. (1986). The philosophical context of a health model of social work. *Social Casework, 67,* 551-559.

Weil, M. O., & Gamble, D. N. (1995). Community practice models. In *Encyclopedia of social work* (19th ed.). Washington, DC: National Association of Social Workers.

Weiner, J. (1994). Financing long-term care: A proposal by the American College of Physicians and the American Geriatrics Society. *Journal of the American Medical Association, 271,* 1525-1529.

Weiner, J. M., & Illson, L. H. (1994). Health care reform in the 1990s: Where does long-term care fit in? *The Gerontologist, 34,* 402-408.

Weiss, J. (1995). Genetic technology, ethics, and the family. In J. B. Rauch (Ed.), *Community-based, family-centered services in a changing health care environment.* Arlington, VA: National Maternal and Child Health Clearinghouse.

Weissensee, M. G., Kjervik, D. K., & Anderson, J. B. (1995). A tool to assess the cognitively impaired elderly. *Journal of Case Management, 4*(1), 29-33.

Weissert, W. G., & Hedrick, S. C. (1994). Lessons learned from research on effects of community-based long-term care. *Journal of the American Geriatric Society, 42,* 348-353.

Weissman, A. (1976). Industrial social services: Linkage technology. *Social Casework, 57,* 50-54.

White, M., Gundrum, G., Shearer, S., & Simmons, W. J. (1994). A role for case managers in physician office. *Journal of Case Management, 3*(2), 62-68.

White, S. W. (1993, Winter). Mental illness and national policy. *National Forum,* pp. 2-3.

Wickizer, T. M., et al. (1993). Activating communities for health promotion: A process evaluation method. *American Journal of Public Health, 83,* 561-567.

Wildon, V. R. (1994). Go beyond "home" to a hometown. *Journal of Long-Term Care Administration, 22*(2), 9.

Willer, B., & Intagliata, J. (1982). Comparison of family care and group homes as alternatives to institutions. *American Journal of Mental Deficiency, 86,* 588-595.

Williams, J. K. (1993). Case management: Opportunities for service providers. *Home Health Care Services Quarterly, 14,* 5-40.

Williams, S. J. (1991). An overview and management introduction. In A. Ross, S. J. Williams, & E. L. Schafer (Eds.), *Ambulatory care management.* Albany, NY: Delmar.

Williams, T. F. (1990). Foreword. In C. Zuckerman, N. N. Dubler, & B. Collopy (Eds.), *Home health care options: A guide for older persons and concerned families* (pp. ix-xii). New York: Plenum.

Wilson, D. (1979). The Iowa experimental swing-bed program. In M. M. Melum (Ed.), *The changing role of the hospital: Options for the future.* Chicago: American Hospital Association.

Winkler, M. E. (1980). Saving face in the status race. *Health & Social Work, 5*(2), 27-33.

Witmer, J. M., & Sweeney, T. J. (1992). A holistic model for wellness and prevention over the life span. *Journal of Counseling & Development, 71,* 140-148.

Wolf, R. S., & Pillemaer, K. (1994). What's new in elder abuse programming? Four bright ideas. *The Gerontologist, 34,* 126-129.

Wolfred, T. R. (1991). Ending the HIV epidemic: A call for community action. In S. Petrow, P. Frank, & T. R. Wolfred (Eds.), *Ending the HIV epidemic: Community strategies in disease prevention and health promotion* (pp. 132-139). Santa Cruz, CA: Network.

Wood, B. (1994, November/December). 18 steps toward image enhancement. *Nursing Homes,* p. 13.

Wood, K. M., & Geismar, L. L. (1989). *Families at risk: Treating the multiproblem family.* New York: Human Science Press.

World Health Organization (WHO). (1958). Constitution of the World Health Organization. In *The first ten years of the World Health Organization* (pp. 459-472). Geneva: Author.

World Health Organization (WHO). (1986). The Ottawa Charter for Health Promotion. *Health Promotion, 1,* iii-v.

World Health Organization (WHO). (1989). *WHO AIDS series 5: Guide to planning health promotion for AIDS prevention and control.* Geneva: Author.

Wortman, C. B., & Lehman, D. R. (1985). Reactions to victims of life crises: Support attempts that fail. In I. G. Sarason & B. R. Sarason (Eds.), *Social support, theory, research, applications.* Dordrect, The Netherlands: Martinus Nijhoff.

Wright, F. D., Beck, A. T., Newman, C. F., & Liese, B. S. (1993). Cognitive therapy of substance abuse: Theoretical rationale. *NIDA Research Monograph, 137,* 123-146.

Yankelovich, D. (1995, Spring). The debate that wasn't: The public and the Clinton plan. *Health Affairs,* pp. 7-23.

Yanni, F. F. (1979). Hospital-sponsored primary care. In M. M. Melum (Ed.), *The changing role of the hospital: Options for the future.* Chicago: American Hospital Association.

Yessne, P. (1994). Home care today (Part I). *Home Health Business Report, 1,* 13-14.

Yoel, W. C., & Clair, J. M. (1994). Never enough time: How medical residents manage a scarce resource. *Journal of Contemporary Ethnography, 23*(2), 185-204.

Young, G. P., & Sklar, D. (1995). Health care reform and emergency medicine. *Annals of Emergency Medicine, 25*(5), 666-674.

Zarit, S. H., & Zarit, J. M. (1982). Families under stress: Interventions for caregivers of senile demential patients. *Psychotherapy: Theory, Research and Practice, 19,* 461-471.

Zastrow, C. (1985). *The practice of social work.* Belmont, CA: Dorsey.

Zavodnick, L., Katz, G., Markezin, E., & Mitchell, A. (1982). Management and organization of ambulatory care in MIS. In G. Katz, A. Mitchell, & E. Markezin (Eds.), *Ambulatory care and regionalization in multi-institutional health system.* Gaithersburg, MD: Aspen.

Zerubavel, E. (1979). *Patterns of time in hospital life.* Chicago: University of Chicago Press.

AUTHOR INDEX

SUBJECT INDEX

ABOUT THE AUTHOR

SURJIT SINGH DHOOPER is Professor of Social Work at the University of Kentucky, Lexington. His professional experience, spread over 32 years, includes both practice and teaching. He has done direct practice as well as administrative and community organizational work in health care settings for 18 years and has taught at both graduate and undergraduate levels for close to 15 years. He has authored/coauthored four books, more than 40 journal articles, and 20 book reviews, and has presented papers at many national and international conferences. He is the consulting editor and/or book reviewer for many professional journals, including *Journal of Social Work Education, Health and Social Work,* and *Journal of Gerontological Social Work.* He is a member of several university, community, and national-level committees such as the National Committee on Racial and Ethnic Diversity of the National Association of Social Workers.